Praise for *Church of Spies*

"Highly readable.... [Riebling's] painstaking research and vivid writing make it a five-cloak/five-dagger read."

—*Washington Times*

"Other scholars ... have written about the Vatican's connection with the German Resistance, but never with the detail, insight, and proof Riebling marshals here."

—*National Review*

"In compelling detail, Riebling looks not only at the strategies that various anti-Nazi officers and other co-conspirators pursued to kill Hitler, but the kind of government structures that would need to be imposed on shattered Germany if the conspiratorial plots succeeded.... Riebling's compelling new evidence should put to rest the propaganda charging that Pius XII was at best a weak reed and at worst a Nazi sympathizer."

—*Crisis Magazine*

"Riebling, in thorough research and documentation, shows that Pius XII, rather than being an acquiescent enabler of the Nazi's genocidal designs, was an active participant in an intrigue whose goal was the assassination of the Führer."

—*The Jewish Week*

"*Church of Spies* sheds light on the secret actions and covert war waged by Pius, the Vatican, the German Catholic Church, and various German Catholic citizens against Hitler and the Nazis.... By weaving together numerous storylines in a chronological fashion from 1939 to 1945, the history of this period reads more like an exciting popular fiction spy novel than an academic work.... [A]n extremely readable and interesting work."

—*H-Net*

"Riebling recounts in a fast, readable style the fumblings, betrayals, and bad luck that plagued attempts to remove Hitler. Through it all, he shows the Vatican looming in the background—the only support on which the conspirators could count, the only consistent contact they had with the Allies, and one of the few moral centers to which they could look."

—JOSEPH BOTTUM, *Washington Free Beacon*

" [*Church of Spies*] adds a mass of new evidence to what we know, now, about what the Pope and the Church did to deal with the mortal threat to civilization posed by Hitler and German National Socialism.... [A] deeply researched study.... It's a great read, so give it on those grounds; but it's morally permissible if you give it to annoy the *New York Times*."

—GEORGE WEIGEL, *First Things*

" [A] blockbuster of a book which not only defends Pius XII ... but utterly demolishes the Black Legend by showing in intricate and meticulously documented detail ... that from the very start of the war the Pope cooperated secretly with anti-Nazi forces in Hitler's thousand year Reich who sought, first, to remove the Führer from power; and when that failed, to kill him.... Riebling's book is beautifully written, and reads like a novel.... [R]iveting."

—*Catholic World Report*

"[T]he wealth of detail the author has unearthed by his meticulous research ... is impressive and absolutely damning against those who mendaciously have attacked Pius XII as either the silent Pope or even a sub rosa ally of Hitler. This book is highly recommended."

—*The American Catholic*

"[F]ascinating ... offers a compelling narrative of the actions taken by Pope Pius to stop Hitler from carrying out his campaign of world domination and ethnic cleansing. Backed by a mass of carefully compiled documentation, Riebling shows that Pius cooperated in a variety of plots, initiated by patriotic, anti-Nazi Germans, to assassinate Hitler and replace the National Socialist regime with a government that would make peace with the west."

—*Breitbart News*

"Moves as swiftly as a novel."

—*Australian Financial Review*

"[A] revealing history of Pius' wartime dealings with the German resistance to Nazi rule. . . . Readers will be surprised at the steady stream of anti-Hitler conspiracies, several of which reached the point where dates were set and bombs assembled."

—*Military History*

"Meticulously researched. . . . A fascinating account of the many Catholics, including priests, who were part of the intelligence network that actively fought the Nazi regime."

—*Newcastle Herald*

"The most impressive thing about *Church of Spies* is that it offers . . . new detail and with plenty of drama and colour. . . . It's a fascinating story . . . a compelling book."

—*Sydney Morning Herald*

"Immensely well-informed and hugely engrossing."

—*Law and Liberty*

"*Church of Spies* is well worth reading for the fascinating story."

—*Aletia*

"Riebling, an expert on secret intelligence, compellingly explores the papacy's involvement in espionage during World War II. . . . This book has much to surprise, especially the many German officers, separately and together, involved in attempts on Hitler's life. . . . Pius, vilified by critics who believed he ignored Germany's atrocities, comes off as a politically savvy man who realized his interference would precipitate Hitler's mortal overreaction against German Catholics. Not only a dramatic disclosure of the Vatican's covert actions, but also an absorbing, polished story for all readers of World War II history."

—*Kirkus*

"Clandestine organizations are hard to reconstruct and Riebling has mined an impressive array of archival sources to tell this fascinating story."}

—*Library Journal*

"Mark Riebling's methodically-researched detective story . . . deserves widespread attention . . . masterful . . . will long remain the definitive account of the papal involvement in the conspiracies to topple Hitler. . . . This is simply the finest work on the subject in print."

—*Contemporary Church History Quarterly*

"Crackles with suspense . . . serves up surprises. . . . This book inspires and cautions. . . . If World War II, the modern papacy, or the 'Pius War' interests you at all, get this book."

—*America*

"*Church of Spies* . . . truly is a treasure trove of surprising information."

—*Catholic News Service*

"*Church of Spies* is the story of a plot against Hitler forged in breathless secrecy—from the chiaroscuro of church crypts, to the hive offices of the Reich—by a network run by the pontiff himself. . . . A timely book about the Hitler era . . . offers valuable insight."

—*RealClear Religion*

"*Church of Spies* shows, with significant research to back it up, that Pope Pius the Twelfth was not, in fact, Hitler's Pope, as he has wrongly been called, but quite the contrary, an enemy of Hitler's who worked behind the scenes against him. Mark Riebling documents how people of faith linked arms against evil that was Nazism and did not turn a blind eye against it. This is a fascinating, riveting, and a deeply important corrective to the false narrative about the Catholic church during World War II."

—Eric Metaxas, *New York Times* 1# bestselling author,
nationally syndicated radio host

"Mark Riebling takes readers into the seldom-explored mysterious world of Vatican espionage with a deeply researched and fresh account that reads like a spy thriller. The crackling narrative of Church of Spies delivers an important and compelling addition to the debate over the legacy of Pius XII, the most powerful and complex Pope of modern times."

—Gerald Posner, author of *God's Bankers:
A History of Money and Power at the Vatican*

"A fascinating contribution to the literature on the Holocaust, the history of the papacy, and the life of Pius XII."

—Sam Harris, author of *The End of Faith*

"While the Pope hesitated to publicly provoke Hitler in foolhardy way, he had no hesitation in secretly opposing the Third Reich and its crimes. The record of the assistance Pius XII provided, through his representatives, to the German resistance, and the actions they took, under his guidance, is extraordinary. Without minimizing the complicity of individual Christians, or the role of Christian anti-Semitism, Mark Riebling shows that the Vatican took a very powerful stance against the Nazis. It is especially important for Jewish people—and I am Jewish myself—that this information is now being gathered for all to see."

—Sir Martin Gilbert,
official biographer of Winston Churchill

"This gripping book, the product of extensive and fine-grained historical research, should change the course of the 'Pius Wars,' if both critics and defenders of Pius XII take its evidence seriously."

—George Weigel, distinguished senior fellow,
Ethics and Public Policy Center

"In this exciting and original work, Mark Riebling has unearthed vital new sources, and he writes elegantly and persuasively on a fascinating subject that has remained hidden in history's shadows."

—MICHAEL BURLEIGH,
author of *The Third Reich: A New History*

"In *Church of Spies*, Mark Riebling provides a groundbreaking and riveting account of Pope Pius XII's secret war against Hitler. This richly documented book makes an important contribution to contemporary scholarship about Pius XII and to our understanding of the historical legacy of his pontificate."

—RABBI DAVID DALIN,
author of *The Myth of Hitler's Pope*

"*Church of Spies* is an incredible book. It is authentic, documented history that reads like a great action novel. Bonhoeffer, Stauffenberg, the pope, and others plotted to kill Hitler and end the war. Riebling takes us inside their meetings (sometimes held among excavations under Vatican City) and meetings of Hitler and his top advisors. The story that emerges is at times terrifying, tragic, and yet ultimately heroic. This is a book not to be missed."

—RONALD J. RYCHLAK,
author of *Hitler, the War, and the Pope*

"Mark Riebling has set himself a high bar in turning conventional wisdom on its head. He has taken on one of the most controversial and polarizing issues in the history of World War II: the role of the wartime Vatican in fighting the Nazis. By combining new archival material with a lively and convincing narrative he has created a new account of a secret war previously overlooked. This is a highly original contribution to intelligence history."

—COL. ROSE MARY SHELDON, Burgwyn Chair
in Military History, Virginia Military Institute

CHURCH OF SPIES

✝ ✝ ✝

THE POPE'S
SECRET WAR
AGAINST
HITLER

MARK RIEBLING

BASIC BOOKS
New York

Books published by Basic Books are available at special discounts for bulk purchases
in the United States by corporations, institutions, and other organizations. For more
information, please contact the Special Markets Department at the Perseus Books
Group, 2300 Chestnut Street, Suite 200, Philadelphia, PA 19103, or call (800) 810-
4145, ext. 5000, or e-mail special.markets@perseusbooks.com.

Designed by Linda Mark

Library of Congress Cataloging-in-Publication Data

Riebling, Mark.
  Church of spies : the Pope's secret war against Hitler / Mark Riebling.
    pages cm
  Includes bibliographical references and index.
   ISBN 978-0-465-02229-8 (hardcover : alk. paper)   ISBN 978-0-465-06155-6
(e-book) 1. Pius XII, Pope, 1876-1958. 2. Catholic Church—Foreign relations—
Germany. 3. Germany—Foreign relations—Catholic Church. 4. World War,
1939–1945—Vatican City. 5. World War, 1939–1945—Religious aspects—Catholic
Church. 6. Anti-Nazi movement—Vatican City. I. Title.
  BX1378.R54 2015
  282.09'044--dc23

                                                                        2015024814

LSC-C

10 9 8 7 6 5 4
ISBN 978-0-465-09411-0 (paperback)

For Robin

How do we represent our religion?
Just as a system, or as glowing fire?
—German Jesuit Father Alfred Delp

CONTENTS

PROLOGUE

IN APRIL 1945, THE NAZIS TRIED TO BREAK THE MAN THEY CALLED "the best agent of the Vatican Intelligence in Germany." On the surface, Josef Müller seemed just a big-eared Bavarian book publisher, who puffed a pipe and collected stamps. Yet since his arrest for giving Jews false papers and money, he had come to figure in a case of sensational significance. The Gestapo claimed that Müller had plotted to kill Hitler "using the spy service of the Catholic clergy."[1]

He refused to confess, however. "Müller had nerves like ropes and dominated the situation," a prison aide recalled. When guards unshackled him, he threw them using jujitsu. His resolve awed other prisoners, who had misjudged him a regular Joe. "To look at," wrote a British spy jailed with Müller, "he was just an ordinary stoutish little man with a florid complexion and drab fair hair cut en brosse, the sort of man, whom you would not look at a second time if you met him anywhere, and yet, one of the bravest and most determined men imaginable."[2]

A one-legged SS giant entered Müller's cell. Sturmführer Kurt Stavitzki chained Müller's leg irons to a bar. Müller's neighbors at Flossenbürg concentration camp then saw him forced to eat his food like a dog from a plate on the floor, with his hands tied behind his back.[3]

Rummaging through Müller's suitcase, Stavitzki seized an envelope. It contained a letter from Müller's wife, trying to learn what had become of him. She had enclosed a letter from his daughter, who told him that she would take her First Communion that coming Sunday. Stavitzki took the letters and tore them up.[4]

He wanted to learn more about Müller's Vatican links. One case file called Müller "an unusually intrepid man of the Jesuit school," through whom dissident German generals "maintained contact with the pope." Pius the Twelfth had told Müller, as captured coup plans recorded, that the prerequisite for peace would be a change of regime in Germany.[5]

Stavitzki confronted Müller with one of the coup plans. Its lead sentence said: "Decent Germans have decided to negotiate with the English via the Vatican." Stavitzki read the text aloud and, whenever he came to the words "Decent Germans," backhanded Müller on the upper lip. Müller's teeth began to fall out. Finally Stavitzki hit him so hard that he knocked over both Müller and his chair. Stavitzki then stomped on him, yelling, "Talk or die!"[6]

By Sunday, 8 April, Müller's face was bruised and swollen. As he paced his cell, shuffling his feet to keep warm, the door flung open. "The show is ending," Stavitzki said. He yelled down the hall, "Is the adjutant in the execution yard?"[7]

The gallows stood on a parade ground. Six stepladders ran up to a row of hooks, holding nooses. "Generally, the persons hanged were stripped naked," a war-crimes report on Flossenbürg found. "Ofttimes they were beaten before hanging till the unfortunate victims begged for immediate hanging to ease the pain. Hanging a person by his wrists with a heavy barrel suspended from his ankles was another method of execution. This caused the person's insides to be torn up and he died."[8]

A Soviet prisoner, General Pyotr Privalov, saw Müller led toward the gallows. Privalov called out, hoping to stand tall with Müller in one last glance. But he spoke in Russian, and Müller did not react at first. When Müller finally looked up, he seemed "content." Then he passed from Privalov's view.[9]

CHAPTER I

DARKNESS OVER THE EARTH

S IX MONTHS BEFORE THE SECOND WORLD WAR BEGAN, THE CAR-
dinals of the Catholic Church convened in Rome. The doors of the
Sistine Chapel swung shut, and the Swiss Guards planted their battle-
axes against all who might try to enter the conclave, or leave it, before
the world's largest religion had named its new leader. By the next day, 2
March 1939, thousands crowded St. Peter's Square, staring at the chim-
ney on the chapel's roof. Twice it churned up black smoke, marking
a vote without a verdict. Suspense rose, as usual, when the smoke did
not; but for the first time in memory, the spectacle drew a crush of foreign press, whose telephoto lenses reminded one witness of "anti-tank
guns." With Europe drifting toward war, the new pope's public words
might sway opinion, his discreet diplomacy turn events. "Never since
the Reformation," wrote one observer, "had the election of a Pontiff
been awaited with so much anxiety by the whole world."[1]

At 5:29 p.m., a white plume rose from the roof pipe. Hats flew, can-
nons boomed, bells pealed. On the balcony of the Apostolic Palace, the
cardinal-dean bent toward a microphone. "I announce to you a great
joy. We have a Pope! Most Revered Cardinal Eugenio Pacelli, who has
taken the name Pius the Twelfth."[2]

With hesitant steps, the new pope came to the balustrade. He was majestically tall and deathly pale, with eyes like black diamonds. He raised a hand. The square quieted, and the crowd sank to its knees. Three times he made the sign of the cross. The crowd rose in a clash of sound: bursts of *Evviva il Papa!* met the sawing cadences of *Pacelli, Pacelli, Pacelli!* He stood on the balcony, making gestures of benediction, his sleeves spread like white wings. Then, suddenly, he turned and disappeared into St. Peter's.[3]

In the palace, Pacelli entered the chamber of a dying friend. Cardinal Marchetti-Selvaggiani tried to raise himself, whispering: "Holy Father." Pacelli reportedly took his hand and said, "Tonight, let me still be Eugenio." But the mantle of Pontifex Maximus, claimed by 257 saints and scoundrels before him, had already claimed Pacelli. From the first moment of his election, he wrote later, he "felt all the great weight of responsible cares."[4]

Returning to his apartment, he found a birthday cake with sixty-three candles. He thanked his housekeeper, but did not touch the cake. After saying a rosary, he summoned his longtime companion, Monsignor Ludwig Kaas. They left the papal apartment, and did not return until two in the morning.[5]

One of the pope's earliest authorized biographers described what followed. Pacelli and Kaas traversed the back passages of the palace, and entered an alcove on the south wall of St. Peter's Basilica. Between statues of Saint Andrew and Saint Veronica, they came to a door. It opened onto a tunnel, leading to another door, heavy and bronze, with three locks. Kaas unlocked the door with his breviary keys, locked it again behind them, and followed Pacelli down a metal staircase, into the Vatican crypt.[6]

The air was hot and dank, moist from the nearby Tiber. A passage curved into the vault, shelved with dead popes and kings. Pacelli gathered his cassock and knelt before a low, box-like structure, which encased an earthen hole. There he pondered and soon after made his first choice as pope. His undersecretary of state later deemed the decision one of the "stars which lighted his arduous way . . . from which he drew strength and constancy, and which gave rise, as it were, to . . . the program of his pontificate." By this choice, Pacelli sought to solve the most vexing of the Vatican's mysteries—and the ghosts he met on this quest would become his guides.[7]

THE RIDDLE PACELLI RESOLVED TO ANSWER WAS AS OLD AS THE Church. Sometime in the first century, Saint Peter had gone to Rome, led a church that upset the state, and died on a cross in the Vaticanum, a marsh known for big snakes and bad wine. The infant Church had then gone underground, literally into the catacombs, and the first pope's successors had prudently kept secret the site of his grave. Romans, however, had long whispered that Peter was buried beneath the high altar of the basilica bearing his name. Rumors centered on a pile of masonry and other unknown materials, twenty feet wide and forty feet deep. No one knew what lay under or inside this mysterious core. Some said it held gold and silver, which medieval pilgrims poured down a shaft. Others said it concealed a bronze casket containing Peter's bones. No one had ever mounted an expedition to test these tales. By the Vatican's own account, a one-thousand-year-old curse, detailed in secret and apocalyptic documents, threatened the worst possible misfortune for anyone who disturbed the rumored site of Peter's grave.[8]

But in 1935 Pacelli had broken the taboo. Pius the Eleventh asked for a plot beneath the high altar, and accommodating his coffin required enlarging the crypt. Pacelli, who among his other duties was grand chancellor of the Pontifical Institute of Christian Archeology, decided to increase the crypt's headroom by lowering its floor three feet. At two and a half feet, papal engineers had brushed the earth from something unexpected: the façade of a mausoleum, decorated with friezes of cranes and pygmies—a pagan allegory of the duel between life and death. The Vatican crypt lay above a lost necropolis, a city of the dead, untouched since imperial times.[9]

Pacelli, believing Peter's bones might lay within, asked to dig deeper. Pius Eleven refused. His cardinals called the project sacrilegious; his architects thought it dangerous. If excavators damaged the piers supporting Michelangelo's massive dome, the largest church in the world could collapse.

But Pacelli, more than any previous pope, put faith in science. As a pious Catholic in a liberal high school, taunted about the injustice done Galileo, he learned a compensatory reverence for adventures of reason. "O scanners of the skies!" he enthused. "Giants when you measure stars and name nebulae." He praised both pure science and its uses: His panegyrics to railroads and factories read like outtakes from *Atlas Shrugged*. No engineering problem would daunt him, no pious curse prevent a quest. "The heroes of research," Pacelli said, would not fear "the stumbling blocks and the risks." Now, on his first night as pope, kneeling at the blind mouth of the halted dig, Pacelli decided to make a full exploration.[10]

The quest prefigured, in miniature, the epic secret enterprise of his pontificate. For here, at the site of this bold project, his aides would meet, with his blessing, to plot an even bolder one. That second venture, like the first, revealed the signatures of Pacelli's rule. Both projects showed a fetish for secrecy. Both relied on German exiles, German lay operatives, and German Jesuits. Both entailed breaches between overt words and covert acts. Both put the largest church in the world at risk. And both would culminate in controversy—making Pacelli's reign seem so ill-starred that some thought he had actually come under the coffin-raider's curse.

As Pacelli prayed in the Vatican crypt, lights burned late at the most feared address in Germany. The five-floor mansion at 8 Prinz-Albrecht-Strasse, Berlin, had once been an art school. The Nazis had turned its sculptors' studios into jail cells. At the grand front staircase stood two guards with pistols and nightsticks. On the top floor worked Heinrich Himmler, Reichsführer of the Schutzstaffel (SS), Hitler's terror corps. In an adjacent office, Himmler's Vatican expert toiled at a typewriter, preparing a dossier on the newly elected pope.[11]

Storm Leader Albert Hartl was a defrocked priest. He had a round face, round glasses, and a knob of hair that looked like a Mohawk top-knot. His wife described him as "taciturn, strict, evasive . . . very moody." He had become a priest after his freethinking father died, to please his pious mother. Trouble ensued when his superiors found him "unsuitable for dealing with girls." He left the Church mysteriously, after betraying his best friend, a fellow priest, to the Nazis.[12]

"He claims that he woke up one morning in January 1934 in the Gestapo headquarters in Munich," a postwar debriefer wrote, "covered with black and blue marks and in intense pain. One foot revealed a large wound and his head was completely swollen and suppurative. His lips were blue and bloated and two teeth were missing. He had been beaten unmercifully but remembered nothing, he claims." Standing over Hartl was a tall man with the oval face of a "fallen angel." SS spy chief Reinhard Heydrich explained that Hartl had been "beaten and poisoned by fanatics of the Church."[13]

Heydrich asked him to join the Nazi secret service. As chief of Unit II/B, Hartl would lead a team of ex-priests who spied on anti-Nazi Catholics—"to harass and hem them in, and finally to destroy them." As Hitler himself had said, "We do not want any other God but Germany." Hartl joined the SS on the spot. As a colleague recalled, he then served "with the whole hatred of a renegade." Hartl wrote in his updated CV, "The fight against the world I knew so well is now my life's work."[14]

The new pope's election gave Hartl a chance to shine. He hoped senior leaders, even Hitler, would read the SS Pius-dossier. Hartl culled secret and public sources, filtered the facts through his own experience, and used the short form busy policymakers preferred.[15]

Pope Pius XII (Cardinal Pacelli)

Biography:

2 March 1876 born in Rome

1917 Nuncio in Munich—intense cooperation in Vatican peace efforts

1920–29 Nuncio in Berlin

1929 Cardinal

1930 Cardinal Secretary of State—travel in America and in France.

Attitude towards Germany.—Pacelli was always very pro-German [*sehr deutschfreundlich*] and known for his excellent knowledge of the German language. But his defense of official Church policy has often led him to duel National Socialism on principle.[16]

The duel had begun with a deal. When the Nazis took power in 1933, Pius the Eleventh praised Hitler's anticommunism, and accepted his offer to formalize Catholic rights. Pacelli negotiated a concordat, funding the Church with annual tax revenues of 500 million marks. "The Pope by signing this concordat pointed the way to Hitler for millions of heretofore aloof Catholics," Hartl wrote. But by mid-decade, Hitler found the concordat a hindrance. Pacelli peppered Berlin with fifty-five notes protesting breaches. It became clear, as one SS officer said, that "it would be absurd to accuse Pacelli of being pro-Nazi."[17]

Pacelli's public statements disturbed Berlin. The 1937 encyclical *Mit brennender Sorge* (*With Burning Anxiety*) accused the German state of plotting to exterminate the Church. The most cutting words, Nazi analysts noted, came from Pacelli's protests: "hatred," "machinations," "struggles to death." With those words, Hartl thought, Pacelli "summoned the whole world to fight against the Reich."[18]

Worst of all, Pacelli preached racial equality. "Christianity has supposedly gathered together all races, whether negro or White, into a single, big family of God," Hartl sneered. "Hence the Catholic church also rejects anti-Semitism." Speaking in France, Pacelli had condemned the "superstition of race and blood." As a result, Nazi cartoonists drew a hook-nosed Pacelli cavorting with Jesse Owens and rabbis, while, Hartl claimed, "the entire Judaized USA press praised Pacelli."[19]

These doctrines were dangerous because they were not just rhetorical. The secret police found Catholics "ideologically un-teachable" in their continued patronage of Jewish merchants. As the SS noted, "in exactly those districts where political Catholicism still holds sway the peasants are so infected by the doctrines of Catholicism that they are deaf to any discussion of the racial problem." Catholic farmers changed a sign saying "Jews not wanted here" to read: "Jews very much wanted here."[20]

Hartl traced the tough stance to a dark cause. A friend from his ordination class, Father Joachim Birkner, worked in the Vatican Secret Archives, ostensibly researching sixteenth-century Church diplomacy. Birkner was in fact an SS spy. He fixed on Pacelli's Jesuit aide Robert Leiber, sometimes called "the evil spirit of the Pope."[21]

"Father Leiber has told the informant that the Church's greatest hope is that the National Socialist system will be destroyed in the near future by a war," the SS reported. "If war does not come, Vatican diplomacy expects a change in the situation in Germany, at the latest, after the death of the Führer." Birkner's report coincided with a plea by Pacelli for Christian heroes to "save the world" from pagan "false prophets," which Hartl considered a call to resist Hitler.[22]

Pacelli, then, seemed at the very center of a war against the Reich. The war would not end soon. "So long as there will be a Roman church," Hartl warned, "its eternal political claims will bring it into combat with any ethnic-conscious state." At issue was not whether the new pope would fight Hitler, but how.[23]

Hitler agreed. As Propaganda Minister Joseph Goebbels recorded: "4 March 1939 (Sunday). Midday with the Führer. He is considering whether we should abrogate the Concordat with Rome in light of Pacelli's election as Pope. This will surely happen when Pacelli undertakes his first hostile act."[24]

ON SUNDAY, 5 MARCH, PIUS PICKED UP THE TELEPHONE ON HIS desk to tell his most trusted aide that he was waiting. Father Robert Leiber entered the papal quarters. Known in papal Rome as "the little asthmatic," the fifty-one-year-old Bavarian Jesuit had the air of a melancholy elf. Though he spoke to Pius twice daily and read nearly everything that crossed his desk, no one knew his title. He was variously described as "an agent for German questions," a papal librarian, a professor of Church history, and a "sort of scientific secretary."[25]

In fact, he had no title. "Father Leiber was never a Vatican official," a Jesuit colleague said. "He was a close collaborator of the Pope, but he was never officially admitted to the Vatican as a member of the Vatican." Leiber kept an office in the Vatican, but did not appear in its directory. He was an unofficial official.[26]

Leiber's lack of a title made him ideal for secret work. As one priest who worked for American intelligence during the Nazi years later explained, "It is evident that official authorities may not be made coresponsible if we make errors or fail. They must be able to declare that they never knew what is being said and done." Since Leiber did not work for the Vatican, it could deny involvement in whatever he did.[27]

Helpfully, Leiber knew how to keep his mouth shut, as fellow Jesuits noted. Especially on Church politics, one who knew him said, "Father Leiber takes an attitude of absolute secrecy." In that respect he seemed the very model of a papal aide, as described by the sixteenth-century Pope Sixtus the Fifth: he must know everything, read everything, and understand everything, but he must say nothing.[28]

When Leiber did speak, he was straightforward. "His word is sharp as polished steel," one diplomat said. In the 1920s, when Pacelli was apostolic nuncio in Munich, Leiber had even called out the future pope for living with a Bavarian nun, Pascalina Lehnert. When a cardinal inspected the nunciature, Leiber described the living arrangements as inappropriate; Lehnert, by her own account, liked to see Pacelli "in riding dress, which suited him extremely well." Learning that the cardinal conveyed the complaint to Pacelli, Leiber offered to resign, but Pacelli said, "No, no, no. You are free to think and say whatever you feel. I am not going to dismiss you."[29]

Yet the candor that attracted Pacelli drove others away. A fellow priest called Leiber's manner cutting, even hurtful, adding: "You see, he became a little bit strange." Asthma drove Leiber to try "living cell therapy"—injections of finely ground tissues from freshly slaughtered lambs. Some described him with a Latin quip: *Timeo non Petrum sed secretarium eius*—"I do not fear Peter [the pope], but his secretary scares me."[30]

On that Sunday morning, Leiber brought Pius an urgent memo-randum. Munich Cardinal Michael von Faulhaber had long pushed the Vatican to publicly resist Nazism, which violated principles that must stand, like the eternal stars, above compromise. But now, in a letter captioned "Most Respectful Suggestions," Faulhaber urged a truce.

He worried that Hitler would break the German Church away from Rome. Many German Catholics "believed in" the Führer—not as Catholics, but as Germans. "Catholics admire Herr Hitler as a hero, despite his hatred for the Church," Pacelli himself had noted. Faulhaber saw a danger of schism in "the country which gave us the Reformation." Forced to choose between Hitler and the Church, many German Catholics would choose Hitler. "The bishops," Faulhaber warned, "must pay particular attention to the efforts to establish a national church." Unless the Vatican sought an accommodation, Hitler might nationalize the Church, as King Henry the Eighth had once done in England."[31]

Meanwhile, the Nazis had themselves become a church. "Their philosophy is a de facto religion," Faulhaber said. They had their own sacramental rituals for baptism and confirmation, marriage and funerals. They changed Ash Wednesday into Wotan's Day, Ascension Day into the Feast of Thor's Hammer. They crowned the Christmas tree not with a star, but with a swastika. The Nazis even made "the blasphemous claim that Adolf Hitler is essentially as great as Christ."[32]

Faulhaber wanted to discuss these bad omens with the pope. Since he and the Reich's three other cardinals had come to Rome for the conclave, Pius invited them to "surface some ideas" in an audience the next day. The meeting, however, posed a problem for Pius, because he distrusted one of the cardinals he invited to attend it.

The primate of Vienna had caused a scandal the year before. When Hitler annexed Austria, Cardinal Theodor Innitzer had said the Church supported the Nazis. Pacelli, then Vatican secretary of state, recalled Innitzer to Rome and made him sign a retraction. Now, as pope, Pacelli remained unsure about Innitzer. The good-natured and sentimental Austrian seemed vulnerable to pressure. With war looming, all who entered the pope's library wanted to leave it saying that God was on their country's side. If Innitzer did not publicly twist the pope's private words, Nazi propagandists might do so for him.[33]

Pius therefore decided to make a private transcript of the cardinals' audience. A master verbatim source would help him refute any distortion of his views. To that end, early in his pontificate, Pius equipped his library with an audio spying system.[34]

THE POPE'S AUDIOSURVEILLANCE WOULD REMAIN ONE OF THE VATIcan's best-kept secrets. Only seven decades later would the last living member of the Church's Nazi-era underground, German-Jesuit Father Peter Gumpel, confirm it. By then, Gumpel had spent forty years managing the case for Pacelli's sainthood.

"There was a hole made in the wall," Gumpel said. "I happen to know this, and on a very high level. . . . [T]he matter is certain. I investigated this, from the immediate environment of the pope."[35]

Audio spying came of age just as Pacelli became pope. Over the next few years, Hitler, Stalin, Churchill, and Roosevelt would all make covert recordings; only days earlier, a sweep of the Sistine Chapel had found a hidden Dictaphone; and the Vatican's own audio prowess matched that of any secular power. The Holy See was hard-wired by Guglielmo Marconi, inventor of the radio.[36]

Pacelli himself had earlier hired Marconi to modernize Church headquarters. Marconi had built, for free, a telephone exchange, a radio station, and a short-wave link to the papal summer villa. Rome, for its part, annulled Marconi's marriage, allowing him to remarry and have a daughter, the aptly named "Electra." A few Marconi engineers still worked for the pope, under a Jesuit physicist who ran Radio Vatican. They did what Church documents called "institutional tasks," such as recording the pope's speeches, and "extraordinary services," such as bugging his visitors.[37]

On paper the job did not seem daunting. The Radio Vatican team knew the site and could control access to it. The pope received visitors in the Papal Library. It shared a wall with two anterooms, where the Marconi-Jesuit techs could work unobserved. Yet with the German cardinals scheduled for an audience on 6 March, the installers had only a day to survey the target, make an entry, insert a microphone, run wires to a listening post, and test the system.[38]

They considered microphone-concealment locations in the library. Picture frames, table lamps, braces below table legs, the telephone, overhead lights—all offered possibilities. In the end, as Father Leiber recalled, the team chose a system that operated "through a contrivance which made it possible to hear everything in the room next door." They drilled a hole, and miked it.[39]

Most likely on the night of 5–6 March, Vatican Radio technicians set to work. To avoid staining the anteroom floor, and to collate their gear for quick exit, they unrolled a rubber mat. On it they set their tools: drills and bits, pipe-pushers, collapsible ladders. Because power tools would draw attention, the team used hand-turned drills. They worked in shifts, each man cranking hard, then resting while another spelled him. At the highest turn rates, however, even hand drills made a telltale din. The techs decided that greasing their bits would reduce the noise. A Jesuit reportedly went to fetch some olive oil, perhaps from the papal apartments. The team then wet its drill heads, and the work progressed quietly. But as the bits warmed, so did the coating oil. Soon the site smelled like fried food. To evacuate the odor, the team had to pause and open a door onto the Cortile del Pappagallo, the Courtyard of the Parrot.[40]

Finally, after some tense and tiring hours, they broke through to the library side. Using a small bit, the techs made a pinhole—creating a passage for audio pickup and a wire. Book spines on the library wall presented natural concealment cavities. It remains unclear whether the techs hid a microphone in a hollowed-out book, which Father Leiber possessed, or whether they enlarged their side of the wall to fit the device. In any case, they apparently used a teat-shaped condenser microphone. They plugged it into a portable pre-amplifier that looked like a brown leather briefcase.[41]

From the pre-amp they ran wires to the recording post. A stable link of coaxial cables passed through a tunnel, beneath an oak grove in the Vatican Gardens, and into a ninth-century dragon-toothed tower.

There, amid frescoes of shipwrecks with Jesus calming the storm, Jesuits operated the largest audio recorder ever built. Bigger than two refrigerators stacked on their sides, the Marconi-Stille machine registered sound on ribboned razor wire, which could break free and behead the operators. They worked it only by remote control from a separate room. A half-hour recording used 1.8 miles of spooled steel.[42]

On the morning of 6 March, the available evidence suggests, an operator flicked a wall switch. A white lamp on the machine lit up. The operator waited a full minute to warm the cathodes, then moved the control handle to the "record" position.[43]

Pius entered the papal library at six minutes to nine. At about that moment, from a cubbyhole in the courtyard of San Damasso, Monsignor Enrico Pucci saw the four cardinals enter the Apostolic Palace. Each wore a red skull-cap, a red sash, and a gold pectoral cross. The cardinals navigated a warren of halls and courts and then rode up a creaking elevator. It opened onto a red-velvet waiting room, decorated with medallions of recent popes. The papal *maestro di camera*, Alberto Arborio-Mella, led the cardinals into the library.[44]

The corner room overlooked Peter's Square. Bookcases ran along the walls, and above them hung twelve paintings of animals. A crystal chandelier pended the ceiling. The room had one plush rug. Three dark portraits by Dutch masters stared down from niches. A mahogany table extended toward the three windows, their curtains parted to let in knives of white light.[45]

Pius sat at a desk, hands clasped, silhouetted by sunbeams. He wore a white cap and red slippers without heels. Only the golden cross on his chest adorned his snow-white robes. By turns they bent to kiss his ring: Adolf Bertram of Breslau—Faulhaber of Munich—Josef Schulte of Cologne—Innitzer of Vienna.

They settled into the cane-backed chairs that faced the pope. A crucifix shared the desktop with ziggurats of documents. Nearby sat a gold-plated rotary telephone, with finger-holes in royal blue. A silver plaque declared the desk a gift from the German bishops for his twelve years as papal agent in Germany.

"We want to use the time while your eminences are here," Pius began, "to consider how the cause of the Catholic Church in Germany can be helped at the present time." He read in Latin a proposed letter to Hitler. Amid the curlicued cordialities of protocol stood the phrase: "God protect you, honorable sir."[46]

Pius asked, "Do you think this document is appropriate, or should we add or change anything?" Three of the cardinals approved it. Faulhaber had an issue.

"Does it have to be in Latin? Considering his aversion to non-German languages, maybe the Führer would rather not have to call in a theologian first."

"We can write in German," Pius said. "We must think of what is right for the Church in Germany. That is the most important question for me."

The pope turned directly to the conflict between Church and Reich. He read out a list of grievances, compiled by Cardinal Bertram. The Nazis had thwarted the Church's teachings, banned its organizations, censored its press, shuttered its seminaries, seized its properties, fired its teachers, and closed its schools. The conflict portended a full-scale persecution. Party officials boasted that "after the defeat of Bolshevism and Judaism the Catholic Church will be the only remaining enemy."[47]

Pius then gave the floor to Faulhaber. He had an even gloomier report. "The prejudice against Catholicism won't go away," Faulhaber warned. He cited Hitler's recent Reichstag speech, which had contained a chilling phrase: "The priest as political enemy of the Germans we shall destroy." Brownshirts had taken these words as a license to behead cathedral statues, use crucifixes for target practice, and smear altars with excrement. A mob had recently surrounded Faulhaber's own home, smashed all the windows, and tried to set the building on fire.[48]

Faulhaber traced the trouble to the 1937 papal encyclical. He himself had drafted the papal protest against Nazi policies—but Pacelli, as secretary of state, had sharpened it. Where Faulhaber had dwelt on suffering, Pacelli changed the theme to combat. He retitled the text, from *With Considerable Concern* to *With Burning Anxiety*. The sharpened text said that "National Socialism has intended the persecution of the Church from the beginning and in principle." Hitler had said in his first speech as chancellor that he wanted peace with the Church, and so "was infuriated by the foregoing words in the encyclical and has broken off relations with the Church authorities almost completely since then." Although Faulhaber stopped short of saying it, Pacelli the cardinal had helped create the crisis now confronted by Pacelli the pope.[49]

Faulhaber questioned another Pacelli barb in the encyclical. The text stated that Germany "celebrated the apotheosis of a cross which is hostile to the Christian cross." Faulhaber protested: "The swastika was not selected by the Führer as an alternative to the Christian cross, and it isn't regarded that way by the people either." A state had the right to choose its flag, and "a rejection of this flag would be perceived as unfriendly." Here again, Faulhaber hinted, hadn't Cardinal Pacelli stoked a fire that Pope Pacelli must now put out?[50]

"Eminence Faulhaber is quite right," Pius said. It was the only point in the meeting at which he singled out any of the cardinals for praise. With that, he sent a subtle signal that he would defer to Faulhaber—not to Bertram, the nominal leader of the German Church—in crafting policy toward Hitler.

Faulhaber's preferred policy had two parts. The first was overt acquiescence. "They [the Nazis] seem so much like combatants that it feels like they would rather look for reasons to fight. Particularly if it is against the Church! But I also believe that we bishops must act as if we are unaware of that." The bishops should not get into a war of words with Hitler—and neither should Pius. "Practically speaking, the Holy Father will have to make some concessions on his part."

"I have forbidden polemics," Pius said. He had already asked the Vatican's daily, *L'Osservatore Romano*, to refrain from attacking German policy. "I have let them know that there should be no more incisive words."

The second part of the policy was backstairs intercession. Countering Nazism required "personal contacts," not formal protests. Trusted collaborators could resolve conflict behind the scenes—if they kept themselves informed. "The German bishops must find a way to send Your Holiness timely and exact intelligence." If necessary, they could bypass the formal bureaucracies.[51]

"It goes without saying," Pius said. He liked to keep important threads in his own hands. "The German question is the most important for me. I am reserving its handling to myself."[52]

That prospect seemed to unsettle the cardinals. "We must make sure Your Holiness is in good health," several said at once.

"I am healthy," Pius said. Then he stood. "Eminences, maybe we can get together again." As the cardinals made to leave, he tried to firm their resolve.

"We cannot give up on principles," the pope declared. "If they want a fight, let us not be afraid. But we still want to see if it is somehow possible to come to a peaceful solution. . . . When we have tried everything and still they absolutely want war, we will fight back." He repeated: "If they refuse, then we must fight."[53]

AT SS HEADQUARTERS, ALBERT HARTL WAS STILL HARD AT WORK. His superiors had asked him to expand his dossier on the new pope, so that they could publish parts of it as a pamphlet. It would lay down the party line on Pius, and it would go to press by the middle of March. Hartl built out his portrait with battle scenarios. If Pacelli continued to fight, it was crucial to know the weapons and tactics he would use.

Pacelli would not act rashly. His public statements against Nazism reflected Pius the Eleventh's stormy style more than Pacelli's. The new pope was not a ranting mystic but a careful watcher, a shrewd perceiver of things that coarser natures missed. "What he does, he hides within. What he feels, he does not show. The expression in his eyes does not change." Pacelli measured each word and controlled each move. That could make him seem superficial, pedantic, or fussy. Only rarely, with Americans or children, did his eyes glow and his voice rise.[54]

Yet Pacelli did not shun direct combat just as a point of style. A political realist, he would avoid playing a weak hand. The Church was "outdated, slack, and powerless" against authoritarian mass movements. Italy's conquest of Abyssinia, and Germany's annexation of Austria, had already revealed deep divisions between the pacifist Vatican and nationalist bishops. Pacelli would find his power over local churches total in theory but partial in practice.[55]

So he would fight indirectly. "Wherever the church does not feel itself in possession of power, it naturally applies more cunning methods." Hartl spotlighted three: militance, mutiny, and espionage; and the greatest of these was espionage.[56]

"Strictly speaking there is no Vatican Intelligence Service," Hartl wrote. Yet the Church did have "intelligence agents"—clergy who submitted reports. By analyzing these reports for decisionmaking, the Vatican gave them "intelligence treatment." The pope's staff, further, assigned "intelligence missions" to clergy and lay agents. Since the Vatican had intelligence agents, analysts, reports, and missions, the pope had "a *de facto* Intelligence Service."[57]

A near-medieval militance marked some of the alleged missions. Hartl reported, for instance, that Cardinal Faulhaber hid weapons for right-wing forces in Munich. While working in the Freising student seminary, from 1919 to 1923, Hartl heard that "a considerable quantity of weapons and ammunition was being kept hidden with the permission of Faulhaber. . . . There were rifles, machine guns and two small artillery pieces." Hartl reported that he saw these weapons himself. "Some of them were stored in a secret hiding place . . . which could be reached by a hidden staircase located under a stone slab near the main altar." Bavarian reactionaries used the weapons in secret military exercises, and perhaps in operations against left-wing terrorists. The Church could abet violence against the Nazis, using similar methods, if pushed.[58]

Militance would then become mutiny. "The Catholic church fundamentally claims for itself the right to depose heads of state," Hartl avowed, "and down to the present time it has also achieved this claim several times." During the Counter-Reformation, Jesuit agents purportedly killed French kings Henry the Third and Henry the Fourth, and plotted to blow up the British Parliament. Hartl already knew that Pacelli's Jesuit aide, Father Leiber, had no *moral* objections to similar moves against Hitler. The SS therefore needed to flush out any militant German Catholics linked to Leiber, and to "break their fighting stance."[59]

Uncovering these links was "extremely difficult," Hartl admitted. Only the pope's inner circle knew details of secret operations. Tracking papal spies, further, was a duty of German Military Intelligence (Abwehr), a rival spy unit rumored to harbor conservative opponents of Hitler. As a result, the SS had only a "meager" knowledge of "personalities in the Vatican Intelligence Service."[60]

Hartl hoped that sex would open windows on the Vatican's secret world. Archbishop Conrad Gröber of Freiburg reportedly had a half-Jewish mistress, and had cooperated with the SS, Hartl thought, "out of fear his love affair might be brought to light." The SS had trapped monks in gay nightclubs. The president of the Catholic charity Caritas, Father Johann Gartmeier, had been caught embezzling 120,000 marks when a ménage-a-trois went wrong: "He fell into the hands of two married women who had broken up their marriage[s] and then blackmailed him," one of Hartl's men reported. But exploiting these lapses had not exposed Church spies.[61]

One way in remained. All secret agents eventually sent intelligence to their handlers. This was the moment of greatest danger for any spy: most failed agents were caught while trying to communicate. As a precaution, agents and their handlers used intermediaries, called "cutouts," as couriers. Hartl therefore sought, as the SS noted, "to break the courier system operated by the Catholic Church."[62]

At first he thought he had penetrated the system. As Hartl reported, a Dr. Johannes Denk "ran a courier station of the Vatican Intelligence in Munich and was at the same time an agent of the Berlin Gestapo." Yet the letters passing through Denk's hands revealed no agents. Hartl deduced that the Church ran a still-uncovered courier system; and, having failed to infiltrate its German end, he turned his agents' eyes toward Rome.[63]

Pius met the Reich cardinals again on Sunday, 9 March. The "esatto" (verbatim) transcript showed the pope's men as outsiders never saw them. Relaxed after more than a week in Italy, the German princes of the Church bantered as if in a kind of clerical locker room. Colorful almost to irreverence, they joked about their prospects for sainthood. Bertram laughed about how Pius might address Hitler: "The Holy Father also says Heil, Heil!"[64]

"If Your Eminences will settle down again," the pope said, "I want to pursue the German question. It is so important."

He raised the lead agenda item, stressing its importance. The first part of the German question needing attention that morning did not bear on the spiritual plight of individual Catholics per se. It related, rather, to a problem of clandestine operations.

"The first question," the pope said, "involves the courier service between the Holy See and the German bishops." He added: "The matter is vital, since a courier link is the only way to get secret messages." Faulhaber's political secretary, Monsignor Johannes Neuhäusler, had sent two proposals. Pius read them out:

a) Periodically (each month or every two months) the Holy See sends a diplomat with whom the most reverend bishops can discuss issues and to whom they can also give written material intended for Rome. The route in this case would be something like: Rome, Vienna, Munich, Freiburg, Cologne, Berlin, Breslau, Rome (via Vienna or Munich).

b) A twofold courier service would be used. First, the one already operating between Rome and Berlin (question as to whether there should be an intermediate stopover in Munich). Secondly, one internal to Germany: Berlin, Munich, Freiburg, Cologne, Berlin. At the intermediate point, the materials intended for Rome would be collected and a courier would bring them to Berlin, from where they would be sent on to Rome via the first-mentioned courier service. Also, the intra-German courier would probably have to have diplomatic status to be assured of access.

Pius then glossed what he called this "technical" subject in plain terms. "It's about a courier, not officially from the Holy See, but who is, however, quite trustworthy. He will travel once a week. He will leave Rome on Saturday and arrive on Monday in Berlin. In the reverse direction, the Holy See will receive messages from Berlin on Monday. This weekly Rome-Berlin link is reliable. We have the best proof of the secrecy of this connection from the time of the encyclical *Mit brennender Sorge*. Nobody knew anything."

The intra-German network was more problematic. Episcopal agents had to elude the Sicherheitsdienst [SD], the SS spy service. "That's the big evil," Cardinal Bertram said. The group discussed how to link disparate dioceses with Berlin.[65]

CARD. BERTRAM: We have to do it clandestinely. When Saint Paul had himself lowered over the city wall at Damascus in a basket, he didn't have permission from the police either.[66]

HOLY FATHER: Yes, we have a good precedent there. Pius XI had already approved paying for the costs of the courier from Munich, Breslau and Cologne to Berlin out of the Peter's Pence. The messenger service is possible and easy in this way!

CARD. INNITZER: Yes, and he certainly must also be trustworthy.

CARD. SCHULTE: The courier service was not always provided by the same person. It would be better if it was always the same person.

CARD. FAULHABER: We change them often in Bavaria, because otherwise the police catch on. That's easy to do in Munich. The Europäische Hof is where traveling clergy stay; one almost always finds someone from Berlin there.[67]

HOLY FATHER: What about Vienna?

CARD. INNITZER: It works essentially the same from there.

CARD. FAULHABER: The bishops don't know when the courier goes to Berlin from Rome.

HOLY FATHER: Every Saturday, every week.

CARD. FAULHABER: May we tell that to the bishops?

HOLY FATHER: Sure! I always receive the pouch from Berlin on Monday evening. Quite regularly, certainly and securely. As I said, Pius XI had let me know that the bishops' expenses for the courier can be paid for quite readily out of the Peter's Pence.

Secure links would be critical if the Church had to fight the Nazi Party. Pius asked, "Are there any perceptible signs on the other side that they want to make peace with the Church?"

Innitzer saw the trend as "quite bad." In the countryside, the party tried to keep priests from teaching religion classes. But some farmers had resisted. "The school, they say, belongs to us. If there are no more religion classes, we will riot."

"We must not lose our nerve," Pius said. "We can't simply give up."

Cardinal Bertram warned, "The danger is great."[68]

At six in the morning on Sunday, 12 March, a procession snaked toward the bronze doors of St. Peter's. Swiss Guards led the line, followed by barefoot friars with belts of rope. Pius took his place at the end, borne on a portable throne. Ostrich plumes stirred silently to either side, like quotation marks.

Pius entered the basilica to a blare of silver trumpets and a burst of applause. Through pillars of incense he blessed the faces. At the High Altar, attendants placed on his shoulders a wool strip interwoven with black crosses.

Outside, police pushed back the crowds. People climbed onto ledges and balanced on chimneys, straining to see the palace balcony.

At noon Pius emerged. The cardinal deacon stood alongside him. Onto Pacelli's dark head he lowered a crown of pearls, shaped like a beehive. "Receive this Tiara," he said, "and know that you are the father of kings, the ruler of the world."[69]

Germany's ambassador to the Holy See, Diego von Bergen, reportedly said of the ceremony: "Very moving and beautiful, but it will be the last."[70]

As Pacelli was crowned, Hitler attended a state ceremony in Berlin. In a Memorial Day speech at the State Opera House, Grand Admiral Erich Raeder said, "Wherever we gain a foothold, we will maintain it! Wherever a gap appears, we will bridge it! . . . Germany strikes swiftly and strongly!" Hitler reviewed honor guards, then placed a wreath at a memorial to the Unknown Soldier. That same day, he issued orders for his soldiers to occupy Czechoslovakia.[71]

On 15 March the German army entered Prague. Through snow and mist, on ice-bound roads, Hitler followed in his three-axle Mercedes, its bulletproof windows up. Himmler's gang of 800 SS officers hunted undesirables. A papal agent cabled Rome, with "details obtained confidentially," reporting the arrests of all who "had spoken and written against the Third Reich and its Führer." Soon 487 Czech and Slovak Jesuits landed in prison camps, where it was "a common sight," one witness said, "to see a priest dressed in rags, exhausted, pulling a car and behind him a youth in SA [Storm Troop] uniform, whip in hand."[72]

Hitler's seizure of Czechoslovakia put Europe in crisis. He had scrapped his pledge to respect Czech integrity, made at Munich six months before, which British Prime Minister Neville Chamberlain said guaranteed "peace in our time." Now London condemned "Germany's attempt to obtain world domination, which it was in the interest of all countries to resist." Poland's government, facing a German ultimatum over the disputed Danzig corridor, mobilized its troops. On 18 March, the papal agent in Warsaw reported "a state of tension" between the Reich and Poland "which could have the most serious consequences." Another intelligence report reaching the Vatican called the situation "desperately grave."[73]

Perhaps no pope in nearly a millennium had taken power amid such general fear. The scene paralleled that in 1073, when Charlemagne's old empire imploded, and Europe needed only a spark to burn. "Even the election of the pope stood in the shadow of the Swastika," Nazi labor leader Robert Ley boasted. "I am sure they spoke of nothing else than how to find a candidate for the chair of St. Peter who was more or less up to dealing with Adolf Hitler."[74]

THE POLITICAL CRISIS HAD IN FACT PRODUCED A POLITICAL POPE. Amid the gathering storm, the cardinals had elected the candidate most skilled in statecraft, in the quickest conclave in four centuries. His long career in the papal foreign service made Pacelli the dean of Church diplomats. He had hunted on horseback with Prussian generals, endured at dinner parties the rants of exiled kings, faced down armed revolutionaries with just his jeweled cross. As cardinal secretary of state, he had discreetly aligned with friendly states, and won Catholic rights from hostile ones. Useful to every government, a lackey to none, he impressed one German diplomat as "a politician to the high extreme."[75]

Politics were in Pacelli's blood. His grandfather had been interior minister of the Papal States, a belt of territories bigger than Denmark, which popes had ruled since the Dark Ages. Believing that these lands kept popes politically independent, the Pacellis fought to preserve them against Italian nationalists. The Pacellis lost. By 1870 the pope ruled only Vatican City, a diamond-shaped kingdom the size of a golf course. Born in Rome six years later, raised in the shadow of St. Peter's, Eugenio Pacelli inherited a highly political sense of mission. As an altar boy, he prayed for the Papal States; in school essays, he protested secular claims; and as pope, he saw politics as religion by other means.[76]

Some thought his priestly mixing in politics a contradiction. Pacelli contained many contradictions. He visited more countries, and spoke more languages, than any previous pope—yet remained a homebody, who lived with his mother until he was forty-one. Eager to meet children, unafraid to deal with dictators, he was timid with bishops and priests. He led one of the planet's most public lives, and one of its loneliest. He was familiar to billions, but his best friend was a goldfinch. He was open with strangers, pensive with friends. His aides could not see into his soul. To some he did not seem "a human being with impulses, emotions, passions"—but others recalled him weeping over the fate of the Jews. One observer found him "pathetic and tremendous," another "despotic and insecure." Half of him, it seemed, was always counteracting the other half.[77]

A dual devotion to piety and politics clove him deeply. No one could call him a mere Machiavellian, a Medici-pope: he said Mass daily, communed with God for hours, reported visions of Jesus and Mary. Visitors remarked on his saintly appearance; one called him "a man like a ray of light." Yet those who thought Pius not of this world were mistaken. Hyperspirituality, a withdrawal into the sphere of the purely religious, found no favor with him. A US intelligence officer in Rome noted how much time Pius devoted to politics and how closely he supervised all aspects of the Vatican Foreign Office. While writing an encyclical on the Mystical Body of Christ, he was also assessing the likely strategic impact of atomic weapons. He judged them a "useful means of defense."[78]

Even some who liked Pacelli disliked his concern with worldly power. "One is tempted to say that attention to the political is too much," wrote Jacques Maritain, the French postwar ambassador to the Vatican, "considering the essential role of the Church." The Church's essential role, after all, was to save souls. But in practice, the spiritual purpose entailed a temporal one: the achievement of political conditions under which souls could be saved. Priests must baptize, say Mass, and consecrate marriages without interference from the state. A fear of state power structured Church thought: the Caesars had killed Peter and Paul, and Jesus.[79]

The pope therefore did not have one role, but two. He had to render to God what was God's, and keep Caesar at bay. Every pope was in part a politician; some led armies. The papacy Pacelli inherited was as bipolar as he was. He merely encompassed, in compressed form, the existential problem of the Church: how to be a spiritual institution in a physical and highly political world.[80]

It was a problem that could not be solved, only managed. And if it was a dilemma which had caused twenty centuries of war between Church and state, climaxing just as Pacelli became pope, it was also a quandary that would, on his watch, put Catholicism in conflict with itself. For the tectonic pull of opposing tensions, of spiritual and temporal imperatives, opened a fissure in the foundations of the Church that could not be closed. Ideally, a pope's spiritual function ought not clash with his political one. But if and when it did, which should take precedence? That was always a difficult question—but never more difficult than during the bloodiest years in history, when Pius the Twelfth would have to choose his answer.

On 1 September 1939, Pius awoke at around 6:00 a.m. at his summer residence, Castel Gandolfo, a medieval fortress straddling a dormant volcano. His housekeeper, Sister Pascalina, had just released his canaries from their cages when the bedside telephone rang. Answering in his usual manner, "E'qui Pacelli" ("Pacelli here"), he heard the trembling voice of Cardinal Luigi Maglione, relaying intelligence from the papal nuncio in Berlin: fifteen minutes earlier, the German Wehrmacht had surged into Poland.[81]

At first Pius carried on normally, papally. He shuffled to his private chapel and bent in prayer. Then, after a cold shower and an electric shave, he celebrated Mass, attended by Bavarian nuns. But at breakfast, Sister Pascalina recalled, he probed his rolls and coffee warily, "as if opening a stack of bills in the mail." He ate little for the next six years. By war's end, although he stood six feet tall, he would weigh only 125 pounds. His nerves frayed from moral and political burdens, he would remind Pascalina of a "famished robin or an overdriven horse." With the sigh of a great sadness, his undersecretary of state, Domenico Tardini, reflected: "This man, who was peace-loving by temperament, education, and conviction, was to have what might be called a pontificate of war."[82]

In war the Vatican tried to stay neutral. Because the pope represented Catholics in all nations, he had to appear unbiased. Taking sides would compel some Catholics to betray their country, and others their faith.[83]

But Poland was special. For centuries, the Poles had been a Catholic bulwark between Protestant Prussia and Orthodox Russia. Pius would recognize the exiled Polish government, not the Nazi protectorate. "Neutrality" described his official stance, not his real one. As he told France's ambassador when Warsaw fell: "You know on which side my sympathies lie. But I cannot say so."[84]

As news of Poland's agony spread, however, Pius felt compelled to speak. By October, the Vatican had received reports of Jews shot in synagogues and buried in ditches. The Nazis, moreover, were targeting Polish Catholics as well. They would eventually murder perhaps 2.4 million Catholic Poles in "nonmilitary killing operations." The persecution of Polish Gentiles fell far short of the industrialized genocide visited on Europe's Jews. But it had near-genocidal traits and prepared the way for what followed.[85]

On 20 October Pius issued a public statement. His encyclical *Summi Pontificatus*, known in English as *Darkness over the Earth*, began by denouncing attacks on Judaism. "Who among 'the Soldiers of Christ' does not feel himself incited to a more determined resistance, as he perceives Christ's enemies wantonly break the Tables of God's Commandments to substitute other tables and other standards stripped of the ethical content of the Revelation on Sinai?" Even at the cost of "torments or martyrdom," he wrote, one "must confront such wickedness by saying: '*Non licet*; it is not allowed!'" Pius then stressed the "unity of the human race." Underscoring that this unity refuted racism, he said he would consecrate bishops of twelve ethnicities in the Vatican crypt. He clinched the point by insisting that "the spirit, the teaching and the work of the Church can never be other than that which the Apostle of the Gentiles preached: 'there is neither Gentile nor Jew.'"[86]

The world judged the work an attack on Nazi Germany. "Pope Condemns Dictators, Treaty Violators, Racism," the *New York Times* announced in a front-page banner headline. "The unqualified condemnation which Pope Pius XII heaped on totalitarian, racist and materialistic theories of government in his encyclical *Summi Pontificatus* caused a profound stir," the Jewish Telegraphic Agency reported. "Although it had been expected that the Pope would attack ideologies hostile to the Catholic Church, few observers had expected so outspoken a document." Pius even pledged to speak out again, if necessary. "We owe no greater debt to Our office and to Our time than to testify to the truth," he wrote. "In the fulfillment of this, Our duty, we shall not let Ourselves be influenced by earthly considerations."[87]

It was a valiant vow, and a vain one. He would not use the word "Jew" in public again until 1945. Allied and Jewish press agencies still hailed him as anti-Nazi during the war. But in time, his silence strained Catholic-Jewish relations, and reduced the moral credibility of the faith. Debated into the next century, the causes and meaning of that silence would become the principal enigma in both the biography of Pius and the history of the modern Church.

Judging Pius by what he did not say, one could only damn him. With images of piles of skeletal corpses before his eyes; with women and young children compelled, by torture, to kill each other; with millions of innocents caged like criminals, butchered like cattle, and burned like trash—he should have spoken out. He had this duty, not only as pontiff, but as a person. After his first encyclical, he did reissue general distinctions between race-hatred and Christian love. Yet with the ethical coin of the Church, Pius proved frugal; toward what he privately termed "Satanic forces," he showed public moderation; where no conscience could stay neutral, the Church seemed to be. During the world's greatest moral crisis, its greatest moral leader seemed at a loss for words.

But the Vatican did not work by words alone. By 20 October, when Pius put his name to *Summi Pontficatus*, he was enmeshed in a war behind the war. Those who later explored the maze of his policies, without a clue to his secret actions, wondered why he seemed so hostile toward Nazism, and then fell so silent. But when his secret acts are mapped, and made to overlay his public words, a stark correlation emerges. The last day during the war when Pius publicly said the word "Jew" is also, in fact, the first day history can document his choice to help kill Adolf Hitler.[88]

CHAPTER 2

THE END OF GERMANY

O N 22 AUGUST 1939, TEN DAYS BEFORE GERMANY INVADED PO-
land, Hitler called his commanders to his private Bavarian
mountain. After passing through the security checks, the generals and
admirals entered Hitler's chalet, the Berghof, and settled into chairs
in the reception hall. A picture window lowered hydraulically into the
floor, opening the room to such an immense alpine panorama that one
guest felt suspended in space. In the distance gleamed the teeth of the
Untersberg Alps, guarding the rumored grave of Charlemagne. Hitler,
leaning on a grand piano, spoke with barely a glance at the notes in his
left hand.[1]

At the back of the room sat a mouse-like man, nervous and intense,
with piercing blue eyes and a shock of white hair. He pulled out a pad
and pencil. As chief of German military intelligence (Abwehr), Admiral
Wilhelm Canaris could make notes on secret German military briefings. Other attendees later affirmed the substantial accuracy of his transcript, which would become an exhibit in the Nuremberg war crimes
tribunal.[2]

"I have called you together," Hitler said, "to give you some insight
into the factors upon which I have decided to act. It was clear to me that
a conflict with Poland had to come." Germany would never regain her

honor or restore her prestige until she reclaimed all lands lost in the last war. Therefore, Hitler had decided to attack. Though the British had pledged to protect Poland, they would probably not intervene: "Our enemies are *kleine Würmchen* [little worms]." Referencing a Radio Vatican appeal for peace talks, which the pope had made in Rome that morning, Hitler said he worried only "that at the last moment some pig-dog will yet submit to me a plan for mediation."[3]

Hitler spoke for another hour, going into operational details, and then they all broke for lunch. After caviar on the terrace, served by SS officers in snow-white summer uniforms, Hitler resumed in an even more fanatical mode. Canaris's pencil sped across the paper again. "We must shoulder this risk. . . . We are faced with the harsh alternatives of striking or of certain annihilation. . . . Eighty million people must obtain what is their right. Their existence must be made secure. . . . The moment is now favorable for a solution, so strike! . . . Execution: Harsh and ruthless! Close your hearts to pity!"[4]

What Hitler said next shocked his generals. Canaris dared not put it to paper, but Field Marshal Fedor von Bock later confided the details to a colleague. Special SS Death's Head formations, Hitler revealed, would snuff out the least flicker of Polish strength by liquidating thousands of Catholic priests. As one of Bock's colonels recounted, Hitler asserted "that the Poles would be treated with merciless severity after the end of the campaign. . . . [H]e did not want to burden the army with 'liquidations' necessary for political reasons, but rather to have the SS undertake the destruction of the Polish upper stratum, that is, above all the destruction of the Polish clergy."[5]

"The victor will not be questioned afterwards whether his reasons were just," Canaris's transcription continued. "What matters is not to have right on our side, but simply will to win." Hitler ended by saying: "I have done my duty. Now do yours."[6]

There followed a long beat of what Bock remembered as "icy silence." Finally Walther von Brauchitsch, commander in chief of the armed forces, said, "Gentlemen, return to your posts as soon as possible." Canaris closed his notebook and went back down the mountain.[7]

THAT NIGHT HITLER PACED THE TERRACE, STARING AT THE HORIzon. "The eerie turquoise colored sky to the north turned first violet and then blood-red," his adjutant recalled. "At first we thought there must be a serious fire behind the Untersberg Mountain, but then the glow covered the whole northern sky in the manner of the northern lights. Such an occurrence is exceptionally rare in southern Germany. I was very moved and told Hitler that it augured a bloody war."[8]

"If it must be so, the sooner the better," Hitler replied. "No one knows how much longer I shall live. Therefore, better a conflict now. . . . Essentially all depends on me, on my existence, because of my political talents. Probably no one will ever again have the confidence of the German people as completely as I have. My existence is therefore a factor of great value. But I might be eliminated at any time." He feared that "some fanatic armed with a telescopic-sighted firearm" would shoot him.[9]

Hitler did not think an attacker would act alone. If he suspected there was a plot to remove him, he told his deputy Martin Bormann, he would take urgent measures against the one faction he suspected would most likely sponsor a coup. "Spiritual factors are decisive," Hitler had said in his speech that day. Neither bourgeois nor Marxist elements could motivate true idealists, willing to risk their lives to kill him. The greatest danger would instead come from "assassins whipped up by the black crows in confessionals." The "dunderheads" who opposed him, Hitler said, included "particularly [the leaders] of political Catholicism." If anyone ever tried a coup, he vowed, he would "round up all the leaders of political Catholicism from their residences, and have them executed."[10]

THE NEXT DAY, BACK IN BERLIN, CANARIS BROODED IN HIS ABWEHR office. While his dachshunds slept on a blanket-piled cot, Canaris worked his notes into a coded digest of the Führer's remarks. Then, in a meeting with his closest colleagues, Canaris read out the crucial passages in his characteristic slight lisp. Only then did they notice the extent of his despair. "He was still utterly horrified," Abwehr officer Hans

Gisevius wrote. "His voice trembled as he read. Canaris was acutely aware that he had been witness to a monstrous scene."[11]

Canaris hated Hitler with the fervor of one who once had loved him. Hitler had promised to preserve Germany's religious and military traditions, but delivered a pagan mockery of the old ideals. Canaris's epiphany came in 1938, when Hitler removed Germany's two ranking generals after impugning their sexual honor. Rather than resign in protest, Canaris stuck to his post as spy chief, giving Hitler's conservative enemies a secret weapon to destroy the monster they had helped create. Directing covert activities, privy to state secrets, Canaris and his comrades were perfectly positioned to damage the Nazis. They could strike at Hitler from within.[12]

After Canaris read out his notes to his colleagues, they debated what to do. His deputy Hans Oster wanted to leak the text of Hitler's speech. Perhaps it would spur the regime's opponents into a peace-preserving coup d'état. If London and Paris reacted sharply enough, Germany's generals might follow the advice of their chief of staff, Franz Halder, who had told the British ambassador to Berlin, "You have to strike Hitler's hand with an ax."[13]

It seemed worth a try. On 25 August Oster smuggled the document to Alexander C. Kirk, the American chargé d'affaires in Berlin, who said, "Oh, take this out of here. . . . I don't want to get involved." Oster then sent a copy to a British embassy official; but the unsigned text, on plain paper, did not impress him. In dealing with foreign powers, Oster decided, the plotters must seek some imprimatur, some stamp of legitimacy, some way of guaranteeing German goodwill.[14]

Canaris meanwhile tried more active measures. Canaris linked with deputy Foreign Secretary Ernst von Weizsäcker, who wrote in his diary after learning that war loomed: "It is an appalling idea that my name should be associated with this event, to say nothing of the unforeseeable results for the existence of Germany and for my own family." On 30 August Weizsäcker met Hitler in the Reich Chancellery and begged for peace. In his pocket he carried a Luger pistol, loaded with two bullets. Later he said that he had meant to kill Hitler and then himself. He lost his nerve and left in a sweat. As Weizsäcker told Canaris's intermediary,

"I regret that there is nothing in my upbringing that would fit me to kill a man."[15]

Hitler issued an order to attack Poland in twenty-four hours. Abwehr officer Hans Gisevius drove to headquarters, raced up the stairs, and met Canaris and other officers descending. Canaris let his companions proceed as he drew Gisevius into a corridor. Choked with tears, Canaris said, "This means the end of Germany."[16]

ON 1 SEPTEMBER 1939, A MILLION GERMANS POURED INTO POLAND. Two days later, Hitler boarded a train to tour the front. There his henchmen began to liquidate what he had called the "spiritual factors" that might inspire resistance. "We will let the small fry off," SS spy chief Reinhard Heydrich said, but "the Catholic priests . . . must all be killed."[17]

Canaris flew to Poland to protest. On 12 September he reached Ill-nau, where Hitler's train had stopped, and confronted General Wilhelm Keitel in the conference car. "I pointed out that I knew extensive executions were planned in Poland," Canaris recorded, noting that "clergy were to be exterminated." Keitel replied "that this matter had already been settled by the Führer."[18]

Hitler himself then entered the meeting. One witness, Lieutenant Colonel Erwin Lahousen, recalled that Hitler deemed it "especially necessary to eliminate the clergy." Lahousen added, "I don't remember the exact term that he used, but it was not ambiguous and it meant 'kill.'" To expedite his plans, Hitler would put Poland under the control of one of his party cronies, attorney Hans Frank. "The task I give you, Frank, is a Satanic one," Canaris overheard Hitler say. "Other people to whom such territories are handed would ask: 'What would you build?' I will ask the opposite. I will ask: 'What did you destroy?'"[19]

The results of these orders Canaris soon saw firsthand. On 28 September he wandered the ruins of Warsaw, where rats ate corpses and smoke turned the sun red. An old Jew stood over his dead wife, shouting, "There is no God! Hitler and the bombs are the only gods! There is no grace and pity in the world!" From the roof of a sports stadium, one of Canaris's friends recalled, Hitler watched his artillery pound the city, "and his eyes nearly popped out of his head and he became quite a different person. He was suddenly seized by a lust for blood." Canaris took to his quarters and vomited. A friend said that he returned to Berlin "entirely broken."[20]

Hitler had by then decided to invade France. "Revolutions by their nature may accelerate but cannot slow down," one of Canaris's colleagues reflected. "It became increasingly clear that, just as a cyclist can only stay aright through forward motion, so Adolf Hitler could only stay in power through continuation of the war." With the attack on France slated for late October, those who opposed it had a four-week window to spike the revolution's wheels. The generals as a group "fought tooth and nail against the French campaign," General Dietrich von Choltitz recalled, while the bolder among them diverted troops to stage a coup in Berlin.[21]

Canaris initialed the coup plan. Two panzer divisions would hold Berlin while sixty Abwehr commandos stormed the chancellery. Although the order stated blandly that Hitler would "be rendered innocuous," the commandos meant to shoot him like a mad dog. The military would install a civilian junta, schedule elections, and open peace talks. To dramatize the change, the new rulers would lift the wartime blackout, and the lights would go on all over Germany.[22]

The plan presented obvious obstacles. It required knowing Hitler's schedule and movements, which he himself often decided at the last minute. The generals, further, would have to break their oaths to Hitler and revolt against civilian authority. They would hardly take such an unprecedented action if it might cause their own defeat and enslavement. They would remove Hitler only if the Allies agreed beforehand to a just peace.

Linking domestic plans to foreign forces posed a further challenge. The plotters faced here a double dilemma: convincing the Allies they spoke the truth, and keeping the Nazis from learning the truth. They needed credibility, and they needed cover. Canaris found an answer to both puzzles in the person of the pope.

CANARIS HAD ROMANTIC AND FANCIFUL VIEWS ABOUT THE CHURCH.
Raised as an evangelical, he came to admire the Roman religion, its organization, the strength of its faith; he deviated into a vague mysticism that led him to wander Gothic cathedrals in mute awe. "He was greatly influenced by Italy and the Vatican," a colleague recalled, and "many of his conspirational activities could be traced back to this influence." By some accounts, Canaris's cross-and-dagger complex dated to the First World War, when he mounted a secret mission to Italy in the company of a priest. In one variant of the story, he escaped an Italian jail by killing the prison chaplain and donning his cassock. Yet these perhaps confused associations did not decide Canaris's view of the pope. His choice lay in realistic calculation.[23]

Canaris knew and trusted Pacelli. During the 1920s, when the future pope was the "best-informed diplomat in Berlin," they had shared horse rides on a mutual friend's estate. Canaris admired Pacelli's realism and discretion—and his dislike for Hitler. If the pope joined the conspiracy, Canaris thought, the plotters would at least have a hearing in the West. Conversely, if Pius could broker peace terms in advance, this might spur the army to change the regime.[24]

In late September, Canaris set out to recruit Pius into the plot. But he needed some way to raise such a sensitive issue with the pope. Canaris himself could not travel to the Vatican without rousing suspicion, even if Pius agreed to see him. The plotters needed a go-between, a "cut-out." Because the Abwehr was an adjunct of the Protestant-dominated Prussian military, Canaris's deputies hardly knew where to look for intermediaries with the Holy Father. As it happened, however, one of the Abwehr's Catholic contacts in Munich yielded the name, and then the file, of a man who seemed born for the mission.[25]

CHAPTER 3

JOEY OX

Josef Müller was a self-made lawyer of sturdy peasant stock, a beer-loving Bavarian with sky-blue eyes, and an Iron Cross hero of the Great War. Because he worked his way through school driving an oxcart, friends ribbed him as *Ochsensepp*, Joey Ox. The nickname aptly captured Müller's robust build, his rural roots, and the strong will that brought him such bad and good fortune.[1]

His life was a wild mix of exploits. Müller led troops, smuggled documents, played politics, plotted murder, wrote sermons, rescued Jews, ransomed bishops, eluded capture, suffered betrayal, endured torture, confounded his captors, married his true love, and went to his grave with grace. Pope Pius the Twelfth said flatly that Dr. Müller "worked wonders." Colleagues in the Bavarian People's Party seldom introduced him without saying that "Joey Ox overcame the prevailing [communist] forces in Bavaria in two days at the age of twenty-one." Political rivals like Konrad Adenauer, the first chancellor of postwar West Germany, dismissed him as a mere "adventurer." But a Bavarian obituary expressed the more general view: "This colorful, jovial, cunning, convivial and hard-drinking democrat was a good man."[2]

Doctor Müller was a godfather figure in Catholic Munich. Through his legal work he came to sit on boards and control companies: he was by turns a brewer, printer, banker, book publisher, and importer of tobacco. On any given day his waiting room might include a Belgian abbot, a Portuguese consul, a professor of cosmology, the boss of a banned labor union, a dealer in precious stones, and a Metternich baron suffering a breakdown. His law office adjoined the former Wittelsbach palace, now the Bavarian headquarters of the SS, and some of his clients owed their lives or livelihoods to Joey Ox. They repaid him with friendship, the jovial appellation *Ochsensepp*, and modest gifts—a cask of Ettaler beer, a tub of personally baked pretzels. It was unstated but understood that he might someday ask a small service in return. For those who fell afoul of the Nazis, he was a fixer and a benefactor, a guardian and advocate—part Oskar Schindler, part Vito Corleone.[3]

By 1939, Müller had bound hundreds to him. He was "a popular comrade," as Gestapo records said—and not just because he did favors. He had what one American spy called "a rather awesome reputation for inexhaustible conviviality." Once he won three trainloads of German war prisoners in a drinking bet with Soviet diplomat Leonid Georgiev. But if his blue eyes sparkled partly from wheat beer, he was not an alcoholic, at least not by Bavarian wartime standards. He drank hard but watched his words. When he poured out his feelings freely, or filled his glass too often, he did so only among reliable friends, like the anti-Nazi regulars at a pub near Berlin's Hotel Kaiserhof. In more sober or less certain circles, he spoke in a semaphore of pregnant gesture. Sometimes, for instance, Müller would grasp the portrait of Hitler that seemed to grace every room in the Reich, set it face down on a table, and say: "He's up there crookedly. He deserves to be hanged correctly."[4]

MÜLLER WAS IN BERLIN ON BUSINESS ON 30 JANUARY 1933, WHEN Germany fell into Hitler's hands. Below his hotel balcony, on the Wilhelmstrasse, thousands of Nazis massed by torchlight, stamping their jackboots, beating drums. He recalled thinking, as he looked down at the flickering faces: It'll be all over if they're ever turned loose. "I sensed for the first time what it means when a collective turns individuals into a nameless mass," he recalled. "It was not a literal fire that had been unleashed here," but a human inferno—the heat of hate.[5]

Five weeks later, the fire spread to Bavaria. At a meeting of the Bavarian Sport Pilots Club, a local airfield commander told Müller that the national government would close the runways the next day. Something was going to happen. Müller's unease deepened when a club member moved to expel the Jewish treasurer. Protesting that they must not abandon loyalty and comradeship for political reasons, Müller threatened to resign. But he did not have the room with him. Nazi Party membership had become a path to professional advancement. The motion carried and Müller quit.[6]

Later that day, he ran into a banker friend with SS links. Because the Nazis had never won Bavarian elections, his friend said, they would seize power there by force. The takeover would happen "tomorrow." Müller rushed to the home of Bavaria's prime minister, Heinrich Held, who had long relied on him for legal advice. As he helped the diabetic Held inject insulin, Müller urged him to mobilize the state guard. But the prime minister hesitated to inflame the situation.[7]

The next morning, as Müller sipped coffee with Held in the prime minister's office, the door flew open. SS chief Heinrich Himmler banged a horsewhip on the desk and demanded that Held cede power. To make Held's "voluntary" resignation more palatable, Himmler offered him the Bavarian ambassadorship to the Vatican. When Held asked for two hours to think it over, Himmler stalked out, vowing to mobilize "the people's will."[8]

Müller urged drastic action. As the head of a state under siege, Held had the authority to form a special guard detail, which could arrest Himmler and put him before a firing squad. But Held did not want to provoke a civil war.[9]

The situation became desperate. Brownshirts surged through the streets. Müller hustled Held into an unmarked car. They drove to the home of Müller's fiancée, Maria, where Held conceded that "the Devil is loose in Bavaria." After dark, Müller drove the prime minister to exile in Switzerland.[10]

IN THE NEXT MONTHS, MÜLLER'S BEST FRIENDS BEGAN TO VANISH. Through discreet inquiries he learned that they had landed in the Reich's first concentration camp, at Dachau. Atrocity tales soon crossed the moors between Dachau and Munich. The SS secretly murdered Jews and humiliated "political Catholics," Müller heard from the camp's chief warden, an old war buddy. He produced a photo showing Held's son with a shaved head, pulling a road roller in a convict's stripes. Müller slapped the photo down on the desk of Bavarian justice minister Hans Frank, another old friend, who asked Hitler to close Dachau. Hitler kept it open.[11]

By early 1934, Müller's intrigues had riled the secret police. His name appeared on an SS list of Catholics opposed to the regime. Dachau's warden warned that Müller himself would soon "arrive" at the camp. A few weeks later, on 9 February, the Gestapo arrested Müller in Munich and charged him with "a treasonous conspiracy . . . punishable by death."[12]

Heinrich Himmler directed the interrogation. With his small eyes darting behind rimless glasses, his manicured hands stroking a receding chin, he seemed more schoolmaster than hangman. A stickler for procedure, he ordered a transcript made of the interview. He opened by saying that there could be no compromise between the Church and the Reich, because each demanded "the whole soul of the man." Müller agreed. His interrogator then noted that Müller had represented enemies of the regime. Müller countered that there was no law against practicing law.[13]

Himmler asked what advice Müller gave Held during the takeover. Müller told the truth. He admitted that he urged having Himmler shot. As the head of government then, Held could have legally ordered it. Wouldn't Himmler have made the same recommendation in Müller's position?[14]

Müller's courage confounded Himmler. An Allied Intelligence officer later posited that Müller, "a tough and two-fisted political infighter," was "the type of man-sprung-from-the-people whom the Nazis loved to claim as their own and who, as an opponent, rather daunted them." Somewhat awed by his prisoner's will, Himmler invited him to join the SS. Müller refused. "I am philosophically opposed to you. I am a practicing Catholic, and my brother is a Catholic priest. Where could I find the possibility of a compromise there?" Himmler congratulated Müller on his "manly defense" and let him go.[15]

Shortly after Müller's release, an SS man called on him. Hans Rattenhuber, a thirty-seven-year-old ex-cop, commanded Hitler's bodyguard. A tall man with plain values, he saw most of the Nazi bosses as corrupt sycophants, and admired Müller for standing up to Himmler. Ever since word went round that he had admitted urging Himmler's execution, Rattenhuber had wanted to meet Joey Ox.

Over steins of beer, they became friends. Rattenhuber cherished their beer brotherhood because it gave him the chance, so rare in a dictatorship, to speak his mind. Müller relished Rattenhuber's rants because they revealed Nazi plans against the Church. Thus developed one of the singular friendships of the Second World War, in which the head of Hitler's bodyguard regularly revealed SS secrets to a Vatican spy.[16]

MUNICH CARDINAL MICHAEL FAULHABER DID NOT ACTUALLY ASK Josef Müller to spy. Though they were fraternity brothers, and addressed each other with the familiar "du," Faulhaber used an intermediary—a husky monsignor with horn-rimmed glasses and a bulbous nose—who also, it seems, did not *directly* ask Müller to engage in espionage. Instead, Monsignor Johannes Neuhäusler, who used the codename "Casanova," asked Müller to help save the Leo Haus, an insolvent holding company for Catholic media. Müller thus became what Vatican officials called "a trusted collaborator." The work became more secret and more dangerous until, by Müller's account, it seemed "almost sacrilegious." But in long walks through the Englischer Garten, Munich's central park, Neuhäusler helped Müller get his mind around the Church doctrine of the *Disciplina Arcani*, the Way of Secrecy.[17]

The Way proceeded from the practice of Christ himself. Preaching in a hostile environment, he ordered his disciples to conceal his identity, his words, and his actions from the uninitiated. He formed his apostles into clandestine cells, led by James and John, whom he called the "Sons of Thunder," and whom he took to a mountain, with his protégé Peter, to discuss secret matters. They met in safe houses, which Jesus accessed by hidden separate entrances, and whose locations they revealed to each other through coded signals, such as following a man with a jug of water through Jerusalem. Christ took these measures not to evade the Roman political authorities, but to elude the Jewish high priesthood, then held by the Annas family, of whom the Talmud records: "A plague on the House of Annas: a plague on their spying."[18]

Church Fathers followed the Way of Secrecy after Jesus died. The faith at first survived only as a clandestine movement in Rome; and since the Gospel writers thought Jesus's return imminent, the early Christians perhaps expected to remain underground operatives until the end of times. For three centuries, until Christianity became Rome's religion, the Church concealed baptism and confirmation, the Our Father, the Holy Trinity and the Eucharist, the creeds and Scriptures— not only from heathens, but even from converts to the faith, who, as one later Church authority explained, "might be spies wishing to be instructed only that they might betray."[19]

The price of betrayal was high. "Some were nailed on crosses, others sewn up in the skins of wild beasts, and exposed to the fury of the dogs; others again, smeared over with combustible materials, were used as torches to illuminate the darkness of the night," Tacitus wrote of Nero's persecutions. The first popes were martyred to a man: the emperors sent some of them to Sardinia, where each had the nerve at the back of his right knee severed, his right eye gouged out and cauterized with molten iron; and then, if under thirty, he endured castration. In the ensuing centuries, scarcely a year had passed when the Church was not at war in the world. One hundred seventy times usurpers drove a pontiff from the city, and thirty-three times killed him on Peter's Chair. The ninth and tenth centuries alone saw John the Twelfth decapitated, John the Fourteenth starved, Adrian the Third poisoned, Benedict the Sixth asphyxiated, Stephen the Eighth dismembered, Leo the Fifth bludgeoned, Stephen the Sixth strangled, Stephen the Seventh garroted, John the Eighth clubbed to death, John the Tenth suffocated under a pillow, and Boniface the Seventh beaten unconscious, left under a statue of Marcus Aurelius, and stabbed to death by passersby.[20]

Popes had therefore learned to defend themselves. By the seventh century, Pope Martin the First had targeted spies against potential kidnappers; and since then, tips from secret papal agents had saved dozens of pontiffs from death or capture. The Church justified these and other secret operations not just by Jesus's example, but also by Aquinas's doctrine, which allowed ambushes and other secret means in the conduct of a just war. During the Counter-Reformation, Jesuits had expanded Aquinas's teaching to justify plots against Protestant kings; and during Italian unification, the Vatican used agents provocateur to lure rebels to Perugia, where Swiss Papal troops beheaded them.[21]

What Neuhäusler proposed seemed by comparison tame. He wanted Müller to hold on to some files. Since Neuhäusler had hired Müller to save the Leo Haus, they could claim attorney-client privilege if the Nazis ever tried to seize the documents. When Müller agreed, he became an agent in a counter-Nazi secret service.

"We need to be prepared for an uphill battle," Cardinal Faulhaber had said at the first meeting of the Munich Ordinariat after Hitler took power. "It will be important that our defense and resistance measures are uniformly directed, and that all the intelligence is collected in one place." Faulhaber asked Neuhäusler to take on that "serious and dangerous job," and to coordinate the project with the Vatican.[22]

In April 1933 Neuhäusler traveled to Rome. Although Cardinal Secretary of State Pacelli had just begun negotiating the Reich concordat, he already saw the need for a central registry of concordat violations. Neuhäusler described the situation as perilous: hooting thugs pummeled street collectors for charities, horsewhipped worshipers as they left Mass, trashed Catholic printers and dumped trays of broken type in the streets. But of these flagrant acts, Neuhäusler brought stories rather than proof. "Send us reliable reports!" he reported Pacelli saying. "Otherwise, we can't help you."[23]

Müller's law office became the central registry Pacelli wanted. Joey Ox collated reports of concordat violations from the Munich archdiocese and from the Bavarian Jesuits, whose Kaulbachstrasse headquarters he passed on his way to work. Although Neuhäusler told his sources to keep their "eyes and ears open for anything," they focused on ten priority targets:

(1) Anti-Christian decrees
(2) Press censorship
(3) Hindrance of clergy
(4) Suppression of clubs
(5) Breakup of meetings
(6) Desecration of crosses
(7) Pressure on Church schools
(8) Proceedings against orders and cloisters
(9) Injury and imprisonment of leading Catholics
(10) Secret trials of Nazi officials for financial and sexual crimes

So much material poured in that Neuhäusler and Müller had to disperse it daily to backup sites in case the SS mounted an illegal search.[24]

Evaluating the intelligence proved harder than collecting and storing it. Since Müller knew the material would go to Rome and inform Vatican views, he did not wish to relay raw or false data. "I wanted to check the veracity of reports to send to the Cardinal Secretary of State," he said. "I felt duty bound to provide intelligence to Eugenio Pacelli with evaluations such as 'with a probability bordering on certainty,' or only 'likely.'"[25]

To verify the information, Müller built a network of agents. He sounded army, college, and law-school friends with access to Nazi officials—a community of the well-informed, who worked in newspapers, banks, and even, as with Hans Rattenhuber, the SS itself. One of Müller's more colorful informants, "Sister" Pia Bauer, ran a charity for Nazi Old Fighters, and styled herself a Nazi nun; the price of information from this harpy was to drink with her in a side room of the Eidenschink bank, and whenever Müller met her, he noted, "she lifted her skirt and showed a scar on her bare ass," which she had received as the only woman to march with Hitler during his failed 1923 Beer Hall putsch, and which she displayed so often that "she was not even wearing a panty."[26]

A final difficulty lay in getting the intelligence to Rome. The Reich Concordat gave the Holy See "full freedom . . . in its correspondence with the bishops," but the Nazis did not give the bishops full freedom in their correspondence with the Holy See. Albert Hartl's SS spies opened the bishops' mail and tapped their phones, keeping a special watch lest their complaints reach the wider world. The nuncio in Berlin, Cesare Orsenigo, saw Hitler as merely a German Mussolini, and so "could not execute normal operations," as Müller recalled, "not even in his reports to the Vatican." These communication obstacles presented a special, classical problem, because to propagate the faith, the Holy See was "peculiarly dependent upon freedom of speech and writing," as Müller said. Paul and Peter spread the faith by writing letters; Peter perhaps even built the Church in Rome because all roads led there; and so, among his other functions, the pope was in a nontrivial sense the postman of the West. To send and receive messages, the Vatican had long resorted to ingenious devices. In the Renaissance, it pioneered coded communications, inventing a mnemonic key to mix a cipher alphabet, a practice that secular powers later copied. In the Reformation, the Semaphore of the Holy See flashed messages across Europe, from one hilltop to another, with mirrors by day and flares by night. In the 1930s a radio tower, soon nicknamed "the Pope's Finger," arose in the Vatican gardens, and was then the most powerful transmitter in the world. After some deliberation, however, Neuhäusler opted for the oldest and simplest means of all.[27]

He trusted people. One was film critic and children's author Ida Franziska Sara Schneidhuber (nee Wasserman, pseud. Thea Graziella), a convert to Catholicism, whom one Church official later described, with a loaded sigh, as "Jewish, divorced, and probably a lesbian, but devoted to the faith." Vital reports flowed to her through Munich Jesuit Father Rupert Mayer, "who was able to visit Frau Schneidhuber inconspicuously," as Neuhäusler noted, so that "much valuable intelligence found its way . . . to Rome. For many years this intelligence channel worked quickly and well," until finally, in 1941, the SS arrested Schneidhuber as a non-Aryan, and in 1942 killed her in the concentration camp at Theresienstadt.[28]

The key courier, however, was Joey Ox. "He did a lot of dangerous things," a Jesuit priest later said of Müller. "He was a brave man. He needed to have a firm character. He was flying this tiny little sports plane from Germany into Italy, bringing over these documents to Merano, and there he gave them to somebody who would take them to Pacelli in the Vatican." Neuhäusler called Müller "my lion-hearted mailman," adding: "I must gratefully admit that without him I would not have been able to fulfill my mission of constantly informing the Holy Father of all important matters. . . . He was one of the most dedicated opponents of the Third Reich. That gave him courage, coolness and skill. There was nothing he could not be trusted to handle. 'Just give it here!' he would say, and he often put letters with 20 or more enclosures into his suitcase or briefcase, which he stowed in the cockpit." Although Müller buried the most sensitive items amid innocuous Church materials, this hardly reassured his episcopal handler. "I could hardly sleep on many a night when Müller was on his way to Rome with dangerous materials," Neuhäusler recalled. "I knew that if that material was discovered the two of us would lose our heads."[29]

Müller's secret services soon came to Pacelli's attention in Rome. As a reward, Pacelli arranged for Müller to marry his fiancée, Maria, above the rumored tomb of Saint Peter in the Vatican crypt. On 29 March 1934, Father Neuhäusler wrapped his stole around Josef and his bride's joined hands, tightly and for a long time, to emphasize the strength of their union.[30]

Pacelli used Müller's bulletins to write protest notes to Berlin. Father Leiber then stowed the reports on a high shelf in Pacelli's library, in the secret cavity of a big red book. One of the red book's reports especially haunted Pacelli.[31]

Hitler had created special schools for his new elite. He called them "order castles," and staffed them with trusted SS instructors. Speaking at Order Castle Sonthofen in 1937, Hitler vowed: "I'll step on the Catholic Church like a toad!" One of the lapsed-Catholic cadets, stricken by conscience, related the remark in a letter to his bishop. Soon afterward, the cadet and a friend of like sympathies died in a purportedly accidental fall from the Munich-Berlin express train. The Vatican's new secret source in the SS, Hans Rattenhuber, said the tragedy fit Himmler's known methods of dealing with suspected traitors.[32]

Himmler still suspected Müller, too, of treason. Rattenhuber provided regular warnings. Although the SS seemed unaware of Müller's Vatican work, they knew his law firm represented many Jews, who sought to emigrate after the November 1938 Night of Broken Glass.[33]

Müller wondered whether he also should leave, but he did not want his family to become dependents and beggars. He chose to stay and fight, and made a pact with Pacelli. Müller would work harder for him, offering that work to God, and Pacelli would pray for him every day. This covenant consoled Müller, especially after Pacelli became pope. The Holy Father seemingly had pressed a talisman into his hand. Müller drew strength from it on Thursday, 27 September 1939, which started for him like any other day, but became the most fateful of his life.[34]

AROUND EIGHT IN THE MORNING, MÜLLER KISSED HIS WIFE AND HIS daughter good-bye. He lit his pipe, set out from his mustard-colored Munich row house, and walked to his law office on the Amiraplatz. Later that day, he got a call from William Schmidhuber, a shady importer/exporter. Schmidhuber said that Admiral Canaris's office wanted to see Müller at once.[35]

Müller flew to Berlin, wondering what Hitler's spy chief could want with him. He shuffled along the dead leaves of the Landwehrkanal, worried that his secret Church work had endangered his family. At 74/76 Tirpitzufer, the doors of an old elevator rattled shut behind him and he rode up to the second floor. Guards unlocked a folding grille and he ventured into a hall that echoed with paratroopers' boots and foreign accents.[36]

A dashing cavalry officer stepped forward. Colonel Hans Oster, head of Section Z, showed Müller into an office and shut the door. The two men studied each other. Then, as Müller recalled, Oster began by saying, cagily: "Being that we are an espionage organization, we know a lot more about you than you do about us."[37]

He opened a dossier and ticked off particulars. Oster knew that Müller had traveled often to Rome to discuss "business matters" with Pacelli. He knew that, through Pacelli's graces, Müller had been married at the tomb of Saint Peter. A transcript in the folder recorded Müller's arrest and questioning by Himmler. Finally, Oster noted that Müller had given free counsel to Church leaders, who dueled the party in games of legal chess.[38]

Those peacetime games must now end, Oster said. The party was on war footing and would show no mercy. What would become of Müller's wife and daughter if things did not end well for him? If, by contrast, he cooperated, everyone would gain. His Church connections, in fact, would make him uniquely valuable to the Abwehr in Vatican City. Admiral Canaris needed an agent with access there. The Abwehr would overlook Müller's past if he would visit Rome as a confidential agent to seek the pope's views on "certain matters."[39]

Müller refused. Precisely because the Abwehr had such accurate intelligence about him, he said, they must know that he wouldn't spy against the Vatican or the pope.

Oster insisted that he had "just the opposite" kind of project in mind. He paused, as if letting the implications percolate. Finally, he said that he regarded Müller as so reliable that he would speak plainly. "Now, Dr. Müller, I will tell you something which presupposes my very great trust in you, because if I didn't know you so well based on the intelligence we have about you, I wouldn't be able to tell you what I am about to tell you without exposing myself to incalculable danger."[40]

The words that came next marked a passage between worlds. "After this prologue—there may have been one or two more sentences yet— Oster said to me: Well, Dr. Müller, here you are in the headquarters of German military intelligence. We even hope that someday you will be a part of the leadership of this headquarters. The leadership of this Abwehr headquarters is, at the same time, the headquarters of the German military opposition to Hitler." Oster added: "I, myself, favor knocking off that criminal by assassination."[41]

In the first week of October, Josef Müller stared at the Roman skyline, dominated by the dome of St. Peter's. He felt safe at the Hotel Albergo Flora, on the Via Veneto. It was a favorite stopping place for German officers, Oster had said, and some of its personnel were in Abwehr pay. Müller had taken a room overlooking the courtyard, so that he'd be spared the street noise. Still, as he replayed his meeting with Oster, he couldn't sleep.[42]

"The dice had fallen," Müller recalled thinking. "Oster had actually put his own head in the noose, so to speak, and had plainly said, Yes indeed, he'd wanted to remove Hitler. . . . He'd wanted to remove Hitler because Hitler had persecuted the Christian churches and wanted to exterminate the Jews."[43]

Oster knew about the murder of Jews in Poland. He had opened a dossier on Nazi crimes there, to justify Hitler's assassination. Since the SS had killed Catholic priests as well as Polish Jews, Oster thought the Vatican should know about the atrocities as well. He asked Müller to present some of the proof to Pius.[44]

Germans must unite in Christ to restore peace, Oster went on. He himself was a Protestant, a pastor's son; but Christians must do more than pray. "A criminal like Hitler can only be removed by force. And the only ones who can oppose force with force are the people of the military opposition." Yet the military would only remove Hitler if they knew that doing so would produce a fair peace with the West.[45]

That was where the pope came in. No one could more discreetly and credibly link Hitler's internal and external enemies than Pius. As perhaps the most prestigious figure in Europe, above party pressures, he had the greatest advantage a ruler could possess: he was the one trusted power amid powers nobody could trust. Only he had the influence and reputation to broker peace—and persuade the Allies that the German resistance was not, as a British spy claimed, "a creature as fabulous as the centaur and the hippogriff." If the continent came under Axis control, neutral Vatican City might yet offer the plotters a channel to the West. Would Müller approach the pope on their behalf?[46]

After Oster lobbied him for three hours, Müller joined the plot. They sealed the pact by shaking hands on oaths of honor. Either Hitler died, or they would. But if either of them were caught, he would die before betraying the other. He would go to the gallows alone.[47]

When Müller made those vows, he had felt euphoric and free. Yet ever since his plane took off, his stomach had been in knots. "A feeling of contending against diabolical powers comes home strongly," he later said, "when you are sitting in an airplane, when you have left the ground, and then you try to collect your thoughts up there."[48]

ON HIS SECOND NIGHT IN ROME, MÜLLER SAT IN THE SHADOWS OF a wine garden. It looked over the Quo Vadis chapel on the Appian Way. There he met an old friend, Monsignor Ludwig Kaas, one of the few who carried the keys to the pope's apartments. Formerly the chairman of the now banned German Catholic Center Party, the portly, bespectacled Kaas advised Pius on German affairs while living in quiet exile as keeper of the Vatican crypt.[49]

Müller and Kaas talked about what might happen if Hitler became master of Europe. Would he make good on his promise to squash the Church like a toad? Müller wanted to tell Kaas about his contacts with the German resistance, but fear held him back. Instead, he listened as Kaas described his crypt excavations for the lost tomb of Saint Peter. As they lingered over dessert, Müller recalled, he gazed at the lighted white Quo Vadis chapel. Kaas told him the legend behind its name.[50]

As the story went, Saint Peter had mounted a jailbreak. As he fled Rome, Christ passed him on the Appian Way—reportedly, just where the chapel now stood. Peter asked Christ, "Quo vadis?" (Where are you going?), and Christ said he had come to endure a second crucifixion because Peter would not die in his name. Ashamed, Peter hurried back and then asked his executioners to nail him to the cross upside down because he did not deserve to die like Jesus.[51]

Hearing that simple legend, Müller later said, banished his fear. Despite the sociology classes he had taken with Max Weber, despite the wool suits he wore and the corporate boards he graced, Joey Ox kept his peasant creed. Once, when then cardinal Pacelli asked how he had stayed calm under SS interrogation, Müller confessed that Catholic theology hadn't helped. Instead, he relied on the "country catechism" of his father, who, before every wagon journey, would take his whip and trace in front of the horses the sign of the cross, saying, "In God's Name."[52]

Müller passed Kaas the plea from the German resistance. By his own account he also shared the Abwehr dossier on SS atrocities in Poland. They agreed that Müller should henceforth consider himself bound by a *Secretum Pontificium*, a vow of papal secrecy. "I'll bite off my tongue," he said, "before I reveal anything!" He meant those words, he later said, "quite literally." Kaas promised to brief the Holy Father and to relay his response.[53]

CHAPTER 4

TYRANNICIDE

I N MID-OCTOBER 1939, MONSIGNOR KAAS DROVE DOWN THE AP-
pian Way to Castel Gandolfo, where Pius was polishing his encyclical. Why Kaas waited two weeks before making this excursion remains
unclear. The delay may have merely proceeded from the *pazienza*, the
slower Roman pace that Müller and other Germans noted. Or perhaps
Müller did not impart, and did not know, that Hitler intended to attack
France that month. In any case, Kaas conveyed the plotters' plea no later
than 16 October.[1]

The pope spent a day in reflection. Father Leiber recalled that Pius
always pondered things for a long time before saying yes or no. Leiber
could therefore scarcely believe it when, after less than a day of med-
itation, the pope gave him an answer for the German plotters, cast in
resolute form. At least one historian of his pontificate found the answer
"thoroughly out of character." In fact, it was of a piece with his whole
career.[2]

THIRTY-EIGHT YEARS BEFORE HE WAS CROWNED POPE, PACELLI BE-
came a spy. So said the dossier of the Nazi Vatican expert, Albert Hartl;
and though hardly a full description of Pacelli's duties, it was not wholly

wrong. Pacelli was twenty-four, a newly ordained priest living with his parents in Rome, and reportedly was playing the violin, accompanied by his sister on piano, when a startled maid announced the "man from the Vatican." The thin hands clutched the mute violin; the portly monsignor lit a cigar. They talked all night by the tangerine glow of the brazier. Monsignor Pietro Gasparri discoursed on socialist and nationalist dangers to the Church. Pacelli begged for a pastoral career. At dawn, the bells of St. Peter's cast in bronze italics the appeal: "We need watchdogs to chase away the wolves that prey on the flocks of the Lord." Finally the sigh, the nod, and afterward the same superflux of doubt that paralyzed the Apostle Thomas, creasing the soul of the talked-out priest reciting an awesome pledge of secrecy.[3]

A few days later, he climbed 294 steps from St. Peter's Square to the palace attic. In the old-fashioned rooms, decorated with maps of medieval Europe, Pacelli sat down in an uncarpeted cubicle and began deciphering cables in the Sacred Congregation for Extraordinary Ecclesiastical Affairs, the papal foreign service. Though he began as a clerk, larger forces set him on a fast track. His prominent family marked him as promising, Gasparri's sponsorship provided protection, and the patronage of Pope Leo the Thirteenth groomed him for power. Pacelli had hardly started work when Leo chose him to carry condolences to London after the death of Queen Victoria. Just two years later he cut a dashing figure as a newly minted monsignor—caped in black, with a violet sash and silver buckled shoes. By 1905, not yet thirty, he ran the Congregation's France desk. There, however, he found himself at the center of a crisis—and the lessons he drew from it would guide his approach to papal foreign policy for the next four decades.[4]

Pius the Tenth had broken diplomatic relations with France. After Catholic newspapers accused Jewish artillery officer Alfred Dreyfus of treason, the ruling French socialists had closed fourteen thousand Catholic schools and expelled their clergy. Jesuits doffed their habits and nuns fled to Belgium with only a few minutes to pack their things; priests without parishes busied themselves in beekeeping.[5]

The shuttered Paris nunciature was left in the hands of Monsignor Carlo Montagnini, ostensibly a caretaker for furnishings and files.

Actually he served as Vatican secret agent, cultivating sympathizers in the French police and warning the faithful of impending persecutions. French troops in Savoy, sent to evict monks and nuns from their monasteries and convents, found their way blocked by hundreds of peasants holding sharpened sticks. Suspecting Montagnini of subversion, French police raided the nunciature and seized its archives. The papers included messages Montagnini had sent Pacelli. One cable reported that a French politician urged the Church to fight anticlerical laws by paying bribes.[6]

Pacelli wrote up a postmortem. Detailing what had gone wrong in France, the document flagged problems in the papal intelligence system. Nuncios ran narrow networks—relying mainly on bishops, diplomatic colleagues, and local officials handling religious issues. As a result, Vatican agents kept Rome well informed about local religious matters but failed to cultivate well placed political sources. The Congregation could widen its secret horizons, however, by exploiting the intelligence potential of Catholic laity. The Church could cultivate influence-agents in political parties and exert indirect influence through labor, media, and other "front" groups—a practice Church officials termed "Catholic Action."[7]

Pius the Tenth took at first a different tack. He worried less about external threats than about modernist moles within the bosom of the Church. He asked Monsignor Umberto Benigni, undersecretary for extraordinary affairs, to set up a central vigilance committee. Benigni rolled out a worldwide network of informants, handwriting experts, and code breakers, creating, Gasparri recalled, "a secret espionage association outside and above the hierarchy . . . a sort of Freemasonry in the Church, something unheard of in ecclesiastical history." A backlash arose, however, when Benigni accused prominent Jesuits of heretical leanings because they used electric lights. By 1914 Benigni had resigned and Gasparri was named Cardinal Secretary of State. Pacelli, who had prudently kept to the curial shadows, became the Congregation's undersecretary, and found his chance to leverage lay agents during the First World War.[8]

Pope Benedict the Fifteenth (1914–1922) strove to keep the Vatican neutral. He hoped to broker and influence the terms of peace and secure a pro-Catholic postwar order. Pacelli thus initially planned to penetrate the foreign political-military circles from which any armistice would emerge. But Benigni's years had left the Congregation behind the curve of events, lacking talent spotters who could plausibly approach men of affairs and recruit them to the Catholic cause.[9]

So Pacelli played a defensive game. He modernized papal codes and created a formal training program for diplomat priests. The Vatican also hunted foreign spies, and in 1917 it caught one. German Monsignor Rudolph Gerlach, Pope Benedict's *guardaroba* (wardrobe keeper), also worked as a secret agent for the kaiser, reporting what he saw and heard to Berlin. Even more scandalously, Gerlach had served as a paymaster for German saboteurs who had blown up Italian warships.[10]

The pope's sympathies, and Pacelli's policies, shifted against Germany. The secret wing of Catholic Action soon sheltered Matthias Erzberger, leader of the German Catholic Center Party, who had become disillusioned with the war. He met Pacelli in Roman monasteries, crypts, and even back alleys. Pacelli began conspiring with Erzberger to halt Prussian militarism by proposing peace talks directly to the German parliament and people.[11]

But events cut short the game almost before it began. Since they perceived Pacelli as favoring the Allies, clerics from the Central Powers intrigued against him. Wanting to make peace in his own house, especially after the divisive Gerlach affair, the pope consecrated Pacelli a bishop *in partibus infidelium*, "in the lands of the infidel," and sent him to run papal operations in Germany.[12]

PACELLI SPENT SEVERAL MONTHS STUDYING THE CONGREGATION'S dossier on Bavaria. The nunciature there had an unusually rich tradition of covert actions. In the eighth century, the first Bavarian nuncio, Saint Boniface, had exchanged so many coded messages with Rome that he made crucial breakthroughs in cryptography, before heathens killed him. During the Counter-Reformation, Munich nuncio Peter Canisius, a Jesuit, held off Lutheranism with methods that one chronicler called "sly and stealthy, like the steps of a cat." But since 1872, when Bismarck expelled the Jesuits for political conspiracy, Rome had relied on the Catholic Center Party and its ally, the Bavarian People's Party, to protect Church interests. Pacelli made restoration of the Jesuits a priority. In 1917, through the influence of his key asset, Erzberger, the Reichstag repealed its anti-Jesuit laws.[13]

Pacelli resumed his peace intrigues. According to one postwar German intelligence report, Pacelli conspired to thwart a 1917 offensive that Prussian General Erich Ludendorff planned in France. Erzberger visited the Jesuit superior-general in Switzerland. Soon afterward, French Jesuit Michael d'Herbigny tipped off the Allies, who moved up reserves and dealt Ludendorff a crushing defeat. German morale collapsed, the kaiser abdicated, and Erzberger signed the armistice ending the war.[14]

Pacelli stayed at Munich during the storm that followed. "The state of things looks uncertain and grave," he cabled Cardinal Gasparri after Marxists declared Bavaria a soviet republic. In April 1919, Red Guards stormed the nunciature and put a pistol to Pacelli's chest; they stole his car but spared his life. Right-wing paramilitary bands soon seized power, but Pacelli found these nationalists just as "faith-hostile" as the socialists. They executed Catholic workers as "communist sympathizers" and raked the nunciature with gunfire. When General Ludendorff, leader of the right-wing forces, called on Pacelli and asked for help in hunting "reds," Pacelli demurred. Ludendorff began to denounce "the Church of Rome" as un-German and unpatriotic, branding Erzberger a "November criminal" who intrigued for peace and signed the surrender.[15]

The police warned Erzberger that right-wing hit squads had targeted him. He told his daughter before she entered a convent, "The bullet that will kill me has already been molded." Friends had urged him to carry a Luger and learn how to shoot, but he had replied, "I do not want to learn how to kill." In August 1921 his enemies followed him to Bad Greisbach, in the Black Forest. As he walked along an isolated road after Sunday Mass, two men fired revolvers into his chest. Erzberger jumped thirty feet down a ravine, clutching at tree roots to break his fall. The assassins fired three more shots, piercing his lungs, stomach, and upper thigh. He sought shelter behind a pine tree before collapsing. The men then stepped down the slope, bent over Erzberger, and dispatched him with three final shots to the head. At the bottom of the slope police found a ring Pope Benedict had given Erzberger, which the killers had torn from his hand.[16]

Pacelli had lost his key lay collaborator. To reassert Catholic political influence, he aligned with the Archbishop of Munich-Freising, Cardinal Michael Faulhaber, and with Bavarian People's Party deputy Franz Matt. They sought closer Bavarian ties with Rome, but told little to their trusted aides; one of Pacelli's confidantes called their tri-cornered collaboration a "diplomatic mystery play." As all three men dined in the nunciature on 8 November 1923, they heard that Adolf Hitler had declared himself leader of a new government.[17]

PACELLI KNEW LITTLE ABOUT HITLER. THE CASHIERED CORPORAL reportedly gave good speeches, but his past remained a mystery. When Hitler became politically active in late 1919, he impressed Jesuit Father Rupert Mayer, but soon alienated him and most of the clergy with anti-Christian rhetoric. By 1921 future Bishop Clemens von Galen of Münster had condemned Nazi doctrines. When Hitler forged an alliance with the anti-Catholic General Erich Ludendorff in 1923, Cardinal Gasparri ordered Pacelli to have both men "closely watched." Pacelli's surveillance failed to detect that the young corporal and old general would take the Bavarian cabinet hostage in a beer hall.[18]

Pacelli sent a situation report in cipher to Rome. Ludendorff's influence, if the coup succeeded, would mean an anti-Catholic regime, and would jeopardize chances for a concordat guaranteeing Church rights in Bavaria. The Vatican's reply revealed the quintessence of Catholic covert action, the model Pacelli would follow as pope. Because secular powers tried to break the Congregation's codes, this telling language was rare in cable traffic, which tended toward generalities and ellipses; but as a Vatican archivist later wrote, "once in a while a shaft of light illuminates the real situation." Gasparri's message disclosed that Rome would influence events indirectly, keeping its own role concealed. He cabled the order: "Keep Catholics from supporting the putsch. Refrain from public statements, but allow local priests to speak. Leave direct involvement to the Catholic Bavarian People's Party (BVP)."[19]

BVP deputy Matt established a rump government in Regensburg. A certain Father Sextel spied on rebel officers' meetings. Another priest publicly branded Hitler a "bandit, scoundrel, and traitor." But Jesuit Father Mayer, a former army chaplain, made the most impact. Bavarian soldiers adored him for saving many wounded during the war: he lost a leg in the process, and he wore the Iron Cross on his black robe. His widely publicized statement that a "Catholic cannot be a Nazi" turned the Bavarian military against Hitler.[20]

The putsch failed. Ludendorff and Hitler stood trial for treason, but received light sentences. Cardinal Gasparri worried that the Bavarian clergy had taken sides too blatantly, and he feared the Nazis would hold a grudge. Pacelli confidently cabled to Rome his prediction that Hitler was unlikely to achieve any real power. Hitler, meanwhile, had learned the importance of keeping the Church silent.[21]

ON 18 AUGUST 1925, PACELLI BOARDED A TRAIN FOR BERLIN. POPE Pius the Eleventh (1922–1939) had named him nuncio to Germany, and tasked him with improving the situation of Catholics in Protestant Prussia. "All eyes were immediately attracted to the tall figure clad in scarlet and purple damask," wrote society reporter Bella Fromm. "His countenance is ascetic, his features resembling those carved on an old cameo, and only rarely does the shadow of a smile scamper across them. His even-handed tranquility enchanted me." When time allowed, he visited new friends on an estate in the Eberswalde Forest and rode horses with German military personalities—Wilhelm Canaris, Ludwig Beck, and Hans Oster.[22]

In late 1929 Pacelli returned to Rome to become secretary of state. By then he had negotiated a concordat guaranteeing Church rights in Prussia. For the first time since Bismarck unified Germany, Prussian priests could study in Rome. The state agreed to compensate the Church for properties seized in Martin Luther's era. After four hundred years, the Counter-Reformation had officially ended.

But Pacelli's problems in Germany had barely begun. The Nazis were climbing to power even as he left Berlin. The world financial crash of October 1929 and the subsequent global depression gave Hitler his opening. After the apparent failure of capitalism, most German voters felt compelled to try socialism. Given the choice between Stalin's international socialism and Hitler's National Socialism, they chose Hitler's. Less than a year after the economic crisis began, the Nazis had more than quadrupled their share of seats in the Reichstag, from 4.6 percent to 18.3 percent. Although the German bishops forbade Nazi Party membership, following Pacelli's 1930 guidance from Rome, many Protestant ministers and churchgoers affiliated themselves with Nazism, and Catholics felt increasingly pulled by the national tide. As the Depression deepened, the date of Hitler's eventual triumph came to seem merely a math problem, until finally, on 30 January 1933, he reached his goal.[23]

Hitler's appointment as chancellor dismayed Pacelli. He regarded that event, as he told Father Leiber, as "more ominous . . . than a victory by the socialist left." Pacelli pronounced himself in agreement with Konrad von Preysing, then Bishop of Eichstätt, who observed: "We are now in the hands of criminals and fools."[24]

Stunned by Hitler's victory, the pope tried to work with him. At six in the evening by the bells of St. Peter's, on 20 July 1933, Cardinal Pacelli initialed a concordat with the Reich. Building on the agreement he had negotiated with Prussia, the treaty guaranteed Catholic rights throughout Germany. But any Vatican illusions about Hitler disappeared on 30 June 1934, the Night of the Long Knives.

While purging party rivals, the SS also killed lay-Catholic leaders. Steel-helmeted SS agents smashed down the doors of Catholic Vice Chancellor Franz von Papen's office, blew open the safes, and gunned down his press secretary. They executed the president of Catholic Action, Dr. Erich Klausener, after making him sign a faked suicide note, and dragged Klausener's deputy, Edgar Jung, to a suburban wood and shot him in the back of the head. They beat to death the pious Catholic

Dr. Fritz Gerlich, editor of the anti-Hitler magazine *Straight Path*, and shot the national director of the Catholic Youth Sports Association, Adalbert Probst, while he "fled from arrest." They broke the spine and put three bullets in the heart of Father Bernhard Stempfle, who had at first backed Hitler and then denounced him. They cremated their victims, in defiance of Catholic doctrine, and the dead men's relatives received the ashes in the mail.[25]

By late 1936, the Church and the Reich seemed on course for a showdown. Party officials removed crucifixes from Catholic schools, calling them "symbols of superstition," and began merging Catholic and Protestant school systems. Only 3 percent of Munich children attended Catholic schools, down from 65 percent three years before. During the Christmas holidays, the pope reportedly felt so depressed that he sat in silence for hours each day by his bedroom window.[26]

In January 1937, Pacelli called five German bishops and cardinals to Rome. Asked how the Vatican might alleviate Nazi harassment, Cardinal Faulhaber advised that only a papal protest, "a word of redemptive truth," could reverse "an unstoppable sinking into the abyss."[27]

The pope thought the time seemed ripe. Respectable Germans resented Nazi harassment of Catholics. Pacelli did not think that Hitler, concerned with international opinion, would respond with violence, so long as the document referred just to Germany and avoided mentioning Nazism by name.[28]

Twelve secret presses printed the text in Germany. A clandestine network of couriers carried copies to every parish. Catholic youth used backpack caravans and hiked through the Bavarian Alps, the Black Forest, and along the Rhine. Altar boys pedaled bicycles at night. High school athletes ran across barley farms. Nuns rode motorcycles to remote villages. In church confessional booths, the couriers delivered their cargo to priests. The priests locked the text in their tabernacles, and on Palm Sunday, they read it from every pulpit in the Reich.[29]

The Nazis reacted sharply. "The Reich does not desire a modus vivendi with the Church," Hitler ranted, "but rather its destruction." Himmler staged mass trials of monks in Berlin. Party thugs invaded the cardinal's palace in Vienna. They desecrated his chapel, burned his vestments, and broke a curate's legs by throwing him out a second-floor window.[30]

The horizon darkened further in 1939 as Pacelli became pope. Despite an apparent détente, threats and pressures swirled. "The election of Pacelli is not welcomed in Germany, since he has always been hostile to National Socialism," Berlin declared, adding ominously: "In the end, worldviews are decided by weapons."[31]

Yet the Reich cardinals had urged Pacelli to avoid confrontation. Speaking out had only worsened conditions for the Church in the Reich, they said. Whatever he did against Hitler, he would do in the shadows.

AT CASTEL GANDOLFO, PIUS WALKED THE SAME PATH EACH AFTER-noon. It curved through rose gardens, past the broken columns of a villa built by the Roman emperor Domitian. Amid these vine-wrapped ruins, the pope pondered the most fateful decision of his young pontificate. Could he, the deputy of Christ on earth, become accessory and agent in a military plot to remove a secular leader?[32]

Church teaching stated the conditions under which citizens could kill tyrants. Catholic doctrine permitted capital punishment; and though a priest himself could not shed blood, a Christian knight could wield the sword of justice at the bidding of a priest. Accordingly, over the centuries, Catholic theologians had developed a nuanced doctrine of tyrannicide, covering virtually every conceivable context. They divided tyrants into two classes: usurpers, who seized power illegally, and oppressors, who used power unjustly. Hitler, who held office legally but ruled unjustly, had become an oppressor. He therefore fell into the class of evildoers whom—as Aquinas and some Jesuit theologians argued—citizens could assassinate.[33]

But Catholic ethics strictly limited political violence. The tyrant's executioners must have good grounds for believing his death would actually *improve* conditions and would not cause a bloody civil war. The tyrant himself must not merely stand revealed as the primary instigator of unjust policies; his assassins must have sufficient reason to believe that those unjust policies would end with the tyrant's life. If another tyrant would likely continue those polices, the assassins had no moral basis to act. Finally, the assassins must have exhausted all peaceful means for removing the tyrant.[34]

The plot against Hitler seemed to meet these terms. First, the conspirators intended to secure an honorable peace under a strong but anti-Nazi government, so that Hitler's removal would not mean chaos or more Nazism under Göring or Himmler. Second, Hitler could only be removed by violence, because he had abolished the democratic process through which he claimed power. As Josef Müller reported Nazi ideologist Alfred Rosenberg saying, "We National Socialists have created this State; we are going to hold on to this State; and we shall never let go of this State." Finally, and most fundamentally, Müller's intelligence indicated not only that Nazi policies were wicked, but that Hitler himself directed those policies.[35]

The wickedness of the policies was plain from Müller's dossier on Poland. As a Vatican priest later summarized this evidence, "Hundreds of priests were arrested and shot by the Germans during the first month, while Catholic intellectuals, clerics or laity were arrested and sent to concentration camp Oranienburg near Berlin. . . . The basis of this program was the elimination of the intellectual elite and the traditional influence of the clergy." Müller recalled the dossier as including proof also of "the systematic extermination of the Jews," such as "movies, photos, reports, e.g. of naked Jewish men, women and children, packed in trenches they had to dig themselves, machine-gunned like sardines in a can; and, in one photo, a police officer shooting a child clamped between his knees."[36]

Pius believed that Hitler directed these policies. Some German bishops, as the pope later lamented, still viewed Hitler as the defender of Christian values. In fact, believing that Christianity had undermined Germany's manly tribal traditions, Hitler wished that Muslims had conquered Europe: "It's been our misfortune to have the wrong religion. Islam would have been much more compatible to us than Christianity. Why did it have to be Christianity with its meekness and flabbiness?" As Hitler elsewhere said, "Our whole deformity and atrophy of spirit and soul would never have come into being, except for this oriental mummery, this abominable leveling mania, this cursed universalism of Christianity which denies racialism and preaches suicidal tolerance." Pius had not forgotten the Führer's vow to crush the Church like a toad; Himmler reportedly hoped to publicly execute the pope to inaugurate a new soccer stadium; and Father Leiber's red book brimmed with indications that Hitler encouraged and sponsored the atrocities. Although harsh measures were invariably ascribed to "the mistake of some subordinate," Müller acidly noted, they were "not a mere episode or a temporary tactical method, but an essential element of National Socialism, something systematic and calculated." Thus Pius wrote Cardinal Schulte around this time, it was "the Party" that directed the attack on the Church; and probably for that reason Pacelli had reportedly described Hitler, according to one contemporaneous note by an Allied diplomat, as "not only an untrustworthy scoundrel but as a fundamentally wicked person."[37]

WHEN THE POPE AROSE THE NEXT MORNING, HE HAD MADE UP HIS mind. He would engage the German military resistance and encourage a conservative counterrevolution. He would serve as secret foreign agent for the resistance—presenting and guaranteeing its plans to the British. He would partner with the generals not just to stop the war, but to eliminate Nazism by removing Hitler.[38]

The decision stunned his aides and others who later learned of it. "Never in all history," pronounced one ecclesiastical historian, "had a Pope engaged so delicately in a conspiracy to overthrow a tyrant by force." A wartime US intelligence officer would term the pope's quick consent to act as a conspiratorial intermediary "one of the most astounding events in the modern history of the Papacy." Father Leiber thought Pius went "much too far." The dangers, both to the pope and the Church, seemed almost foolhardy. If Hitler learned of Pius's role, he might punish Catholics, invade the Vatican, and even kidnap or kill the pope.[39]

But Leiber could not talk Pius out of his decision. Pius told him, "The German Opposition must be heard in Britain." Leiber fell into line. He began to make notes, so that he could tell Müller: Here are the exact words of the pope. Pius himself provided the governing phrase, the leitmotif for the events of the next five years. Asked what kind of government Germany should work toward, Pius answered, according to Leiber's notes: "Any government without Hitler."[40]

CHAPTER 5

SOMEONE TO KILL HIM

B Y 17 OCTOBER JOSEF MÜLLER HAD RECEIVED THE POPE'S REPLY.
The Vatican crypt-keeper, Monsignor Ludwig Kaas, brought
Müller up to date, probably in a tavern near Pius's villa. The next day,
as Müller flew to Berlin with the pope's answer, he felt the agonized
jubilation of the successful secret agent, carrying good news he could
tell almost no one.[1]

Müller presumed his handlers would proceed with due discretion.
He was a civilian, and they were professionals. It would have shocked
him to learn that on Friday, 20 October, an Abwehr officer privy to the
secret wrote it down.

Major Helmuth Groscurth opened his safe, removed his diary,
and spread it on his desk. He linked the Canaris-Oster cell with anti-
Nazi generals; he had procured explosives for assassination plans; and
he transcribed the results of Müller's mission, not from any Teutonic
record-keeping compulsion, but for two considered reasons. First, military intelligence officers were trained to write down information from
contacts and store it safely for reference, because otherwise one's memory could play tricks. Second, some of the plotters wished to prove for
posterity that a Decent Germany existed, so that if they failed to kill

Hitler, they would still have shown the possibility of fighting tyranny. Thus, in their very losing, they would have found a way to win.[2]

"The Pope is very interested and holds an honorable peace to be possible," Groscurth wrote. "Personally guarantees that Germany will not be swindled as in the forest of Compiègne [where an armistice ended World War One]. In these peace feelers one encounters the categorical demand for the removal of Hitler."[3]

ON THAT SAME FRIDAY, AT HIS VILLA, PIUS SIGNED HIS FIRST EN-cyclical. Although he had reportedly finished it by 8 October, the *New York Times* announced on 18 October that its publication had been delayed. The *Times* gave no explanation, but its correspondent filed the story on 17 October—just as Pius pledged to help the German resistance. A wartime remark by Josef Müller suggests that Pius's covert actions delayed, changed, and finally muted his public stance on Nazi crimes.

The plotters asked the pope not to protest. According to a document found among President Franklin Roosevelt's papers, the coup planners urged Pius to "refrain from making any public statement singling out the Nazis," as Müller told an American diplomat, since "this would have made the German Catholics even more suspected than they were and would have greatly restricted their freedom of action in their work of resistance."[4]

During the encyclical's delay, Pius did weaken its words. He diluted or deleted phrases criticizing "unrestrained expansionism," the conception of "relations between peoples as a struggle," and the "rule of force." Pius did keep the admonition that, for human-rights purposes, "there is neither Gentile nor Jew." But that was the last time he publicly said "Jew" during the war.[5]

AT ABWEHR HEADQUARTERS, MÜLLER'S MENTORS BEGAN PLANNING his Vatican "show." In spy jargon a show meant the whole composed of two halves—a secret operation and its cover. Canaris would cover Müller's Vatican contacts as an Abwehr project. Despite Hitler's looming attack in the West—by now postponed to November—the aim was not quick results, but a standing capacity under a protective guise. The plotters would not plan on luck; or rather, they would plan only on bad luck. Nazism was a problem that might take years to solve, and for as long as that took, the show must have some plausible cause to go on.

The cover would build on Nazi preconceptions. Hitler saw the Italians as wobbly allies, and the plotters played on his fears. The Abwehr would send Müller to Rome to monitor Italian pacifism. He would pose as the agent of disgruntled Germans seeking peace through Italian channels. This would ostensibly let him sound out gossipy Italians through plugged-in Vatican officials. The Abwehr would tell the Gestapo in advance that Müller was posing as a conspirator. Canaris could even send the resulting reports on feckless Italians to Hitler. To all bureaucratic appearances, Müller would advance the war effort by pretending to talk peace.

But he would only be pretending to be pretending. He would actually be the plotter he was pretending to be. He would be a plotter, covered as a spy, covered as a plotter. He would do a kind of triple backflip without moving a muscle.

This was classic Canaris. It was his signature move, this hiding in plain sight. He would use it repeatedly, though never in the same way, to extract the plotters from difficulties. The results until the war's last month could only be described as death-defying. How well the cover worked in Müller's case seems clear from a later CIA assessment, estimating that he visited the Vatican at least 150 times for the would-be assassins during the war's first three years, always with the consent of the government he sought to overthrow.[6]

Before returning to Rome in late October, Müller met Canaris. As soon as he entered the admiral's office he felt at home. He saw an old Persian carpet, and, in one corner, a dachshund sleeping on a cot. On an ink-stained nineteenth-century desk sat a model of the light cruiser *Dresden*. Canaris held out his hand, as though to an old friend, and asked Müller to have a seat.[7]

They spoke about Hitler. Though the Führer had awarded himself the title Greatest Warlord of all time, to Canaris he seemed "the greatest criminal of all time." Canaris had expressly warned Hitler that the Western powers would stand by Poland, but Hitler had started the war anyway.[8]

Worse yet, he was planning a blitzkrieg against the Netherlands, Belgium, and France. Hitler's disregard of international law, Canaris said, amounted to criminal negligence.[9]

But all that paled, the admiral said, compared to what went on in Poland. Whole provinces faced devastation by a rabble resembling the ravens that followed the march of any army. Like a band of pirates, the SS acted under no authority known to the law. Yet clearly, the party, and above all Hitler, encouraged and sponsored them.[10]

Canaris knew so from his own spies in the party security apparatus. The Gestapo's conscience-stricken chief criminal investigator, Arthur Nebe, had turned over many secret reports.[11]

Canaris thus knew about actions planned against the Church—not just in Germany, but in Rome as well. Four separate organizations competed to spy on the pope, on his inner circle of advisers, and on the Vatican secretariat of state. The Reich government had broken the papal diplomatic codes, and Rome's religious institutions swarmed with informants. Canaris promised to provide supporting evidence, to show his willingness to help the pope.[12]

The admiral then got down to discussing Müller's future missions. He stressed three points. First, he did not wish Müller's secret work to burden his conscience. Müller would receive no commands unless he volunteered for a task.[13]

Second, Müller would ask the pope to make contact only with the British. To avoid all suspicion that they played the Allies against each other, the plotters should not negotiate with more than one government at a time. If they could have only one link, it must be with London. The English were more dependable diplomats. Though tenacious negotiators, they kept their word.[14]

Finally, Canaris asked Müller to include, in each of his reports from Rome, a section headed "Current Possibilities for Peace." Müller would make coded reference to the removal of Hitler only in this section. Canaris would detach everything written under that heading and deliver it secretly to others. That would provide a certain protection if a report ever fell into the wrong hands.[15]

Canaris then spoke reverently of Pius. The reverence surprised but pleased Müller. He sensed that Canaris and Oster, though Protestants, considered the pope the world's most important Christian, and placed in him an almost childlike trust. They sought out the Holy Father not only for clandestine support, but for solace and hope. Canaris quoted the pope's veiled warning to Hitler, issued a week before the war: "Empires not based on peace are not blessed by God. Politics divorced from justice betrays those who wish this to be so." The admiral punctuated this papal wisdom by pouring schnapps into shot glasses and proposing a toast: "Wir gedenken des Führers, uns zu entledigen!" (We are thinking of the Führer, that we may be rid of him!")[16]

THE POPE'S PARTICIPATION IN THEIR COUP PLANS ENERGIZED THE plotters. Especially in the cell of civilian plotters led by former Leipzig mayor Carl Goerdeler, the news produced euphoria. Goerdeler had prepared a radio speech to the German people and had begun to fill cabinet seats in a shadow government. Müller thought the excitement misplaced. When Oster passed him a list of ministers and secretaries, he returned it unread. "Keep it, Hans," he sighed. "If we succeed, we have more ministers and secretaries of state than we could ever want. What we need now is someone to kill him."[17]

Not just who but also how to kill Hitler remained an issue. Arguments swirled about the ethics of assassinating him, imprisoning him, putting him on trial, or having him declared insane. Some Protestant plotters opposed killing on religious grounds. Even generals and ex-generals, who had made violence their profession, objected to the use of force. "In particular, the Lutheran Christians within the military opposition refused to support an assassination for religious reasons," Müller recalled. "They referred to a sentence by St. Paul, according to which 'all authority comes from God,' so he [Hitler] could therefore demand obedience." Resting their case largely on Romans 13, Martin Luther and John Calvin had argued against all resistance to rulers. "I would rather suffer a prince doing wrong than a people doing right," Luther had written. As he put it, "Disobedience is a greater sin than murder."[18]

Catholics drew on a different tradition. Following Aquinas, Jesuit theologians considered political violence not only sometimes allowable, but even necessary. "One thing alone is forbidden to the people," wrote the French Jesuit Jean Boucher in 1594, "namely, to accept a heretic king." In such cases, argued the Spanish Jesuit Martin Anton Delrio, the Christian must "make the blood of a king a libation to God." With some logic, then, the plotters looked to Rome for moral sanction, and found in lay Catholics their triggermen. Catholics would go where Protestants feared to tread. An Abwehr contact therefore asked Müller to seek the pope's formal blessing for tyrannicide.[19]

Müller knew the Vatican did not work that way. He disabused his Protestant collaborators of their hopes that the pope would directly endorse violence. Worried, as he later said, about "misuse of the papal authority and position," he called tyrannicide "a matter for the individual conscience." Pressed whether he would raise the problem with his own confessor, Müller said he favored shooting Hitler like a deranged dog, and let the matter rest there.[20]

A key Catholic general meanwhile seemed poised to join the plotters. Knowing that the army's commander in chief and chief of staff opposed Hitler's planned attack in the West, Colonel-General Ritter von Leeb assured them: "I am prepared in the coming days to stand behind you fully with my person and to draw every necessary and desired conclusion." Yet because the devout Leeb had once publicly snubbed Alfred Rosenberg, the Nazi apostle of anti-Christianity, Himmler had put Leeb under SS watch. That surveillance prevented the plotters from bringing Leeb into their plans.[21]

By late October, momentum nevertheless gathered for a coup. German Catholic clergymen who knew Müller began to whisper about Hitler's imminent demise. After an extended call at Müller's home on 24 October, Benedictine Abbott Corbinian Hofmeister told a fellow priest that the war would end by Christmas, since a powerful military plot would by then have rid the country of Hitler. By the end of the month, a Catholic plotter in the Foreign Ministry, Dr. Erich Kordt, had decided to take Hitler's life.[22]

Kordt's conscientious decision stemmed from an offhand remark. "If only [the generals] had not sworn an oath that bound them to the living Hitler," Oster said as they left a secret meeting. It occurred to Kordt that Hitler's death would release the generals from their oath. He did not share his Protestant friends' perplexities about tyrannicide. A phrase from Aquinas became his motto: "When there is no recourse, one who liberates his country from a tyrant deserves the highest praise."[23]

On 1 November, Kordt followed up with Oster. "We have no one who will throw a bomb in order to liberate our generals from their scruples," Oster groused. Kordt said that he had come to ask Oster for the bomb. As an aide to Foreign Minister Joachim Ribbentrop, Kordt had access to Hitler's anteroom. He knew Hitler's habit of stepping out to greet visitors or give orders.[24]

Oster promised him the explosive by 11 November. Hitler had scheduled his attack in the West for the twelfth. Kordt began to visit the chancellery on pretexts, to accustom the guards to his presence.[25]

CHAPTER 6

LUCK OF THE DEVIL

Germany's generals did not want to widen the war. On 5 November, the army commander in chief, Walther von Brauchitsch, tried to present the military's pessimism to Hitler. Flustered by the Führer's proximity, Brauchitsch did not get far. "When I confront this man," he once said of Hitler, "I feel as if someone were choking me and I cannot find another word."[1]

Brauchitsch had prepared a paper on the attack plan. Troop morale could not sustain a new offensive, he warned. In Poland, officers had lost control of enlisted men, who staged "drunken orgies" on troop trains. Court-martial reports described "mutinies."[2]

Hitler erupted—dressing him down, Brauchitsch recalled, "as one would not do even to the stupidest recruit." Even the secretaries outside heard his tirade. Which units lacked discipline? Where? He would fly there tomorrow to enforce the death sentences. No, Hitler screamed, the troops would fight; only their leaders worried him. How could they condemn the whole army because of a few excesses? "Not one frontline commander mentioned any lack of attacking spirit in the infantry to me. But now I have to listen to this, after the army has achieved a magnificent victory in Poland!"[3]

Brauchitsch offered to resign. Hitler shouted back that the general must do his duty like every other soldier. Alluding to the compound outside Berlin where the army general staff worked, Hitler warned that he would not ignore the defeatist "spirit of Zossen." He cursed the army's cowardice until he ran out of breath. Then he snatched Brauchitsch's memo, tossed it in a safe, and stalked out of the room, slamming the door and leaving it to echo in the great hall.[4]

Brauchitsch staggered out. Army chief of staff Franz Halder, waiting for him in the anteroom, recalled Brauchitsch emerging "chalk-white and with twisted countenance," incoherent and terrified, choking between clenched teeth, "looking convulsed." Brauchitsch related Hitler's threat to crush defeatists. Had Hitler learned of their putsch plans? At any moment, the SS might descend on Zossen. No one had forgotten the Night of the Long Knives. Returning to headquarters, Halder ordered all coup-planning papers burned.[5]

It soon became clear that Hitler knew nothing of the plot. But Oster's colleague Hans Gisevius warned Müller not to count on a renewed push by the generals. "They're only playing chess with the people," Gisevius said over beer at the Kaiserhof, just before Müller boarded a train back to Munich. "These gentleman riders will go right up to the hurdle, but never jump it!" He urged Müller not to oversell the military at the Vatican.[6]

In Rome, on 7 November, Müller entered Father Leiber's apartment at 4 Piazza della Pilotta. Unlike the warm and blunt Kaas, Leiber—a whisper of a priest in a black soutane—revealed little of himself behind an enigmatic and worldly smile, born of long service in secret matters. Expressing concern that Pius had decided to join the plot, the Jesuit éminence grise schooled Müller in the rules of the game.[7]

Pius could not meet with Müller while the conspiracy unfolded. Hartl's SS spies prowled the schools and rectories of papal Rome. What if one of them blew Müller's cover? To retain plausible deniability, Pius must be able to say that he never met Müller during the plot. Instead,

Müller would liaise with Pius through Father Leiber, their "common mouth." Müller took these words, he later said, as a "gracious yet well-reasoned command."

Finally, Pius wanted personal control of the channel between London and Berlin. He did not want to devolve responsibility in any way to the Church. The plotters could involve the Holy Father, but not the Holy See. The dynamic must have a plain symmetry: just as Hitler, not the German state, was the target of the plot, so Pius, not the Roman faith, would be its abettor. "Leiber said, by the order of the pope, that he requested that, when discussing the authority to convene the peace talks, they [the military conspirators] should cite the 'pope' and not the 'Vatican,'" Müller recounted. "Because he himself [Pius] had made a point of drawing a clear distinction between the pope who, in a certain sense, was entitled and obligated to do everything for peace, and the Vatican, which had a more political status." What might seem like scholastic hairsplitting to outsiders had a compelling logic to Pius. The German generals, and their prospective British interlocutors, were Protestants; they liked and trusted Pacelli, but retained a certain reserve toward the Roman Catholic Church, and especially toward the Vatican. Pius therefore felt it opportune to say, in essence: you people on both sides of the war know me; you know that I am reliable. For my part, I know that you have some misgivings or some problems with the Vatican as such. Let this delicate business then be done under my name, which you credit, rather than that of my institution, which you doubt. So that this proposal be taken seriously, whether it should succeed or fail, I offer my personal reputation as collateral. Strictly speaking, then, the intrigues that followed would not be the Church's covert campaign against the Reich, but the pope's secret war against Hitler.[8]

He took a personal interest in operational details, including code names. Müller would go by "Herr X." Father Leiber, who taught at the Gregorian University, would use the handle "Gregor." They would both call Pius the "Chief." Müller asked Leiber whether the pope knew his own code name. "Of course," said Leiber. "But isn't it a little sacrilegious?" Müller asked. "How did he take it?" Leiber assured him that the

Holy Father had only smiled, and had even seemed pleased. The code name "Chief" showed, he thought, that the pope returned the trust the plotters placed in him.[9]

WHILE MÜLLER SAT WITH LEIBER IN ROME, HITLER RODE IN HIS private train to Munich. Every year on 8 November he spoke at the Bürgerbräukeller, marking the anniversary of the 1923 beer-hall putsch. But he felt uneasy about the security risks involved in annual public appearances, believing an irregular routine the best safeguard against assassination.[10]

As Hitler arrived in Munich, his border police made an arrest. Georg Elser, a thirty-six-year-old Swabian watchmaker, had tried to cross illegally into Switzerland at Lake Constance. In his pockets police found a pair of pliers, pieces of a bomb fuse, and a picture-postcard of the Bürgerbräu's interior. Concealed under his lapel the officers discovered a badge of the former "Red Front" Communist movement. Not until several days later would Elser tell SS interrogators why he had tried leave Germany that night. Knowing Hitler spoke every 8 November at the beer hall, Elser had hidden a bomb there. He was not a member of the Canaris group. Elser worked alone. Nevertheless, he planned the attack expertly. He had taken a job at a quarry to steal donarit, an explosive with the properties he required. For thirty-five nights he managed to hide without detection in the hall. In the paneled column behind the dais, he cut a hole and then disguised it by making a door from a matching piece of paneling. Inside he placed a bomb improvised from a stolen 75-millimeter shell. On 5 November, Elser installed two Westminster clocks, cased in cork to muffle the ticking.[11]

At eight o'clock, Hitler entered the beer hall. Three thousand Nazis cheered as he stepped to the flag-draped platform. When the room hushed, Hitler spoke for only one hour, instead of his usual three. He excoriated England. London would soon learn: "We National Socialists have always been fighters. This is a great time. And in it, we shall prove ourselves all the more as fighters." Afterward he greeted the party officials who thronged forward. Some in the audience sat around drinking; others filed out of the hall.[12]

Eight minutes later, at 9:20 p.m. the pillar behind the podium vanished in white flame. The blast hurled tables and flung party veterans to the floor. Beams from the collapsed roof crushed to death eight people and injured more than sixty, including the father of Hitler's mistress, Eva Braun. The beer-hall proprietor recalled "a tremendous explosion, which caused the ceiling to fall and crash with a terrific roar. There were screams and the air was filled with dust and an acrid smell. Bodies lay under the debris and there was a great struggle as the injured tried to struggle free and the uninjured tried to find a way out."[13]

Hitler had left the building eight minutes earlier. He had already boarded his train back to Berlin when the word spread to his coach that something had happened. At Nuremberg station, the facts filtered through. Hitler declared it "a miracle" that he had been spared, a "sure sign" that Providence favored his mission. The incident also showed, as his adjutant wrote, "that Hitler had enemies who would go to any lengths to get rid of him."[14]

JOSEF MÜLLER SPENT THE EVENING OF 8 NOVEMBER IN ROME. He was sitting with Monsignor Johannes Schönhöffer, in the offices of the Sacred Congregation for the Propagation of the Faith, when news came that Hitler had survived a bombing attempt. "An Italian and a French priest in the room with us stared at me inquiringly," Müller remembered. The looks suggested that Müller had at least established his "cover" as an agent of dissident Germans. He himself wondered whether his friends had planted the bomb.[15]

Four days later, in Berlin, Müller found his comrades in confusion. The bombing had totally surprised Oster's group. As far as they could glean, Elser was a lone-wolf communist. Because he worked alone, no one could betray him; the SS had virtually no way to penetrate his plot. If Hitler had not inexplicably shortened his speech, Elser's bomb would have killed him. Not for the last time, Müller found himself thinking that Hitler had "the luck of the Devil."[16]

The Bürgerbräu incident wrecked Erich Kordt's plan. Late in the afternoon of 11 November, he went to Oster's home to get the bomb he meant to use that evening. Though Hitler had postponed his western offensive, citing weather reasons, Kordt remained determined to strike. Oster met him with the sad words: "I am unable to give you the explosive." After the bombing, party police had placed all munitions depots, including the Abwehr's, under surveillance. Kordt said softly: "Then it will have to be tried with a pistol." Oster grew agitated. "Kordt, do not commit an act of insanity. You do not have one chance in a hundred. You cannot see Hitler alone. And in the anteroom in the presence of adjutants, orderlies and visitors you would hardly get a chance to shoot."[17]

THE MUNICH BOMBING DISTURBED THE POPE'S MEN. MONSIGNOR Kaas found it "inexplicable," an "enigma," especially because Müller could relate only the Abwehr's conjectures. Kaas thought the Nazis themselves might have staged the attack, as they allegedly did the Reichstag fire, for their own ends. That no one seemed to regard the event as astonishing or abnormal showed, Kaas thought, that Hitler and Stalin had made gangsterism a generally accepted state of affairs.

In Berlin, the papal nuncio carried an envelope to the Foreign Ministry. The pope's secretariat of state relayed congratulations to the Führer for surviving the attempt on his life. Hitler doubted the pope's sincerity.

"He would much rather have seen the plot succeed," Hitler told dinner guests soon after. Polish governor Hans Frank protested that Pius had always proved a good friend to Germany. Hitler said, "That's possible but he's no friend of mine."[18]

THE FAILED ASSASSINATION HAD ONE GOOD RESULT FOR THE PLOT-ters. It excited the British about regime change. Josef Müller's messages through Vatican channels gained credibility. British Prime Minister Neville Chamberlain had said that for London to support anti-Nazis, "Germany must do some deed as evidence of good faith." Now a German had done a deed. The day after the bombing, therefore, the British sent two spies to meet a German officer, who promised to detail a plan to remove Hitler and end the war.[19]

They met at the Dutch-German border town of Venlo. The British officers, Payne Best and Richard Stevens, did not know the true name of the man they would meet. They knew him only by the code-name "Schaemel."

A SENTRY RAISED THE BARRIER AND THE BRITISH DROVE INTO no-man's-land. Only a few trees fringed a customs house and a café. Schaemel emerged on the café's porch just as the gate on the German side rose. He waved to indicate an all-well.[20]

Without warning, a car shot through the German gate. SS officers on the running boards leveled machine-pistols at the Englishmen. Schaemel ordered Best and Stevens out of their car. Their Dutch driver, Dirk Klop, drew his revolver and ran away, shooting at the SS as he went. The Germans returned fire, and Klop fell dead into a row of trees. Schaemel disarmed Best and Stevens and marched them into Germany.[21]

The British had fallen into a Nazi trap. An SS intelligence officer, Walter Schellenberg, had posed as an oppositional general—Schaemel—to feed the British disinformation. After the beer-hall bombing, Himmler saw a chance to rally Germans around Hitler by claiming that Elser had worked for British intelligence. He ordered Schellenberg to arrest the British agents and declare them Elser's handlers. The Nazis hoped thereby to stir popular support for an attack in the West, while discrediting any true resistance in Allied eyes. They failed in the first goal, but succeeded in the second: London became reflexively skeptical about alleged plots to remove Hitler.[22]

The Venlo affair also dismayed the Vatican. On 21 November the British ambassador to the Holy See, D'Arcy Osborne, cabled London after speaking with Monsignor Kaas. The Vatican crypt keeper seemed "friendly as ever," and made clear his hatred of Hitler and his Nazi regime. But "Kaas took a very gloomy view" about the prospects for regime change. Germans were "by nature subservient," and, after long regimentation, almost incapable of organizing a revolt. They remained mostly united behind Hitler, even though many deplored Nazi principles and methods. The success of the campaign against the hated Poles had dazzled even critics of the regime. The Nazis had stunned and battered the rest into acquiescence.

Osborne appreciated Kaas's realism. Hoping to keep the Vatican channel open, he asked London to keep his talk with Kaas confidential. The monsignor's name should "on no account be mentioned." Sensing that Kaas had resistance contacts deep within Germany, Osborne urged his Foreign Office superiors to pursue any leads the Vatican offered, pending proof that they would not lead Britain into "another Venloo" [*sic*].[23]

Josef Müller spent the second half of November seeking that proof in Berlin. He found it hard to come by. Army Chief of Staff Franz Halder supported the coup planners, but remained paralyzed by Hitler's vow to vanquish "the spirit of Zossen." Müller heard from Hans Rattenhuber, the head of Hitler's bodyguard, of increased security-patrols in the chancellery gardens, a new command post outside Hitler's rooms. Partly for that reason, Kaas told Osborne that a "numbed fatalism" afflicted the conspirators. Then the picture changed again. The plotters' situation went from gloomy to catastrophic. An SS spy had uncovered the pope's role in the plot.[24]

CHAPTER 7

THE BLACK CHAPEL

I T WAS JUST A MATTER OF TIME. TOO MANY KNEW TOO MUCH, TOO
many said and did too much to escape the notice of Albert Hartl and
his spies. The defrocked priest who ran SS intelligence Unit II/B had
watched Josef Müller for years. Hartl not only suspected that Müller
was a secret Jesuit, of the sort that had once infiltrated Elizabethan
England in plainclothes, but believed that Pacelli had granted Müller
a dispensation, permitting him a wife and family. By the war's third
month, one of Hartl's agents learned about Müller's Roman missions.[1]

Hermann Keller was born with a hole in the heart. Barred from military service, he became a Benedictine monk in Beuron Abbey, which
commanded the Danube like a castle. For eight centuries, Beuron's
black-clad monks had obeyed the Rule of St. Benedict, praying seven
times daily and once at night. Bored by this routine, Brother Keller
sought excitement in alcohol, love affairs, and espionage. "Keller . . .
was one of the best foreign agents of the [SS] Vatican Referat," Hartl
recalled. Most helpfully to Hartl, the monk hated Müller, and needed
no encouragement to case him.[2]

Their feud went back years and it involved the Jews. In 1933, Beuron's
Archabbot, Raphael Walzer, had sent Rome an appeal by Edith Stein,
a convert from Judaism who became a Carmelite nun. She pleaded: "Is

not the campaign of destruction being conducted against Jewish blood a profanation of the most holy humanity of our savior?" After Pacelli passed the text to the pope, the Nazis intrigued to remove Walzer. Hartl supplied trumped-up evidence that the archabbot had broken currency laws. While Walzer stayed out of SS range in Switzerland, Keller's peers put him in charge of Beuron.[3]

Suspicious Benedictine leaders asked Müller to investigate. From a prosecutor friend, Müller learned that the state had no plans to prosecute Walzer. The SS had concocted the charges to install its agent, Keller, in Walzer's place. The irate Benedictines transferred Keller to their abbey on Mount Zion, in Palestine.[4]

Müller sensed that he had not heard the last from the Nazi monk, however. "Keller could become dangerous for me," Müller remembered thinking at the time. "Intelligent as he was, he had found out that I had thwarted his plans and vindicated Archabbot Walzer. Keller was out for revenge."[5]

The monk continued to spy for Hartl. In Palestine, he penetrated the entourage of the anti-Semitic Grand Mufti of Jerusalem. Returning to Germany in 1937, Keller began reporting also to the Abwehr's Stuttgart station. "It was his custom to disguise his intelligence activity," Hartl recalled, "by posing as a collector of photostats of medieval manuscripts." By November he was in Switzerland, stalking Berlin lawyer Alfred Etscheit, one of Müller's friends.[6]

Etscheit was a minor but earnest resistance agent. A frequent guest at General Halder's home, he had eased Müller's entry into the cabal. Canaris had sent Etscheit to sound Allied diplomats in Switzerland, under cover of a military commission to buy milk for German children, and there Etscheit ran into Keller, perhaps not by chance. During a jolly night of brandy and cigars, Etscheit let slip that the war would soon end, because certain generals planned a coup. They had already sent an emissary to the Vatican, to seek peace terms through the pope.[7]

Seeking a big scoop, Keller rushed to Rome. Questioning some Benedictine contacts, he learned that his old nemesis, Joey Ox, had been to Vatican City several times in the last weeks. Rumors linked him to dissident generals. Keller, however, showed so much interest in Müller that senior Benedictines again became suspicious. They warned Müller about the inquiries when he was next in Rome.

Pius had by then learned of Keller's mischief from another source. His nuncio in Berne, Monsignor Filippo Bernardini, received a tip from one of Keller's former brothers at Beuron. Carl Alexander Herzog von Württemberg, known as Dom Odo, was a character worthy of the pen of Evelyn Waugh, full of ambitious schemes and claiming personal contacts with President Roosevelt, whose name he could not spell. Dom Odo ran into Keller in Berne, and related their talk to the nuncio. On 22 November, Bernardini cabled Cardinal Maglione in Rome:

> With great circumspection I pass on the following intelligence to Your Eminence: Person named in Your Eminence's message No. 5152 of August 18 last [Dom Odo] begs me insistently [phrase incomplete] to inform you that a serious military plot is being organised in Germany to overthrow Hitler and National Socialism and to conclude peace with Britain and France. For prudence sake I am not putting on paper the names and details given to me.[8]

Keller had already returned to Germany and briefed his handlers. Because the case had foreign connections, the monk's report found its way to Abwehr headquarters. When Müller was back in Berlin, Oster showed him Keller's statement.

"We reckoned that they would snipe at you from all possible directions," Müller recalled Oster saying, "but we hardly feared having to shield you from men of the cloth." Worse yet, Keller had made a second report, to Hartl, claiming that Müller had access to the papal apartments, and positing that he worked as a papal intelligence courier. That report had caused such a stir that Heydrich had summoned the monk to Berlin to debrief him. The SS spy chief had reportedly remarked that Müller would be arrested within days. Oster warned Müller to avoid Rome until the Abwehr sealed the security breach. They had best see Canaris.[9]

Müller feared the worst, but the admiral just patted his dogs. He said he would handle their SS friends. At first Müller could not understand what the admiral asked him to do. Canaris asked him to sit down and write what he dictated—an ostensible "secret intelligence report from the Vatican," detailing plans for a military coup "shortly before the war." Referencing Keller's report, Canaris warned that some generals wanted to overthrow the Führer. Vatican sources, Canaris continued, did not know the conspiracy's size, but had heard the name of General Werner von Fritsch (subsequently killed in the Polish campaign and thus out of harm's way). Canaris told Müller to add the name of General Walter Reichenau, a known Hitler supporter. When Müller objected that Reichenau would never resist Hitler, Canaris said that was the whole point. Hitler would back Reichenau and reject the report—discrediting Keller's charges.[10]

Some days later, Müller asked about the faked report. Canaris related how he had presented Hitler "the report of a particularly reliable agent in the Vatican." When Hitler read Reichenau's name, he threw the paper down and exclaimed, "*Schmarren* [nonsense]." Canaris then called at Heydrich's house. "Just imagine," Canaris had said with a glum look, "here I thought I was bringing the Führer something really important in the shape of a report from Dr. Josef Müller, my ace man in the Vatican, about plans for a military coup. Then, when he finished reading it, the Führer threw it down."[11]

For the moment, the plotters had averted disaster. But the scare produced inconvenient echoes. A Swiss newspaper claimed that Halder and other generals would soon try to remove Hitler. For most of December, Müller stayed away from Rome. The plot stalled.[12]

Brother Keller kept the pressure on. With Hartl's help, he sent another Benedictine, Damasus Zähringer, to Rome. Zähringer probed Father Leiber about Müller's doings and even tried to learn from Sister Pascalina Lehnert, head of Pius's household, whether Müller entered the pope's apartments. Pascalina replied that she could say nothing about the pope's visitors.[13]

Undeterred, Keller sent a second spy to the Holy See. Swedish journalist Gabriel Ascher, a Jewish convert to Catholicism, had come under Hartl's Nazi influence and control. Ascher managed to get an introduction to Monsignor Kaas, whom Keller suspected of serving as Müller's pipeline to Pius. But Kaas did not trust Ascher and turned him away.[14]

Hartl then sent Keller himself back to Rome. Müller's contacts saw the monk drinking like a sailor at the Birreria Dreher, a tavern catering to Mussolini's German allies. To throw Keller off the track, two Benedictines said they did not trust Müller because of his "pro-Nazi views." Finally Keller did himself in by boasting too openly about his links to German intelligence. Canaris reported the indiscretion to Heydrich, who transferred Keller to Paris, where no more news of Müller's intrigues reached him.[15]

Yet Heydrich remained suspicious. One night he called in his deputy, Walter Schellenberg, and motioned for him to sit down. "For almost a minute we sat round the table in silence," Schellenberg recalled. In his high, nasal voice Heydrich opened the conversation by asking, "What about the investigation of those Abwehr men in Munich—Josef Müller . . . and the others? Isn't it pretty clear that this is the circle which started the peace feelers via the Vatican?"[16]

Schellenberg knew only what Keller had reported. Müller had direct access to the highest levels of the papal hierarchy. He was "a very clever man and, although one could not quite trust him, his reports were not without interest."

Heydrich nodded thoughtfully. "See to it that this whole circle is closely watched." The case file carried the code name *Schwarze Kapelle*, or Black Network, after the color of priestly cassocks. Since *Kapelle* also meant "chapel," that double meaning became an SS metaphor for treason tracing to the Vatican. Heydrich would save what he called his Black Chapel "ammunition pack" until the time seemed right for the killing blow.[17]

CHAPTER 8

ABSOLUTE SECRECY

A S THE DANGER OF DISCOVERY SEEMED TO FADE, PIUS REJUVE-
nated the plot. Late in 1939, he began showing his secret cards
to London. After lunching with Monsignor Kaas, British ambassador
D'Arcy Osborne cabled London on 1 December about a plot to remove
Hitler and make peace through the pope.

Kaas said an agent of German military circles had approached him.
The agent, whom Kaas evidently knew and trusted, had asked to use the
Vatican as intermediary in securing a "fair and honourable peace." If
Germany could be guaranteed fair treatment, the conspirators "would
subsequently take over control of the country from the Nazi regime."

Pius would "always gratefully welcome" what the plotters proposed.
Yet he would demand the greatest caution by the Vatican, and avoid
direct political intervention. Osborne's comment to London, like Gasparri's 1923 cable to Munich, shone a rare shaft of light on papal secret
policy: "This is the usual assertion of the Vatican's nonpolitical principle; in practice I think it could always be surmounted, so long as there
was no *obvious* lapse from impartiality" [emphasis added].

Kaas then shared his own views. He thought the suggestion of peace
talks premature. Negotiations would require conclusive guarantees not

only of the plotters' intent to remove Hitler, but also of their ability to do so. Just how they proposed to deal with Hitler remained unclear.

Osborne agreed that the plan seemed "nebulous." Before fruitful talks could occur, in any case, London needed assurance that Germany would abandon its present policy of rape on the installment plan. "At the same time I did not exclude the eventual possibility of an establishment of contact through the Vatican, or at least through Vatican circles," Osborne recorded. He hoped Kaas would report any further contacts with the plotters. When Osborne asked whether he might report their talk to London, Kaas consented, "as long as secrecy was carefully guarded."[1]

MÜLLER'S VATICAN LINKS MEANWHILE THWARTED HITLER IN SUR-prising ways. In January a report reached Abwehr headquarters that he might invade Switzerland to cover his left flank. Müller saw Canaris nearly choke with wrath. "This fool now wants to pull in the Swiss too," the admiral lisped. German honor would never recover, he said, if the world's greatest ruffian (*Weltlump*), already conspiring to violate the Low Countries, now also attacked Europe's iconically neutral state. If that happened, he said, no one in the future would "accept a piece of bread from any German."[2]

Canaris considered ways to warn the Swiss. Could they stimulate enough visible Swiss military movement to deter Hitler from an attack? Müller suggested using Abwehr agent Hans Bernd Gisevius, who had an assignment in Zurich and knew the Swiss scene. But that contradicted Canaris's operational principles. "You must keep one thing in mind," he said. "If you want to be helpful to a nation you must not do it in the country itself. If I have one of my people in Switzerland do this, he will be too much exposed thereafter. So Gisevius cannot do it as well as you." Müller took the mission but stressed that he must avoid doing anything that could compromise the Vatican.

In Rome, Müller tried several approaches to the problem. First, he met with Paul Krieg, the chaplain of the Swiss Guard. But Krieg wanted to know too much, and Müller shied off. Müller then decided to work through Italian foreign minister Galeazzo Ciano, whose relative pacifism and distrust of Berlin was well known to the Abwehr. Müller got a message to Ciano through an intermediary. Ciano sent a warning to Berne, and the Swiss began military maneuvers.[3]

Canaris magnified these to Hitler as a "partial mobilization." Knowing how Hitler's mind worked, Canaris followed with reports on Alpine defenses, noting that they came from "a high ecclesiastical authority." The intelligence purportedly came from Müller's friend and frequent travel companion, Abbott Corbinian Hofmeister of Metten. He was in Switzerland on Church business often enough to make such a side activity appear plausible, and, through his fictive studies of Swiss defense measures, he appeared on the Abwehr's rolls as a "secret agent." Using these reports, Canaris argued that a full conquest of Switzerland would take more than the six weeks some suggested. Hitler abandoned the Swiss plan.[4]

On 8 January, Monsignor Kaas learned that Müller had returned to Rome. Kaas alerted Osborne that same day, reiterating "the Vatican's willingness to act as intermediary," as Osborne recorded. The coup planning seemed newly urgent because Nazi labor leader Robert Ley, when recently in Rome, had bragged that Hitler would launch a great attack.[5]

Three days later, Pius summoned Osborne. "He told me that he had received the visit of a German representative," Osborne wrote London. The agent spoke for German army chiefs, whose names the pope preferred to keep secret. Pius felt duty-bound to relay what he had learned. "At any rate he had felt that his conscience would not be quite easy unless he sent for me," Osborne wrote. "A grand German offensive has been prepared down to the last details for the middle of February, or possibly even earlier," Osborne paraphrased Pius as saying. The attack would occur through Holland. "It will be violent, bitter and utterly unscrupulous."

But it need not occur. If the generals could be assured of a fair peace with Great Britain—they did not mention France—they would replace the present German government by a *verhandlungsfähige Regierung*—a government capable of negotiating. They would wish to retain Austria, but would restore Poland and Czechoslovakia, and would also "deal with" Russia, by which Osborne understood at least the breaking of Hitler's pact with Stalin.

Osborne remained skeptical. The vague plans reminded him of the Venlo affair. "His Holiness had said that he could answer for the good faith of the intermediary," Osborne wrote, but he could not guarantee the good faith of the principals. Still less could he guarantee that they could effect the change of government they indicated or that they would be any more reliable than Hitler if they did.

Yet Pius proceeded as if he believed in the plotters. He assured Osborne that the German principals were in no way connected with the Nazi Party. Should London wish to send the pope any message for the German plotters, Osborne could ask to see him at any time. Further, "he begged me to regard [the matter] as absolutely secret. If anything should become known the lives of the unnamed generals would be forfeit."

Osborne promised discretion. He would report on the audience only in a confidential letter to the foreign secretary, Lord Halifax, sent by courier pouch, so that no cipher officer or stenographer would see it. Osborne would type the letter himself and keep no copy.[6]

Though Pius acted discreetly, he did not hide Hitler's attack plans under the proverbial bushel basket. During the second week of January 1940, a general fear gripped Western diplomats in Rome as the pope's aides warned them of the German offensive, which Hitler had just rescheduled for the 14th. On the 10th, a Vatican prelate warned the Belgian ambassador at the Holy See, Adrien Nieuwenhuys, that the Germans would soon attack in the West. Nieuwenhuys called the Vatican the next day and questioned Undersecretary of State Giovanni Montini, the future Pope Paul the Sixth.[7]

At first Montini confined himself to generalities. When the Belgian pressed him, however, Montini gave way. "We have indeed received something," Montini said. Because of the sensitivity of the source, he urged the ambassador to raise the matter at a higher level. Taking that advice, Nieuwenhuys called on the cardinal secretary of state, Luigi

Maglione. Treading carefully, Maglione hinted that a German attack loomed, but attributed his views to private guesswork, rather than to secret agents. Nieuwenhuys and the French ambassador to the Holy See, François Charles-Roux, suspected that Pius had received some special reporting on 9–10 January, but was proceeding with care to protect a German source.[8]

Charles-Roux did some diplomatic snooping. On 16 January, he called on the undersecretary for extraordinary affairs, Domenico Tardini, who deftly avoided admitting to any secret intelligence. Tardini referenced only rumors from Berlin: Hitler found himself in a trap, his prestige demanding that he strike the Allies in the spring or even before. Tardini's circumlocution only deepened Charles-Roux's belief that the pope possessed intelligence from a secret cell in Germany.[9]

Pius had in fact already shared the warning, while shielding its source. On 9 January, Cardinal Maglione directed the papal agent in Brussels, Monsignor Clemente Micara, to warn the Belgians about a coming German attack. Six days later, Maglione sent a similar message to his agent in The Hague, Monsignor Paolo Giobbe, asking him to warn the Dutch.[10]

That same month, Pius made a veiled feint toward public protest. He wrote new details on Polish atrocities into Radio Vatican bulletins. But when Polish clergy protested that the broadcasts worsened the persecutions, Pius recommitted to public silence and secret action.[11]

AGAIN THE POPE APPROACHED THE BRITISH AS THE PLOTTERS' agent. On 7 February, he summoned Osborne for another audience. The Vatican had imposed elaborate new secrecy measures. "This time it was all very Phillips Oppenheim," the envoy wrote, name-checking a then-popular spy novelist. The pope's *maestro di camera*, the head of his private household, called first at Osborne's apartment. He asked Osborne to come to the Vatican office at half-past midnight. The maestro would wait in the Papal Apartments, to which an intermediary would lead Osborne. Then the maestro would discreetly conduct him to the pope. Osborne must not dress for an audience. The Church would not announce his visit and keep no record of it. If anyone asked, Osborne should say he had come to see the maestro. To make that lie technically true, Osborne could ask the maestro something London might plausibly want to know.

At the appointed hour, Osborne showed his credentials to a Noble Guard. The maestro approached silently on a thick carpet. Motioning that Osborne should imitate him, he genuflected just inside an adjoining door. Osborne found himself in a book-lined corner room, with three tall windows, overlooking St. Peter's square.

His Holiness sat at an oak desk, flanked by a white typewriter and a white telephone. He spoke from four pages of German typescript notes.

"The Pope told me that he had been approached again by the 'reliable intermediary' of German military circles," Osborne recounted. "I pressed him as to the identity of these, but he would give me no name; he would only say that a well-known and important General was concerned. He withheld the name as he did not wish inadvertently to be the cause of the man's death if it should come out. But he assured me that he was of sufficient importance to be taken very seriously."

Pius dissected a mysterious incident to underscore the agent's importance. In the foggy dawn of 10 January, two confused Luftwaffe officers crash-landed in a Belgian field. One of the officers carried secret papers, which he only partly succeeded in destroying. Belgian officials recovered plans for a German attack through the Low Countries. Allied commanders suspected a German trick; Osborne had thought the episode staged to pressure Belgium.[12]

The plotters' agent described the documents as genuine. Hitler refused to cancel the invasion, despite the security breach. Only the extreme cold delayed him. He would attack in the spring, the pope warned: "Hitler is boasting that he will be in the Louvre by summer and that one of his first cares will be to find a more worthy site to set up the Venus of Milo [*sic*]!"

Pius now came to the crux. "A part of the army (proportion and influence unspecified) would like a change of government and to get rid of Hitler." They would not start their coup in Protestant Berlin, but in Catholic Munich, Cologne, and Vienna. The Reich would have at first two governments, and probably a civil war. The anti-Hitler group would install a military dictatorship, then replace it with a democratic state. Once the new regime could speak with authority, it would make peace. The plan's backers wanted to know whether "the continued existence of the Reich plus Austria" provided a basis for talks.[13]

Osborne remained skeptical. He told Pius the new approach seemed open to all the old criticisms. It contained no guarantees of authenticity, or of success, or that a new German Government would be more trustworthy or less aggressive. The vital question—whether the rebels wanted to start talks before the coup—seemed obscure.

Pius did not disagree. The plot amounted, at most, to a hope. Yet "his conscience would not allow him to ignore it altogether, lest there might conceivably be one chance in a million of its serving the purpose of sparing lives."

The pope reemphasized the need for extreme secrecy. He insisted that Osborne put nothing on paper, except a report to London, which the envoy would type himself, and of which he would make no copy. Pius begged further that British Prime Minister Neville Chamberlain brief the French only orally. The pope stated that even his own secretary of state must know nothing. If the British had any messages for the plotters, Osborne should repeat that night's clandestine ballet, making contact through the maestro.

Pius clearly took the plot in dead earnest. "I think that His Holiness' urgent insistence on the most absolute secrecy is a measure of his own belief in the bona fides of his informants," Osborne wrote. Pius seemed so committed to the plot that he came off almost as pushy. He even asked whether Lord Halifax could not personally guarantee the territorial integrity of post-Hitler Germany: "He was most reluctant to abandon this idea."

The pope's passion made an impact. "I derived the impression," Osborne typed, "that the German initiative was more important and more genuine than I had believed." Pius had lobbied so hard for the coup, Osborne sensed, that London would probably have to respond.[14]

THE POPE'S PLEA GAINED A HEARING AT THE HIGHEST LEVELS IN London. Lord Halifax sent a copy of Osborne's report to King George the Sixth. His Majesty mused that something seemed afoot in Germany: two weeks before, he had heard through his cousin, Queen Marie of Yugoslavia, of a plot to "bump off" Hitler. By 15 February, Chamberlain jotted guidance for future contacts through the pope: "G. B. [Great Britain] would be willing to discuss any conditions asked for," the prime minister wrote, "if convinced that business was meant."[15]

While awaiting a formal reply, Pius gave another nudge. This time he used an official ritual for clandestine business. Lord Halifax's wife and son visited Rome on 16 February; Pius gave them an audience, and Osborne joined. The Holy Father "drew me aside at the end," Osborne wrote, "to tell me that the German military circles mentioned in my previous letters had confirmed their intention, or their desire, to effect a change of government." Even if the regime changed, however, Osborne did not think Britain could leave the German war machine intact. Besides, if the plotters really wanted regime change, why didn't they "get on" with it? Pius countered that they awaited British assurances. He then cut the talk short, because Lady Halifax was waiting. But Osborne honored a promise to relate what Pius told him.[16]

Halifax gave Osborne the green light the next day. "I have reflected on your [7 February] letter and have discussed it with the Prime Minister." That opening chord showed that London now took the plot seriously. An even surer sign that the British endorsed the plan was that they proposed not to give the French "any account of what passed."

Halifax cited the pope's personal stake as the reason for going forward. "In view of the importance attached by His Holiness to the approach which has been made to him, we think that you should get in touch with him again through the channel indicated to you, and convey to him an indication of our reaction." If the principals in Germany had both the intention and the power to perform what they promised, His Majesty's Government would consider any inquiries they might make. Halifax invited the plotters to develop the idea in concrete terms. He proposed an exchange of ideas with the German resistance through the pope.[17]

In the last week of February, Osborne relayed the British answer. "Today O was with the Chief, and told him something which will induce you to go home at once," Father Leiber scrawled on a calling card at Josef Müller's hotel. "We must have a talk yet today." When they met that night, the Jesuit whispered: "It's going ahead."[18]

CHAPTER 9

THE X-REPORT

A FTER MONTHS OF BACK-CHANNEL DIPLOMACY, PIUS HAD LINKED the Reich's internal and external enemies. In March 1940, he refereed their parley. Each side made seven statements. The negotiations unfolded in a tense atmosphere, for Hitler might attack in the West at any moment.[1]

The pope established an intricate communications chain. Oster submitted yes-or-no questions to Müller, who passed them to Pius, who shared them with Osborne, who cabled them to London. The British answers flowed back in reverse. The Vatican remained the crossroads in the plot to kill Hitler: all roads truly led to Rome, to the desk with a simple crucifix overlooking the fountains on St. Peter's Square.[2]

As cutouts, Pius relied on his closest deputies. Father Leiber managed the German channel, meeting with Müller on the roof of the Jesuit College or obscure Roman churches. Typically, Leiber passed him oral messages. But when Leiber saw the pope late at night, and Müller needed to leave the next day, Leiber would leave notes on block paper, initialed "R.L." (Robert Leiber), at Müller's hotel. That practice did not strike the Jesuit as risky. In most cases, he could encapsulate the British answers in brief replies under the numbered headings of the German questions, and Müller burned the messages after reading them.[3]

Monsignor Kaas handled the British end. His apartment abutted Ambassador Osborne's, on the Vatican Gardens, so they could meet without great fear of detection. By late February they had begun direct talks.

One point Kaas made struck Osborne as important. If, after eliminating Hitler, the plotters accepted humiliating peace terms, their position would become precarious. Osborne recorded: "The elimination of the *furor Germanicus* of Hitlerism will leave particularly among the younger and restless generation, a spiritual vacuum which will have somehow to be filled if another explosion is to be avoided." As an alternative order-principle, the Vatican proposed European unification. An economic federation, Kaas argued, would prevent autarchy, exacerbated patriotism, aggression, and war.[4]

Some in London remained skeptical. On 28 February, Foreign Office Undersecretary Alexander Cadogan slammed the "ridiculous stale story of a German opposition ready to overthrow Hitler, if we will guarantee we will not 'take advantage.'" He said it was "about the 100th time" he had heard that story. Four days later, the Foreign Office warned against another Venlo: "We have reason to believe that the Gestapo have a hold on Mgr. Kaas." London sent Osborne a Most Secret warning that the monsignor might have come under Nazi influence through German seminarians in Rome.[5]

"I know Mgr Kaas quite well," the envoy shot back, and "there is little doubt that he is strongly anti-Nazi." Osborne thought Kaas too busy managing St. Peter's to see German seminarians, who seemed unlikely spies: "They are dressed in the brightest possible scarlet from head to foot, which does not conduce to the work of secret agents."[6]

Pius received London's final terms about 10–11 March. The conditions the British required to negotiate with a post-Hitler Germany included the *conditio sine qua non*: "elimination of the National Socialist regime." Leiber handed Müller a full-page summary on Vatican stationery, watermarked "P.M.," for "*Pontifex Maximus*," and, in the upper-left corner, the sign of a fish, after Saint Peter, a former fisherman.[7]

Leiber expected Müller to burn this paper after making coded shorthand notes on it. But Müller thought the whole plan might hinge on the impact Britain's terms produced in Germany. Believing the world perhaps hung in the balance, he made a snap decision to keep rather than burn the watermarked document. About 14 March, he took the pope's notes with Leiber's calling card to Abwehr headquarters, where Hitler's would-be killers rejoiced. Müller considered that moment the climax of his Vatican intrigues.[8]

"Your slips of paper [*Zettel*] have been very useful to me," Müller told Leiber when next in Rome. The Jesuit lost his temper. "But you promised me that you would destroy them," he protested, and demanded their return. Müller said that he had passed them on and no longer had control over them. Because of these materials, he said, he felt more sanguine about the impact in Berlin: "The results of the mediation are regarded as most favorable in Germany." The coup could occur as early as mid-March. Müller sounded so positive that Leiber felt reassured. The pope and the initiated few in the Vatican settled down to wait.[9]

THE PLOTTERS PREPARED A FINAL ACTION PACKAGE FOR THE GENERALS. Father Leiber's single page and an oral presentation would scarcely suffice for the decisive gambit. A supreme attempt to propel the military into mutiny merited a final report covering the entire operation.

The paper emerged from a frenzied all-night effort. Müller holed up in the house of Oster's deputy, Hans von Dohnanyi. In the guest bedroom, Müller spread the results of the pope's maneuvers on the bed usually reserved for Dohnanyi's brother-in-law, evangelical pastor Dietrich Bonhoeffer. Besides Father Leiber's paper, Müller had his own coded notes in Gabelsburg shorthand on paper towels, as well as a half-inch stack of Dohnanyi's notations. Dohnanyi dictated a report to his wife until late into the night. The next morning Müller reviewed the result, which totaled about twelve typed pages.[10]

For security reasons, the document lacked heading, date, and signature, and it referenced Müller only as "Herr X." It became known among the plotters as the "X-Report." The report delineated the British conditions for peace talks with "the Decent Germany." There were seven: (1) removal of Hitler; (2) "rule of law" in Germany; (3) no war in the West;

(4) Austria stays German; (5) Poland is liberated; (6) other territories self-determine by plebiscite; and (7) an armistice through the pope. The subtext of these protocols later became the subject of debate: Moscow would allege, for instance, that the report contained a Vatican-Anglo-German deal to smooth the way for an attack on the Soviet Union. But on one point, all who saw the report agreed. The pope, as one reader noted, had "gone astonishingly far" to help the conspirators. Pius had coaxed London to meet the plotters more than halfway, and covered the British terms with the mantle of his authority. He had brought the plans to the edge of action. General Halder began hiding a pistol in his pocket when he saw Hitler.[11]

Yet by late March Hitler was still alive. On the 27th Osborne saw Kaas, whose "German military contacts seem to have abandoned their peace plans for the time being," the envoy recorded. A dejected Kaas portrayed his countrymen as too obedient to organize a revolt.[12]

Three days later, the pope summoned Osborne. When the envoy asked whether His Holiness had heard anything from the conspirators, the pontiff said that he had heard nothing since relaying the final British terms, about twenty days before. Pius said he sensed that London had begun to lose hope. Osborne admitted that only Hitler's removal could now assure "the bona fides of the German principals." Still, he insisted that London "would always receive with interest, and treat with respect," any messages the plotters sent through Vatican channels. Osborne sensed that Pius "was much disillusioned."[13]

During the meeting, Osborne received a message from Halifax. He conveyed it to Pius, who seemed "very pleased," and asked Osborne to send his best wishes and thanks. This note, perhaps later destroyed on the Vatican's request, may have simply repeated London's willingness to deal with the German military after Hitler's death. Three days later, just such an assurance reached the plotters through Müller.[14]

At that pivotal point, however, the Protestant plotters wavered. Christian scruples moved their hearts but stayed their hands. Chief of Staff Halder fingered the pistol in his pocket, but "as a Christian" he could not shoot an unarmed man. To loosen Lutheran strictures, Müller asked former Saxon crown prince Georg von Sachsen, now a Jesuit priest, to speak with Halder. Sachsen, known for clicking his heels in front of the Communion host, stressed the Christian moral right to rebellion and seemed to put some spine into the general. After rebuffing initial approaches, Halder finally agreed to read the X-Report.[15]

A snag then occurred over who would bring and brief the text. The plotters first chose Ulrich von Hassell, a former German ambassador to Rome, who had known of coup plans since before the war. On 16 March, as Hassell wrote in his diary, he saw "extraordinarily interesting papers about talks of a Catholic confidential agent with the Pope. . . . The general assumption naturally is a change of regime and a commitment to Christian morality." Yet Hassell just then came under SS suspicion, and the plotters had to put him aside.[16]

The task of lobbying Halder fell instead to General Georg Thomas. On 4 April, Thomas carried the documents to Halder. The package by now included a statement from the Vatican that the British still adhered to their terms, as well as a memorandum by Dohnanyi stressing the need to disassociate the army from SS crimes.[17]

These materials intrigued but perplexed Halder. The report struck him as long-winded, and yet vague on key points. He felt unable to assess the credibility of the German figures involved, since the report did not identify them or their Vatican cutout, "Herr X."[18]

Still, Halder felt the X-Report deserved a hearing. He took the package to his superior, the army commander in chief, Walther von Brauchitsch, and asked him to read it overnight.

The next morning Halder found his boss in a bad mood. "You should not have shown this to me," Brauchitsch said, handing the paper back. "We are at war. That one in time of peace establishes contact with a foreign power may be considered. In war this is impossible for a soldier." Indicating the X-Report, Brauchitsch said: "What we face here is pure national treason [*Landesverrat*]." As Halder recalled, Brauchitsch "then demanded that I have the man who had brought this paper arrested. . . . I replied to him at that time: 'If there is anyone to be arrested, then please arrest me.'"[19]

Brauchitsch grew quiet and pensive. Looking at the X-Report, he sighed: "What am I to do with this scrap [*Fetzen*] which is without date and without signature?" After some fretting, he and Halder decided to study the Vatican materials for another ten days. During that period, the prospects for action dramatically changed.[20]

HITLER HAD FOR SOME MONTHS PLANNED TO INVADE NORWAY. Foreseeing a long war against the Allies, especially after he invaded France, Hitler wanted secure access to Scandinavian metals and other strategic resources before the British could. The nascent Norway crisis presented the coup planners with a new opportunity: a warning to the Allies might prompt a British show of naval force that might deter Hitler or deal him a defeat. Joey Ox therefore warned the pope about Hitler's plans through a guarded telephone call to Monsignor Johannes Schönhöffer. At the end of March, Kaas warned Osborne about a possible German move against Norway, and Osborne relayed the information to London. But the English did not respond before 9 April, when Hitler struck.[21]

At Abwehr headquarters, Josef Müller and others studied a map of the North Sea. They made bets among themselves as to just where the British fleet would blow German ships out of the water. Canaris, however, predicted that the British would never stake their fleet until an existentially critical moment had arrived. Events proved Canaris correct: the English did not react in force.[22]

Hitler's popularity soared. He had won yet another victory at almost no apparent cost. Veteran generals who had dismissed Hitler as a Bohemian corporal began to revise their judgment. Halder lost his nerve and entangled himself in a glutinous web of second guesses. In the middle of April, he returned the X-Report to General Thomas without comment.

Around that time, a dejected Müller returned to Rome. The generals, he said, lacked the will for a coup. "All was ready," he told Father Leiber. "The other day I sat at my desk at five o'clock and waited for a call. But none came."[23]

The news disillusioned Pius. Months of intrigue had produced nothing. But in the last days before Hitler finally attacked in the West, the plotters risked a bold new mission to restore the Holy Father's trust.[24]

CHAPTER 10

WARNINGS TO THE WEST

HITLER HAD FINALLY FIXED A DATE FOR HIS WESTERN WAR. Learning in late April 1940 that the attack would come in early May, the Nazis' secret German enemies again felt obliged to warn the victims through the pope.[1]

But the stakes seemed higher now. Because the Vatican intrigues had not yet prompted a coup, the plotters needed to burnish their bona fides. Unless they compensated for any excessive optimism they had generated, London might assume that the plotters were really Nazi agents. Then not only the British but the pope too might close Vatican channels. If, instead, they could effectively alert the Allies to Hitler's war plans, the conspirators might at least keep the papal conduit open for a future coup. Canaris therefore saw the need for a redeeming Roman mission. As one of his deputies put it: "We must stand there with clean hands."[2]

On 1 May, Josef Müller arrived in Rome. He traveled with Abbot Corbinian Hofmeister of Metten, ostensibly on Church business. The Canaris group had carefully formulated the message Müller gave Father Leiber for the pope. "The discussions cannot continue with any prospect of success. Unfortunately the generals cannot be persuaded to act," Müller recalled the text saying. "Hitler will attack and this action lies just ahead."[3]

After giving Leiber the message, Müller hurried to another address. He wanted to warn a close Belgian friend, Norbertine Abbot-General Hubert Noots, what lay in store for his country. Two days later, Müller gave Noots an even more detailed picture, then flew out of Rome on 4 May.

During a layover in Venice, paranoia seized him. Sensing how deeply he had imperiled himself by leaking the war plans, Müller tried to cover his tracks. In Venice, through which he passed several hundred times during the Nazi years, he had earned the friendship of a customs officer with cigars and other gifts. From this officer Müller now borrowed an official rubber stamp. He used it to smear in his passport the dates on which he had entered and left Italy.[4]

Hitler meanwhile kept changing the dates for the attack. On 1 May he fixed it for the fifth; on the third, he moved it to the sixth; on the fourth, he moved it to the seventh; on the fifth, he moved it to the eighth. As the situation evolved, Canaris saw the need to update the pope. But on 4–5 May, Müller had just returned to Berlin, and there seemed little sense in his racing back to relay a few words—especially since another Abwehr agent, Wilhelm Schmidhuber, was about to leave for Rome. Müller gave him a note for Leiber, stating only the date then set for the offensive, 8 May. If the date changed again, Müller would phone Schmidhuber at the Hotel Flora. Since they both sat on the board of the Eidenschink Bank, Müller would reference the purported dates of its board meetings as a coded way of conveying the attack dates.[5]

Schmidhuber flew to Rome and warned Leiber on 6 May. On the 7th and the 8th, Schmidhuber received calls from Müller, changing dates for the "board meeting." In each case, Father Leiber briefed the pope.[6]

Pius responded swiftly. As he remarked to an aide, the accuracy of the recent Norway warning led him to accept the latest intelligence at once. The approaching violation of neutral lands roused his special indignation. On 3 May, Pius directed the cardinal secretary of state, Luigi Maglione, to send warning telegrams to papal agents in The Hague and in Brussels. To give his alerts more weight, the pope personally relayed the grim prediction in a private audience on 6 May with Belgian Princess Marie José.[7]

More momentous was his warning to the Allied powers. Because they had declared war on Germany, the Vatican could not couch alerts to them as humanitarian gestures. Betraying Hitler's designs to Paris and London meant taking sides in the war.

For this delicate action, the pope chose an aide who himself later became pope. On 7 May, Monsignor Montini, the future Paul the Sixth, spoke solemnly to Osborne and to French diplomat Jean Rivière. Before the week's end, he said, Germany would invade the Low Countries. Montini furnished tactical intelligence on the expected style of operations, including the use of paratroopers and sabotage.[8]

Father Leiber opened yet another warning line. He tipped Jesuit Father Theodor Monnens, a Belgian colleague at the Gregorian University. Monnens rushed straightway to the Belgian ambassador, Adrien Nieuwenhuys, who had received almost the same warning from Abbot-General Noots. The envoy took notice, dispatching on 2 May a ciphered telegram warning Brussels of an attack the next week. The Belgian Foreign Ministry demanded more details, so Nieuwenhuys sent a fuller account to Brussels on 4 May, just as Josef Müller was smudging his passport in Venice. The warning, Nieuwenhuys stressed, was not mere opinion, but intelligence from a "compatriot"—a Belgian—tipped by a "personage who must draw his information from the General Staff."[9]

This person, who left Berlin 29 April, arrived in Rome 1 May, Friday evening had a new discussion of several hours with our compatriot [Noots] to whom he confirmed that the Chancellor [Hitler] had irrevocably decided to invade Holland and Belgium, and that, according to him, the signal for this attack will be given very soon without declaration of war. . . . He added that the war will be conducted with all means: gas, bacteria, total pillage, including bank deposit boxes. . . . To degree external aspects permit a judgment, I find difficult believe this development as near.[10]

The recipients dismissed all these Vatican warnings. "I do not attach particular faith to their present prediction," Osborne noted when he cabled the pope's alert. "[T]hey have had similar expectations before." On 19 March, for instance, Osborne had expected an attack in less than a month; Pius's most recent intelligence placed the attack about mid-April. After six months of Vatican intrigue, Lord Halifax seems to have mentally filed the May alerts under the heading of the pope who cried wolf.[11]

Hitler invaded Holland and Belgium on 10 May, and then sliced into France. After five days, France considered itself beaten. The Allies began a five-week retreat that would climax with the British evacuation at Dunkirk, and end with the swastika flying from the Eiffel Tower.

WHEN PIUS HEARD ABOUT THE INVASION, HE PREPARED A PROTEST. Cardinal Maglione drafted a brief statement for his signature, which could run that evening in the Vatican daily, *L'Osservatore Romano*. Pius rejected it as too mild. A second draft by Maglione received the same verdict. By eight o'clock that night the deadline for even a delayed edition of the paper had nearly passed. The pope then took the more direct step of writing one-paragraph condolences to the invaded sovereigns, condemning the invasion's "cruelties" as "against all justice," and ordered them published in the paper's next edition. He pecked out the notes on his white Olivetti typewriter and corrected them himself. Because of the late hour, he forged Maglione's counter-signature.[12]

The notes provoked an Axis backlash. Perhaps spurred on by Berlin, Mussolini tried to intimidate the pope. On 13 May an audience Pius gave Italian envoy Dino Alfieri crackled with spite. Mussolini saw not only the notes themselves, but their publication in the Vatican paper, as "a move against his policies," Alfieri said. Given the anger in Fascist quarters, Alfieri could not exclude "serious things happening." In response to this veiled threat, Pius said he did not fear "going to a concentration camp or into hostile hands."[13]

He then tendered his own warning. As pope he "should speak in fact against what is happening in Poland," an aide recorded him saying. "We would like to utter words of fire against such actions and the only thing restraining Us from speaking is the fear of making the plight of the victims even worse."[14]

HITLER'S TRIUMPH LEFT THE VATICAN AN ISLAND IN AN AXIS SEA. In June, as Italy entered the war on the German side, Pius offered Allied diplomats sanctuary in his city-state, where Osborne felt "like a trapped animal." Mussolini viewed the Holy See, with its warren of diplomats, as "a cave of spies" (*un covo di spie*) and boasted that he could invade it at any time. Müller warned Father Leiber of an SS plot to place the pope in protective custody. After the Vatican newspaper published Pius's sympathy notes to the invaded neutrals, Fascist goons beat up the newsboys and threw the papers into the Trevi Fountain. When Pius ventured out into Rome to say Mass, fascists waylaid him at a crossroads, rocking the papal limousine and yelling, "Death to the pope!"[15]

Pius tightened his perimeter. The Vatican police created a plain-clothes Special Section for counterespionage. The Swiss Guards retained their plumed hats and antique swords, but stockpiled gas masks and submachine guns. Vatican engineers built air-raid shelters and a steel-armored room to protect rare books and manuscripts.[16]

Anxiety rose in the Vatican about Pius's links with the German resistance. Father Leiber's clandestine actions produced some panic in high Jesuit quarters. When the order's superior-general objected that Leiber's "nebulous and dubious intrigue" jeopardized Jesuits in the Reich, Pius moved Leiber's meetings with Müller to a suburban rectory. Smoke rose above Roman chimneys as Müller's contacts burned their papers. But when Leiber and, later, Monsignor Kaas suggested that Pius should break all contact with the plotters, Pius sharply commanded them to "mind their own business."[17]

Pius insisted that he did not fear for his own safety. Apparently referencing the communists who raided his Munich nunciature in 1919, he told Alfieri: "We were not frightened by pistols pointed at Us once and We will be even less frightened next time." But in the coming months, as his resistance links put him again in SS crosshairs, Pius would realize just how perilous his position had become.[18]

CHAPTER 11

THE BROWN BIRDS

A N SS OFFICER CALLED IT "THE WAR'S MOST IMPORTANT CASE OF high treason." Josef Müller learned of it on 17 May 1940, when he got an alarming telephone call over the Abwehr's special secure network in Munich. A Canaris confidant told Müller to come at once to Berlin. He must travel by car, avoiding train and plane to prevent later tracing of his movements.[1]

Müller called Monsignor Johannes Neuhäusler, and they arranged a meeting in Munich's Englischer Garten. "Giovanni," Müller said, using his friend's Italian nickname, "I think I'm lost." He asked the priest to look after his family, especially his daughter. He worried that life would be tough for the child of a condemned traitor.[2]

In Berlin, Müller went to Hans Oster's home. The chief of Abwehr Section Z looked at him mournfully. Müller recalled him asking, "Do you remember what we promised ourselves? If one of us screws up, he goes to the gallows alone." When Müller said that of course he remembered, Oster said, "Well, now, we're both in deep shit." He wouldn't go into more detail. "But keep your chin up," Oster said, "and may God help us."[3]

Müller went over to the Abwehr headquarters, where he ran into Canaris. The admiral was just then going into the daily meeting of the department heads. Müller noticed at once that Canaris was agitated. He whispered and used the familiar *Du*. "The Brown Birds!" he hissed. "Read the Brown Birds." Müller's confusion deepened when Canaris asked him with narrowed eyes, "Are you the one?" Müller said. "Who am I supposed to be?" But Canaris turned away without answering the question.[4]

Finally, in the office of Oster's deputy, Müller learned the truth. Years before, Hans von Dohnanyi explained, Luftwaffe chief Hermann Göring had created the Research Office of the Reich Air Ministry to read foreign communications. The office intercepted and decoded messages and sent the results to interested departments. Because the decrypts circulated on brown paper, imprinted with a Reich eagle, Abwehr officials called them "Brown Birds."

The office had decoded two cables sent by the Vatican's Belgian envoy. Transmitted by Adrien Nieuwenhuys on 2 and 4 May, the messages detailed Hitler's war plans. One text sourced the warning to a Belgian "compatriot," tipped by a "personage" who "left Berlin 29 April, arrived in Rome 1 May."[5]

"Is that you?" Canaris asked when he returned. Müller replied evenly: "Maybe." Canaris said, "Come on, you would have to know that!" Then he smiled, put a hand on Müller's shoulder, and praised his composure amid the chaos. The admiral asked: "Are you prepared to receive an order from me?" Müller said that depended on the order. "I order you to go to Rome on special assignment and investigate this leak there," Canaris said.

Müller must go at once. As soon as the plane took off, Canaris would launch a manhunt for the "personage" and impose frontier controls for all travel to Italy: "I must take charge of that before Heydrich gets his hands on it." In Rome Müller should call at Abwehr headquarters, where the colonel in charge would have orders to help him. The whole probe would lie in Müller's lap. It only remained for Canaris to assure Hitler, when he demanded a leak inquiry, that he had the right man on it—one Josef Müller, with peerless Vatican connections. As Müller later said, "The admiral had turned me into the leader of the investigation against me."[6]

Once more Müller flew to Rome. He called first on Father Leiber and briefed him. They agreed that the telegrams' author, Belgian ambassador Nieuwenhuys, must vanish for a time in the thousand-roomed Apostolic Palace. Then Müller and Leiber must find some way to divert attention from Abbot-General Noots, who had relayed Müller's warning to Nieuwenhuys. Müller would slip into the abbot-general's home after dark.

Next Müller called at the Abwehr office. There he asked Colonel Otto Helferich for the file summarizing the leak probe to date. To Müller's relief, it contained nothing of urgent concern. He then asked for and received a list of Abwehr and SS agents spying on the Vatican. Finally, knowing that his friends would worry about him, and needing to impress Helferich with the importance of his mission, Müller phoned Canaris, in the colonel's presence, saying that Helferich had the inquiry well launched and that they had a very "satisfactory conversation." Helferich, a relaxed type, seemed glad that Müller had taken on the extra work. Müller thus commandeered the local Abwehr apparatus to advance his purpose—the investigation of himself.[7]

Things fell into place. Müller called on Noots and warned him to keep a low profile. That night Müller saw Leiber and gave him the windfall list of Nazi spies. It included Keller's Benedictine friend, Damasus Zähringer; Gabriel Ascher, the Jewish convert to Catholicism; and Father Joachim Birkner, Hartl's mole in the Vatican Secret Archives.[8]

The next morning Müller met the beaming Leiber. "I have had an inspiration," the Jesuit said with elfin mischief. "One of our fathers, a Belgian, has left for the Congo and is well beyond reach. Why not shove everything onto him as the 'compatriot' referred to by Nieuwenhuys? That should serve to draw attention away from Noots."[9]

Müller now had a plausible story to tell Berlin. He had framed someone else for Noots's role as the Belgian "compatriot." Müller returned to Colonel Helferich, glowing with unfeigned satisfaction. He had learned through his Vatican connections that a Belgian Jesuit, Theodor Monnens, had fled Rome and gone into hiding. Here, clearly, was the Belgian "compatriot" mentioned in the intercepts.

The problem remained only half-solved, however. Müller still had to frame someone else for his own role as the "personage" who warned the "compatriot." Here Abbott Noots helped craft a legend that leveraged Nazi preconceptions. SS chief Heinrich Himmler hated German Foreign Minister Joachim von Ribbentrop and also disliked Italian Foreign Minister Galeazzo Ciano. Reportedly, Ciano ran a social espionage ring in Rome's cocktail and dining circuits. Müller would credit Ciano's spies with ferreting the war plans from Ribbentrop's thirty-five-person travel entourage, which included legal and economic experts, two hairdressers, a masseur, a doctor, and a gymnastics coach. From Ciano the tip could have flowed to Belgian Crown Princess Marie José, who moved in his social circuit; and from the Belgian princess, it could have reached the Belgian Jesuit Monnens.[10]

Still, the danger had not passed. An Abwehr counterespionage officer, Colonel Joachim Rohleder, had learned of the intercepted messages. He did not belong to the Canaris cabal. Rohleder studied the roster of three dozen persons who crossed the frontier toward Italy at the time in question. He saw Josef Müller's name.[11]

Rohleder decided to put an agent on Müller's trail. He learned that Gabriel Ascher had earlier helped Hermann Keller gather intelligence on Müller. Since Ascher still had friends in high papal places, Rohleder gave him money and sent him to Rome.[12]

Two weeks later, Ascher returned with a damning report. It contained what Rohleder called "logically convincing" evidence against Müller. Ascher cited an impressive list of supposed agents, including priests in Milan and Genoa, and a Vatican personality who knew Father Leiber. Armed with these data, Rohleder visited Oster, who dismissed Ascher's claims as petty gossip from a rival clerical group, jealous of Müller's access. Rohleder then appealed to Canaris, who called the case "inconclusive."[13]

The plotters again called Müller to Berlin. In a discreet nook near the main railway station, Müller had a confidential talk with Hans Dohnanyi, who showed him Ascher's report and Rohleder's resulting accusation. For the record, Müller must sign and swear a counterstatement. Müller went to the office of a lawyer friend, Max Dorn, who owed him a favor. While Dorn typed, Müller dictated a rebuttal for delivery to Canaris.[14]

The admiral called in Rohleder. Having considered all angles, he thought it advisable to drop the whole business and dump Ascher. The colonel protested, especially against Oster's continued use of Müller. When Canaris insisted, Rohleder saw no choice but to obey.

The near-disaster chastened Pius. Through Müller, he implored the conspirators to destroy any papers implicating the Church in their plans. But retired general Ludwig Beck balked at burning any resistance documents, which his protégé Oster kept in a safe at Zossen. Beck wanted to preserve proof for posterity that a Decent Germany had existed. Müller protested, through Oster, that this would imperil the plotters both in Rome and in Germany. He asked Oster to promise, on his word of honor, to destroy the Leiber papers. In Müller's presence, Oster asked an underling to do so. Only later did Müller realize that Oster hadn't actually given his word of honor.[15]

HITLER'S WIN IN THE WEST DEMORALIZED BOTH HIS FOREIGN AND his internal enemies. The plotters saved their honor but lost their moment. Instead of attacking Hitler, the Wehrmacht had attacked the Allies—first in the north and then in the West. The British cabinet, now under Winston Churchill, would not parley further until the Germans removed Hitler. The German masses, drunk with victory, did not want Hitler removed. The Battle of Britain further soured Churchill on the very idea of a "Decent Germany." Toward the German resistance, he ordered: "Our attitude . . . should be absolute silence."[16]

Still, Pius kept the channel open. Although he could not extend British commitments, he kept in touch with the German plotters. Müller continued his Vatican mission, positioning the resistance for some lucky turn of fortune's wheel. Perhaps as early as September 1940, Müller briefed Roosevelt's personal representative to Pius, Myron Taylor, on the basics of the plot.[17]

With Leiber under SS suspicion, Müller met more with Kaas. As the danger of surveillance increased after the fall of France, they began to convene in the Vatican crypt, where the excavations for Peter's tomb continued. Müller descended the stairs and slipped through a narrow passageway in the foundations of the church—a few seconds' journey returned him to the Rome of the second and third centuries. In the mosaics on the walls, he could not avoid seeing allusions to his own life and mission. In one pastoral scene, two oxen awaited their master, yoked to a grape-laden wagon. A red, white, and blue emblem, worked into the design of a cross-vault, evoked the British Union Jack. Beneath it, the freedman Flavius Agricola had inscribed: "When death comes, earth and fire devour everything." Nearby, Jonah fell from a ship into the mouth of the whale. In the depths of the vault, directly beneath the high altar of the basilica, someone had written: *Petr[os] en[i]*, "Peter is here within."[18]

In the summer of 1940, Josef Müller learned more about the plotters' leadership. He began meeting with retired General Beck. These meetings brought the pope's most trusted political agent in direct contact with the designated regent of the Decent Germany's post-Hitler regime. In long talks, Müller won Beck over to the idea of "a European Economic Union as a fundamental step toward a united Europe, which would make exaggerated nationalism and war between the separate states impossible." This idea became integral to resistance plans for post-Hitler Europe.[19]

A second idea developed with Beck was the need to make the resistance more ecumenical. Because Lutheran generals kept more strictly to their loyalty oaths, potential allies in Germany saw the coup plan as a Catholic Center Party scheme; and because the pope had fronted for the plot, prospective foreign friends viewed it as a Vatican project. As Müller recounted, Beck wanted to "modulate" that predominantly Catholic "resonance."

To that end, the resistance recruited Protestant theologian Dietrich Bonhoeffer. His sister, Christel, had married Hans von Dohnanyi, and Bonhoeffer had learned contours of the plot from his brother-in-law. Bonhoeffer joined the Abwehr's Munich office, and Müller became his handler. By October 1940, he had ensconced Bonhoeffer beyond the Gestapo's reach, in the Benedictine monastery at Ettal, around which the winds of the Alps broke.[20]

Mountains blocked the sun, which only touched the abbey at noon. Father Johannes Albrecht—a master beer-brewer in a hooded black tunic—gave Bonhoeffer a key to the library. There he spent most of each morning writing his *Ethics*, which fused Catholic and Protestant precepts.[21]

Around this time, Bonhoeffer adopted the Catholic view on tyrannicide. Jesuit Father Rupert Mayer, then lodged at Ettal, may have encouraged Bonhoeffer to abandon the Protestant doctrine of nonresistance; from Bonhoeffer's Ettal stay, in any case, comes the earliest clear proof that he abandoned it. Müller's Church intelligence contacts, Abbott Hofmeister and Monsignor Neuhäusler, became the pastor's closest new companions; he began adverting to Catholic themes, such as the "Unity of Christendom"; and in letters to his trusted associates, he began to speak elliptically, using new-testament Greek terms to urge "boldness joined with prudence." Echoing Ignatius's *Spiritual Exercises*, he wrote of "Christ [as] the destroyer," who saw his enemies as "ripe for burning." In "grave situations," Bonhoeffer now argued with Jesuitical casuistry, treason became "true patriotism," and what normally passed for patriotism had become treason.[22]

At Christmas 1940, Christian resistance agents convened at Ettal to plan their next move. They met in the abbot's private dining room, and sat up half the night around the fireplace: Müller, Dohnanyi, Father Mayer, Father Albrecht, and Pastor Bonhoeffer, along with Schmidhuber and Captain Heinrich Ickhardt from the Munich Abwehr. By some accounts, the Vatican sent three prelates to the meeting, including Leiber, and possibly Jesuit Father Ivo Zeiger, rector of the German college in Rome.[23]

Over sweet Franconian ice-wine, their talk took a sober turn. They wondered whether the pope could renew contacts with the British. The Jesuit hoped so. But Müller warned his friends not to expect too much. The whole environment had now changed. With Italy in the war on the Nazi side, and the British in a real shooting war against Germany, the time for talk had passed. The Decent Germans must act. If they did, the pope would help them. If they did not, then no help from the pope would matter. With Hitler everywhere triumphant, Europe was becoming a pagan empire. Deputy Führer Martin Bormann had just launched the *Klostersturm* (Cloister Storm), confiscating religious properties, removing crucifixes from schools, and melting down Church bells for bullets. Father Albrecht shared the deepening concern of the pope, who feared "the equivalent of a death sentence for the Catholic Church in Germany."[24]

When the priests retired for the night, the spies weighed their options. They would have to keep trying to make contact with the Allies. But the real push, all agreed, must come in Germany. Müller had already discussed with Bonhoeffer how to build on small communities of committed Christians. Dohnanyi would then seek a way to link these Christian cells with labor and military circles in a militant popular front.[25]

In rural Bavaria, there were already flickers of revolt. When party bosses removed crucifixes from rural schools, pious women launched a wave of civil disobedience. Often they marched together to replace a crucifix after a Mass for a fallen soldier. In the village of Velsburg, five hundred women pushed into the mayor's house, pinned him down as he reached for his pistol, and forced his wife to hand over the classroom keys. Women rallied their husbands in other villages, where the public squares filled with peasants brandishing pitchforks. Perceiving "a front of psychological resistance" and "almost a revolutionary mood," the Bavarian government restored the crosses.[26]

Unarmed women had faced down the world-conquering Nazis. The episode inspired and shamed the Ettal plotters. They now felt compelled to spearhead direct action within Germany itself.

But guerilla warfare was no game for old men. "Old people would rather let everything go on just the way it has been, and like to avoid unpleasantness at all costs," a young priest from Passau wrote that month to the eighty-one-year-old chairman of the German bishops, expressing the newly militant mood. "How very necessary and important it is, in such offices of far-reaching responsibility, to have the decisiveness and energy to make vigorous and intrepid interventions, and the courage even to be prepared to die." In just that spirit, as the onus of Catholic action shifted from the Vatican to the German Church, the Ettal conspirators would align with a corps of younger, more daring priests in a new round of plots against Hitler.[27]

CHAPTER 12

FORGING THE IRON

F RANCE SEEMED "STRUCK AT INTERVALS BY A FIST," ABWEHR officer Helmuth James von Moltke thought. Touring the occupied
West in August 1940, surveying the Maginot Line, Moltke lamented
"the waste of money and the waste of land" used for guard posts, bar-
ricades, tank traps, blockhouses, and barracks, stretching from Belgium to Switzerland. "In this entire region," he wrote his wife, Freya,
"nothing grows but thistles and other weeds, and the wind just blowing
across it was carrying whole consignments of mature thistle seed, to
spread like a plague." After watching the wind blow thorns, Moltke reflected: "Such a defense system is inorganic and diseased. If we cannot
manage without such things, in Europe, I mean, then we deserve no
better."[1]

Moltke's melancholy deepened as he mixed with the French. He
found them "sickeningly friendly." Relying on their physical fortifications, they had failed to cultivate the spiritual qualities required to fight.
Describing the "moral debacle," Moltke lamented that French women
"were positively queuing up to get a German soldier into bed, evidently
from a feeling that he was the stronger and that it was more fun with the
stronger man." The French soldiers, meanwhile, had become "simply
refugees in uniform; when a plane was heard approaching, they jumped

yelling from their vehicles, pushed aside women, children, old people, and took cover in the fields."[2]

Moltke drew the lesson that "totalitarian war destroys spiritual values. One feels that everywhere. If it destroyed material values, the people, whose thinking is mostly limited by their perceptions, would know how and against what to defend themselves. As it is, the inner destruction has no correlative in the perceived world of things, of matter. So they fail to grasp the process and the possible means of countering it or renewing themselves."[3]

Returning to Berlin, Moltke began to work for regime change. On 14 August, he met for the first time with Abwehr archivist Hans von Dohnanyi, who was then preparing a text on the right to disobey immoral orders. Proceeding reflectively at first, recruiting trusted friends one at a time, Moltke built a circle that by late 1941 transformed the German opposition. For to Moltke the fight against Hitler was not mainly military or political, but meta-ethical: his French sojourn had convinced him that resistance to tyranny hinged on "how the image of man can be replanted in the breasts of our countrymen."[4]

The quest for a new image of man led the Protestant Moltke to the Catholic Church. He knew and liked Josef Müller, had lost sleep over his friend's Vatican mission, and saw a "silver lining" when Hitler's enemies befriended the pope. Seeking a spiritual basis for a post-Hitler government, Moltke found that papal social encyclicals not only offered a coherent program but filled him with a deep, inner calm. Yet as he looked around for partners in his project, he found that leading non-Catholic ministers still resisted resistance. "Whereas [Muenster Bishop Clemens von] Galen and the Bishop of Trier [Franz Rudolf Bornewasser] have preached bravely in opposition," one of Moltke's Protestant contacts recorded, "there is no leadership on the Evangelical side." At a 28 September 1941 dinner with General Beck, Moltke therefore urged—and Beck approved—a "forging of the iron" along Catholic lines.[5]

On 13 October 1941, a Jesuit priest entered Abwehr headquarters in Berlin. Short and stocky, the son of a locomotive driver,

Father Augustinus Rösch had fought in the First World War. An artillery barrage had temporarily buried him alive, and sometimes his limbs involuntarily trembled and twitched, as if still trying to claw him out. Restless, turbulently busy, always in motion, Father Rösch had a flair for spinning webs and making alliances. Father Leiber would hail him as "Catholicism's strongest man in Germany." On his shoulders rested the burden of leading the Bavarian Jesuits in a time of persecution.[6]

Father Rösch had come to see a good friend from Munich. Ludwig von und zu Guttenberg, former editor of the banned Catholic-monarchist *Weisse Blätter*, had joined Military Intelligence, where, like his good friend Josef Müller, he carried out missions for Oster's resistance group. Now, while Father Rösch visited military offices in Berlin, ostensibly to discuss the status of army chaplains, Guttenberg offered to introduce him to yet another member of the resistance.[7]

Guttenberg imposed elaborate security precautions. He would go on ahead to the *Treffpunkt*, the meeting point, with Rösch following about fifty meters behind. When Guttenberg stopped at a garden gate and lit a cigarette, the priest should go through the next garden gate. He should wend through a large garage, loop behind the building, and climb a stairway on the rear wall. A hidden apartment was located above the garage, Guttenberg said. "Ring, and my name is the password." Rösch followed those directions, recalling that he "had to look around a little to find the stairway." He rushed upstairs and rang.[8]

Helmuth von Moltke opened the door. "I would never forget that first meeting," Rösch wrote. He remembered Moltke as "a gaunt man with a finely-chiseled head," so tall that he had to bend down to get through the door. Moltke led Rösch amiably into a big room, simply furnished but with "a splendid library." On one wall hung a well-known Wehrmacht propaganda poster, captioned: "The Enemy Is Listening."[9]

Guttenberg joined them. Moltke sat his guests at a polished wood table and disappeared. He returned with cups and plates, coffee, rolls, an alcohol stove, and batter in a bowl. As Moltke fried up apple pancakes, Guttenberg predicted that harassment of the Church would soon intensify, for the war seemed all but won. Moltke interrupted to disagree. "It's going terribly for Germany, indeed the war is already lost for us . . . if leadership is not taken from the hands of Hitler."[10]

Moltke then sketched his own coup plans. "Our officers could declare a cease-fire and make peace in the west; then there can be an acceptable peace and Europe will be saved," Rösch recalled him saying. "We must be ready to take the military leadership from Hitler. . . . The man is really sick. . . . And if our officers should fail us—I still don't believe it—then Germany is lost."[11]

They discussed the Nazi war on religion. Moltke granted Hitler's "satanic hatred of the churches, above all the Catholic," the fury against the Jesuits, against everything Christian. He lamented that, whereas the Catholic Church had forbidden Nazi Party membership, following then-Cardinal Pacelli's 1930 guidance from Rome, many Protestant ministers had affiliated themselves with Nazism. Because of the Catholic Church's more disciplined stance, which it maintained precisely *because of* its hierarchical structure and the supremacy of the pope, Moltke believed that the Church must lead the Christian resistance to Hitler. According to Rösch, Moltke underlined that idea by saying: "I want to tell you the conclusion I have come to as a Protestant Christian. Christianity in Germany can only be saved by the German bishops and the pope."[12]

Moltke had ambitious ideas along those lines. He wanted Rösch to bring the Catholic Church into the planning for a post-Nazi order. Assuming that the military could depose Hitler, public safety would require a provisional government, which should build on Christian social views. "We must think like Christians and must plan and prepare to rebuild again. . . . We must fight, and do everything to save what can be saved," Moltke reportedly said. The words made a great impression on Rösch, who often later repeated them. "And now I ask you, Father Provincial: You are ready for it? Are you willing to cooperate in this way? Will you cooperate?"[13]

Rösch asked for time to think about it. He could not simply agree on the spot, for Moltke clearly "expected a great deal of direct help from the Catholic Church." The hierarchical structure that Moltke hailed would oblige the Jesuit provincial to consult Rome. Moltke traveled often to Munich; they agreed to continue their talks there. As Moltke showed his guests out, he said, *"Guten Tag,"* and Rösch answered *"Grüss Gott"* (go with God). According to Rösch, that pleased Moltke so much that he said, "From now on, I will also always say '*Grüss Gott*.'" Those words, sealing the partnership between Count Moltke and Father Rösch, marked the formal beginning of Catholic involvement in the second round of wartime plots against Hitler.[14]

THE SECOND SET OF CONSPIRACIES HAD CRYSTALLIZED EVEN BEFORE 22 June 1941, when 3 million Axis troops attacked Stalin's empire. Canaris had already tipped the Vatican to what Hitler called Operation Barbarossa. Father Leiber remembered this warning with great clarity; he had received several updates as plans developed, dating to late 1940. The Jesuit assured the Pope in each case that the intelligence came from Canaris.[15]

An alarming notice came in late April 1941. Josef Müller called at Abwehr headquarters and Oster handed him an order from the Führer, for issuance two months hence. A key sentence in the instructions ran: "In the struggle against bolshevism, we must not assume that the enemy's conduct will be based on principles of humanity or of international law." Two other lines jumped out at Müller: "Political commissars have initiated barbaric, Asiatic methods of warfare. Consequently they will be dealt with immediately and with maximum severity. As a matter of principle they will be shot at once, whether captured during operations or otherwise showing resistance." Guerrillas and suspected civilian supporters, which in party parlance meant mainly Jews, must die on the spot.[16]

The army must now do in Russia what the SS had done in Poland. Brauchitsch, though outraged, would neither confront Hitler nor resign. Like Halder, he would stay in his post to prevent something worse from happening. They might save a few thousand lives by special order, Müller and Oster agreed. Yet even the appearance of acquiescence stained the army's honor.[17]

Oster took Müller to see Canaris. The old man's dogs barked at them, and Canaris came in from the terrace above the Tiergarten, where he had been feeding birds. He waved Müller to a seat and sank into a worn armchair. Worried that the new commissar order would blight them forever, Canaris asked Müller to seek, through Pius, "the old formulations" for peace. He meant the British terms of March 1940. As Canaris patted his dachshunds, he predicted: "Contrary to the fantasies of the dreamers," who thought Russia would be defeated in six weeks, Hitler would meet his doom there just like Napoleon.[18]

HITLER HID IN HIS BUNKER. ONCE THE RUSSIAN CAMPAIGN BEGAN, he rarely left the Wolf's Lair, his command post near Rastenburg, East Prussia. A triple perimeter in a dark wood cut him off from the world. Only his travel offered a chance to get at him.[19]

Oster had planned to have Hitler shot during an earlier victory parade in Paris. But when Hitler arrived, on 23 June 1940, he saw the Louvre and skipped the parade. During another march of German divisions down the Champs-Elysées in May 1941, two officers at the saluting base planned to shoot Hitler, while a third would toss a bomb from a hotel balcony. But as the parade date neared, Hitler canceled the trip. He stayed on his Bavarian mountain to plan his Russian war. Only later in 1941, as the enormities of the Russian campaign emerged, would a new group of younger military staffers decide to resist Hitler.[20]

An operations officer in the east, Major General Henning von Tresckow, led the cabal. Seeing the Wehrmacht as "a mere puff of wind on the vast Russian steppes," Tresckow regarded German defeat "as certain as the Amen in church." Yet he also believed, he told a deputy, that Hitler's crimes would weigh on Germans for a hundred years—"not just on Hitler alone, but on you and me, your wife and mine, your children and my children, the woman crossing the road now, and the boy playing with a ball over there." In September 1941, just after the Nazis started making Jews wear yellow stars, Tresckow sent an emissary to the Canaris group.[21]

Canaris aligned with Tresckow, but feared civil war. They must make provisions to fill the power vacuum, Tresckow agreed, "like one navigates a whirlpool." Before removing Hitler, they must fuse military, civilian, and religious "nuclei," creating the political preconditions for a coup.[22]

At just that time, and to just that end, Moltke linked hands with Father Rösch. As Moltke's letters show, he rightly believed the Jesuit provincial "very in with the Vatican." Less clear is whether Moltke knew that Rösch would bring more than the Catholic viewpoint on church and state. In any case, Rösch furnished a turnkey ecclesiastical espionage service, readily adaptable to the cause of Hitler's death.

CHAPTER 13

THE COMMITTEE

T HE ORIGINS OF THE BAVARIAN-JESUIT SPY NETWORK—AND ITS links to Pacelli—stretched back to the earliest years of the Reich. The apparatus grew from Josef Müller's Munich intelligence depository. Father Rösch, who dueled daily with the SS over Church prerogatives, had tipped Müller to Nazi plans, and Müller had ferried Rösch's reports to Rome. Thus a secret and secure pipeline already linked Pius with religious orders in the Reich by Christmas 1940, when the locus of Catholic resistance moved from Rome to Germany.[1]

That shift should have meant increased reliance on the Berlin nunciature. But Pius considered his Berlin agent soft on Nazism—and even suspected the nuncio's deputy of spying for the SS. The pope therefore looked to the German bishops. But Albert Hartl's moles had burrowed into the episcopacy too, even obtaining minutes of its closed-door conferences at Fulda.[2]

One option remained. The German branches of the Catholic orders, such as Jesuits, Dominicans, and Benedictines, would serve as papal proxies. They did not report through the local bishops but rather to the orders' leaders in Rome—who themselves answered only to the pope. Though the Benedictines seemed susceptible to Nazi cooptation, the Dominicans and especially the Jesuits showed a martial spirit. Branded "enemies of the Reich," they feared deportation to the East. From their ranks arose a younger, more militant corps of clergy, who accepted what the Vatican termed, in the title of a text on martyrdom, *Invitations to Heroism.*[3]

They accepted this invitation at a closed-door conference in Berlin. On 26 May 1941, the leadership of the German Jesuits and Dominicans pledged "to endure and preserve our Catholic honor, before our consciences, before the people, before history, the Church and the Lord God." In that spirit, they formed themselves into a seven-man group that did not officially exist, but merely fronted for a "Church intelligence service" (*kirchliche Nachrichtenwesen*). Among themselves, they called it the Orders Committee, or just the Committee.[4]

Father Rösch was the Committee's driving force. He traveled through Germany, organizing a courier service between the bishops, transmitting warnings, advising on countermeasures, and building up a group of like-minded men. They learned about Nazi plans from secretaries, telephone operators, government clerks, military officers, and even members of the Gestapo. The intelligence all came together in the Jesuit provincialate at Munich. After Rösch linked with Moltke, his priests worked closely with the military plotters.[5]

Committee operatives worked by camouflage and disguise. They received special dispensations to wear nonpriestly garb and to live, as required, "beyond the regulations of the order." The Dominican courier, Father Odilo Braun, concealed his cassock beneath a light-colored duster; the Jesuits wore black-gray wool coats. Some operatives kept secret second residences; Braun had a room in the house of a female friend in Berlin, where he hid documents. They took to role-playing to avoid detection, as when the Jesuit courier, Father Lothar König, and Braun's secretary, Anne Vogelsberg, promenaded under an umbrella at the Berlin railroad station, posing as lovers to fool Gestapo surveillance. Or Vogelsberg would buy a ticket and hold a seat for a Committee priest on a waiting train, while he, to avoid traveling under his own name, merely got a platform pass; then, shortly before the train left, the priest would board, Vogelsberg would disembark, and they would inconspicuously exchange tickets as they passed in the aisle. When Committee priests corresponded or telephoned, they did so in code; they referenced Bishop Johannes Dietz, for instance, as "Tante Johanna" (Aunt Joanne).[6]

Rösch set the strategy, but left most tactical operations to a key aide. His secretary and courier, Father König, became a critical intermediary between resistance groups throughout the Reich. By February 1941, König had developed stomach cancer, but he refused Rösch's pleas to rest in the rectory, insisting "the fight comes first." That year alone he logged 77,000 kilometers traveling on Committee work, usually by train at night. His soft, soothing manner concealed unpriestly urges. Once, as König drove a truck, Hitler's motorcade swept past, and the hair rose on the priest's neck as he thought how much evil he would prevent, if only he could run over Hitler.[7]

Rösch had already reached out to the military plotters on the pope's behalf. As early as April 1941, Father Rösch and his Munich Jesuits had begun visiting the dissident Wehrmacht chief of staff, General Franz Halder. They discussed how to remove Hitler, as Halder recalled, and whether military methods "would be appropriate." The ever-wavering Halder said that he agreed with everything the Jesuits planned, but could do nothing himself; nobody around him would cooperate. "After this disappointing observation," Halder recalled, "we spoke about the methods which the Catholic Church had at its disposal for the fight against Hitler. . . . That always stuck in my memory, because I could not conceive of how these spiritual dignitaries could be effective against a dictator."[8]

IN APRIL 1942 THE COMMITTEE RECRUITED ITS MOST CHARISMATIC and vital agent. Jesuit priest Alfred Delp wore secular clothes, a suit and tie, which gave him an owlish and rumpled look, and he seldom appeared without a cigar in his hand and a wreath of smoke around his head. He became important in the resistance as a kind of people's tribune. Parishioners took down his sermons in shorthand, sharing them on paper folded to the size of a thimble to escape detection.[9]

Delp had the spirit of a freethinker. Before converting from Lutheranism, he had flirted with Nazism; his Protestant roots and political interests gave him a perspective unique among the Bavarian Jesuits. In his first book, he held the Christians Luther and Kant responsible for the "total disintegration of human personality"; the atheist Nietzsche, on the other hand, had prepared the way for new Christian developments. Delp thought, for instance, that the churches had mistakenly encouraged a "collectivist" view of democracy. He bore into questions and theories, and loved to debate. Delp spoke often of Saint Peter, seeing in him a combination of impetuousness, frailty, and passionate trust—qualities that defined Delp himself, and caused his Jesuit superiors some headaches.[10]

His combative manner alienated some other Jesuits, and even his friends found him difficult. "Don't let my mother tell any 'pious legends' about me," he wrote to a friend. "I was a brat." When the provincialate postponed his final vows, for unknown reasons, people whispered about Delp's friendships with women. A rare maverick in the regimented Jesuit order, he urged his civilian contacts to move against Hitler. "Whoever doesn't have the courage to make history," he wrote, "is doomed to become its object. We have to take action."[11]

THE ORDERS COMMITTEE KEPT IN CLOSE TOUCH WITH THE VATIcan. Josef Müller provided the primary link. Six of the Committee's seven clerics had used him as a courier since the mid-1930s. Most of the group's members had their own lines to Rome as well. Father Rösch often used his Jesuit colleague, Father Leiber, as a back channel to the pope. The Vatican knew, through these pipelines, about the Committee's work. Father Rösch accepted Moltke's offer only after "I . . . discussed it with important people," while Moltke's letters buoyantly referenced Rome's "great hymn in praise of Rösch: he was Catholicism's strongest man in Germany."[12]

Pius took a more-than-casual interest in the Committee's work. On 30 September 1941, two days after General Beck approved Moltke's "forging of the iron" along Catholic lines, Pius gave the Committee written guidance, calling for Church collaboration with the military resistance. The pope's letter specifically urged the Committee to seek a "unity of convictions and actions" against Nazism through the "concentration of all forces." Since the Tresckow-Beck alliance had just invited the Committee's participation in that very project, the pope's directive came at a pivotal time. Judging by later events, the pope's letter evidently did not inhibit Rösch's Committee from intriguing to remove Hitler.[13]

In Autumn 1941, during a general Wednesday audience with about eighty people, including German soldiers, Pius received an exiled German Jew. According to a wartime account in the Zionist *Palestine Post*, the non-Aryan visitor—later identified as Heinz Wisla—asked the Holy See to help shipwrecked Italian Jews reach Palestine. After inviting Wisla to return the next day with a written report, Pius reportedly said, "You are a young Jew. I know what that means and I hope you will always be proud to be a Jew!"[14]

Pius had by then begun to regret not saying such words more publicly. By 7 October, reports had spread that a Catholic chaplain officiated in St. Hedwig's Cathedral, Berlin, with a yellow star on his vestment, just like the Jews were now compelled to wear. Meeting three days later with papal diplomat Angelo Roncalli, the future Pope John the Twenty-Third, Pius fretted that his "silence about Nazism might be badly judged."[15]

Perhaps from guilt or frustration, then, Pius reportedly raised his voice to the Jewish emissary. "My son, whether you are worthier than others only the Lord knows, but believe me, you are at least as worthy as every other human being that lives on our earth." According to the press, Pius ended the meeting by telling Wisla, "Go with the protection of the Lord."

Then, as after each audience, Sister Pasqualina disinfected Pius's bishops' ring. It had a diamond in it, and could puncture his skin when people pressed his fingers; "and there was one particular reason why he [sic] had to be disinfected," as the relator for his sainthood later said. "Namely, people took his hand very firmly, and pressed on the ring, and not rarely the pope returned to his private apartment with blood on his hands."[16]

Father Rösch and Helmuth Moltke made a good team. From a quiet start in 1941, they drove events in eighteen months to a shattering climax. During that span, the second plot against Hitler progressed farther and faster than the first. Without Rösch's intelligence service, the plot might not have progressed at all.

The Committee became the plotters' postwar planning board. Moltke decided to convene leading social thinkers at Kreisau, his Silesian estate, to write a political platform. Father Rösch agreed to moderate the dialogue and distill its consensus, much as Alexander Hamilton had done during the American Revolution. Moltke, immersed in the *Federalist Papers*, encouraged the parallel.[17]

Rösch set himself the tall task of brokering agreement on all questions in advance. Because security concerns precluded phone or mail contact, Rösch's secretary, Father König, became a key operative, arriving and departing in night and fog, never saying where he went or whence he came, lifting spirits with maxims like "there is no such thing as I cannot."[18]

Father König opened a new frontier of resistance, which promised for the first time to unleash mass support for a coup. "A great problem, insoluble up to now, is where we can find names that carry weight with the workers," conspirator Ulrich von Hassell wrote in October 1941. By that month's end, König had linked the Berlin and Munich networks with leaders of the banned Catholic Workers Movement in Stuttgart and Cologne. The labor kingpins, in turn, recruited key figures in the outlawed Catholic Center Party.[19]

Plans proceeded so smoothly that by November Beck and Admiral Canaris approved an overture to President Roosevelt. As their channel, the plotters chose Louis Lochner, the Associated Press bureau chief in Berlin. Meeting a dozen resistance leaders at the home of a Center Party stalwart, Lochner saw the conspiracy as almost a Church social; Catholic labor leader Jakob Kaiser struck him as the circle's leading figure. The conspirators gave Lochner a secret code for radio communication between FDR and General Beck, and Lochner agreed to approach the White House over Christmas.[20]

By December, momentum had built to a crossover point. Army commander in chief Walther von Brauchitsch, disquieted by the persecution of the Jews, began asking resistance leaders to tea. Hasso von Etzdorf, liaison officer between the Foreign Office and the High Command, described a charged scene during that first Christmas of the Russian war. In an address to officers, NCOs, and men of headquarters, Brauchitsch had pointed to the Christmas tree in the middle of the square and declared: "You will have to choose between these two symbols—the blazing flames of the Teutonic yuletide fire and the radiant Christmas tree. For myself I have chosen the symbol of Christianity." In conclusion, he had asked his audience "to think of the man on whose shoulders rests the entire responsibility." The implication was not misunderstood. There were cries of "scandalous" and "the man [Hitler] should be shot."[21]

The pieces for a coup fell into place so neatly that Müller sent lay Catholic operative Charlotte Respondek to Father Leiber in Rome. Oster then called Müller to Berlin to coordinate the Vatican's role in the regime change. By one account, not deeply documented but not implausible, the Dohnanyis had made plans for an evening at the opera, and when Müller arrived, they quickly arranged a reservation for him, too. When they left the hall at intermission, they met Oster in the lobby. The colonel suggested they step out for a moment. Outside, where the walkways crisscrossed beds of barren rosebushes, he said he had just received word from an Abwehr runner: the Japanese had bombed the United States fleet at Pearl Harbor.[22]

AMERICA'S ENTRY INTO THE WAR BOTH DOOMED AND SAVED HITLER. Over the longer term, as Pius's advisers now perceived, the Axis could only lose. But for the moment, the German resistance could not win. Hitler's declaration of war on the United States made White House officials reject Lochner's approach, he recalled, as "most embarrassing."[23]

The Christmas plot collapsed. Already reeling from this blow, the resistance suffered another on 19 December, when Hitler blamed the increasingly oppositional Brauchitsch for the stalled Moscow offensive and sacked him. Yet these losses only briefly crippled the conspirators. They recovered because Father Rösch replanted, in their breasts, "the image of man."[24]

It happened on 22–25 May 1942, at Kreisau, Moltke's Silesian estate. During that Pentecost weekend the plotters lived for three days in the new world they sought. Moltke's two dozen guests would recall with unanimous warmth the idyllic setting—the lilacs in the sun, the sheep and the sugar beets, the late-night talks by the fireplace. The feast of the Pentecost spurred the spirit of renewal, with its tradition of the Holy Spirit appearing, in tongues of flame, to the apostles meeting secretly in Jerusalem. The plotters saw themselves as latter-day apostles in a new Babylon, and Father Rösch coached them. He taught them how to resist interrogation, based on his more than one hundred confrontations with the Gestapo. He offered the simple advice of "praying to your guardian angel." That set the primitive Christian tone that infused the weekend—the ethos of the catacombs, the rejuvenating purity of a return to the roots. Moltke's wife wrote of Father Rösch: "We really felt quite reborn because of him."[25]

Rösch was too seasoned and discreet to suggest that he fronted for the pope. But the Vatican precoordinated and preapproved the Kreisau agenda, as Helmuth Moltke's secret writings showed. On 8 May, "a man came from Rösch who wanted to know various things and furthermore came from meetings with the Pope [*Besprechungen beim Papst*]," Moltke recorded, and "one of the main questions from Rome was, 'What can you say on the question of the economic order?'" Moltke had a day of morning-to-midnight talks with the Vatican envoy, whom he identified only as "the stranger." Through Moltke, the stranger relayed questions about the post-Hitler order to Berlin Bishop Konrad von Preysing; and through Moltke, in turn, Preysing answered the pope. In the end, they made "a lot of progress," Moltke thought: "P[reysing] was obviously satisfied, and so was I." The resulting conference manifesto, drafted by Jesuit Father Delp and edited by Rösch, hewed strictly to Catholic social teaching as set forth in Pius the Eleventh's 1931 encyclical *Quadragesimo anno*, which Moltke had long admired.[26]

When Rösch read the manifesto to the gathering, it made an impact. Rejecting much political thinking since the fourteenth century, the document denounced the "deification of the state" (*Staatsvergöttung*) and lamented its progressive expansion into "a python hug that had succeeded in laying claim to the entire man." In opposition to this anonymous monster, Rome proposed a communitarian localism—"the largest possible number of the smallest possible communities." The

Christenschaft, a union of Christians, would become the basic atom of this new order. Germany would return to the theory of the "organic state" that had vanished with Charlemagne. Rösch persuaded Protestant resistance leaders and socialist union bosses that this model suited the German future. Almost as if Pentacostal fire had descended over their heads, a reactionary romanticism took hold. Rösch imparted the vision of a New Christendom, built on social democratic rather than military-feudal lines; and this political nostalgia fed into a feeling that the Reformation had been a grave error, because the decline of the Church had allowed the rise of the absolute state. Though a somewhat monistic explanation of Germany's predicament, it oriented the conspirators in their ruined world. Energy they had once devoted to explaining Hitler could now be devoted to fighting him.[27]

Rösch reviewed the Catholic take on tyrannicide. Aquinas had stressed that a tyrant's removal must not cause civil war. In that sense, the Kreisau group, created precisely to prevent internal strife after Hitler, legitimized the plot. "There was talk that somehow another attempt against Hitler's life had been made again, of which nothing was made public," Rösch recalled.[28]

The plotters pledged themselves brothers in war and Christ. As the weekend closed, they sealed their honor with a secret sign. Much as the first Christians scrawled the sign of the fish in the Roman catacombs, the Kreisauers would know each other by their own symbol: a circle enclosing a cross. The circle represented their *Freundeskreis*, a closed circuit of friends who trusted each other with their lives. The cross stood for their belief in Christ. Together the circle and cross, their faith and friendship, formed a crosshairs.[29]

The religious transport of Kreisau galvanized resistance. Plotting sped forward in the months to come. But the realities that would undo the plotters took shape even as the Circle did. Events in Prague, just beyond the mountains that sheltered Kreisau, had for a third time put the SS on the trail of the conspirators' links to the pope. Having escaped twice before, the Canaris group now made careless lapses that led them, eventually, into torture cellars, and, finally, to death at the gallows.

CHAPTER 14

CONVERSATIONS IN THE CRYPT

I N JULY 1942, JOSEF MÜLLER BROUGHT DIETRICH BONHOEFFER TO Rome for talks with the pope's deputies. The dialogue aimed at bridging interfaith gaps, so that Christians could coordinate their fight against Hitler. Müller introduced Bonhoeffer to Father Leiber and Monsignor Kaas, who subtly proselytized by initiating the Protestant into the quest for Peter's Tomb.[1]

The crypt talks conjured the prospect of a reunited Christendom. Bonhoeffer savored Catholic teaching—on the church in the world, on Christ taking form in current events, on the place of the Church in the valley of death. Taking up where the Kreisau talks left off, the conferees agreed that the Protestant-Catholic split had gone "way beyond what the reformers had actually been striving for." Father Leiber conceded that the Catholic Church had "lost some balance when it lost northern Europe, because it then came under the influence of Italian novels about mother-child love, which created the whole cult of the Madonna." Bonhoeffer, for his part, granted that Protestant princes had exploited the Reformation to seize Church assets. He ventured further that Catholic priests, as celibates, made better fighters against Hitler, for they lacked dependents on whom the Nazis could take revenge.[2]

Müller's report on the crypt dialogues influenced Church resistance in Germany. A revised Committee mission statement stressed that Catholics must "intercede not only for the Christian churches in purely denominational, canonical, or spiritual matters, but above all in the defense of people as human beings." Father Delp took those words as a call to save non-Aryan lives. He wrote into the Vatican-approved agenda for a second Kreisau conference, in October 1942: "Restoration of basic human rights (especially the Jews)." His Munich rectory became a station in an underground escape-route to Switzerland.[3]

Müller and others in the Canaris group were also helping Jews. During the war's first months, his Abwehr circle had spirited the leading orthodox rabbi, Chabad Lubavitcher Joseph Isaac Schneersohn, from Warsaw to Brooklyn; and by 1942 Dietrich Bonhoeffer was exfiltrating Jews to Switzerland under a special Abwehr operation, code-named U-7. Anxious to save some Jewish acquaintances, Canaris had given Hans von Dohnanyi the task of supervising their escape, on the pretext that the Abwehr could use them as agents, ostensibly for infiltration into America. Müller and Munich Abwehr agent Wilhelm Schmidhuber arranged a "ratline" for the refugees—lubricated by American dollars that Schmidhuber smuggled for the Jews' temporary support, and using a network of monasteries stretching from Slovakia to Italy.[4]

But that ratline could become a noose. At Pentecost 1942, German customs began to uncover the rescue scheme when they arrested a black-marketer for illegal currency exchanges at a railway station in Prague. Searching the man's briefcase, police found precious stones. The suspect confessed that Schmidhuber had asked him to fence the gems and currency to wind up some financial dealings with Jews. The chief customs investigator phoned a colleague and asked him to arrest Schmidhuber in Munich. But the colleague, who sympathized with the resistance, instead placed calls to Schmidhuber and Müller. They warned Canaris than an avalanche was bearing down on them.[5]

Schmidhuber had laundered cash to rescue Jews. Dohnanyi had asked him to smuggle $100,000 to twelve elderly Berlin U-7s, for whom Bonhoeffer had secured sanctuary in Switzerland. Schmidhuber, however, had seen the chance to make some money on the side, thereby jeopardizing the wider circle. Although Schmidhuber did not know about the pope's role in the assassination plots, he had helped Pius leak Hitler's war plans—taking Müller's calls at the Hotel Flora, and passing Leiber the updated attack dates. If Schmidhuber talked, Hans Oster warned Canaris, he "could bring us all to the gallows with ease."[6]

THE JEWS' PLIGHT MEANWHILE PUSHED PIUS TO THE VERGE OF PRO-test. On 20 January 1942, SS spy chief Reinhard Heydrich chaired a meeting in the Berlin suburb of Wannsee, to plan the liquidation of European Jewry. Five weeks later, Father Pirro Scavizzi reported that the Germans had begun exterminating whole populations. As a military chaplain of the Maltese Order, Scavizzi had accompanied an Italian military hospital train through occupied Poland and Russia, where conscience-stricken officers told him of "the deportations into concentration camps from which, they say, few return alive. . . . In these camps thousands and thousands . . . are exterminated, without any judicial process." Near Auschwitz, the chaplain's informants said, they could smell crematoria smoke in nauseating whiffs. Scavizzi made a report for the archbishop of Krakow, who ordered him to destroy it, lest the Germans discover the text and "shoot all bishops and maybe others." The priest obliged, but first made a secret copy by hand, for the pope's eyes only. When he shared the report in a 12 May audience, Scavizzi later claimed, Pius broke down, raised his hands to heaven, and "wept like a child."[7]

By that summer, the world had still heard only rumors of the genocide, but Pius had a stack of reports. Nuncio Giuseppe Burzio cabled from Slovakia that 80,000 Jews vanished in Poland. Angelo Rotta, the nuncio in Budapest, wrote that the Slovakian Jews had "gone to a certain death." Gerhard Riegner, the representative of the Jewish World Congress in Geneva, told the nuncio in Bern of Jews massacred by "gas and lethal injection." Even Orsenigo, the pro-Axis papal agent in Berlin, credited "macabre suppositions" about the deportees' fates, adding: "All well-meant intentions to intervene on behalf of the Jews are impossible."

Holland's bishops, however, issued a public condemnation; the Nazis responded by deporting 40,000 Dutch Jews.[8]

The Dutch debacle put Pius under pressure. One evening—probably in late July or early August 1942—Father Leiber walked into the kitchen of the papal apartment and saw two sheets of paper bearing the pope's distinctive cursive script. The pages contained the Vatican's strongest protest yet against the persecution of Jewry. The pope planned to publish it in *L'Osservatore* that very evening. But Leiber urged His Holiness to remember the Dutch bishops' pastoral letter. If it had cost the lives of 40,000 Jews, an even stronger protest, from even more prominent lips, could cost the lives of many times more. The pope would do better to keep a public silence and do whatever he could in secret. Two witnesses later said they saw Pius throw the pages into the kitchen fireplace and watch them burn.[9]

But a few months later, Pius did protest the genocide. In his annual Christmas message, he denounced "the many hundreds of thousands of innocents put to death, or doomed to slow extinction, sometimes merely because of their ethnicity." Although he did not say "Jew," he used a word for "ethnicity"—*stirpe*—which Italians used as a euphemism for Jewry. Though Allied diplomats felt that Pius had not gone far enough, they did not object—or even seem to notice—that he failed to use the word "Jew." They complained rather, as Vatican documents noted, that he had not "mentioned the Nazis" by name.[10]

The Nazis responded as if they had been named. German foreign minister Ribbentrop had phoned Ambassador Diego Von Bergen in Rome. An SS intelligence analysis of the pope's text pronounced it "one long attack on everything we stand for. . . . God, he says, regards all people and races as worthy of the same consideration. Here he is clearly speaking on behalf of the Jews. . . . He is virtually accusing the German people of injustice toward the Jews, and makes himself the mouthpiece of the Jewish war criminals." Protestant pastor François de Beaulieu, a sergeant radio operator in Zossen, was arrested for dispersing clandestine copies of Pius's Christmas message instead of destroying it. A military tribunal accused Beaulieu of disseminating a "subversive and demoralizing document," and of being "spiritually attracted to Jewish environments and sympathetic toward Jews." Spared a death sentence through the intervention of his superiors, Beaulieu later disagreed with those who said Pius should have made a bolder gesture. "Of what use would it have been for the Pope to set himself on fire in front of the Vatican? What was needed was the revolt of all priests and Protestant pastors in Germany."[11]

By late 1942, plans for a Christian revolt were gathering force. Interfaith unity became an operational axiom as the pope's secret policy crept forward in Munich, Cologne, and Berlin. The crypt talks continued to buoy Committee outreach. "The Church is obliged to regain contact with her ever-widening alienated circles through the use of our ideologically driven and integrated personnel," Father Delp wrote. Marking the new ecumenism that inspired him to broker an alliance between underground Catholic and socialist labor leaders, he stressed: "We should try to coordinate the efforts of extra-ecclesiastical groups for the removal of the system by sufficiently powerful forces."[12]

But while Delp coordinated those forces, Canaris faced a moral dilemma. Willy Schmidhuber's unraveling ratline endangered an enterprise that might save the lives of millions. By some accounts, Oster urged Canaris to liquidate the not-very-virtuous Schmidhuber before he betrayed them. But Canaris refused, haunted by his post-facto complicity in the 1919 murder of revolutionary Rosa Luxemburg. Panicking, Schmidhuber fled to a hotel in Merano; Italian police returned him to Munich in handcuffs.[13]

The sand now began to run in the hourglass. "The 8 weeks ahead of us will be filled with tension as seldom, perhaps never before in our lives," Moltke wrote his wife on 25 October, as his meetings with Müller and the Jesuits became especially frequent. "Strange how infinitely many things suddenly depend on a single decision. Those are the few moments when one man can suddenly really count in the history of the world."[14]

CHAPTER 15

SHOOTOUT IN THE CATHEDRAL

I T WAS JUST AFTER PENTECOST, AND PRAGUE WAS QUIET, SO QUIET that one could almost hear the coach-and-fours of a lost age rattling over the cobbled roads. Admiral Canaris had come to the city the week before. He had walked its walled and winding streets, admiring the ornate churches; even the spires had spires. His agents showed him the secret city, the basement restaurants only locals knew. After carafes of Tokaj wine, Prague was both more sinister and more beautiful, as one of Canaris's Jesuit contacts remembered, "with its shadows and specters," with its "memories of something sunken," and with only the blurred outlines of towers gleaming through the moonlit mist. "It was a magical sight, because one could not see the supporting walls of the shiny golden domes which seemed to hover there all by themselves, shrouded in holy mystery."[1]

Canaris had made Prague a cay in his covert archipelago. He spent nearly two years building up this reef of resistance; the SS needed only a month to destroy it. Yet in the Czech Protectorate, Hitler's secret enemies would find, just before their downfall, a stunning triumph, in which Hitler would claim to see the secret hand of the Catholic Church. Like the floating domes of Prague itself, the events seemed more marvelous because their supporting apparata remained unseen, and the facts seemed to hover on their own, their foundations hidden in hallowed secrecy.[2]

SS spy chief Reinhard Heydrich lived in Prague. From Hradschin Castle, he managed both the party's campaign against the Catholic Church, and the murder of Europe's Jews. On 18 May, Canaris called Heydrich to discuss a division of secret labor between military and party spies, known informally as the "ten commandments." During the meeting, Heydrich adverted darkly to "the leakages through the Vatican in 1940." He had not closed his dossier on the Black Chapel.[3]

Five days later, Czech resistance agents learned Heydrich's travel schedule. They decided to kill him as he rode to his castle, at a hairpin bend where his driver would have to brake for the turn.[4]

At 9:30 a.m. on 27 May, two Czech guerillas stood by the road. Under their raincoats, Jan Kubiš and Jozef Gabčík hid submachine guns and grenades. A third man crouched behind a hedge, to signal with a mirror as Heydrich's car approached.[5]

The mirror flashed at 10:31. As Heydrich's dark-green Mercedes came into view, Gabčík stepped forward to shoot. But his gun jammed. Kubiš then threw a grenade at the car. A wounded Heydrich staggered out of the wreck, drew his pistol, and then collapsed. A week later he died.[6]

The Czech agents fled into the crypt of Prague's cathedral. They slept in the niches in the stone walls built to hold the corpses of monks. Members of the underground planned to escape into the Moravian mountains, whence they could exfiltrate to England. They would stage a memorial at the cathedral, honoring victims of the Gestapo purge that Heydrich's killing provoked. No one would suspect that the agents would be spirited away in caskets.[7]

But someone betrayed them. As SS detective Heinz Pannwitz recalled, Atta Moravec, an agent in the assassins' support network, broke down when interrogators "showed him his mother's head floating in a fish tank." Moravec confessed that he had been told to hide in the cathedral if he ever got in trouble.[8]

Pannwitz ringed the church with SS troops. He posted guards by every manhole cover and roof in the area. Hoping to learn the full scope of the conspiracy, Pannwitz ordered the assault teams to capture the suspects alive.

The Germans entered the church at 4:15 a.m. on 18 June. "We summoned the priests," Pannwitz remembered, "but they denied knowing anything about secret agents." Chaplain Vladimír Petřek could not explain, however, why one of the iron bars on his windows was missing. The raiders took Petřek along as they probed the half-dark cathedral. They had just crossed the nave when they came under fire from the choir loft.[9]

The barrage hit one of the detectives in the hand. Waffen SS infantry returned fire from the sanctuary with machine-pistols. The Czechs were pinned down and could not take any aimed shots. They threw out a grenade, setting the sanctuary drapes on fire. The Germans tried to storm the loft, but could only reach it by a narrow spiral staircase, putting them in the sights of the gunmen above. So they lobbed up grenades, as Pannwitz recalled, until the defenders "slowly fell silent." An SS team in steel helmets warily circled up the stairs.[10]

In the loft they found three men. Two were dead and the other was dying. The dying man was Kubiš, who had thrown the grenade that killed Heydrich. Attempts to keep him alive failed after twenty minutes. "The state's main witness was dead," as Pannwitz put it, and he found it "a heavy loss."[11]

The roadside shooter, Gabčík, remained at large. But the Germans had not yet searched the catacombs. Chaplain Petřek now admitted that he had sheltered seven men in the church. Four were down in the crypt. By removing some skeletal remains, they turned the caskets into sleeping compartments. The other three only went up to the loft because they became claustrophobic in the coffin niches. Petřek sketched the layout of the tombs and said there was only one way in and out of them. He lifted a flagstone and showed the Germans a trap door.[12]

Pannwitz called Petřek to the hatch, hoping he could talk the men out. The Czechs said they would never surrender. "They were well armed down there," Pannwitz remembered. "Anyone who put as much as a leg through the hatch would immediately be shot."[13]

Pannwitz called in a fire brigade to flood the crypt with water. The Czechs tossed out the hoses and fired pistols ferociously at the SS. Tear gas proved problematic because it seeped through floor joints and overcame the Gestapo detectives. Finally, a three-man assault squad tried to force its way down. The Czechs shot up the team, and a backup force had to rescue them. Standing knee-deep in water, the SS troops shot into the coffin holes. Gabčík and his friends fired back until they ran low on ammunition. Down to their last cartridges, they shot each other, in turn, until the last man shot himself.[14]

The clergy's role in hiding the killers enraged Hitler. That the priests in question were Eastern Orthodox rather than Roman Catholic mattered little to him. The denominational difference seemed just an ingenious Vatican disguise. The pope had in fact issued a secret *Motu proprio*, allowing Orthodox priests to keep their conversions to Catholicism secret. The SS Vatican expert, Hartl, claimed that the pope coordinated operations with the Czech Orthodox Church through a monastery in the Dukla pass of eastern Slovakia. According to Hartl, Pacelli had since the 1920s supervised a major project to penetrate Central and Russian Europe, using Jesuits disguised as Orthodox priests. One of these priests, Hartl suspected, was Matěj Pavlík, who converted from Catholicism in 1921 to found a Czech national church. Pavlík remained friendly with Rome, and the grounds for his separation from the Church seemed superficial: he wanted to minister to Czech Legionnaires who returned from the Great War with Russian wives. He became Bishop of Prague, and it was in his cathedral that Heydrich's assassins hid.[15]

Pavlík admitted that he helped the plotters. He was executed later that year, with his chaplain, Petřek. Liquidated also for supporting the assassins was Robert Johannes Albrecht, a German military translator in Prague who confessed to being secretly a Jesuit. Though an SS probe failed to link the plotters to Pius, Hitler cited the episode to explain why he intended to "settle accounts" with the pope.[16]

"One need only recall the close cooperation between the Church and the murderers of Heydrich," Hitler told Martin Bormann. "Catholic priests not only allowed them to hide . . . but even allowed them to entrench themselves in the sanctuary of the altar."[17]

Priestly assassins flitted through Hitler's paranoid daydreams. He told three officers on 16 November that "there were designs against his life; so far, he had managed to make life miserable for those who were out to get him." One of the officers recalled Hitler saying: "What was particularly sad about it all was that they were by no means fanatical communists, but in the first place members of the intelligentsia, so-called priests."[18]

IN NOVEMBER 1942 DR. MANFRED ROEDER, A LUFTWAFFE JUDGE-advocate, began interrogating Abwehr agent Willy Schmidhuber. "He claimed to have traveled to Rome on orders from the Munich military intelligence office, to establish contacts with influential members of the German clergy in the Vatican," SS officer Walter Huppenkothen testified after the war.

> The intent had not only been the exploitation of such relationships for the acquisition of intelligence of military and general political content, but also of establishing contact, via the Vatican, with opposition circles to explore the possibilities for peace. Schmidhuber said further that the Munich lawyer and reserve first lieutenant, Dr. Josef Müller, who had particularly good access in the Vatican, conducted similar missions in Rome. He knew that there was a "clique of generals" behind that activity, but he did not know who their members were. The officer in charge of these matters was the Reich Justice von Dohnanyi in Oster's office, who had also made many trips to Rome himself, where Müller put him in contact with influential Vatican personalities. Schmidhuber provided all this on his own, without prompting. . . . Nevertheless, we evaluated this information cautiously at first. Due to Schmidhuber's insecure and unconvincing personality, we had to consider that he might be manipulating us to win leniency in criminal proceedings, by putting pressure on higher-placed personalities, including Canaris, who might also come under investigation.[19]

Because of Canaris's position, his enemies had to move carefully. Himmler would require high-command General Wilhelm Keitel's permission to break the seal of secrecy over the Abwehr offices, which Canaris so jealously guarded. A mere charge of currency irregularities would not suffice. But if the case involved more than that, Roeder vowed, he would uncover it. He had a reputation as a bloodhound: his recent prosecution of the Rote Kapelle, a communist resistance group, had brought death sentences to its leaders.[20]

On 27 November, Dohnanyi flew to Rome. There, in his continuing talks at the Vatican, he had hoped to get Allied backing for a post-Hitler government. Specifically, he sought approval for a list of *Landesverweser*, or regional commissioners, who would assume interim responsibility after Hitler's removal. But now Dohnanyi had to warn the pope's advisers that Schmidhuber's arrest had placed Oster's group, and its links to Pius, under new scrutiny. Father Leiber again demanded that the military plotters burn all papers implicating Pius, especially the papal note stating British peace terms. "The documents are destroyed," Dohnanyi reportedly said. He lied. The military had merely moved its main documents deep underground, into a cellar in army headquarters in Zossen.[21]

While Dohnanyi was in Rome, Müller faced questions in Munich. Fortunately for him, Luftwaffe judge-advocate Karl Sauermann seemed skeptical about the Schmidhuber case. It emerged that Müller had borrowed money from Schmidhuber to buy Slovakian postage stamps, but Müller could show that his stamp-collecting hobby covered meetings with Abwehr sources. When Sauermann suggested that some officers around Canaris might be disloyal, Müller feigned outrage: "Do you think [the Führer] would have allowed the admiral to remain in his position if there had been even a grain of truth to that? Do you consider the Führer to be that naive?"[22]

After the interrogation, Canaris sought out Müller in Munich. In the lobby of the Hotel Regina, at the foot of the curving grand stairs, Müller peered through an archway into the restaurant and saw a table reserved for the admiral and his entourage. Three SS men sat at an adjoining table, watching the door. Müller recognized one of them as

Heydrich's successor, SS spy chief Ernst Kaltenbrunner—taller than the rest, with a long scar down his cheek.[23]

Müller went upstairs to Canaris's room. Canaris did not seem quite himself, and the report of Kaltenbrunner's presence seemed to unhinge him. He started knocking on the walls, looking for microphones. He took the pictures down and scrutinized the areas behind them, then ran his hands under the edges of the tables and the chairs. Apparently satisfied, Canaris put his coat over the telephone and asked about the interrogation. Müller said that they had asked about his Vatican missions, but he had purged all his files before Sauermann arrived. They found nothing. But Canaris worried about the money Dohnanyi had given Schmidhuber for U-7. They seemed trapped. The admiral sank into a chair and muttered, half to himself, "This constant strain." His nerves seemed shot.[24]

Müller saw only one way out. Canaris should reconsider Keitel's offer to let military intelligence set up its own internal policing unit, so that Canaris could investigate crimes within his own service. In their current straits, that certainly would help them control the probe.[25]

Canaris would not consider that. The Rosa Luxemburg case haunted him. After Luxemburg's assassination by a paramilitary Freikorps in 1919, Canaris had served as a junior officer at the court-martial, which imposed a strangely lenient judgment on the perpetrators. Some suspected him of complicity in Luxemburg's death. He wanted nothing to do with "manhunts," he told Müller. He already had enough emotional burdens from "the old days." Rising abruptly, he suggested that they go downstairs to eat.[26]

Müller suggested they eat elsewhere, given the SS stakeout. Canaris disagreed. They should always do the unexpected. When a sniper had someone in his sights, he said, the target must break cover to confuse him. As they descended the stairs, however, Canaris grabbed Müller to steady himself. "That criminal," he said in a loud voice, "is still sacrificing millions of people just to prolong his miserable life." Startled, Müller pulled him back into the room to recompose. When they stepped out into the hall again, Canaris slung an arm around him and said, "My nerves, my nerves! I can't stand it anymore." No one knew what he had endured since 1933. He murmured about a tightening noose and then forced his face into a mask of normality. Together they descended to the restaurant to meet the enemy over a four-course meal.[27]

Canaris sat down and nodded to Kaltenbrunner. Müller sat by Canaris. They all talked like old friends. The surreal dinner had the feel of a parlay between the Greeks and Trojans. When it ended, the war resumed. Over the next months, Müller would return to the Vatican, and the pope would again become an active conspirator—as the plotters accelerated their plans to destroy Hitler before he could destroy them.[28]

CHAPTER 16

TWO BOTTLES OF COGNAC

"COME ON! LET'S GO! WAKE UP!" JESUIT FATHER ALFRED DELP spoke those words in his 1942 Advent sermons, and spoke them so often in daily life that they might have been his motto. He yearned for a "shaking that goes to the heart, right down to the bones," a parishioner recalled. "A sudden awakening. Something that would force people to wake up and come to their senses."[1]

For most of 1942, Germans sleepwalked with Hitler. As the Wehrmacht slashed into the Caucasus, as Rommel rolled toward Cairo, Hitler seemed invincible. Then, at year's end, everything changed.[2]

Russian tanks encircled the Sixth Army at Stalingrad. By Christmas, the SS reported mutterings of domestic discontent. The average German now sensed that a retreat had begun which would not stop at Germany's borders.[3]

The plotters saw their chance. Major-General Tresckow planned to lure Hitler to Army Group Center at Smolensk. There the plotters controlled the terrain, and could better elude Rattenhuber's bodyguard. Tresckow's deputy, Fabian von Schlabrendorff, visited Berlin to link with Oster and Müller and—through them—with the Allies, via the Vatican. An American spy who met Schlabrendorff during the war found him "highly intelligent," noting that whenever he talked about something that interested him, his eyes "flickered like a snake's." A lawyer in civilian life, he earned the resistance code name *Der Schläger*, meaning "the hit man."[4]

Oster summoned resistance members to his office and drew a circle around Stalingrad on his military map. He sent an emissary to Tresckow, who spoke of "arresting" Hitler, a euphemism for killing him, when he next visited Smolensk. Shortly thereafter Tresckow arrived in Berlin, with the result that General Friedrich Olbricht, head of the Home Army General Office, pledged to build up a secret military shadow organization capable of seizing power as soon as Hitler died.[5]

The civilian plotters huddled to freshen their plans. In December, Josef Müller and Helmuth Moltke met every few days with the Munich Jesuits. Committee priests saw the need for a political coalition to augment the coalescing military plot. But the civilian resistance, Father Delp argued, had one main problem.[6]

His name was Carl Goerdeler. Admittedly, he did not lack courage or charisma. Wearing a soft gray hat and billowing overcoat, carrying a gnarled cane, Goerdeler looked like an itinerant preacher and exuded a missionary zeal. In 1937 he had resigned as mayor of Leipzig when the Nazis destroyed a statue of Jewish composer Felix Mendelssohn. Goerdeler had even written Pacelli in 1939, asking him to help overthrow both Hitler and Mussolini.[7]

Yet as putative chancellor of the Decent Germany, Goerdeler was a jinx. Former leaders of banned unions and political parties found him reactionary. Many also considered him a security risk. Introducing himself to Berlin Bishop Konrad Preysing, Goerdeler said, as they shook hands: "The Nazi regime will of course have to be eradicated." Munich Cardinal Michael Faulhaber and Vienna Cardinal Theodor Innitzer reported similar encounters. Müller doubted whether Goerdeler would prove discreet enough to achieve their shared goals. Moltke and Delp had therefore tried to keep labor barons out of Goerdeler's camp.[8]

But Delp thought Goerdeler could still prove useful—even vital. The Kreisauers needed to light a spark with a united political leadership the generals trusted. Since the generals trusted older conservatives like

Goerdeler, everyone else had to accept him. Delp had worked too hard to ignite the coup and effect Hitler's death to let this chance slip away.[9]

So he urged and won a fresh approach. In one move, the younger faction both reached out to Goerdeler's group and united the forces against him. Dominican Father Laurentius Siemer became a liaison to Goerdeler, coordinating Catholic labor elements with his coup plans. Delp meanwhile negotiated a pact between Catholic and socialist labor bosses, so that Goerdeler found himself aligned with forces that outweighed him. Ultimately they would lead the leader.[10]

But where would they lead him? Delp answered that question in his Declaration of German Peace Ideals. It hewed to the doctrines set forth by Churchill and Roosevelt in their 1941 Atlantic Charter. The "boldness of an inner twist in Germany" would bring peace only if the Allies did not fear that "reactionary militarist elements" still pulled strings. To defuse that distrust, Germans must accept "an equal union of all European States" and restore "basic human rights, especially [for] the Jews."[11]

Delp then urged a sit-down to unite civilian forces. On 8 January 1943, Moltke's younger group met Beck's older faction in Berlin. Delp helped organize the meeting at Kreisau plotter Peter Yorck's house, but did not attend.[12]

Beck chaired the gathering and let the older faction speak first. Ulrich von Hassell, Germany's former ambassador to Rome, lamented that they had already waited too long, and any new regime would become "a liquidation commission." Goerdeler offered optimism and pieties and tried to avoid drilling too deeply into contentious issues that might complicate consensus. Refusing to characterize their plans as an assassination or coup, Goerdeler suggested that they operate under the assumption that he, Goerdeler, could persuade Hitler to resign.[13]

Moltke and his younger group found Goerdeler evasive and naive. They wanted a critical airing of realistic ideas—on church and state, capitalism and socialism, dictatorship and democracy. Protestant Pastor Eugen Gerstenmaier responded sharply to what he later called Goerdeler's "pedagogic obscuration of the issues." Moltke offended the elders by muttering "Kerensky," implicitly comparing Goerdeler to the figurehead whom V. I. Lenin had exploited and then discarded during the Russian Revolution. As Moltke confessed the next day to his wife, "I shot off a poisoned arrow that I'd kept in my quiver for a long time."[14]

The younger faction's unity made it dauntless. Adam von Trott zu Solz, a Foreign Office hand, articulated Delp's plea for a united Europe. Moltke urged cooperation between the churches and unions along the lines Delp had drawn. The younger group got its way. As Moltke recorded, "The affair ended dramatically, and luckily not flat[ly]." Those attending ratified Delp's declaration of ideals for a unified civilian front. The Kreisau Circle and Beck-Goerdeler group would work as one with the military plotters. Over yellow pea soup with slices of bread, Beck said portentously that they must assess the operational strength of their forces. All agreed that a coup must occur soon.[15]

WHILE THE JESUITS FORGED CONSENSUS, THEIR MILITARY CONFEDerates built bombs. Tresckow commissioned intelligence officer Freiherr von Gersdorff to obtain explosives on the eastern front. Gersdorff visited the Abwehr's depots and asked for a demonstration of plastic explosive "clams," captured from British commandos. The clams used silent acid fuses no bigger than pocket Bibles. In one test, a clam blew off the turret of a Russian tank and hurled it twenty yards.[16]

Gersdorff took four clams and Tresckow prepared to hide them in Hitler's Mercedes. If that did not work, he would smuggle a package onto Hitler's plane. The plotters just had to get Hitler to Smolensk.[17]

Tresckow intrigued to make it happen. "Hitler was to be persuaded to leave his headquarters in East Prussia," Tresckow's deputy recalled, and visit Army Group Center. "Tresckow wanted to have Hitler in a place familiar to us but unknown to him, thus creating an atmosphere favorable to the planned initial spark."[18]

IN FEBRUARY, MÜLLER DROVE OUT TO BECK'S VILLA IN BERLIN-Lichterfelde. As they talked, Hans von Dohnanyi joined them. But Beck sent Dohnanyi into the garden, saying he wanted to speak privately with Müller.[19]

They spoke for three hours. Beck thought the Allied demand for Germany's unconditional surrender, issued at Casablanca on 23 January, changed everything. As Müller remembered their talk, "The question then was, could we use Casablanca to our advantage, to forestall an invasion by a coup? . . . The overthrow would have to take place before any invasion. That was also one of the main reasons why the Tresckow assassination attempt had rushed along." Beck had approved Tresckow's plan. "The generals on ethical grounds feel themselves obliged to act. Count on it," Beck said. "I now have my finger on the button [*ich habe jetzt den Finger auf dem Knopf*]; it will finally happen."[20]

They discussed how to again contact London through the Vatican. Müller stressed that the chances of success had fallen since 1939–1940. Yet Beck decided that they must try to get London aboard. He gave Müller the mission of informing Pius about the imminent coup—and of asking the Holy Father to serve, again, as their secret foreign agent.[21]

MÜLLER SPENT THE NEXT TWO WEEKS IN ROME. EXTRINSIC EVI-dence suggests that he flew out of Berlin just after 9 February and did not return before the 22nd—perhaps his longest Roman sojourn during the war. In addition to briefing Pius on the coup plans, Müller carried out two other important assignments.[22]

The first was to convey an urgent situation report from Father Rösch. Addressed to Father Leiber in care of the deputy Jesuit general, it alluded to Committee plans against the regime. During the "grave [and] impending events [in] coming weeks," Rösch reported, his Jesuits would not only coordinate "labor forces," but would function as the "pope's storm troopers." If they failed, Rösch expected that they would be "deported like Jews." He would keep Father Leiber abreast, and, if the plans seemed too risky, "let him reverse me." If anything, Rösch candidly confessed, he could use more rather than less guidance from Rome, especially since "well-connected circles" had remained "silent about the fate of the Jews."[23]

A second Müller mission in Rome related to atomic weapons. "I got a detailed report from someone who was employed by the Vatican and the U.S., on the state of the atomic research," he said later. "I had also discussed that with Canaris. The two of us talked about the circumstance of Hitler's having caused the emigration to America of Jewish researchers and chemical engineers, and how they would revenge themselves against Hitler." Müller may have received the "detailed report" from one of the five American physicists who advised the Pontifical Academy of Sciences, where on 21 February Pius himself described how a nuclear explosion might occur—going into such detail that his prescience attracted the astonished notice of both Hartl's SS Church unit and the British Secret Service.[24]

But Müller's main business in the Holy See was the imminent overthrow. He approached the pope through Leiber and probably also through Kaas. "General Beck gave me the order to notify the Holy Father of the imminent revolution in Germany and of asking him again to strive for an acceptable peace," Müller recalled telling Leiber. "The generals feel obliged to eliminate this criminal gang which has plunged the whole world into misfortune." The Decent Germany wanted Pius to know its new postwar plans, which Müller summarized as follows:

> It will be necessary to establish a military dictatorship in Germany for one year after Hitler's downfall, until democratic groups can be established, which will no longer resemble political parties in the old sense. German troops will remain temporarily in the occupied countries, until they can make contact with resistance movements that will form the new governing forces. This will not be a pretext for continued occupation of the conquered lands. Rather, Admiral Canaris has accurate intelligence (for example from the Prefect of Police in Paris) that an uncontrollable anarchist movement will develop after any abrupt withdrawal of German troops.

Müller shared not only the plotters' after-plans, but their preparations. As Leiber told a US spy the next year, the plot "resulted directly from the Stalingrad disaster," and, compared to previous efforts, it was

> far more serious and extensive in the support it obtained. Its leader was General Ludwig Beck, and its civilian adherents included . . . all political elements under the Weimar Republic except the extreme

Right and the extreme Left. [Konrad] Adenauer, former Centrist mayor of Cologne, refused to join the movement, since he believed that the Nazi regime should bear the onus of losing the war before the opposition should attempt its overthrow. The key figures in the conspiracy were to have been the generals on the Eastern Front, under the leadership of [Field] Marshal [Erich] von Manstein. Immediately after the Stalingrad defeat, these generals had despaired of holding the front together.

Leiber doubted the generals would do anything. But he thanked Müller "in old friendship" for the message and promised to pass it to on.[25]

Pius responded promptly on three fronts. First, he gave his moral sanction, agreeing that the plotters faced "diabolical powers"—underscoring even, as Müller recalled, that they would be morally justified in blowing up Hitler's plane, "since we had to wage our war against the powers of evil." Müller could therefore reassure General Beck that assassination was allowed "in a moral emergency, to help preserve the free will of the people, which had been given them by their Creator."

Second, Pius made practical plans to recognize the Post-Hitler regime. He suggested speeding matters by seeking the customary formal agrément—the statement of willingness to receive a proposed envoy—before an actual coup. He proposed that, in the event of an overthrow, Müller should be recognized as the Vatican's special emissary to the post-Hitler government, with the title and status of ambassador-designate. That would show the world that Germany had made a fresh start. The new regime should then send Müller to petition Pius to mediate peace.

Third, Pius would seek a separate peace with the Western Allies. Although the Casablanca declaration made papal mediation unwelcome, Pius opposed the Allied unconditional surrender policy: "No nation would accept that," Leiber recalled him saying. "To threaten Germany with it will only lengthen the war." Pius sought a quick peace for many reasons, including to prevent a Soviet advance into Europe. He assured Müller that chances for peace were good if they ousted Hitler before an Allied invasion. Perhaps based on that assurance, General Tresckow soon spoke of agreements with the Western Powers for a separate surrender in the West.[26]

The British made no such agreement with Pius. Monsignor Kaas approached Ambassador Osborne, but the X-Report terms of 1940 were no longer on offer. Churchill, who felt hemmed in by Roosevelt's unilateral declaration at Casablanca, might nevertheless have winked at what Müller proposed. But Churchill never got the chance, because a Soviet spy in British intelligence, Kim Philby, shared the proposal with his handlers in Moscow instead of his superiors in London.[27]

Washington received the overtures more warmly—or at least received them. By 11 February, Leiber had begun passing Müller's messages to an American Jesuit in Rome, Father Vincent McCormick, who relayed them to US Vatican diplomat Harold Tittmann. Through a separate chain of intermediaries, including exiled German-Jesuit Father Friedrich Muckermann, Müller reported to the European chief of the US Office of Strategic Services, Allen Dulles, in Berne. A postwar OSS report on Müller stated flatly: "he was our agent and informant during the war with Germany." Despite Roosevelt's refusal to negotiate, Dulles and OSS chief William Donovan not only pursued contacts with Müller, but hinted broadly that Hitler's death would nullify the Casablanca declaration overnight.[28]

That was just what the German generals wanted to hear. "It was intended that a British-American invasion in the West should not be opposed; German troops were to be withdrawn to the interior of the Reich and to reinforce the Eastern front," recalled Major General Alexander von Pfuhlstein. During the coup, while Pfuhlstein's elite Brandenburg Division liquidated the SS in Berlin, the conspirators would "establish contact with America and England through the Vatican, with the purpose of negotiating for an armistice," Pfuhlstein said in 1944, adding: "I think that the Vatican was chosen as the neutral meeting place for the diplomats concerned." That Pius asked, in the bargain, for a free hand in naming German bishops for fifteen years gave the counterfactual scenario a texture of reality. Although Müller tried not to overpromise, he thought that Rome's readiness to mediate inspired his friends "in Germany's darkest hour."[29]

Müller also brought from Rome the guidance Rösch requested. As if expecting to be out of contact for some time, perhaps during the chaos following a coup, Pius sent a flurry of letters to the German bishops in February, and then none at all for the next six weeks. Before that hush of a great held breath, on 24 February, Pius had endorsed what Father Odilo Braun called the Committee's plans for "manly intercession." At that time, Father Delp mischievously remarked to lay aides that "no tyrant has ever died in his bed. That's no trouble to us." Delp added: "Watch out, the whistle will be blown by the workers."[30]

The pope's role in the plotting created some problems, however. Chief among them was the need to hide his role. "We could not portray the pope as a direct accessory to an assassination," Müller recalled.

> Consequently, in the statement formulated by Beck and me—we had discussed exactly how I should draft it—everything had already been prepared so that in the event of an overthrow, the pope would seem ignorant about everything. . . . But we had to consider what we would do if such a thing was aborted. The pope couldn't just immediately be standing by, visibly ready for a regime change—he'd look like a guilty schoolboy. . . . At that moment, much would depend on the demeanor of the pope."[31]

Needing someone to front for Pius, Müller called on the Bishop of Berlin. Would Preysing, in the event of an overthrow, agree to become a papal legate? Preysing promised to conscientiously discharge whatever mission Pius entrusted to him, but could not conceal his skepticism. "The generals will hesitate until the Russians are in Berlin," he told Müller, "and then maybe they will try to do something."[32]

Even as Preysing spoke, however, events were in train that would prove him wrong.

On 18 February, the SS arrested two college students in Munich. Hans Scholl and his sister Sophie led a resistance cell that became known as the White Rose. Working at night in the woodshed behind their apartment, the Scholls printed leaflets—"white roses"—denouncing Hitler. They rode trains to other cities, carrying the leaflets in suitcases, and mailed them in post boxes, or scattered them on streets and in railroad stations. Once, the police opened Sophie's luggage, but they did not find the leaflets hidden in her underwear.[33]

The Scholls became careless, however. In exuberant defiance, Sophie scattered handbills over the University of Munich quadrangle from a balcony. As the leaflets floated down, a janitor saw the Scholls flee. The Gestapo brought them to their headquarters in the former Wittelsbach palace. To compel Hans to betray those who supported them, they interrogated Sophie in front of him. An SS man shoved a leaflet into his face and demanded to know who wrote it. Hans confessed that he wrote it and begged them to leave his sister alone.[34]

Four days later, People's Court Judge Roland Freisler arrived from Berlin to try the Scholls. Sophie testified that they had only written what many believed but dared not say. Freisler knew as well as they did that Germany could not win the war, she said. Why didn't he have the courage to admit it? Freisler erupted, declaring that the SS must have treated her too leniently. They should have broken every bone in her body. But he would not fail to dispense justice. Sophie declared that God's justice transcended the state's; Freisler responded by reading out the state's sentence: death. The Scholls' mother screamed and collapsed in the gallery. That day the Gestapo beheaded her children.[35]

They died without revealing their links to the Catholic resistance. The Scholls had begun their underground work distributing a sermon by Bishop Clemens von Galen, denouncing Hitler's gassing of the infirm and insane. Sophie Scholl had obtained episcopal permission to reprint the text and distribute it at the University of Munich. Father Delp had kept in touch with the Scholls through a friend. Moltke received the final, fatal handbill, probably through Josef Müller, who knew its author, Professor Kurt Huber. "A White Rose [pamphlet] was brought to my residence upstairs and presented to me by Prof. Huber," Müller recalled. "I had then taken the White Rose [pamphlet] to Rome along with other things, and from there it had gone to England and arrived back here via Radio London." Its ties to Müller and Delp made the White Rose almost a student chapter of the Black Chapel.[36]

The Scholls' case shook the coup plotters. Some thought the Nazis had meant the trial as a warning. Why else would a Supreme Court judge have come out from Berlin?[37]

TWO WEEKS LATER, IN EARLY MARCH, HITLER FELL INTO THE PLOT-ters' trap. Hitler agreed to visit Smolensk. Cavalry officers there volunteered to shoot him as he sat down to lunch or ambush him while he drove through the woods. Tresckow decided instead to sabotage Hitler's flight home. On 7 March, ostensibly to hold an intelligence conference, Canaris and Oster flew to Smolensk with a pack of explosives. Tresckow's aide, Schlabrendorff, locked the bomb in a case for which he had the only key.[38]

"A simple pressure on the head of the igniter broke a very small bottle releasing a corrosive substance," Schlabrendorff recalled. The acid would eat a wire, and a firing pin would snap forward to ignite the bomb. "In order to be sure of the effect, we took not one but two packages of explosives and wrapped them into one package which looked like a package containing two bottles of cognac."[39]

Hitler would arrive on 13 March, in the morning. The plan seemed all set. Father Rösch's Committee had prepared the political grounds in Berlin, Munich, and Vienna. General Olbricht told Schlabrendorff: "We are ready; it is time for the spark."[40]

IN THE SISTINE CHAPEL, ON FRIDAY, 12 MARCH, PIUS CELEBRATED the fourth anniversary of his coronation. The Roman diplomatic corps attended en masse. The US chargé d'affaires, Harold Tittmann, recalled that the British and American representatives to the Holy See, D'Arcy Osborne and Myron Taylor, exchanged meaningful grins. Tittmann attributed the smiles to the tonic effect of Mussolini's daughter. Edda Ciano caught attention with her flashing eyes, sable cape, and "curls like small horns arising from her forehead." Only later would there seem another plausible cause for his colleagues' knowing glee. Both had received indications—Osborne through Kaas, and Taylor through Müller—that action against Hitler was imminent.[41]

On the next day, 13 March, Hitler flew to Smolensk. Hans Rattenhuber's bodyguards, in field-gray SS uniforms, leveled their submachine guns as Hitler's Focke-Wulf Condor landed. The stairs were lowered, the door opened, and Hitler descended, bent and tired. After a tense meeting with his generals, he got back on the plane. As Lieutenant-Colonel Heinz Brandt followed Hitler aboard, Schlabrendorff stopped him on the stairs.[42]

The propeller wash swirled snow around them and they had to shout to hear each other. Schlabrendorff asked whether Brandt would carry along some cognac for General Helmuth Stieff. Brandt said he would do so gladly.[43]

Schlabrendorff handed him a package and wished him a safe trip. As the plane took off, Schlabrendorff stood back and watched until it vanished in the falling snow.[44]

CHAPTER 17

THE SIEGFRIED
BLUEPRINTS

JOSEF MÜLLER SPENT 13 MARCH IN A PUB NEAR MILITARY INTEL-
ligence HQ in Berlin, waiting for the code word of Hitler's death.
Admiral Canaris's personal plane stood fueled at Tempelhof airport,
ready to fly Müller by the fastest route to Rome. Once within the Vatican's walls, if all went as planned, Müller would present his credentials
to Pius and receive the pope's official recognition of the post-Nazi government. The hours passed. With each stein of beer, Müller's hopes fell.
The code word never came.[1]

In Smolensk, Tresckow was sitting with Schlabrendorff. They expected one of the fighters escorting Hitler's plane to radio an emergency. With the fuse set for thirty minutes, the bomb should have
exploded after about 125 to 150 miles, somewhere above Minsk. But
they heard nothing until three hours later, when the phone rang and
Tresckow snatched it up. Hitler had landed safely in Rastenburg.[2]

Schlabrendorff called Berlin with a code word for failure of the attempt. Then he realized in a panic that they must at all costs retrieve the
package right away. Otherwise, the unwitting General Stieff might still
open it, expecting to pour himself an after-battle cognac. "We were in
a state of indescribable agitation," Schlabrendorff recalled. After some

frantic deliberation, Tresckow called Brandt and casually asked him to hold the package, pleading some kind of mix-up.

The next morning Schlabrendorff flew to Mauerwald, in East Prussia. He nervously passed the security checkpoints and remembered how Brandt, "ignorant of the subject at hand, smiled and presented me with the bomb, shaking the package so violently I feared it might explode yet since the ignition had been set."

Schlabrendorff hurried to a train that lodged guests on a siding. "I got into the compartment reserved for me, locked the door and cautiously opened the parcel with a razor blade. As I removed the wrapper, I could see that the condition of both loads had remained unchanged. I uncocked the bomb carefully and took the fuse out."[3]

Acid had eaten through the wire. The striker had hit the detonator, burning the cap. Yet by some fluke the bomb had not gone off. It was wet and cold. Perhaps because the cabin's heating system had failed, or because the plane's luggage bay had no heat, the trigger switch had caked with ice.[4]

A FEW DAYS LATER, THE ASSASSINS HAD A SECOND CHANCE. BY coincidence one of the conspirators, Colonel Baron Rudolf von Gersdorff, was detailed for duty at a Berlin Heroes' Day ceremony, where Hitler would review captured Russian weapons. Gersdorff pledged to make an attempt on Hitler's life—at the cost of sacrificing his own.[5]

He would blow himself up with Hitler. Gersdorff's wife had died, the war was lost, and he wanted his own death to mean something. To that end, he naturally wanted to know that the coup would progress as planned. Tresckow said that the pope had made arrangements with the Western Powers for a separate surrender in the west, while German Jesuits had laid plans for a democratic form of government.[6]

On the night of 20/21 March, Tresckow told Schlabrendorff of the plan in a code which no outsider could have understood. Tresckow learned Hitler's timetable from General Staff contacts on pain of the strictest secrecy and with repeated references to "the death sentence." He inferred that Hitler had allotted half an hour for the visit.

Early the next morning, Schlabrendorff went to the Hotel Eden. Gersdorff was still sleeping. "I woke him," Schlabrendorff recalled, "and handed him the bomb before he had had any breakfast."[7]

Gersdorff went to the ceremony with the bomb in his coat pocket. He would serve as Hitler's guide, explaining the displays. As Hitler passed through lines of war-wounded into the Zeughaus museum, an orchestra played solemn music in the flag-decked hall. Gersdorff set the bomb—two clams wrapped together—to detonate in ten minutes. Hitler, however, rushed through the exhibition, hardly glancing at the Soviet materiel. He left after three minutes. Gersdorff rushed into a bathroom, smashed the detonator, and flushed it down the toilet.[8]

THE MARCH 1943 FAILURES FRUSTRATED THE JESUIT PLOTTERS. "Even Fathers Rösch and König, who really should have learnt, from their discipline, to wait, are incapable of it," Moltke wrote, "and when an action is followed by an inevitable setback, they become restless and don't see that beyond the valley is another height." After eighteen months of political advance work, the Orders Committee Jesuits did not wish to tarry—especially since they saw the chance of getting to Hitler literally in their own backyard.[9]

In the suburb of Pullach, ten miles south of Munich, Hitler had built four underground bunkers, comprising thirty rooms, with a ventilation system to protect him against gas attack. This alternate Führer headquarters, code-named Siegfried, bordered the Jesuits' modern and spacious Berchmanskolleg, which the Nazis had tried to commandeer. To keep their college out of party hands, the Jesuits had retained Josef Müller, who outflanked the party by negotiating a deal with the army, allowing it to use parts of the campus as a hospital. But this had not ended the disputes in Pullach. Hitler's SS bodyguards at the Siegfried bunker threatened a lawsuit, claiming that Jesuit sewage had polluted their drinking water. Father Rösch had again hired Müller to fend off the party.[10]

Then Hitler himself showed up. When he stayed in Siegfried for the first time, from 9–12 November 1942, his proximity to those plotting his death prompted some creative, goal-oriented thinking. It occurred to the Jesuits that their quarry had essentially taken an apartment in their complex. Father Delp urged that priests excluded from military service should join Organization Todt, which maintained the Führer bunkers. Thus, they could gain access to plant a time bomb in HQ Siegfried. Delp asked military contacts whether they could get him into the Todt corps.[11]

A breach in Hitler's security had already emerged, however. Negotiating with the SS over the leaking sewage, Father König obtained copies of the architect's plans for the Siegfried bunker. He passed the blueprints to Müller. Through his beer brotherhood with Hans Rattenhuber, the head of Hitler's bodyguard, Müller knew top secret details of Hitler's protection procedures, but had never seen a good way past Rattenhuber's guards. Having blueprints to the creature's lair changed everything. Vents, shafts, doors, ducts—here lay a draftsman's brew of possibilities. Müller alerted Oster, who thought of eliminating Hitler in the bunker under cover of an air raid. By Müller's account, he had a copy of the blueprints in the desk at his home on 4 April 1943, as the Führer's special train barreled through the Thuringian wood toward Munich, where Hitler would stay at least through 5 April. But on that day, just as all those factors converged in the plotters' favor, the SS dealt them a lethal blow.[12]

WILLY SCHMIDHUBER TALKED. ROUGHED UP AFTER HIS EXTRADI-tion from Italy, he unloaded about Operation U-7, the plotters' plan to rescue Jews. As a result, at 10:00 a.m. on 5 April, Luftwaffe investigator Manfred Roeder and SS Inspector Franz Sonderegger swooped into Oster's office. Roeder displayed his search warrant, asked Dohnanyi to open his desk drawers, and told him that he proposed to search the room for incriminating documents. He bore down on a green safe adorned with embossed scrolls and demanded the key, which Dohnanyi grudgingly produced after at first denying that he had it on him. Roeder removed files from the safe and deposited them on Dohnanyi's desk. They contained code words for disguising secret missions abroad, as well as reports on the exfiltration of Jews.[13]

Dohnanyi stared at a folder labeled "Z Grau." He glanced meaningfully at Oster, who stood by the desk, and mouthed silently: "Those papers, those papers!" Camouflaged as "intelligence material," they explained the failure of the 13 March coup attempt. Accompanying notes, made out for General Beck, informed him that on 9 April Pastor Bonhoeffer would accompany Müller to Rome to discuss the plots with Father Leiber.[14]

Oster reached behind him to extract the sheets. Roeder swung round, and later described what happened. "By arrangement between Oster and Dohnanyi, Colonel Oster stood facing the chief investigator with his left hand behind his back, removed the said papers and . . . concealed them beneath his civilian suit. Having been observed by . . . Sonderegger . . . and the chief investigator, he was promptly challenged."[15]

Roeder arrested Dohnanyi. Oster escaped, for the moment, with house arrest; Canaris considered his days numbered. The plotters could no longer strike at Hitler from within—and their enemies now had written proof of their contacts, through Müller, to the pope.[16]

MÜLLER RACED HOME AS SOON AS HE LEARNED OF DOHNANYI'S ARrest. Toward noon, the Munich Abwehr telephoned. Something flat in Lieutenant Colonel Nikolaus Ficht's tone told Müller that his time had come.[17]

He wondered what charges they would bring against him. Ficht said the lead prosecutor for the Supreme Reich Court Martial, Colonel Dr. Manfred Roeder, had issued orders for his arrest. Luftwaffe chief Hermann Göring and Wilhelm Keitel, chief of the German Armed Forces Supreme High Command, had cosigned the warrant. The stated crime was undermining the war effort. The evidence reportedly included Wilhelm Schmidhuber's statements that Müller helped Jews escape with forged papers and cash. Further, according to the SS, Müller was "suspected of being involved in a general conspiracy to overthrow Hitler in collusion with the Western powers."[18]

Stalling for time, Müller asked permission to call Canaris. Try your luck, Ficht said, but Müller could not reach the admiral, only his secretary, Frau Schwarte, who seemed agitated. "It's total chaos," she shouted into the phone. "*They* are here!"[19]

Müller started to clean out the desk in his study. For nearly a year since Schmidhuber's arrest, a sword had hung over their heads. Now it had come down. He wondered whether the Gestapo had more than Schmidhuber had told them. Had they found the papers at Zossen? If so, biting off his tongue would not save anyone. Those files, Müller knew, contained enough proof to hang them all.

With horror he realized he could not remove the most damning evidence from his desk. A hidden, locked drawer contained the blueprints to Hitler's Pullach residence, the Führer bunker at Siegfried, and papers relating to his Vatican missions. As a security measure, Müller never kept the key to the secret compartment in his home. He locked it in a safe at his law office. He doubted he could get there and back before the authorities arrived. His secretary, Anni Haaser, knew the safe combination and could drive the key over, but he had already phoned her and she had begun destroying boxes of files. She could not help him in two places at once.[20]

He packed for prison. Into a traveling trunk he shoved fifteen handkerchiefs, six dress shirts, five pairs of socks, some underwear, two pocket dictionaries, two oranges, a three-piece gray suit, and a green necktie.[21]

Müller kissed his wife, Maria, and held her. He had always tried to keep her out of his intrigues. But he knew from experience that the Nazis would threaten or arrest innocent family members to attain their goals.[22]

He called for his eight-year-old daughter, Christa. They went out onto the porch adjoining the study to feed the canary, Hansi, in its cage. If he had to go to Berlin for longer than usual, he told her, she should not forget to feed the bird.[23]

Kriminalkommissar Franz Sonderegger loomed in the doorway. He was a slim Rhinelander with sloped shoulders and a wrinkled meager face. As Müller made his way downstairs, Sonderegger used police tape to seal the study doors.[24]

On the front stoop, an army officer held out handcuffs. Müller wedged himself into the back seat of the waiting dark sedan. He turned and lifted his manacled fists, waving to his wife and daughter on the front steps. They watched him until he vanished from their view.[25]

CHAPTER 18

THE WHITE KNIGHT

O N 7 APRIL 1943, HANS GISEVIUS CROSSED ST. PETER'S SQUARE. The Abwehr officer approached the Vatican apartment of Monsignor Johannes Schönhöffer, a close friend of Josef Müller. Gisevius let himself in, using a key left under the doormat, and waited in the hall, staring tensely out the window. Suddenly he saw "something black scurry across the yard, quickly like a weasel, so that I could only barely discern the small, gaunt figure, hidden by a big, black Jesuit hat." Gisevius went onto the landing and looked down a spiral staircase. He saw the hat get bigger as it circled up.[1]

Father Leiber came in, coughing. The asthmatic Jesuit described Pius as "full of worry over Müller's fate." Leiber himself feared that the 1940 statement of British peace terms, written on the pope's watermarked stationery, might fall into Himmler's hands. Gisevius promised to raise the matter with Beck. As for Müller, languishing in an army prison, much would depend on his staying out of SS custody. The case against him seemed grave.[2]

Gisevius returned from the Vatican and briefed Admiral Canaris in Berlin. Father Leiber had suggested the plotters coordinate any future plans through his Jesuit colleague in Munich, Father Rösch. With the loss of Müller, Leiber hailed Rösch as "Catholicism's strongest man in Germany."[3]

The arrest of Oster's cadre, alas, left the conspirators with little to do except cover their tracks. "After such wide blows by the Gestapo," Gisevius recalled, "the psychological shock produced paralysis, and created a kind of conspiratorial vacuum."[4]

Yet on the very day that Gisevius met Father Leiber, carnage in North Africa called forth a warrior Catholic on whom all hopes would rest. After years of missed chances and failed schemes, the German resistance would finally cross the threshold of action through the force of one man.

ON 7 APRIL, THE GERMAN ARMY ATTACKED IN TUNISIA. THE DUST and smoke rose so thickly that tank commanders fought standing in their hatches. Too late they saw the white stars on wings of American planes. Colonel Claus von Stauffenberg dove from his jeep to the sand, burying his face in his arms.[5]

Medics found a bullet hole in the jeep's windshield and a dead lieutenant in the back seat. Stauffenberg lay a few yards off, unconscious, bleeding from his head and hands. In a field hospital, doctors amputated his right hand and two fingers of his left. Then they removed his left eye.[6]

Stauffenberg's colleagues at division headquarters missed him. Secret microphones in POW compounds recorded some of their wartime praise: "Stauffenberg was the ideal of the coming German generation," a "good, honest, Christian and courageous man" who "cared for his troops." If he had a fault, it was that he was "incredibly indiscreet," but his comrades considered that "part of his honesty." The first time one met him, "he opened his heart . . . straight away."[7]

Later he became a kind of cult figure. "Claus was a man of such charm," one of his friends recalled, that he "exercised such a spell over all of us who came near him." Even the dour General Halder confessed that he found Stauffenberg "magnetically attractive," while a less reserved confederate called him "radiant and handsome as Alcibiades." Interviewing his former associates in 1947, a British debriefer recorded that their "eyes brightened" and they seemed "bewitched by the mere recollection." Perhaps no German during the Nazi years had such a hypnotic effect on his countryman except Hitler himself. Given what Stauffenberg later did, and how famous he became by doing it, those who knew him tended to recall him in mythic terms; and in his status as countermythical icon lay the key to his charisma. One cannot understand his influence unless one sees him, for instance, in his white summer uniform, with an Iron Cross pinned at his heart, looking, as one of his colleagues recalled, "handsome and strong, like a young war god," sitting up late with junior officers, with his left hand in his trouser pocket and a wine glass in his right, translating Homer's *Odyssey* or criticizing Hitler.[8]

Hitler had alienated him by persecuting the Jews. Like most European gentiles, Stauffenberg was raised on mixed racial messages; but one of his brothers had married a Jewish aviatrix, whose 1936 dismissal from the Luftwaffe made anti-Semitism a family problem. Although Stauffenberg's knowledge of the Shoah deepened his disgust with Nazism, the persecution of the Jews had turned him against Hitler years before. Kristallnacht was the Rubicon: two months later, in January 1939, Stauffenberg walked in the Wuppertal woods with his friend Rudolf Fahrner, a literature professor with wild gray hair and gleaming eyes, who had reacted to the pogrom by taking an ax and smashing a bust of Hitler. When Fahrner asked whether the army would just accept the burning of synagogues, Stauffenberg spoke openly—for the first time—of overthrowing the Nazi regime.[9]

Yet for three years he failed to heed his own call. When the Canaris group approached him, he made excuses: the idea was right, the timing wrong. Only when he lost the chance to act, immobilized by his wounds, did he commit himself to action. When Munich doctors broke open his body cast, a new man emerged. "He became convinced that Hitler . . . was indeed controlled by a diabolic power," recalled Elizabeth, Baroness von und zu Guttenberg, who visited him in mid-May 1943. "He was sure at last in his own mind that in the assassination of

Hitler he would be removing a creature actually possessed, body and soul, by the devil."[10]

His fervor was a function of his faith. Where sympathy for those of another creed made him hate Hitler, the tenets of his own creed helped him resist Hitler. Stauffenberg was a "devout Catholic," an SS probe found, and his "church ties played a *major role* in the conspirator's clique" [emphasis in original]. That he was "a Catholic reactionary," as the Gestapo reported, was clear from more than just the gold cross he wore on a simple neck chain. Since medieval times the Stauffenbergs had been cathedral canons in Swabia; one of the clan had been Prince Bishop of Constance, and another Prince Bishop of Bamberg. His family's links to the papacy were a formative and lasting force on Claus. At age nine, playing Mass at an altar in a castle attic, he sermonized that if Luther had just been more patient, there would now be only one true faith. Even before joining the German resistance, he sought not just to raze the Third Reich but to revive the Holy Roman Empire.[11]

Stauffenberg had a stained-glass mind. His notebooks brimmed with poems eulogizing the medieval Catholic Imperium, and, much as Britons then renewed their founding myths, casting Churchill as Arthur returned from Avalon, so Stauffenberg dreamed that Holy Roman Emperor Frederick the Second, sleeping in a mountain, would awake to rescue Europe. When he lectured cadets, standing among the ruins of tenth-century castles, Stauffenberg spoke not as an intellectual observer but as an original participant, called back to make world-historic choices. Physically he fought in the Second World War, but psychologically he lived in a secret Germany, among secret saints, loyal not to the Nazis' New Order but to Augustine's *Civitas Dei*. To Stauffenberg, as to Father Rösch's Kreisau disciples, Western civilization could only be saved by restoring the ideals that fused to create it under Charlemagne. In that respect certain Catholic ideas belonged together, and no more needed questioning than jewels in a necklace: humanism, classicism, Christendom, aristocracy, tyrannicide.[12]

"Well, I am a Catholic and we have a long-standing tradition that tyrants can be murdered," one of his coplotters recalled him saying. To rationalize breaking the officer's pledge, he cited the concept of a trumping natural law: "As a believing Catholic," one officer remembered him arguing, "I was bound in duty . . . to act against this oath." He justified killing Hitler by quoting Aquinas, but did not rely just on his personal interpretation of doctrine; he consulted Church authorities, including the Orders Committee's Bishop Preysing and Father Delp.[13]

Stauffenberg connected with the Committee soon after his fateful decision. Since he and they were both in Munich then, that was easy enough. He likely linked with the Munich Jesuits while still in the hospital there, through Baroness von Guttenberg. Her husband had introduced Father Rösch to Moltke, in fall 1941; since then, she had hosted weekly lectures by Delp in her Munich home. By 9 May one of Father Rösch's lay operatives, Committee lawyer Georg Angermaier, had learned of Stauffenberg's designs. Angermaier was based in Bamberg, where Stauffenberg lived, and knew of the assassination planners' contacts with the pope through Josef Müller.[14]

ON 7 APRIL 1943, WHILE STAUFFENBERG STILL LAY WOUNDED IN Tunisia, the SS had ransacked Müller's Munich home. SS Inspector Franz Sonderegger suspected that Joey Ox had already cleared out any incriminating papers. Still, he took Müller's wife, Maria, up to the study, hoping she might in her distress betray any hiding places. When she failed to do so, two Gestapo officials grilled her. "They tried to find out from me the names of my husband's associates," she later said, by running through names of suspected anti-Nazis, and asking whether they had ever been in the Müller home. "I always gave evasive answers."[15]

Sonderegger meanwhile examined the desk with a magnifying glass. He discovered the hidden drawer, but could not jimmy it open. Suspecting that it contained substantial evidence of anti-Nazi activities, he made a mental note to summon an SS locksmith. Planning to resume the search later, he again closed the study doors and sealed them with an official notice.[16]

When Sonderegger returned the next day, he found the seal broken. Since only Müller's daughter and mother-in-law remained in the house, he took the grandmother to task for it. She said that their canary, Hansi, had become restless out on the porch, and she had allowed Christa to feed him. Christa had gone through the study and out onto the porch, but climbed back in through a window. Sonderegger said sharply that in breaking the seal they had committed a crime for which he could now arrest them. "So," Sonderegger remembered the grandmother scolding, "you've arrested my son-in-law, and now you also want to lock me up, and maybe even little Christa. The next thing you know, you'll be arresting the canary!" If the family's defiance was any indication, Sonderegger recalled thinking, Joey Ox would be a hard man to break.[17]

Around the same time, Father Albrecht of Ettal visited Müller's office. Müller's secretary, Anni Haaser, opened the door. SS Inspector Sonderegger had already placed her under arrest, but compelled her to remain on the job as part of a sting operation. Hoping to identify Müller's contacts, Sonderegger had stationed a Gestapo agent in the office, answering the telephone as "Dr. Müller" whenever it rang, and he ordered Haaser to show all visitors in. Father Johannes, however, had not come in clerical clothes, but a simple black suit. Sonderegger asked what he wanted. Correctly interpreting a wink from Fräulein Haaser, Father Albrecht improvised. He said he had come to see Herr Doktor Müller "about a divorce."[18]

THROUGH THE POLICE-CAR WINDOW MÜLLER STARED OUT AT BERlin. Everything was murky, blacked out. His captors joked about the workings of the guillotine while he pondered his fate. "I was afraid," he said, "that Henning von Tresckow's assassination attempt had been discovered, and that this had put the Nazi bloodhounds on my trail, and that they had also learned about my most recent contacts with the pope."[19]

The car stopped at the military prison on the Lehrterstrasse. Through the gloom he could just see the gray fort with its watch tower and barred windows. In the reception yard an iron gate banged shut behind the car. "Effective immediately," a sergeant barked, "you are forbidden to say 'Heil Hitler.'" Two guards led Müller through latticed galleries, connected by iron spiral stairs, and shoved him into Cell 7 on Death Row.[20]

The room was nine feet deep and six feet wide. In the left front corner, a brown pail served as a toilet. Cardboard covered the window hatch, its glass blown out by air raids, so the room received no natural light. When Müller put his ear to the wall, he heard weeping.[21]

On Müller's second day in Berlin, around 14 April, the commandant called for him. Colonel Otto Maas worked for General Paul von Hase, an uncle of Dietrich Bonhoeffer and Frau Dohnanyi. "I bring you greetings," Maas said in a friendly voice, "from your boss and your real boss." He could only have meant Canaris and Beck. Müller looked at him, and then asked, "Herr Lieutenant Colonel, are you ready to give me a real old-fashioned officer's word of honor?" Maas assumed a military bearing and held out his hand. Müller said, "Send my greetings to my boss and my real boss, and tell them that I will keep my word of honor!" He thus hoped to assure his friends that he would, if necessary, go to the gallows alone.[22]

The next morning he faced Judge Advocate Roeder at the interrogation table. He wanted to know about Müller's Vatican missions. "You'll lay your cards on the table regarding these Jesuits in Rome." Roeder mentioned Father Leiber and Monsignor Schönhöffer, and ordered Müller to identify his other contacts in the Holy See. Müller insisted that only Canaris could give him permission to speak their names.[23]

Roeder took a sheet of paper from his briefcase. Müller realized at once that the SS had found the plans for Hitler's Pullach bunker. "Where did you get these?" Roeder asked gruffly. Müller said he couldn't discuss the Siegfried blueprints without violating attorney-client privilege, and further, "I would violate my professional secrecy oath even by telling you who could release me from my oath." That bought Müller some time, because Roeder then had to consult the Abwehr.[24]

Two weeks later, the bunker plans came up again. Court-Martial Counsel Erwin Noack had found the originals, with a notation that the City of Pullach had given a copy to Father Lothar König, at the Jesuit Berchmanskolleg. Kommissar Walther Möller, standing in for Roeder, began to scream: "If you don't tell us everything that we want to know. . . ." He made a motion with his hand, as though chopping off a head. Noack warned that they would soon get the truth anyway, as he himself would interrogate Father König in Munich.[25]

Back in his cell, Müller sent for the Catholic chaplain. Father Heinrich Kreutzberg, who helped the condemned prepare for death, was soon at his side. Müller had at first feared him, as he had learned to fear Brother Hermann Keller and all clergy with government links. But after Müller had given Kreutzberg a message for Bishop Preysing's Vicar-General, Maximilian Prange, and Kreutzberg had conveyed, in return, a message affirming Preysing's hatred for the Nazis, Müller had decided to trust him.[26]

Now he told Kreutzberg about the bunker plans. The danger was that König, trying to protect Müller, would doom them all. If cornered by Noack, König should admit that he received the plans during the sewage dispute with the SS—and that he had passed them to Müller, the Jesuits' counsel in the case.[27]

Kreutzberg rode that very night to Munich, on the same train Noack took. The next morning he raced to warn König. Noack arrived at the rectory, only to learn that König had just caught a train to Berlin.[28]

As FATHER KÖNIG RODE NORTH ON THE RAILS, THE POPE SENT Bishop Preysing a secret message. In previous weeks, the Holy See had received a new flood of reports about the fate of the Jews. Father Pietro Tacchi Venturi, the liaison to Mussolini, had tried but failed to save Croatian Jews from deportation, calling it "the first step, as is known, toward a not distant, most difficult death." Cardinal Celso Constantini, the pope's propaganda chief, recorded seeing a "picture of crowds of Jews who, after having dug ditches, were killed wholesale and thrown into the ditches; there were women, children, old people, men. A cold-blooded massacre, a barbarism that is equal to and greater than that of the Bolsheviks." Meanwhile Preysing, who (said Moltke) "showed himself very well informed on the latest developments in the Jewish question," asked Rome to help the persecuted. "There is probably no bitterer trial for us here in Berlin than the new wave of Jewish deportations,"

Preysing wrote Pius on 6 March, noting that the victims included Catholics of Jewish descent. "Would it not be possible for Your Holiness to try again to intercede on behalf of the many unlucky innocents?"[29]

The pope's answer reaffirmed the course he had taken since becoming the plotters' foreign agent. "We leave it to the bishops and archbishops active on the spot," he wrote Preysing on 30 April, "to evaluate whether and to what degree it appears advisable to practice restraint to prevent even greater evils in the face of the danger of reprisals." He regretted that the bishops' secret and temperate protests had proved ineffective, but he did not command them to declaim more vigorously in public. Where some later decried his "rigid centralization," he showed exactly the opposite leaning. Instead of giving orders, he listed wishes.[30]

He wished that German clergy would follow Preysing's lead. "It is never allowed to take human rights from a member of a foreign race," Preysing had said in a recent sermon, underscoring that "it is never allowed to commit cruelties towards any such person." Pius hailed not only those "clear and frank words," but the actions of Preysing's cathedral canon, Bernhard Lichtenberg, who died en route to a concentration camp after publicly praying for the Jews. "It has consoled us," Pius wrote, "that Catholics, and especially the Berlin Catholics, have brought much love to the afflicted non-Aryans."[31]

Pius confessed that he too felt compelled to help the Jews—not by words, but through acts. Working with "the Jewish leadership," he told Preysing, the Vatican diverted "very large amounts of American currency" from its banks to help Jews escape Europe—a vast effort that required global coordination with "Jewish communities from Bolivia, Costa Rica, South Africa, Chile, the Union of Orthodox Rabbis of America and Canada and the Grand Rabbi of Zagreb." For Catholics of Jewish descent, Pius could do far less, since Jewish rescue groups would not accept them: "Unfortunately, in the current situation we can give them no effective help other than our prayers." Still, he said, he saw a "way out"—not just for the persecuted in Nazi Europe, but for the innocents needlessly dying on all sides.[32]

"The recklessly mounting, matter-of-fact cruelty makes the thought of a still longer duration of this mutual murder unbearable," Pius wrote.

"The war question compels us now . . . to operate through secret inter-cession." About these covert actions the pope said little in his letter—especially since Preysing, a member of the Orders Committee, already knew of the intrigues through Josef Müller. Pius did say that his discreet project "required the maximum of patience . . . as well as mastering the ever-emerging diplomatic difficulties." It also required the success of what he obliquely called "the action arms."[33]

CLAUS STAUFFENBERG HAD LEARNED TO TIE HIS SHOES USING HIS teeth. With the remnants of his hand, he wrote Lieutenant General Friedrich Olbricht, pledging to report in three months to the Home Army General Office in Berlin. Olbricht had plotted to bomb Hitler's plane two months before, and Stauffenberg relished the "opportunities for decisive intervention." When Stauffenberg left the hospital in July, his wife found his face heavy, almost menacing.[34]

He spent the next weeks with his two brothers in their ancestral cas-tle. They translated Book 7 of *Odyssey*, with Claus marking its maxim: "In every venture the bold man comes off best." He climbed mountains with a cane, and then without one.[35]

By 19 July he had linked with Moltke's Kreisau circle. Through his brother, Berthold, Stauffenberg absorbed the plans for a ghost govern-ment, which had just taken final form under the guidance of the Munich Jesuits.[36]

JOSEF MÜLLER FELT LIKE HE HAD BEEN SEALED IN A COFFIN, ESPE-cially at night, when all the traffic stopped in the corridors. During the day, the guards would not let him walk in the yard, lest he find some way to synchronize stories with Hans Dohnanyi.[37]

"Everything is still in suspense," Moltke wrote on 20 June. At first, it seemed that the protective hand of Hitler's chief bodyguard, Hans Rattenhuber, would keep Müller from the gallows. But the case had taken a "turn for the worse," leading Moltke to predict: "everything will go wrong in the end." Judge Advocate Roeder had questioned not only the SS monk Herman Keller, but even Canaris. The admiral admitted breaking a rule: Section Z did not have authority to run agents. He could only lamely say that "Dohnanyi's overlapping connections to Müller (because of his connections to circles in Rome) . . . were of benefit to the military and military-political information service."[38]

At that precarious point, Müller got two unforeseen assists. Sergeant Herbert Milkau, a former communist, read Müller's background dossier; and, learning that Joey Ox had once led the Bavarian Peoples' Party left wing, agreed to carry messages between him and Dohnanyi. Then Army Judge Advocate General Karl Sack, a friend of Canaris, tipped Müller to the tactics he would face: "Sometimes I was better prepared for an interrogation than the interrogators." When Roeder claimed that Oster had made a full confession, Müller did not fall for the bluff.[39]

The less progress Roeder made, the more angry he became. He grew abusive and failed to ask logical follow-ups. Müller used that against him, looking for ways to provoke his wrath. When Müller casually mentioned interning for a Jewish lawyer, Roeder flew into such a rage that he lost the whole thread of inquiry and had to break off.[40]

Roeder's tirades became so garish that Sack urged Müller to file a complaint. Müller wrote General Keitel, accusing Roeder of dishonoring the Wehrmacht by slandering Vatican personalities, and of breaking secrecy laws by naming some of Müller's agents—Leiber, Schönhöffer, Hofmeister—before unauthorized ears. Sack supported the petition, insinuating that Roeder aimed to crush the Abwehr, subordinating a key part of the armed forces to the SS.[41]

The complaints succeeded. Keitel called on Himmler, who, according to one SS witness, had "not the slightest interest in the whole affair." Keitel told Roeder to limit his probe to nonpolitical offenses, such as customs violations. Treason charges against members of the so-called Black Chapel—Müller, Oster, Dohnanyi, Bonhoeffer, and Schmidhuber—were to be dropped until further notice. Keitel's 26 July order, further, cited a transformational event that occurred the day before, requiring the commitment of all Abwehr forces.[42]

Mussolini had fallen. That "was the first coup, mediated by Müller's agreement," Dohnanyi's wife later said. Though Müller was jailed before his work succeeded, the results of Fascism's failure would at first excite but then alarm him. "Groups working towards the elimination of Hitler have been greatly encouraged by the developments in Italy, where it has been shown that it is possible to remove a dictator," Allen Dulles wired Washington. In fact, Mussolini's ouster caused Beck to rise from his sickbed, Tresckow to rush to Berlin, and Stauffenberg to cancel his fitting for a false hand. By a pact of honor between the Italian and German resistance, as Mrs. Dohnanyi said, a coup in one country would signal parties in the other, and "the German resistance was accordingly to follow with a similar move." Yet while that move got under way, and also as an effect of Italy's demise, German troops would ring the Vatican, and Hitler would hatch a plan to kidnap the pope.[43]

CHAPTER 19

PRISONER OF THE VATICAN

"THE MOUTH OF A VOLCANO HAD OPENED," CARDINAL CELSO Constantini recalled. On 19 July 1943, he was on a train outside Rome when it stopped with a jolt. The cardinal jumped out with other passengers to find himself in a cloud of smoke, fighting to see and breathe. He stumbled over telegraph wires, a broken crib, and a dead horse as he groped his way back to the Vatican, where he learned that American bombers had killed more than a thousand people and razed treasured monuments. As Constantini lamented, "even the ruins have been ruined."[1]

When Albrecht von Kessel arrived in Rome the next day, it smelled like burning grass and heated stone. Officially, Kessel was the new First Secretary at the Reich Mission to the Holy See; secretly he was the new Josef Müller. For the next year, he would link Stauffenberg to the pope. As shouts of "Down with the Duce!" rose beneath Kessel's hotel window, he thought that the American attack would not only doom Fascism, but undermine Nazism. He was right about these effects, but wrong about their cause. The plot that soon removed Mussolini had in fact been hatched through Vatican channels years before.[2]

"It went something like this," Müller said. "Marshal [Pietro] Badoglio had been Chief of the Italian General Staff and had vigorously opposed Italy's [November 1940] attack on Greece. He was a decided opponent of Mussolini and Hitler." Through a contact in the Vatican Congregation for the Propagation of the Faith, Müller learned that Mussolini circulated a petition to Italian officers, calling for Badoglio's court-martial. Mussolini's maneuver spurred Badoglio to explore contacts with the German resistance. As Müller related, "I was allowed to hope—I must express myself carefully—that we could deal with Badoglio." The marshal declared himself ready to overthrow Mussolini, so long as the king and the pope backed him. Müller brokered a "connecting" agreement between the Italian and German plotters: if one side should pull off a coup, the other would follow in train.[3]

For nearly two years, Badoglio stalled. He waited for the Germans to move first. Finally, the American invasion of North Africa, in November 1942, forced his hand. With the Allies now less than a hundred miles' sail from Sicily, Mussolini's position became insecure. On 24 November, Badoglio sent the Princess of Piedmont to discuss regime change with the pope's deputy Montini. At almost the same time, Canaris met Müller in Munich's Hotel Regina and, after their surreal dinner with Kaltenbrunner, the admiral told Müller "to try to see eye to eye with Badoglio." A month later, on 21 December, Badoglio secretly sent his nephew to meet Cardinal Secretary of State Maglione, seeking the pope's blessing for a treasonous approach to Victor Emmanuel the Third, the Italian king. Through these intrigues, Allied diplomats began to talk peace terms with Badoglio. As Müller remembered:

> At the end of 1942, I received the news, not from Leiber, but from a party from the Vatican sphere, that a renowned Italian personage had extended a peace feeler, a suggestion or a query regarding the terms of a peace, a peace that would be a separate peace with Italy. . . . The answer [to the query]—I believe, it came from Washington, not from London—was: 1. [Italian cession of] the North African Italian colonies. 2. Pantelleria [an Italian island near Tunisia] to England. 3. An offer regarding [Italian evacuation of] Albania. . . . 4. was exciting for us in a certain sense. The wording ran something like this: The [Italian] Tyrol was to become part of a new southern German

state. That had concerned not only us [in the Canaris circle] but, as I had informed Leiber, also him. . . . He had hit his head with his hand, because the partition of Germany [by the Allies] broke sharply with all our [earlier] discussions with England. I had asked Leiber to try to find out from his contacts how the idea was viewed in America, whether they essentially disagreed with it there, or whether they thought the same as England.

The prospect of German dismemberment alarmed coup planners in Berlin. Working through Father Leiber, Müller was still trying to "come up with a definitive reading" of Allied terms when he was arrested in April 1943.[4]

A month later Pius had the threads of the Badoglio plot in his own hands. While Roosevelt publicly advised Italy to leave the Axis, his personal representative to the Holy Father, Myron Taylor, took a parallel secret action with Pius. "You will recall your constant touch over the Vatican Radio from Washington with His Holiness," Taylor later reminded Roosevelt. "The first preparation for the extinction of Mussolini was the day that I brought to you the secret message, in response to one of my own regarding Mussolini's fall and the retirement of Italy from the war, which you characterized 'as the first break in the whole Axis organization' and which came to me through that [papal] channel."[5]

Vatican preparations for Mussolini's "extinction" began on 12 May. Maglione summoned the Italian ambassador to the Holy See, Count Ciano, and handed him a verbal note. The Pope suffered *for* Italy and *with* Italy, Maglione said, and would "do everything possible" to help the country. The pope thus meant to let Mussolini know his mind, while avoiding direct intervention. But as the Vatican's expert on Pacelli, Father Gumpel, later said with a chuckle: "Of course, this is a *discreet* way of saying: Can we be of any assistance as a mediator?" Reading that subtext, Ciano said abruptly, "Well, the Duce won't go for that at all." Mussolini vowed to fight on, but Pius had opened a channel for further talks.[6]

On 20 May, Pius wrote Roosevelt, asking him not to bomb Italian cities. Although he did not say so outright, he saw both Allied and Axis bombing as terrorism; it killed women and children, in London as in Berlin, for political rather than military reasons. The pope's letter revealed his deeper game, however, when he asked Roosevelt to have mercy on Italy in future peace talks—indicating that the Vatican expected the Allies to win the war. Pius had discreetly positioned himself between two opposed parties, to whom he asked the same question: "How can I help?"[7]

Though Pius worked with FDR to remove Mussolini, the Vatican claimed that he had not been an active plotter. "One has to be very careful when speaking about involvement or direct influence," Father Gumpel would later say. "Because it is not the place of the Vatican to meddle so much in the affairs of foreign states. . . . Their way is very discreet. . . . They are more diplomatic, and they act more prudently, to avoid exposing themselves to severe accusations." The 1929 Lateran Treaty banned the Vatican from intervening in foreign politics, and how would Hitler react if Italy, through papal intrigue, quit the war? "The Holy Father is of the opinion that something must be done," his deputy Tardini recorded after receiving a ciphered American message on regime change. "He cannot refuse intervention, but must be *segretissimamente* [secret]."[8]

On 11 June, Pius received some important political intelligence. From an informant he learned that Victor Emmanuel had secretly received two non-Fascist former Italian statesmen. That even the king, a notorious idler, realized he must act, suggested the status quo would soon erode. Six days later, the apostolic nuncio to Italy called on the king and told him the Americans would give no quarter unless Rome stood down first. Pius had intelligence from the highest level, from Roosevelt himself, about what would happen. The king remained unsure what to do.[9]

A month later, on 10 July, the Allies invaded Sicily. Three German divisions fled to the Italian mainland, posing the immediate possibility that Allied troops might follow them. That prospect unnerved not only the Italian people, but also the pope. Neither he nor his aides Maglione, Montini, and Tardini wanted Italy in the war to begin with; and now they worked harder to get Italy out of it. The pope arranged to be informed of Fascist Grand Council proceedings against Mussolini. On 18 July, Cardinal Constantini wrote in his diary, "Italy is on the edge of the abyss."[10]

When Rome was bombed the next day, the die was already cast. Italy had lost the war, and its leaders crossed the secret bridge that Pius built to peace. Six days later, the king had Mussolini arrested, and named Marshall Badoglio to rule in his stead. Pius made no public statement, but an American diplomat thought he seemed "not at all unhappy." He spent the next month as the secret host of talks between Badoglio and the Allies, which led to an armistice on 8 September. In response, Hitler decided to place Italy under German protection and invade Rome.[11]

Marshall Badoglio and Victor Emmanuel fled the next day at dawn. On the morning of the tenth, an Italian officer warned Monsignor Montini that a division of German paratroopers was moving up the Via Aurelia toward the Vatican. They marched in ruler-straight formations with ringing boots and took up positions by St. Peter's Square. Behind them lurked SS men in a limousine, as one witness remembered, with "their jackboots gleaming, and the skull-and-crossbones insignia leering hideously from their lapels."[12]

The Holy See now bordered Hitler's Reich. A white line marked the frontier between the arms of Bernini's colonnades. On one side stood German soldiers in black boots and steel helmets, with carbines on their shoulders and Lugers on their hips. On the other side were the Pope's Swiss Guards, in ruffled tunics and plumed hats, holding medieval pikes in white gloves.

At 10 p.m. on the eleventh, the Vatican received a report that the Germans would put the pope under their "protection." The tip came from Albrecht von Kessel, who said that Hitler blamed Pius for the fall of Italy, because "the Pope had long talked by phone with Roosevelt." Father Leiber began to hide the pope's files under the marble floors of the Apostolic Palace. Key staffers in the Secretariat of State were ordered to keep their suitcases packed, so that they could go with Pius if SS commandos seized him and took him to Munich.[13]

HITLER HAD VOWED TO INVADE THE VATICAN TWO HOURS AFTER HE heard of Mussolini's fall. Just after midnight on 26 July, Ribbentrop's liaison officer Walther Hewel asked how they should handle the Holy See in any plans to restore Fascist Rome.

HEWEL: Shouldn't we say that the exits of the Vatican will be occupied?

HITLER: That doesn't make any difference. I'll go right into the Vatican. Do you think the Vatican embarrasses me? We'll take that over right away. For one thing, the entire diplomatic corps are in there. It's all the same to me. That rabble is in there. We'll get that bunch of swine out of there . . . Later we can make apologies. That doesn't make any difference. . . .

HEWEL: We will find documents in there.

HITLER: There, yes, we'll get documents. The treason will come to light.[14]

By the next night's conference, however, Hitler's advisors appeared to have talked him out of the move. "All of us, including the Führer, now agree that the Vatican is to be exempted from the measures we are contemplating," Goebbels recorded in his diary, after a "debate that lasted until far after midnight."

The Führer intends to deliver a great coup. In this manner: A parachute division now stationed in southern France is to land all around Rome. This parachute division is to occupy Rome, arrest the King with his entire family, as well as Badoglio and his entire family, and fly them to Germany. . . . According to the reports reaching us the Vatican is developing feverish diplomatic activity. Undoubtedly it is standing behind the revolt [against Mussolini] with its great world-embracing facilities. The Führer first intended, when arresting the responsible men in Rome, to seize the Vatican also, but Ribbentrop and I opposed the plan most emphatically. I don't believe it necessary to break into the Vatican, and, on the other hand, I would regard such a measure as exceptionally unfortunate because of the effect our measures would have on world opinion.[15]

Another witness, however, claimed that Hitler had reactivated the plan. The SS commander in Italy, Karl Wolff, said that the Führer had summoned him in September to give him a job of "world-historical importance." He wanted a study made of how troops could occupy the Vatican, secure the archives, and remove the pope, together with the Curia, so that they could not fall into Allied hands. Hitler would then decide whether to bring these Catholic dignitaries to Germany or intern them in neutral Liechtenstein. He thought taking the Vatican would prove difficult, and asked Wolff how quickly he could prepare the operation.[16]

Wolff reportedly said he could not commit to a date, and tried to discourage the plan. The war had stretched his SS forces in Italy to the very limits, and, further, the pope might resist; they might have to kill him. Nevertheless, Hitler said, he placed great personal importance on the operation. He ordered Wolff to study the problem and make a report.[17]

"WHAT WILL HAPPEN IN GERMANY? HITLER'S TIME WILL NOT BE far off," Cardinal Constantini reflected on the day that top Nazis debated Pius's abduction. Mussolini's fall climaxed the setbacks that had begun with the surrender at Stalingrad, and continued with the loss of Tunisia. By midsummer 1943, the Axis faced defeat both in the south and the east. This was the psychological moment for a revolution.

The Nazis knew it. "Knowledge of these events might conceivably encourage some subversive elements in Germany to think they could put over the same thing here that Badoglio and his henchmen accomplished in Rome," Goebbels noted after his marathon meetings in late July. "The Führer ordered Himmler to see to it that the most severe police measures be applied in case such a danger seemed imminent here."

Canaris turned those orders into his final master stroke. Hitler feared an uprising of foreign workers in Germany. On 31 July, the Wehrmacht therefore approved Canaris's counterinsurgency plan, code-named Valkyrie. It provided the perfect cover for Stauffenberg's coup: the designated preventers of the revolution would be the ones preparing it.

As summer turned to fall, Stauffenberg reinvigorated planning for the ghost government. Father Delp wrote new plans for decentralizing power to local vocational groups, and became Stauffenberg's liaison to underground Catholic labor leaders in Cologne. Moltke met Delp and other Munich Jesuits in St. Michael's cathedral in Munich to draw a new map of postwar Germany for Allied approval. Moltke's cousin

Peter Yorck briefed Stauffenberg on the Jesuits' political planning; and Yorck briefed the Jesuits, in turn, about Stauffenberg's contacts with the generals.

Müller and Dohnanyi pressed for action in notes smuggled from their jail cells. Dohnanyi underscored the plotters' "moral duty" to Badoglio's government. Müller impatiently awaited his return to the Vatican, to coordinate peace talks with the Allies. In the meantime, a Franciscan seminarian, Gereon Goldmann, would carry messages from Canaris to Albrecht von Kessel in Rome.

Himmler was watching, even if Roeder's treason probe had stalled. A Gestapo probe later found that Stauffenberg "positioned clergy for the purpose of their use as connection to church circles [and] the Vatican." The SS underscored that "to the pope especially, the planners sent trusted agents, the most adroit diplomats, to facilitate the closest connections." Yet though Hitler's secret police would identify Stauffenberg's emissaries in other cities, in Rome they could detect only "an unnamed person to negotiate with the pope."

Actually, Stauffenberg had two cutouts with Pius in Rome. The first was Kessel; the second was Abwehr agent Paul Franken. Ostensibly as a history teacher for the German-language school on the Via Nomentana, Franken had dealings with the Vatican and had established discreet contacts with British and US diplomats. To cover his military-intelligence activities, Franken received a stipend from the German Research Association in Rome to edit papal nunciature reports. In reality, the Catholic Franken took over Müller's Vatican contacts.[18]

Like Müller, Franken kept a low profile. He avoided the haunts where German agents working against the Vatican might be found: the Reich embassy, the Gestapo offices, and the German ecclesiastical college. Instead, Franken took rooms in a clinic run by German nuns, the Grey Sisters. Twice a week Kaas visited the clinic for treatment of a stomach disorder, and before leaving, he would pay a friendly call on Franken. On Sunday mornings, Franken would take coffee at Kaas's Vatican apartment, often with Father Leiber.[19]

In these meetings, Franken briefed the Vatican on plans to remove Hitler. By autumn 1943, Leiber knew of Stauffenberg's plans. An American intelligence officer who debriefed him in 1944 reported Leiber's knowledge of a plot "c. September-October, 1943. Of this third plot, Father Leiber received a[n] . . . outline from a colonel responsible for cultural affairs in Rome. The attempt was to have taken place by October 15 at the latest, but was to be dependent on a previous stabilization of the Russian front. The absence of such a stabilization evidently resulted in the abandonment of the conspiracy."[20]

Franken laid out the plotters' thinking for the Vatican. If General Olbricht's Home Army could block Hitler's communications center, then only a full-fledged SS counterassault could stop them. To prevent that, the plotters must disarm the SS with lightning speed. Regional military commanders would arrest local party leaders. To ensure secrecy, only one or two men would know every element of the Valkyrie plan. Generals not in the know at X-hour would check with headquarters in Berlin—where Stauffenberg would take their calls. Stauffenberg would free Josef Müller and send him to Rome to ask the pope to call for a worldwide armistice after Hitler's death. The pope should know that this time they would do it.[21]

Relaying these plans to Rome gave Franken pause. His fears crested in an October 1943 meeting, in which Father Leiber made written notes for briefing the pope. Franken warned that Leiber's notes might send them all to the gallows. The next day Leiber reassured him that Pius, after reading the notes in Leiber's presence, had held the papers to a candle on his desk, saying, "You can tell him you saw the pope burn the pages with his own hand."[22]

IN EARLY DECEMBER 1943, HITLER SUMMONED SS OFFICER KARL Wolff. Three months had passed since he had asked Wolff to propose a plan to seize the pope. Hitler wanted a straight answer: Why had nothing happened?[23]

Wolff said that seizing the pope would require an extensive operation. It might create a backlash in Rome. Under German occupation, Italy had so far kept calm. The Church provided Italy's only uncontested authority; Italian women remained devoted to it. Abducting the pope could also spur unrest among French and German Catholics. It would cost Berlin dearly in international opinion.[24]

Hitler postponed the plan, at least until he could stabilize the Italian front. He ordered Wolff to remain ready to act on a moment's notice.[25]

ON 19 JANUARY 1944, CLAUS STAUFFENBERG CALLED AT THE BERLIN home of Moltke's cousin Peter Yorck, who served as a liaison to Father Rösch and the Orders Committee. The SS had just arrested Helmuth von Moltke; someone had carelessly mentioned his name. Through his work with the Committee, Moltke had met with Josef Müller and had known about the Vatican connection. Stauffenberg could only hope that Moltke held out long enough for the rest of them to act.[26]

After Moltke's arrest, Committee priests left his circle and joined Stauffenberg's cell. Through Father Rösch's Jesuits, Stauffenberg began coordinating his operations with Count Preysing, the bishop of Berlin. Stauffenberg met Preysing at least once that spring, at Hermsdorf, reportedly for more than an hour.[27]

They discussed the necessity for a regime change, and at least alluded to the moral case for an assassination. Some later suggested that the meeting played an important part in Stauffenberg's decision to kill Hitler. More likely, they discussed Preysing's role as a papal delegate after the coup, when Josef Müller would seek an armistice through the pope. Perhaps to that end, Father Leiber wrote Preysing in April to discuss the need for better communication by "confidential means."[28]

By all accounts, Preysing sanctioned the plot. Apparently, he said he could not absolve Stauffenberg in advance for what he meant to do. Yet as he later wrote to Stauffenberg's mother, he had not withheld his "personal blessing as a priest."[29]

ON 3 MARCH 1944, MÜLLER STOOD TRIAL AT THE SUPREME COURT in Berlin. He wore his gray three-piece suit and his green tie. The proceedings became a showdown between the military and the SS.[30]

The chief military judge, Dr. Sack, presided. Lieutenant General Biron headed the high-ranking generals on the Senate of Judges. SS Inspector Sonderegger represented the SS. Counselor Roeder led the prosecution.[31]

Roeder alleged that Müller abused his authority as a military spy to conspire, through his Church friends, with the enemy. Müller thereby committed high treason and must die.[32]

Judge Biron said that before they hanged a man with such a good military record, on whose behalf even the chief of Hitler's bodyguard had testified, the court must have solid proof.[33]

Roeder stood on the testimony of witnesses, particularly the Benedictine Brother Hermann Keller. He warned the court that "the highest leadership circles would monitor" the court's proceedings.[34]

Biron retorted that his court would retain its independence. It would not rubber-stamp decisions made "elsewhere." Biron asked Müller what he had to say in his own defense.[35]

Müller said the accusations rehashed hearsay from discredited figures with personal grudges against him. An inquiry investigated and rejected their charges years ago. How, otherwise, could Müller have continued to occupy a most sensitive and confidential intelligence post? He had acted on the orders of his superiors, in the interest of his country, as his bosses had testified. The prosecution had produced no proof to the contrary. If the court recognized this much, then it must set him free.[36]

The panel found Müller innocent. The SS, however, announced its intention to arrest him on new charges. To keep Müller out of Gestapo custody, the Wehrmacht re-arrested Müller and returned him to the Lehrterstrasse prison.[37]

Claus von Stauffenberg sat alone in the gallery as an army observer. He walked down toward Müller as the bailiffs placed him in handcuffs. Seeing the maimed officer, the court guards made way. It took a moment for Müller to recognize Stauffenberg with his eye patch. They shared a knowing glance.[38]

IN LATE MAY 1944 COLUMNS OF SMOKE ROSE FROM THE ALBAN HILLS of Rome. From the top of the Vatican Gardens, Pius and his deputies could see Allied patrols. But Vatican intelligence gave Pius no inkling whether the Germans would defend the city or withdraw. Fearing that Roman civilians and Vatican clergy could die in the crossfire, Pius warned in a 2 June address that "whosoever raises his hand against Rome will be guilty of matricide before the civilized world and the eternal judgment of God." Near midnight, Tiger tanks rumbled past St. Peter's in a long column, headed north. With the Allies approaching, the Germans had started to leave.[39]

As dawn broke the next day, American and German forces still dueled south of Rome. "I remember vividly that in the late afternoon of June 3, we could see that a tank battle was in progress near Lanuvio in the plains below the Alban Hills," recalled American chargé d'affaires Harold Tittmann. From vantage points along the walls of the Vatican Gardens, he saw "a great cloud of smoke and dust [hanging] over the battlefield. . . . A tank would lumber out of the cloud into the open, followed by another, both firing at each other at a great rate. After a few minutes, tanks would return to the mêlée inside the cloud. One could hear at all times the continual roar of the guns." Vatican residents did not sleep well on the night of 3 June, as Tittmann's son wrote in a diary, because of the ruckus made by the retreating troops. "Then began the dive bombing. Dozens of our planes came over and started bombing the Germans just outside of Rome, near enough for us to see the bombs falling out of the planes. We could also see the little spurts of flame on their wings as they began machine gunning the road. It was rather sickening to see tired German boys walking past us and then watch them dive-bombed and strafed."[40]

Late on the night of 4 June, the first Allied patrols entered the city. They slipped like shadows up the pitch-dark streets, cautiously, guns ready. The need for caution soon passed. Morning's light revealed Romans massing in the streets, cheering madly. American tank treads passed over roads pink with rose petals, thrown by the women who swarmed over the jeeps and trucks.[41]

"I found myself having to hold tight to my emotions," the conquering general, Mark Clark, wrote later of his entry into Rome. "The Piazza di Venezia was jammed with a monstrous crowd, and our jeep proceeded at a snail's pace, while flowers rained upon our heads, men grabbed and kissed our hands. . . . I felt wonderfully good, generous, and important. I was a representative of strength, decency, and success." Clark and his men soon lost their way, and, "as generals are last among men to ask directions," they ended up in St. Peter's Square. A priest had to point them to the Capitoline Hill.[42]

Perhaps no one in Rome seemed more unburdened that day than the pope. So certain did he feel that he no longer had anything to fear that he strenuously protested Allied violation of the Vatican grounds. At 10:00 a.m. on 5 June, when he came to his study window to bless the faithful, he saw an American tank parked near one of the Bernini colonnades. After two decades of fascism, the right to vent his unhappiness made Pius happy.[43]

Later that Sunday it seemed that all Rome came to St. Peter's Square. To the peal of church bells, 300,000 people packed the square by five o'clock. "The afternoon's sun slanted across the roof of the Basilica," an American nun recorded in her diary, "spilling torrents of golden light on the sea of color below."[44]

The windows on the balcony opened. Everything stopped and everyone hushed. Pius in his white gown walked out on the parapet alone. The crowd roared. Romans waved and held their children up and cried "Viva Papa!"[45]

Pius then gave one of the shortest and plainest speeches of his reign. He thanked Saints Peter and Paul for protecting the city. Calling on Romans to put aside all thirst for vengeance, he cried, "*Sursum corda!*"— Lift up your hearts![46]

After he left the balcony, throngs hailed him as the "savior of Rome." Hard-boiled American radio reporter Eric Sevareid could not keep his eyes from misting. Although he disclaimed any feelings of awe toward the Vatican, which he regarded as "inclined to fascism," Sevareid found himself moved by the pope's ability to express the grief and hope of the whole human family.[47]

In the next days, Pius gave mass audiences to Allied soldiers. An American officer mentioned a number of Jewish soldiers in his group, so Pius gave a blessing in Hebrew. The gesture was so well received that in future audiences Pius inquired for soldiers of Jewish faith to bless them.[48]

During the German occupation, the SS had arrested 1,007 Roman Jews and sent them to Auschwitz. Fifteen survived. Pius said nothing publicly about the deportations. Over the same period, 477 Jews had hidden in Vatican City, and 4,238 received sanctuary in Roman monasteries and convents.[49]

CHAPTER 20

IT MUST HAPPEN

As the Allies took Rome, Hitler's fears fixed on France. He doubted that an invasion loomed, but the waiting annoyed him. In April, the Abwehr had obtained a proof copy of Eisenhower's still secret proclamation to the French people, announcing the landing of Allied troops. Yet reconnaissance of southeastern England showed few landing craft facing the Dunkirk coast, where Field Marshall Erwin Rommel thought the Allies would strike. Luftwaffe meteorologists forecast several days of bad weather. The field marshal of the Fifteenth Army, charged with guarding the English Channel, was on a hunting party. Rommel returned to Berlin to celebrate his wife's birthday. As Hitler went to bed, after midnight on 5/6 June, he did not suspect that five thousand enemy ships had already sailed for Normandy.[1]

News of parachute and glider landings in Normandy spread that night. Troops on Rommel's West Wall heard ships' engines offshore. No one dared to awaken the Führer; the first reports in war often proved wrong. The situation would not clear up, Hitler's adjutants told themselves, until daybreak.[2]

By then the Allies had won a beachhead. It took the invaders only twelve bloody hours to secure a strip of Europe two miles deep and fifteen miles wide. Allied air supremacy kept German reserves from moving by daylight. When Hitler's noon conference began on 6 June, he had already lost France.[3]

THAT AFTERNOON, FATHER DELP TRAVELED BY TRAIN FROM MUnich to Bamberg. A youth pastor had invited him to address a Catholic youth group. Five months of caution since Moltke's arrest had left Delp restless; he relished the chance to speak. Yet he had more urgent and secret reasons to visit Bamberg. While Delp reviewed his notes on the northbound express, a lay co-conspirator, Bavarian monarchist Franz Sperr, had already begun the advance work.[4]

At 3:00 p.m., Sperr called at one of Bamberg's best homes. Claus von Stauffenberg showed Sperr in. The colonel had taken a few days' leave from Berlin, as he did not know when he might see his family again. He gave Sperr a bleak picture of the war. The lack of manpower reserves put Germany in straits. By Sperr's account, Stauffenberg said: "Peace requires an internal political change—the elimination of the Führer." Sperr had left Stauffenberg's long before 9:00 p.m., when Father Delp finished a lecture at the Kleberstrasse rectory.[5]

The youth pastor, Jupp Schneider, then led Delp into an office. He introduced Delp to a longtime coworker, Toni Müller. Schneider described her as a trusted person who would lead Delp to a certain address.[6]

Müller rode a bicycle, weaving slowly as Delp followed on foot. After 2.1 kilometers, she dropped a handkerchief in front of a home on the Schützenstrasse. Delp knocked on the door. Stauffenberg's wife, Nina, opened it. Her husband seemed to be expecting Delp and received him graciously. Some later accounts portrayed Stauffenberg as furious that the Jesuit had come to his home, since visits by the plotters endangered his family. Yet Sperr's visit that day had prompted no such concerns. Delp and Stauffenberg spoke for two hours, until half-past eleven, when Delp caught the last train back to Munich.[7]

The available evidence gives clues to the contents of their talk. Later, in an intentionally misleading account, Delp wrote that they spoke "in general terms about the state of Germany, the concerns of the bishops, and the relationship between the Church and the government." This version, written for Gestapo investigators, omitted Delp's talk to the Bamberg underground, and the dropped-handkerchief spycraft that led him to Stauffenberg's home. Delp instead claimed that he made a "chance" visit to the north—impelled to travel two hours by train because he felt "personally curious" to learn about the Normandy invasion. Why he expected Stauffenberg to receive him he did not say. During that visit, Delp went on, he decided to ask Stauffenberg whether the Jesuits, excluded from military service, could become members of Organization Todt, the construction corps that built the Führer's bunkers.[8]

From Sperr the Gestapo would get a version that seemed more credible. Delp knew that Stauffenberg planned an assassination, Sperr attested, because Stauffenberg told Delp his plan. Canvassing what Sperr called "questions of resistance," Stauffenberg and Delp discussed how Catholic bishops could help the military plotters. Delp shared "everything he knew about bishops and church organizations in certain cities," Sperr said. Delp further reviewed the political ideas he had developed with Moltke, building on papal social encyclicals. Stauffenberg agreed with Moltke's program, at least as the Jesuit framed it. Workers in post-Hitler Germany would share in decisions about wages and hours, and retain strong welfare protections. Yet Delp, like Stauffenberg, also upheld aristocratic principles. Where Delp rejected Nazi "leveling" and urged rule by a "creative élite," Stauffenberg had written a conspirator's oath that declared: "We scorn the lie of equality and we bow before the hierarchies established by nature."[9]

Stauffenberg would likely have told Delp little about *how* Hitler would die. Yet to help the plot, the bishops had to know not only *that* the coup would happen, but *when*. In fact, after Delp met Stauffenberg, the Munich Jesuits knew the planned and revised coup dates. Delp himself apparently encouraged the project; he told a friend, business professor Georg Smolka, that he had stressed to Stauffenberg "the desire of many for action as soon as possible."[10]

Before returning to Munich, Delp had stopped in Jupp Schneider's rectory. Schneider recalled an excited Delp saying: "I believe that today

I have done more for my fatherland and all of you than in my whole previous life. Pray that everything goes well."[11]

The next day, Delp spoke even more suggestively. In the rectory of the Church of the Precious Blood in Bogenhausen, he talked "twice in half a night directly about the rights to resistance," his friend Hans Hutter recalled. "Father Delp was convinced that Christians must have a right to resist for reasons of conscience, if various conditions were met. In particular, there had to be a guarantee that the ones who wielded this right to resistance were in a position to break the power of the dictator and to take over the government. During our conversations, and I still recall this very exactly, he emphasized that a resistance was absolutely necessary politically in order to prove to the world that forces were still alive in Germany which could overcome a dictatorship from within." In the context of those remarks, Hutter attached a specific meaning to Delp's parting words—"It must happen"—and to what Delp inscribed in a gift copy of his book *Man and History*: "Whoever doesn't have the courage to make history becomes its poor subject. Let's do it."[12]

IN EARLY JULY, DIETRICH BONHOEFFER'S UNCLE VISITED JOSEF Müller in jail. Paul von Hase, military commandant of Berlin, had joined the plotters. In the event of a coup, Hase said, he would seal off the government buildings. The Home Army would supply the troops. It would happen soon.[13]

A few days later, Stauffenberg's circle passed Müller a message. It came through the Lehrterstrasse prison commandant, Major Maas, who had likewise joined the plot. In the event of an overthrow, Maas would release Müller. Stauffenberg would have a plane fueled and waiting to fly Müller to Rome. There Müller would partner with Pius to initiate peace talks with the Allies. To speed matters, as in the March 1943 plot, Pius had again granted a formal *agrément* stating his willingness to receive a proposed envoy before the actual coup. Müller's "friends in Rome" had preappointed him special emissary of the new government to the Holy See, with the title and status of ambassador-in-waiting.

Where some had seen the Vatican as the first foreign power to recognize Hitler's rule, now the Vatican would be the first foreign power to legitimize its downfall.[14]

ON THE NIGHT OF 19 JULY, STAUFFENBERG ENTERED A CHURCH IN Berlin. He dipped his good hand in holy water and made the Sign of the Cross. Werner von Haeften sat in a rear pew while Stauffenberg moved through the candlelit nave to a confessional. By some accounts, he knelt at the grille of secrecy and asked for Saint Leo's Absolution, granted to Catholics in danger of imminent death. After a few minutes, he emerged from the church and stepped into a waiting car.[15]

Getting out at home, he told his driver to return at 6:30 the next morning. Then, safely inside, Stauffenberg drew the bedroom curtains and packed his briefcase with two 975-gram lumps of plastic explosive.[16]

CHAPTER 21

HOLY GERMANY

Stauffenberg was at Rangsdorf airfield in Berlin by 7:00 a.m. on 20 July. On the tarmac, he met Haeften, who carried a briefcase identical to his own. They boarded an idling Heinkel 111 and then traded cases. Fog delayed their takeoff. Stauffenberg told the pilot that they had to leave by 8:00 so that he could be in Rastenburg by noon to brief the Führer on matters of the greatest import.[1]

Hitler awoke at 9:00 and shaved with shaky hands around his moustache. In the sitting room beyond, his personal servant, Linge, set a tray on the coffee table. Hitler shuffled over and, as Linge recalled, suspiciously eyed some cream puffs. He asked Linge to have them tested for poison. Linge said that Rattenhuber's people had tested them. Hitler wanted them tested again. As Linge left with the tray, Hitler phoned his adjutant, Nicholas von Below, and asked him to change the location of that day's war briefing. They would meet in the barracks map room, not in the usual concrete bunker.[2]

At 10:30 a.m., the Heinkel touched down in East Prussia. Stauffenberg and Haeften stepped off the plane, got into a staff car, and rode through the dark pines. As trusted staffers of the High Command, they passed routinely through two checkpoints, their briefcases unsearched. They pulled up to the General Staff bunker, where some plump officers breakfasted at a picnic table under a tree. Inside the bunker, Stauffenberg and Haeften found an anteroom and shut the door. A fan blew hot air around. Stauffenberg hung up his cap and jacket, removed his belt, and mussed his hair. Then he reported to Field Marshal Wilhelm Keitel. The field marshal looked up from his desk and commented that the colonel seemed a bit casual for a Führer conference. Stauffenberg said he would clean up before the briefing; he just wanted to keep his uniform from getting sweaty, since the bunker always became so hot during briefings. Keitel advised him that Hitler had moved the briefing to the wood barracks.[3]

By 12:15, Stauffenberg had returned to the anteroom to "clean up." He allowed extra time to set the explosive fuse. The delicate task required him to crush a glass capsule containing acid. He used tongs custom-fitted to his artificial hand. The change of venue meant they should prime two explosive lumps: wooden barracks would not trap the blast force like a concrete bunker. But Stauffenberg had just finished priming the first lump when someone knocked at the door. "Stauffenberg, come along!" an escort officer called from the hallway. They would have to use just one charge.[4]

At 12:30, Stauffenberg followed the escort officer into the briefing barracks. Keitel and the plump officers stood round a table as Stauffenberg came in. Someone droned on about the eastern front. Hitler, toying with a magnifying glass, looked up. "Colonel Claus Schenk von Stauffenberg," the escort officer announced. "Home Army chief of staff, Hero of the Campaign in Tunisia." Hitler shook the fake hand and gave Stauffenberg a piercing look. The plump officers made room for the crippled hero. Stauffenberg positioned himself at Hitler's right. He set down his briefcase and shoved it under the table with his leg. The droning resumed. Hitler leaned over to examine a map position. Stauffenberg eased casually away, close to Keitel, and mumbled that he had to make a phone call. Keitel nodded, but tapped his watch, as if to say: Hurry![5]

In the hallway, Stauffenberg cradled a phone. The escort officer watched him briefly and then returned to the map room. Stauffenberg hung up, hurried down the corridor, and met Haeften on the lawn outside. They had walked about fifty yards from the barracks and were nearing the picnic table when they heard an explosion.[6]

Bluish-yellow flames burst from the barracks. Bodies went hurtling out of the windows. Shards of glass, wood, and fiberboard rained down. Officers and orderlies scurried amid groans and shouts for medics. Someone carried out a still body on a stretcher, covered by Hitler's summer cape.[7]

Stauffenberg and Haeften jumped into their car. As they rode toward the airfield, Haeften threw the unused explosive lump into the woods. At the first checkpoint, the guards let them pass; at the second, someone had sounded the alarm. A lowered gate blocked the car and the sentry fingered his gun strap. Stauffenberg stepped out, phoned a guard captain he knew, and handed the phone to the sentry. Moments later, the gate rose.[8]

When they reached the airfield, the pilot had the engines warm. At 1:15 p.m., the Heinkel took off and banked west, for Berlin.[9]

OUTSIDE THE BARRACKS, CHARRED BODIES LAY ON STRETCHERS IN the grass. Hitler's physician Theo Morrell moved down the line, doing triage. Dead, dead, mortally wounded, dead. He came to one prone form and stopped. The trousers hung in ribbons down the burned legs. Dust and wood fiber coated the skin. The singed hair stood up like cactus spikes. But the victim had sustained no traumatic wounds, lost no blood. In the face masked by soot, blue eyes blazed with life. A gentle rain began to fall. Morrell gathered droplets in his handkerchief and wiped around the world's most famous moustache.[10]

AT 4:30 P.M., STAUFFENBERG CLIMBED THE GRAND STAIRS AT HOME Army headquarters. In a second-floor office on Bendlerstrasse, he met Major Ludwig von Leonrod and the retired General Beck. They all loosened the safety catches on their Lugers, then burst into the adjoining office of the Home Army commander, Friedrich Fromm. The Führer was dead, Stauffenberg announced. He knew because a bomb went off and he was there. They must activate Plan Valkyrie to maintain order.[11]

Fromm refused. Without official word, he said, they must assume the attempt failed. According to the later testimony of Fromm and other witnesses, there followed an exchange along these lines:

STAUFFENBERG: Nobody in that room can be alive.
FROMM: How can you know that?
STAUFFENBERG: Because I planted the bomb.
FROMM: You!
STAUFFENBERG: You generals talked but would not act. The time for tea parties and debates is over.
BECK: I agree.
FROMM: This is treason! [*Landesverrat*].
STAUFFENBERG: No sir. It is *high* treason [*Hochverrat*].
FROMM: I declare all of you under arrest.
STAUFFENBERG: It is we who are arresting you.[12]

They scuffled. Haeften shoved a pistol into Fromm. The general submitted and Major Leonrod led him off. Stauffenberg picked up a phone and got the communications center. At 4:45 p.m., according to his orders, Home Army headquarters cabled a top secret message to field commanders throughout the Reich: "The Führer Adolf Hitler is dead."[13]

FROM HIS LEHRTERSTRASSE CELL, JOSEF MÜLLER HEARD THE BOOTS on the streets. General Hase's guard battalion, Grossdeutschland, had begun maneuvers.[14]

Late that afternoon, prison commandant Maas came to see Müller. "Hitler is dead," he announced. "He's been assassinated." At last, Müller recalled thinking. An Abwehr plane stood ready at Rangsdorf, he knew. By dawn, if the coup succeeded, he would find himself back in the Vatican.[15]

Jesuit Father Lothar König spent the night of 20 July in Munich-Pullach. In the Berchmanskolleg, he huddled around a radio with Home Army officers loyal to Stauffenberg, who had requisitioned the Jesuit school as an alternate command post. At 6:38 p.m., the radio music stopped and an announcer broke in. "There has been an assassination attempt on the life of the Führer, but he was not seriously injured. I repeat, he was not seriously injured. No details are available at present." The bulletin repeated every fifteen minutes until nine o'clock, when the announcer promised that the Führer himself would soon speak.[16]

Rain streaked the windows of the tea bunker in Führer headquarters. Hitler sat in his favorite chair dressed in a formal suit, bandaged, his arm in a sling, happy. Dr. Morrell, kneeling, took his pulse. Secretaries sobbed all around. To Morrell's amazement, Hitler's pulse remained normal.[17]

"I am immortal!" Morell recalled Hitler as saying. "I am the child of Fate. If I hadn't moved the briefing, I'd be dead. You see, the wood frame let the explosion escape. This is the greatest luck I've ever known! Now I have those bastards. Now I can take steps!" He got to his feet in a burst of anger. "Exterminate them! Yes, exterminate them!"[18]

A phone rang. Himmler wished to extend congratulations and sympathies. Then came more rings, from generals trying to verify rumors of the Führer's death. Hitler's mood changed. He approved a radio announcement that he had survived an attempt on his life, but refused to take more calls. He lapsed into brooding silence, listening to the rain drum on the windows.[19]

By 10:00 p.m., Stauffenberg had worked the phones for five hours. From the Bendlerstrasse he called commanders all across the Continent, trying to catalyze the coup. But by nightfall, reports had spread that Hitler had survived. Often these reports reached commanders at the same time as Stauffenberg's orders from Berlin. The generals did not wish to activate Valkyrie until they knew for sure that Hitler had died. They stalled. When Stauffenberg's co-plotters questioned the wisdom of fighting on, he pointed down to his desktop, to a photograph of his children. "I'm doing this for them," he said. "They must know that there was a Decent Germany."[20]

The situation had already escaped the plotters' control. In another part of the building, a group of loyalist officers, armed with submachine guns and grenades, freed General Fromm and led him to his office. Fromm convened a three-general court-martial, which instantly condemned the plotters to death. An arrest party converged on Stauffenberg's command post. He clamped his pistol to his side and cocked it with the three fingers of his left hand. Someone let off a shot. Stauffenberg staggered, hit in the left shoulder blade. He retreated into the anteroom of Fromm's office. Haeften burned papers. Beck stared suicidally at his own gun. Stauffenberg took off his eye patch and rubbed the empty socket. With an indescribably sad expression he said, "They've all left me in the lurch."[21]

The arrest force poked its weapons through the doorway. Stauffenberg and Haeften threw down their guns. In a few clipped sentences, Stauffenberg assumed full responsibility for the coup. All the others, he said, had merely followed his orders. Fromm, unmoved, gloated: "I am now going to do to you all what you should have done to me this afternoon."[22]

At thirteen minutes past midnight, guards marched Stauffenberg outside. In a courtyard, they stood him before a sand pile. Officers' drivers lit the yard with their cars' high beams. Reich armaments minister Albert Speer, sitting in his own car nearby, recalled: "In totally blacked-out Berlin . . . [the courtyard] seemed a movie backdrop lit inside a dark studio. . . . The long, sharp shadows made for an unreal and ghostly scene." A ten-man guard battalion raised its rifles. Stauffenberg pressed to his lips the gold cross he always wore about his neck. He cried out, "Long Live Holy Germany."[23]

CHAPTER 22

THE TROVE

R ADIO BERLIN BROADCAST HITLER'S RASPY VOICE AT I:00 A.M. on 21 July. "My German comrades," he said,

If I speak to you today it is first in order that you should hear my voice and should know that I am unhurt and well, and secondly, that you should know of a crime unparalleled in German history. A very small clique of ambitious, irresponsible and, at the same time, senseless and stupid officers have concocted a plot to eliminate me and, with me, the staff of the High Command of the Wehrmacht. The bomb, planted by Colonel Count Stauffenberg, exploded two meters to the right of me. It seriously wounded a number of my true and loyal collaborators, one of whom has died. I myself was entirely unhurt, aside from some very minor scratches, bruises and burns. I regard this as a confirmation of the task imposed upon me by Providence. The circle of these usurpers is very small and has nothing in common with the spirit of the German Wehrmacht and, above all, none with the German people. It is a gang of criminal elements, which will be destroyed without mercy. Every German, whoever he may be, has quite the same duty to ruthlessly confront these elements, and either arrest them immediately or—if they should somehow resist arrest—to wipe them out without further thought. The command has gone out to all our troops. You are to carry out [this command] blindly, in accordance with the obedience to which the German army is accustomed.[1]

WHEN FATHER KÖNIG HEARD HITLER'S SPEECH, A WITNESS SAID, HE went pale. König knew that Father Delp had met with Stauffenberg a few weeks before. Both priests knew the Catholic colonel's plans. König asked a fellow Jesuit, Father Franz von Tattenbach, to warn Delp to hide.[2]

Tattenbach bicycled in the dark to the rectory in Bogenhausen. He leaned his bike against a tree and threw pebbles at Delp's window. Delp appeared at the window in a track suit. Tattenbach climbed up a ladder and briefed him. Father Delp said spontaneously: "Damn it all."[3]

To avoid the appearance of guilt, he would remain at St. George's and say Mass. If Delp needed to escape, he assured Tattenbach, he could use a secret door in the rectory wall. It opened into Herzog Park, where Delp could meet contacts. They would smuggle him to a farmer's house.[4]

SS GUARDS STRUTTED THROUGH THE LEHRTERSTRASSE PRISON. ALL through the predawn hours of 21 July, they hooted and taunted the prisoners, shouting that the Führer lived. An imprisoned private, whose cell flanked Müller's, blurted out that he wished Hitler had died. An SS guard heard and dragged him out of the cell, screaming that the private would pay for his words.[5]

Müller and other jailed plotters wondered what had gone wrong. They knew that communications between the plotters in East Prussia and Berlin had failed. No one knew why. But when Stauffenberg reached Berlin, still believing he had killed Hitler, almost four critical hours had passed. When the conspirators finally got their troops moving, some Nazi leaders had recovered and alerted loyal commanders. The coup collapsed before it began.

Handcuffed generals streamed into the Lehrterstrasse. Trading glances with the monocled General Stieff, Müller held up his own shackles in solidarity, as if to say that they must stand together, to the last consequence.[6]

FATHER DELP'S FELLOW PRIESTS URGED HIM TO RUN FOR IT. BY LATE July, SS detectives had probed the perimeters of the Jesuit's secret circle. But Delp said he didn't want to leave his parishioners during "these difficult times of night air raids." He also didn't want to jeopardize his final profession of vows, scheduled for mid-August. But Delp's deepest concern probably remained averting the suspicion that would fall on him or others if he fled, as he had told Father Tattenbach the night the coup failed. So he remained at St. George's, visibly tense. Father Braun, who visited Delp and Rösch "immediately after" 20 July, remembered: "Something like a foreboding anticipation weighed on us all. No one knew how great or how close the danger was. But we didn't speak of it. Only several times, when we clearly weren't being watched, did he [Delp] wink at me. His look summarized everything: The question: what's going to happen?" On 26 July Delp's friend Georg Smolka urged him to hide in a Bavarian farmhouse. The priest, smiling, pulled open a drawer and revealed a revolver, "for defense." Berlin contacts would warn him in code, through trusted cutouts, if danger loomed.[7]

On 28 July the warning came. Dr. Ernst Kessler, head of the legal department at the Bavarian Motor Works, received a telex for Delp from "our friends in the resistance in Berlin." The prearranged danger message stated, as Kessler recalled, that "the secret discussion between Father Delp and his Social Democratic friends had been cancelled for security reasons." Kessler got into his car and sped to the early Mass at St. George's to deliver the message.[8]

When Kessler arrived, the service had already begun. Delp read the day's gospel: "You will be betrayed even by parents and brothers, by relatives and friends; and they will put some of you to death."[9]

Kessler left the church and entered the sacristy through the side door. In the most urgent terms, he asked the Vincentian nun assisting at the Mass to give Delp a slip of paper at the altar. As Delp said the Suscipe Pater prayer, the sacristy door opened a crack and then softly closed. The sacristan could not bear to interrupt the Offertory, as Delp held up the paten and bread, saying: "Receive, O Lord, all my liberty. Take my memory, my understanding, and my entire will." Kessler later posited that a "guardian angel . . . impressed by this sacred action," caused the sacristan to retreat, likely sparing Kessler and the nun the noose. For though no one yet knew it, two plainclothes Gestapo agents had already entered the church.[10]

After Mass, the sacristan handed Kessler's note to Delp in the sacristy. Delp read the note and then swallowed it. He left the church by the sacristy door, went into the garden, and lit the stub of a cigar. The sun slanted through oak leaves and lit up the smoke. Delp decided to carry on normally. Two men in hats and trench coats approached him.[11]

In front of the church, parish regulars cleared bomb rubble. "It was a steel-blue, cheerful day, and everything seemed so unreal, that is if one would have even been able to comprehend it," parish secretary Luise Oestreicher remembered. Delp emerged from the rectory with the two men, wearing an overcoat in the summer heat. His complexion had turned gray and he looked ill. "I'm under arrest," he said in a low, strained voice. "God be with you. Goodbye."[12]

On 24 July, a military jeep pulled into St. Peter's Square. Raymond G. Rocca, an X-2 (counterintelligence) officer with the US Office of Strategic Services (OSS), entered the offices of the Vatican secretariat of state. He had an appointment with an American Jesuit, Father Vincent McCormick. Rocca had won McCormick's cooperation by sharing with him a dossier on Gestapo penetration of the Gregorian, the Jesuit university where McCormick served as rector. McCormick led Rocca down a back passage, through the basilica, and down some stairs into the crypt. There Rocca met Monsignor Kaas, who seemed preoccupied with excavations. Rocca knew that the bespectacled German émigré had once chaired the Catholic Center Party, and that he still advised Pius on German affairs.[13]

Rocca explained his business. Briefly, X-2 wanted to confirm the bona fides of some interned Germans who represented themselves as anti-Nazis. Rocca sought especially to verify claims by Albrecht von

Kessel, deputy Reich ambassador to the Holy See, that the entire embassy had been in on the plot against Hitler. If deported to Germany, they would be "as good as dead as soon as they re-entered the territory of the Reich."[14]

Kaas backed Kessel—and then said something that floored Rocca. The monsignor knew about two earlier coup plots. Rocca could not grasp how a senior churchman could have mixed in such dangerous matters. When Rocca tried to learn more, Kaas referred him to another German émigré—Father Leiber.[15]

In OSS offices on the Via Sicilia, Rocca traded cables with X-2/London. Needing anti-Nazis to rebuild Germany after her defeat, Rocca's bosses asked him to pursue the leads from Kaas. But when Rocca tried to see Father Leiber, intermediaries told him to wait. Father McCormick suggested that someone at a higher level, perhaps even the pope personally, had to approve the interface. In the meantime, Rocca cabled the OSS Research and Analysis Division in Washington for background traces on the Catholic resistance.[16]

The trace netted some surprising reports. To Rocca the most surprising came from German émigré Willy Brandt, who later became chancellor of West Germany. Though staunchly Protestant and socialist, Brandt wrote flatly: "The Catholic Church is the most widespread and best organized opposition in Germany." Because clerics interacted with all levels of society, they could maintain contacts, even in military circles, without arousing Gestapo suspicion. The Church resisted most fiercely in Catholic Bavaria, where the Munich Jesuits oversaw "a well-built organizational apparatus." The outlawed Catholic Center Party's trade unions had also "for years been engaged in underground activities."[17]

But because the Catholic resistance worked in great secrecy, the OSS knew little about specific operations and still less about coordination and control. "The German Church opposition has some representatives abroad," Brandt observed, "but they work very cautiously." Father Leiber's reluctance to meet with OSS agents seemed to underscore that caution. Rocca therefore felt honored and grateful when on 18 August Leiber agreed to see him.[18]

Leiber admitted to links with the plotters. They had "almost invariably kept him informed of their activities," Rocca recorded. The Jesuit detailed three plots predating 20 July. Among the conspirators, Leiber named General Franz Halder, the former Wehrmacht chief of staff, known to OSS as "a strong figure in Catholic circles." Leiber implied, but did not state outright, that he had shared his knowledge of the conspiracies with the pope.[19]

Rocca suspected that Leiber knew far more than he would tell. How, Rocca wondered, had Leiber kept abreast of the plots? Did the Vatican have a special courier or intermediary with the German resistance? If so, could OSS get to him? Most fundamentally: Why should the plotters have gone to such extreme lengths to keep the pope's closest aide informed of their designs?[20]

In August the German government launched Operation Thunderstorm, a broad attack on suspected traitors. The Wehrmacht ejected the surviving coup leaders, so that instead of receiving courts-martial, they stood before Judge Roland Freisler in the People's Court. Hitler's wrath also fell on the Church conspirators.[21]

The SS tortured Delp, and issued warrants for König and Rösch. König hid in a coal bin at Pullach. Rösch hid in a grain silo in rural Bavaria, and then on the farm of a family whose Jesuit son had died on the eastern front.

Himmler's hunt for Committee priests broadened to the Dominicans. On the night of 16/17 September, Provincial Laurentius Siemer was awakened about 1 a.m. by a phone call from the gatekeeper of the Schwichteler convent. Two men wanted to talk to him. Siemer replied that they should come back in the morning and went back to sleep. As the two men then tried to climb through the window, the gatekeeper again awakened Siemer, who now realized that the visitors were Gestapo. He consulted Dominican Father Otmar Decker, and they conceived a diversion. While Siemer left the convent by the garden gate, Decker approached the secret policemen and they pounced on him, as expected. Decker led them to the Provincial's room on the second floor, so that Siemer gained time and reached the forest. Siemer sneaked into the village of Schwichteler and hid at first in a woodshed, and later in a pigsty.

The Gestapo tried to get to Siemer through his aide, Father Odilo Braun. On 7 October a female Gestapo agent, Dagmar Imgart, better known as "Babbs" or "Babsy," appeared on the doorstep of Braun's Berlin office. A few days earlier, she had asked him to intercede for a jailed pacifist Catholic priest, Max Josef Metzger. Braun found the request suspicious, because the Nazis had beheaded Metzger six months before. On the other side of the street stood a man observing everything. Braun told his secretary to stall the woman at the door. He then rushed upstairs, went out a gable hatch, and escaped to the adjoining Dominican cloister by jumping across the rooftops.[22]

ON 22 SEPTEMBER, THE SS SEARCHED AN ABWEHR ANNEX AT ZOSsen. They drilled into a safe and found evidence of the Vatican's role in the plots. The trove included a note on papal stationery, describing British conditions for an armistice with Germany—listing the sine qua non as "elimination of Hitler."[23]

Four days later, the guards withdrew from the hall by Müller's cell. Commandant Maas approached Müller for a private talk. The SS had uncovered incriminating material at Zossen, Maas whispered. They would not stop until they tore Müller to pieces. But one of the guards, Milkau, could lead Müller out to a proletarian section of the city. Former members of the Social Democratic Party would hide Müller there. The SS might think to hunt for him in a Bavarian monastery, but not in a Red sector of Berlin.[24]

Müller thanked Maas but declined the offer. It would put his wife behind bars and his friends under suspicion. Maas nodded, as if he had expected that answer. He said he would leave his own Luger on Müller's bed. But Müller again protested. As a devout Catholic, he deemed suicide a mortal sin.[25]

ON THE MORNING OF 27 SEPTEMBER, HITLER REFUSED TO GET OUT of bed. He spurned food and showed no interest in the war. His alarmed adjutants had never seen him so listless. "It seemed to me," recalled his secretary, Traudl Junge, "that he had just laid down and said, 'I will not do anything anymore.'"[26]

For six days, Hitler stayed in bed, sometimes crying out in agony. Dr. Morrell examined him and concluded that nothing physical caused his pain. The Führer just seemed depressed.[27]

Morrell asked the inner circle what might have shattered Hitler's spirits. They let him in on a secret. The Gestapo had recently discovered the assassination plotters' secret archives in a safe at Zossen. Since learning about the contents of the files on 26 September, Hitler had changed. Whatever the documents contained (no one told Morrell), Hitler had barred from the People's Court. He himself would decide the outcome of the affair.[28]

While Hitler brooded in bed, Allied armies neared the Rhine. His senior staff needed to rejuvenate him. Morrell summoned Dr. Erwin Giesing, an ear, nose, and throat specialist, to examine Hitler.[29]

Giesing saw a broken man lying on his bed in a nightgown. Hitler raised his head in greeting and then dropped back to the pillow. His eyes looked empty and he complained of pressure in his head. He spoke of "the continuous nervous strain of the last month." After all, at some time the twentieth of July was bound to affect him. "Up to now I'd had the will to keep all this inside me—but now it's broken out."[30]

Giesing removed a glass vial from his case. The vial contained a 10 percent cocaine solution, which Giesing had administered to Hitler since August. Giesing swabbed a cotton dipper into the vial and then brushed around the edges of Hitler's nose. The Führer soon felt better. He got out of bed, paced the room, and launched into a monologue. He'd read the last letters the hanged plotters sent their wives. General Stieff wrote that he had converted to Catholicism. With a hearty laugh Hitler said he was "happy to give the pope this devil's black soul but only once he'd been hanged."[31]

After half an hour of euphoric ranting, Hitler's words began to fade. His eyes fluttered. He took Giesing's hands, pressed them tightly, and requested more of "that cocaine stuff." Giesing grasped Hitler's pulse and found it rapid but weak. The Führer had fallen back onto the bed, unconscious. Giesing let him sleep. He packed his kit and returned to

Berlin, leaving Morrell to wonder what so upset Hitler in the Zossen documents. Only after the war would survivors of the inner circle learn what the files showed. Since the war's first month, according to an SS final summary of the Zossen papers, Hitler's prospective killers "had maintained connections with the pope."[32]

CHAPTER 23

HELL

O N 26 SEPTEMBER, THE GESTAPO CAME FOR JOSEF MÜLLER. Warned by Maas, he had prepared. He had set all his affairs in order, as far as possible. He kept a few possessions with him—Maria's letters, a snapshot of Christa in her school uniform. As he packed his things, he saw Sergeant Milkau's anxious face outside the door. Müller looked for a long moment into the faithful guard's eyes, trying to convey his thanks. Milkau had already promised that whatever happened, he would get word to Müller's daughter and wife.[1]

The drive through Berlin revealed more ruin than Müller had imagined. Some streets evoked the photographs of contested Stalingrad. The houses in the West End, once the center of the city's intellectual and social life, were burned out and stared menacingly with empty windows. Water stood in bomb craters, with bubbles of gas rising from shattered pipes, as the car circled the Kaiserhof Hotel and entered the gate of SS headquarters at 8 Prinz-Albrecht Strasse.[2]

Inside, two SS men put machine-pistols at Müller's back. They herded him down the steps to a small room and told him to strip. When he asked why, one of them punched him in the face. At the touch of their searching hands, Müller focused on the door beyond. Perhaps they wanted to make sure he had not concealed a vial of poison in his anus.

They ordered him to dress and took him to the basement lined with the infamous former sculptors' studios. At Cell 7, they removed the cuffs and pushed him in.[3]

A bare ceiling bulb lit the windowless room. It contained a stool, a folding bed, and a tiny table. If not for his shackled wrists, Müller could have stood in the middle and touched each wall.[4]

An air-raid siren wailed. Doors flew open, and voices ordered him out. In the gloom, Müller saw Canaris and Oster.[5]

On 27 September, Müller met Oster in the toilets. They could not talk there because a guard paced in front of them. But they managed to whisper in the cold showers, their words covered by the spray. Müller asked about Zossen. Yes, Oster said, someone led the SS straight there. The Gestapo had the whole trove and would just try to wring out whatever they could, especially names, before killing them. They must string the SS along—false leads—anything to drag it out until the Allies reached Berlin.[6]

Heading back to Cell 7, Müller heard screams. When he thought they had ended, the screams grew louder again. They continued for a long time, each more terrible than the last, then changed into whimpers and moans.[7]

In the hall he passed Canaris. The admiral, always slight, now looked emaciated. His eyes glowed like embers in an ash pit. He whispered: "Herr Doktor, this place is Hell."[8]

In late November 1944, an SS man led Müller to an elevator. Far up the shaft the cables rattled. At the third floor, they got off and walked down a long hall to an anteroom, where a guard with a machine gun stood by the door. From the double doors, a guard's voice summoned him. In an adjoining room, Müller found himself standing before Franz Xavier Sonderegger.[9]

Müller had played a clever game until now, Sonderegger said. But the SS had known all along that Canaris protected a traitors' nest. Now they could prove it. They knew what Müller had hatched with his friends in the Vatican—yes, even the pope. Sonderegger took a bulging folder from a drawer and laid it on a table. Müller should read this before making any more denials.[10]

He looked at the dossier. Proclamations Dohnanyi had written for Beck and Goerdeler, Oster's handwritten study for the coup d'état, Müller's Vatican reports. Yes, Müller said, feigning relief: This all seemed to be material his superiors had used to entrap the Allies and collect intelligence on their willingness to fight. Müller had played a role in that. As he had been saying for a year and a half now, he had come to the Abwehr in the first place because his Vatican contacts could supply helpful intelligence for the Wehrmacht.[11]

Sonderegger said that Müller could no longer hide behind that story. He should not thwart the SS once too often before things went to the next level. Life would no longer prove so pleasant for Müller, Sonderegger said. The SS now had custody of him, and it would take a tougher approach than the army. They had found many compromising documents in the army safe at Zossen. Müller might as well consider himself a dead man.[12]

Müller said evenly that he could accept that. Death meant "just a passage from this life to the next," Sonderegger later quoted him as saying. Sonderegger asked Müller whether he prayed. Müller said he did. Did he pray for the SS, too? Sonderegger asked. Müller said yes, he prayed for his enemies most of all.

Sonderegger fell quiet for a moment. Then, saying he would return "in three minutes," he put a sheet of paper on the table.[13]

There lay Father Leiber's note. On papal stationery, watermarked with the sign of the fisherman, Leiber had scrawled the sine qua non for ending the war. Pius guaranteed a just peace in return for the "elimination of Hitler."[14]

Müller tore the paper into pieces and shoved them in his mouth. When Sonderegger returned, Müller had choked the whole note down.[15]

"I definitely don't want to die, there's no doubt about that," Moltke wrote. "Flesh and blood rebel against it wildly." For a long time, he had felt, as had his Prussian forebears, that "one must not make a fuss about dying by execution." But back in October, the Gestapo had formally accused him of conspiring to overthrow the regime, a charge that carried the death penalty. Since then, the work on his defense had given "a mighty stimulus to my will to get round this thing."[16]

The Catholic network helped Moltke cover his tracks. Orders Committee Bishop Johannes Dietz smuggled in messages, helping him synch his story with what other suspects said. Still, Moltke faced "grave danger," as his wife gleaned.[17]

She went to Gestapo headquarters to plead for clemency. But an interview with SS General Heinrich Müller left no doubt that they wanted to kill her husband. After the First World War, Germany's internal enemies had survived and taken over, the Gestapo chief said. The party would not let that happen again.[18]

IN THE FIRST WEEK OF 1945, FATHER DELP TRIED TO DECODE HIS own fate. "This is a moment in which the whole of existence is focused at one point and with it the sum total of reality," Delp reflected on 6 January, the feast of the Epiphany. Finding himself "in the very shadow of the scaffold," he learned that the presiding judge, the red-robed Roland Freisler, hated Catholics and priests.[19]

"Things seem clearer and at the same time more profound," Delp wrote. "One sees all sorts of unexpected angles." In his New Year's stock taking, the war became both an expression and indictment of modernity. "Far more than a civilization or a rich heritage was lost when the universal order went the way of medieval and ancient civilizations." Yet few saw "the connection between the corpse-strewn battlefields, the heaps of rubble we live in, and the collapse of the spiritual cosmos of our views." Europe now faced the ultimate expression of modern nihilism, the prospect of life under Stalin's boot. Communism, however, would serve as "a donkey for an imperialism of limitless proportions. . . . The Slavs have not yet been absorbed by the west and are like a foreign body in the working of the machine. They can destroy and annihilate and carry away enormous quantities of booty, but they cannot yet lead or build up."[20]

Could the Church then rebuild Europe after the war? "So far as concrete and visible influence goes, the attitude of the Vatican is not what it was," Delp regretfully wrote. He worried that the papacy had lost its moment, despite going through the moral motions.

> Of course it will be shown eventually that the pope did his duty and more, that he offered peace, that he explored all possibilities to bring about peace negotiations, that he proclaimed the spiritual conditions on which a just peace could be based, that he dispensed alms and was tireless in his work on behalf of prisoners of war, displaced persons, tracing missing relatives and so on—all this we know and posterity will have documentary evidence in plenty to show the full extent of the papal effort. But to a large extent, all this good work . . . leads nowhere and has no real hope of achieving anything. That is the real root of the trouble—among all the protagonists in the tragic drama of the modern world there is not one who fundamentally cares in the least what the Church says or does. We overrated the Church's political machine and let it run on long after its essential driving power had ceased to function. It makes absolutely no difference so far [as] the beneficial influence of the Church is concerned whether a state maintains diplomatic relations with the Vatican or not. The only thing that really matters is the inherent power of the Church as a religious force in the countries concerned. This is where the mistake started; religion died, from various diseases, and humanity died with it.[21]

ON 9 JANUARY DELP AND MOLTKE STOOD TRIAL IN A COMMANdeered kindergarten. Watching "average" Germans pack the room in their Sunday suits reminded Delp of "a prize giving in a small school that hadn't even the proper room for it."[22]

Judge Freisler entered wearing a red robe. Since 20 July, he had courted Hitler's favor by modeling the People's Court on Stalin's show trials. "Leaning far back in his chair, with a majestic gesture of his right arm he swore to the world . . . that National Socialism and its

Reich would remain eternal—or would go down fighting to the last man, woman, and child," recalled Protestant pastor Eugen Gerstenmaier, who stood trial with Moltke and Delp. When Freisler worked himself up, the blood rose to his face and blushed his bald head; he shrieked so loudly that a sound engineer warned him he would blow out the microphones.[23]

Delp stood trial first. "You miserable wretch, you sanctimonious little sausage," Freisler began. "You rat—one should flush out and step on someone like you." Freisler went on to abuse the Church more generally: "Scandals, bishops who are said to have had children, etc.; the Latin language, Jesuits' corrupt dealings, etc.—this kind of thing came up in every other sentence." Finally, Freisler demanded to know why Delp had become "one of Helmuth Graf von Moltke's most active traitorous assistants. . . . Come on, answer!"[24]

The Jesuit said, "As long as people must live in inhuman and undignified conditions, we must work to change those conditions." Freisler asked: "Do you mean that the state has to be changed?" Delp said, "Yes, that's what I mean."[25]

Decrying those words as "high treason," Freisler proceeded to the charges. He cited the priest's dealings with Stauffenberg, this "subsequently treacherous assassin." Delp had, furthermore, arranged for the coup plotters to meet on Church properties, acting "with the authorization of the Jesuit Provincial of Southern Germany, Father Rösch." Even Delp's absence from resistance meetings at his rectory, Freisler turned against him. In a "typically Jesuitical" way, Delp had "temporarily disappeared like a [cathouse] madam, so that he could then wash his hands of the matter," Freisler charged. "By that very absence you show that you yourself knew exactly that high treason was afoot and that you would have liked to keep your tonsured little head out of it. Meanwhile you may have gone to church to pray that the conspiracy should succeed in a way pleasing to God."[26]

The trial continued the next day, with Moltke in the dock. Accusing him of "consorting with Jesuits and with bishops," Freisler banged on the table and roared:

A Jesuit Father! Of all people, a Jesuit Father! And not a single National Socialist [at the Kreisau meetings]! Not one! Well, all I can say is: now the fig leaf is off! A Jesuit Provincial, one of the highest officials of Germany's most dangerous enemies, he visits Count Moltke in Kreisau! And you're not ashamed of it! No German would touch a Jesuit with a bargepole! These people who are excluded from military service because of their attitude! If I know there is a Jesuit Provincial in a town, it is almost a reason for me not to go to that town! . . . And you visit bishops! What is your business with a bishop, with any bishop?

Freisler capped his tirade with what Moltke considered a profound truth: "Only in one respect are we and Christianity alike: we demand the whole man!"[27]

ON 11 JANUARY, FATHER RÖSCH SAID MASS AT A FARMHOUSE. HE had just finished when the door burst open and three SS officers strode in. Untersturmführer Heinz Steffens put a pistol to Rösch and placed him under arrest. Steffens "immediately began to pump me for names, and accused me of about fourteen allegations in under two minutes," Rösch recalled. "I explained that as a Catholic priest, naming names was out of the question for me on principle. So he hit me with all his strength."[28]

Around 5:00 p.m. Steffens loaded Rösch into the open bed of a truck. With the Catholic family that sheltered him, Rösch rode in a snowfall to Dachau. The Munich police registry tersely reported the "arrest of the Jesuit Provincial August Rösch . . . for his participation in the events of 20 July 1944." The camp barber shaved off Father Rösch's hair, and Steffens bound his hands, saying, "We will never let you out of these shackles until we have hanged you."[29]

AT FOUR O'CLOCK THAT AFTERNOON, FREISLER SENTENCED MOLTKE and Delp to death. Delp showed no emotion as he heard the verdict, but in the police van afterward, his composure broke. He fell into a frenzy of laughter, sputtering one-liners between manic gasps. The others sat subdued and still. To Gerstenmaier, whom Freisler had spared but branded a "blockhead," Delp said, "Better a blockhead than no head at all."[30]

The condemned were locked up and left alone, as if nothing had happened. During these lonely hours, Delp scrawled on scraps of newspaper and toilet tissue a final testament. "To be quite honest I don't want to die, particularly now that I feel I could do more important work and deliver a new message about values I have only just discovered and understood," he reflected. "I am internally free and far more genuine than I realized before. . . . When I compare my icy calm during the court proceedings with the fear I felt, for instance, during the bombing of Munich, I realize how much I have changed."[31]

The January cold seeped through Delp's barred window. Days passed and tedium returned: bound hands, harsh lights, the indecipherable noises. He wondered why his tormentors didn't hang him right away and free up the cell for a fresh victim. Had Hitler decided to save him for some Neronian circus of persecution? If so, with Russian troops nearing Berlin, perhaps the Reich would collapse before these festival killings could occur. Thus Delp dared, once more, to hope.[32]

"Things always turn out differently from what one thinks and expects," he wrote on 14 January. "I'm sitting on my cliff, focused totally on God and his freedom. . . . Waiting for the thrust that will send me over. . . . I believe that a lot depends on August [Rösch] not losing his nerve and remaining silent."[33]

CHAPTER 24

THE GALLOWS

O N 13 JANUARY, THE GESTAPO TRANSFERRED FATHER RÖSCH from Munich to Berlin. The Jesuit Provincial now found himself in the same Lehrterstrasse prison where Josef Müller had spent the first year and a half of his internment. The guards confiscated his breviary, rosary, and military medals. For the next six weeks he was bound day and night and during most of the interrogations. His cell remained lit all night, except during air raids. Countless red crosses adorned the walls, drawn with the blood of smashed bedbugs.[1]

Denied mail privileges, Rösch availed himself of the secret Catholic prison post, run by two lay laundresses, both named Marianne. In clandestine letters, he coordinated his story with Fathers Delp and Braun, listing some of the "tactical lies" he told his interrogators. Rösch said, for instance, that he knew "nothing at all about an assassination planned for 20 July." But since the SS clearly knew about his contacts with Moltke, Rösch admitted conferring with him about plans for a reconstruction, "in case the war had an inauspicious ending." Asked "where he stood" with respect to National Socialism, he said he took the same view toward Nazism that Nazism took toward the Church: "I reject it 100 percent." Would he say that to Judge Freisler? "Absolutely, as often as bells ring." The guards didn't beat him after that, concluding that they lacked leverage over a priest who, by his own account, had prayed for the "honor of a bloody martyrdom" every day since his First Communion.[2]

Rösch took up what he termed his "catacomb pastoral duties." In one case, a Jew and a Jehovah's Witness staged a power failure, allowing him to perform last rites in the cells of the sick. But in the main, Rösch found his chance during exercise hour. "Sometimes, if we were led on a walk around the yard, Father Rösch would overtake us in our ranks with hasty steps, and speak to his parishioners in a whisper, asking who wanted to receive the Sacrament," recalled Dietrich Bonhoeffer's protégé Eberhard Bethge. "Then, he asked us to arrange for clandestine written confession. And in the mornings, if he said his Mass unobserved, we carried the consecrated wafer to the designated cells. His community grew."[3]

THE SS INTERROGATORS PLANNED THEIR INTERROGATION OF FAther Rösch carefully. At 6:00 p.m. on 1 February, their questions fell like darts around the pope's role in the plots. The Jesuit later wrote down the line of inquiry from memory. "We still have to deal with the following complex issues with you: Your relationship with the pope and the Vatican; with the curia of your order; with Fr. Leiber." Rösch felt "secretly pleased at this." So long as the SS still sought answers to those questions, they might keep Father Delp alive. They had not given any reason for delaying Delp's execution; perhaps they wanted to interrogate the two Jesuits together and confront them with contradictions in their stories.[4]

Father Braun managed to speak with Rösch during a walk in the prison yard. "Father, they hate the Catholics here," Rösch recalled the Dominican saying. "But against you Jesuits there prevails an excruciating hate, a gruesome hate." The guards told Rösch more than once: "We can't wait to hang you alongside König and Siemer—that will be a beautiful day." Rösch thought Father Siemer's escape, which embarrassed the Nazis and removed a key suspect and witness, "had a lot to do with the [show] trial being postponed."[5]

On 2 February Gestapo guards led Delp into the interrogation room at Plötzensee. Beneath his orange-and-gray striped pajamas, stamped with the number 1442, he seemed just a rack of bones. The prison had scheduled his death for noon.[6] SS officer Karl Neuhaus would supervise the Jesuit's final hours. A Plötzensee colleague recalled Neuhaus, a former Protestant theologian, as "a gaunt man with a face like a bird of prey." It fell to Neuhaus to interrogate Catholic clergymen suspected of conspiring to kill Adolf Hitler on 20 July 1944.[7]

"I wanted to know what Father Delp had to say about the attempted assassination," Neuhaus said later, "and how he reconciled this violence with his convictions as a Catholic priest and Jesuit Father. I knew that he had some contacts with Stauffenberg. A witness had incriminated Father Delp. All of that was known and was already in the files when I interrogated him." Yet Neuhaus did not know—and his SS superiors had ordered him to learn—just how closely Delp and his Catholic confederates had conspired with the pope. Having already grilled Father Rösch about his Vatican links, Neuhaus now subjected Delp to the same line of inquiry.[8]

He placed Delp's fingers in a clamp lined with spikes. While Neuhaus shouted questions, his assistant, SS Hauptsturmführer Rolf Günther, turned a screw, driving the spikes into Delp's fingertips. When that procedure produced no answers, Günther began to beat Delp from behind with an oak club larded with nail heads. With each blow, Delp fell forward on his face, but he refused to speak. Günther then enclosed Delp's legs in tubes lined with steel needles and slowly drew the tubes tighter, so that the spikes gradually pierced the flesh. At the same time, to muffle the screams, he pushed the priest's head into a metal hood and covered it with a blanket. When the screams penetrated even the hood, Günther put on a phonograph record of children's songs and turned up the volume as high as it would go.[9]

Five hours later, when Father Delp had still not implicated the pope, Neuhaus helped him across the courtyard to the death hut. Sunlight slashed through two arched windows. Six meat hooks hung from a ceiling girder. Atop a tripod sat a 16-mm sound camera, crowned with lamps and loaded with color film. On a table stood a bottle of cognac, two glasses, and a coil of piano wire.[10]

The executioner and his assistant fortified themselves with cognac. The assistant, Johann Reichart, worked the wire into a noose. The executioner, Hans Hoffmann, looped it around Delp's neck and drew it tight. They lifted the priest onto a hook and let him fall. The wire noose did not break his neck, but merely sliced into his windpipe. They left him there, twitching and twisting, for twenty-five minutes. Later, scrawled on a prison laundry form, an orderly found Father Delp's last known words: "Thank you."[11]

DELP'S DEATH SHOOK FATHER RÖSCH, LAY WORKER MARIANNE Hapig recalled. For the next months, the Jesuit provincial cut a "miserable figure." Having recruited Delp into the plots, Rösch blamed himself for Delp's death. As a Jesuit Provincial, charged with protecting and guiding his young priests, Rösch found the guilt hard to bear.[12]

In this demoralized state, Rösch endured more Gestapo questioning. A dark pressure suffuses one secret letter he wrote during these days, relating the line he had taken with his interrogators. "Those in question can come to grave harm. A whole complex of questions is yet to come about the role of the Papal Curia. . . . The hatred against us is very great."[13]

Cagey as ever, Rösch bent the situation to his benefit. His frail health gave him the chance to work in the prison office, where he found his own file card. It recorded an order to kill him without trial. "So, it was possible for him, in conspiracy with some of the guards, to save himself and many others besides, by manipulation of the files," a fellow priest recalled. A sympathetic prison official had Rösch "transferred to the list of those who had already been executed."[14]

ON 3 FEBRUARY BERLIN ENDURED ITS WORST AIR RAID OF THE WAR. Josef Müller jostled with other prisoners in the basement on Prinz

Albrecht Strasse. He looked at the ceiling, worried it would collapse. Water spouted from broken pipes, the lights went out, and soon Müller felt the February cold.[15]

Three days later, guards told him to pack up. In the rubbled courtyard, prisoners massed by transport trucks. With the Gestapo prison ruined, they were going to a concentration camp. No one expected to return. SS officer Walter Huppenkothen ordered Müller and Bonhoeffer kept handcuffed. As the truck rattled out of Berlin, they promised each other: let us go calmly to the gallows, as Christians.[16]

MARIA MÜLLER TRIED TO BRING HER HUSBAND A BIRTHDAY PACKage. She went to 8 Prinz Albrecht Strasse, but could hardly breathe because of the ash and smoke. People stumbled around like sleepwalkers. In the air hung the sickly sweet smell of bodies under wet stone. At Gestapo headquarters, the grand entry steps led up to empty space. The secret police had set up an alternate headquarters, in the crypt of the ruined Dreifaltigkeit Church on the Mausterstrasse. There Maria learned that the prisoners had been taken south to a concentration camp, ostensibly to protect them from air raids. Gestapo officials claimed not to know which camp. Maria went to see Franz Sonderegger. He said Müller had gone to Buchenwald, Dachau, or Flossenbürg. She wrote and telephoned all three. Clerks checked the prisoner lists, or at least went through the motions. They could find no record of Josef Müller.[17]

MÜLLER'S MAKESHIFT CALENDAR READ 26 MARCH. HE KNEW THAT since he would turn forty-seven the next day, his wife might try to visit him. He hoped not. He did not want Maria near Buchenwald, did not want her dirtied by it.[18]

Buchenwald overflowed with the dead and the living dead. The SS had run out of crematorium coke and had begun dumping bodies into a pit. Others lay in the streets where they had died. Blood had congealed in the coarse black scabs where starving prisoners had torn out the guts of the corpses for food. Müller was locked in a basement, which stank from its makeshift toilet, a vase sprinkled with lime.[19]

In that basement, Müller made a friend. Vassili Kokorin, a nephew of Soviet foreign minister V. M. Molotov, had tried to escape from Sachsenhausen by crawling through a tunnel, along with Stalin's son, but SS German shepherds had tracked them down. Kokorin began teaching Müller Russian, and Müller taught Kokorin Christianity. Since the Soviets had raised Kokorin to regard religion as a tool of capitalism, Müller "tried to make it clear to him that Christ had always taken the side of the oppressed; true Christianity had always tried to help the weaker social classes." On 13 February, they found themselves debating the Gospels as the sky darkened with hundreds of Allied bombers. Only later did they realize that the planes had firebombed Dresden, burning perhaps 25,000 civilians alive.[20]

During those weeks, Müller found solace in a letter from his daughter. An SS officer had handed it to him just before they left Berlin. Christa had gone to stay with relatives in Röttingen. The medieval town, surrounded by fortifications and towers, hid a ghastly secret: Röttingeners had killed twenty-one Jews in 1298. This infamous pogrom had happened on 20 April, Hitler's birthday; Röttingen's Jews had died for allegedly profaning the Communion host. Now Christa's letter announced that she would take her First Communion there. On 8 April, in a special dress her grandmother had made, Christa would walk down the aisle, kneel in the nave, and receive the body and blood of Christ. Müller carried Christa's letter with him, knowing it might remain, as he reflected, "the last sign of life of his loved ones."[21]

As Hitler made his last stand in Berlin, new army staffs sheltered in Zossen. The die-hards included infantry general Walter Buhle, who moved into the former Abwehr premises and looked around for more office space. Surveying the storage rooms on 4 April, he came across a safe containing five black, cloth-covered binders. Each held between eighty and two hundred pages, handwritten and dated. Buhle had found a chronicle of Nazi crimes and attempts to stop them, prepared by Hans Dohnanyi and other Abwehr officers, officially covered as the "diaries" of Admiral Canaris.[22]

Buhle felt no qualms about denouncing a disloyal officer. Standing near Hitler on 20 July, he had been injured when Stauffenberg's bomb exploded. Buhle gave the diaries to Hans Rattenhuber, who passed them to Ernst Kaltenbrunner, Himmler's deputy.[23]

On 4 April, the guards at Buchenwald loaded Josef Müller and fourteen other prisoners into a wood-fueled van. Vassili Kokorin wedged in next to Müller. Pastor Bonhoeffer sat in back. They chugged southward, stopping every hour to fill the firebox.[24]

Müller wormed his way back toward Bonhoeffer. Knowing the SS had "worked on" Bonhoeffer at Buchenwald, Müller wanted to know what they had asked—and, especially, what he had answered. Bonhoeffer said, defensively, that he lacked Müller's nerves. Well, Müller pressed, what had Bonhoeffer told them? "They put me under duress," Bonhoeffer said. "They threatened that something would happen to my fiancée. I said that I'd been classified *uk* [military service exempt] so that I could organize a domestic intelligence service for Oster." Müller's heart sank. That was exactly what Bonhoeffer should *not* have said, because it broke the "ten commandments," the SS-Abwehr pact banning military spying at home. The Gestapo had Bonhoeffer on a technicality—but they had him. "Dietrich, why didn't you hide behind me?" Müller asked. The Abwehr would have covered for them. "They blackmailed me," Bonhoeffer repeated. "My fiancée."[25]

As the van rattled south in the dark, Müller recalled their trip to Rome. During their dialogues in the crypt, Bonhoeffer had ventured that Catholic priests, as celibates, made better fighters against Hitler, because their deaths would disadvantage no dependents.[26]

Kaltenbrunner stayed up late that night, reading the Canaris chronicles. He found the contents so sensational that he brought the notebooks to Hitler's war conference the next day at noon.[27]

Hitler immersed himself in the revelations. Reading the SS-marked passages in the notebooks, he became convinced that his great mission—now under threat from all sides—had not failed of its own accord. Instead, traitors in his own ranks had betrayed him by intrigue, lies, and sabotage. His anger exploded in a volcanic outburst: "Destroy the plotters at once."[28]

AT DAWN THE VAN PASSED THROUGH HOF, NEAR MÜLLER'S HOME-town. He weighed an escape attempt. In the Franconian forest, he could perhaps hide with a woodsman. But the transport guards had a dog, which stood behind the prisoners with bared teeth whenever they got out to urinate. About noon they reached Neustadt, where the road forked for Flossenbürg. Knowing Flossenbürg's reputation as a death camp, Müller prayed they would not make the turn toward it. The van stopped and the guards went into what looked like a police hut. They returned and said that Flossenbürg did not have room for new arrivals. Müller thanked God as the van drove on. Suddenly, two SS officers on motorcycles pulled alongside. The van eased over to a ditch and stopped. A rough voice called out for Müller. An urgent telex from Berlin had ordered him diverted to Flossenbürg.[29]

He got out of the truck. Vassili Kokorin bounded down and ran after him. Sensing that the Nazis had marked his friend for death, Kokorin wanted to say farewell. He hugged Müller and kissed his cheeks in the Russian way.[30]

The guards herded Müller into a green van. It reeked of lime and chlorine, with an odor of corpses. They drove up an incline, past clustered houses and a chapel. The camp spread across the spine of the hill: towers, barracks, barbed wire. A ravine gashed the ridge like a moat.[31]

Müller passed through an arched gate to a dusty yard. Several gallows stood under a canopy, screening them from general view. The guards forced him onto a cobbled road and led him to a low brick building that resembled a motor lodge. In one of the cells, the guards chained Müller to the wall and locked the door. The spartan space contained just a plank bed and a stool. Only a stray clanking of chains broke the silence.[32]

One of his neighbors told him Flossenbürg's secrets. General Hans Lunding, the former Danish military intelligence chief, had been in the camp almost a year. Through a crack in his cell door, he had seen hundreds of prisoners led to their deaths in the execution yard. Lunding could also see the narrow footpath inmates used to cart the corpses to the crematorium in a valley outside the camp. He had seen seven or eight thousand borne off, two per stretcher. In winter, the bearers would sometimes slip on the frozen trail, and the corpses would fall off the stretchers and roll down the mountain. Over the last month, the rate of executions had overtaken the capacity of the crematorium, so the SS had started stacking the bodies in piles, drenching them with gasoline, and setting them on fire. Other inmates died by deliberate starvation, or, when the famished showed a stubborn will to live, the SS held their heads underwater.[33]

ON 8 APRIL, SS COLONEL WALTER HUPPENKOTHEN ARRIVED AT Flossenbürg. In what normally served as the camp's laundry, he set up a court to try the Canaris plotters. Black shades blocked the windows. Naked bulbs glared above two tables. Huppenkothen sat by Otto Thorbeck, a fat man in a judge's robe. Storm Leader Kurt Stavitzki stood behind them. The court did not provide any counsel for the defense.[34]

Huppenkothen proceeded first against Hans Oster. After mock formalities, Judge Thorbeck asked Stavitzki to read the charges—high treason and treason in the field during wartime. The prosecution confronted Oster with Admiral Canaris's diary. Did Oster admit to having participated in this plot? Oster saw no point in lying now. Yes, he said, he did it for Germany.[35]

The court dismissed him and called Canaris. The admiral insisted that he had only played along with the plotters to learn their plans. He had intended to roll up the group before it could act. Military intelligence had to insinuate itself into any plot directed against the public safety. The SS could hang him for doing his duty, but if given the chance, he would do it again.[36]

Judge Thorbeck interrupted the proceedings and recalled Oster. When Thorbeck told Oster what Canaris had pleaded in his defense, Oster indignantly protested. His signature move—hiding in plain sight, pretending to be a pretender—had finally failed him. With a desperate look he insisted that he did it all for the Fatherland. He had not committed treason. Surely, Oster must have known that the admiral only *pretended* complicity. He did it for show, he cried desperately. Didn't Oster understand that?[37]

No, Oster snapped, that's wasn't true. They should not pretend anymore. The SS would kill them in any case. They should stand up for what they did. Canaris should confess it proudly, as Oster had done. When Thorbeck asked whether Oster had falsely accused him, Canaris quietly replied, "No."[38]

STORM LEADER STAVITZKI UNLOCKED MÜLLER'S CELL. "YOU WILL be hanged right after Canaris and Oster," he taunted. As the guards let Müller out, Stavitzki called after him, "Good luck, gallows-bird!"[39]

Müller prepared for death. He sank to his knees in his striped orange and gray pajamas, whispering the Our Father. Then he motioned to one of his fellow prisoners, Russian General Pyotr Privalov, and asked him to memorize a message. Knowing that the last words of the condemned sometimes reached the outside world, he told Privalov he would shout to the hangman: "I die for peace!"[40]

Müller then spoke about his daughter's First Communion. He had fought to keep the German Church intact, so that she could live to see this day. Now she would grow up without a father. But he clung to one consoling thought. On the same day he walked to the gallows—perhaps, even at the same hour—she would walk toward the altar to receive the bread of life.[41]

DIETRICH BONHOEFFER AWAKENED TO THE BARKING OF DOGS. A KEY turned in the lock and two men stood in the doorway. It was time. The guards followed him down the hall to the guardroom, where Oster and Canaris waited. They followed orders to undress. A door opened, chill air blew in, and the guards took Canaris. The barking intensified. A shadow ran. The door closed. After a long, long time, the door opened. The guards took Oster. The door closed. After a short time, the door opened again. The guards took Bonhoeffer.[42]

Arc lights glared. To Bonhoeffer's left stood Huppenkothen, Stavitzki, and a man with a stethoscope. To the right, guards restrained dogs. The executioner bound Bonhoeffer's hands behind his back, and then beckoned to him. Bonhoeffer mounted the three steps and turned. Someone put a noose around his neck. The executioner kicked the steps aside.[43]

CHAPTER 25

A DEAD MAN

A SPADE PUSHED THROUGH A VAULT IN THE VATICAN CRYPT. THE pope's excavators had discovered a grave. Coins from medieval Christendom glinted on the floor. At one end of the vault lay some bones. Monsignor Kaas summoned Pius the Twelfth, who sat on a stool beside the cavity. Jesuit Father Engelbert Kirschbaum handed out a breastbone, then half a shoulder blade. He could not find the feet or skull.[1]

Paradoxically, the missing bones convinced Kaas that he had found what he sought. A Dark Age legend said that the Church had removed Peter's skull from its original grave, to adorn the nearby basilica of Saint John Lateran. The missing feet, too, conformed to an old tale. If the Romans had crucified Peter upside down, they would likely have hacked the body off his cross by severing the legs at the ankles.[2]

The tomb tiles dated from Vespasian's reign, a generation after Peter's death. Pius's personal physician decided that the remains had belonged to a "robust" man. Among the bones, Kirschbaum discovered traces of a distinctive purple garment, interwoven with fine threads of gold. The Vatican later announced that the relics were the remains of Saint Peter.[3]

On 12 April 1945, President Roosevelt died of a cerebral hemorrhage in Warm Springs, Georgia. The news gave Hitler a few hours of ecstasy. Goebbels telephoned, screeching with joy. "My Führer, I congratulate you! Roosevelt is dead! It is written in the stars that the second half of April will be the turning point for us. It is the turning point!"[4]

But his government had begun to flee the city. A hope of fighting from the Alps formed in his mind. He ordered his staff to study the possibility of moving munitions factories to the Tyrol, along with the special prisoners he was saving for postwar show trials. Despite the Black Chapel hangings, General Halder and other suspected plotters still remained alive; they must go south, first to Dachau and then into the Alps. Before the Allies found the camps, the SS should have all other political prisoners "done away with."[5]

The chief American spycatcher in Rome, James Jesus Angleton, sent an agent into the Vatican on the day Roosevelt died. James S. Plaut, formerly of the Fogg Museum at Harvard, served in the Office of Strategic Services as director of the Orion Project, trying to recover art looted by the Nazis. At Angleton's request, Plaut visited Albrecht von Kessel, still nominally the first secretary in the German embassy at the Holy See. Kessel had written a manuscript detailing his role as Stauffenberg's Vatican agent, and he gave Plaut a copy.[6]

The loss of his comrades in the 20 July coup haunted Kessel. But he saw their sacrifice as a "secret seed," from which something good might grow. "My friends loved their people," Kessel reflected. "They were committed to Western civilization and wanted to reawaken it in us and our neighbors; they bowed down before God and fought against the evil ones with a holy fury. . . . They are now at rest, who knows where, under the Mother Earth. But the seed they sowed will rise, and of their efforts and desires people will say, in the years or decades ahead: the stone which the builders rejected, has become the cornerstone."[7]

Pius entered his study just before 9 a.m. on 15 April, in keeping with his routine. He pressed a button to summon his undersecretary for extraordinary affairs. Monsignor Tardini reported that the new American president, Harry S. Truman, would extend the tenure of Myron Taylor, Roosevelt's personal representative to Pius. Taylor had hailed the pope's support for Roosevelt's crowning legacy, a postwar United Nations, which would convene for the first time in San Francisco.[8]

Pius then signed a new encyclical, *Interpreter of Universal Anguish*. "Too many tears have been shed, too much blood has been spilled," he had written. "It is hardly enough to pour out many prayers to heaven; we must use Christian morals to renew both public and private life. Change the heart and the work will be changed."[9]

THE RED ARMY UNLEASHED A MASSIVE ARTILLERY BARRAGE ON BERlin. On 16 April thousands of shells boomed down. Hitler's secretary Christa Schroeder asked him whether they should leave.

"No," he sullenly said. "Calm down—Berlin will always be German!"

Schroeder insisted that she did not fear death and regarded her own life as done. But the door was closing for the Führer to continue the war from the Alps. American forces had reached the Elbe River, just sixty miles to the west. With the Americans on one side and the Russians on the other, the western and eastern fronts would soon be separated by a subway.

"Time!" Hitler raved. "We've just got to gain time!"[10]

AT LEHRTERSTRASSE PRISON, A GUARD UNBOLTED FATHER RÖSCH'S door. The Jesuit fled into the basement bomb shelter as the Soviet barrage began. Two minutes later, an artillery round destroyed his cell. "Because of the pending conquest of Berlin, which grew ever closer, a great uneasiness naturally arose among us," Rösch remembered. As the prison came under artillery fire, the guards seemed disoriented. They tightened the prisoners' shackles, but returned their possessions, including their now worthless Reichsmarks.[11]

During the barrage, Rösch ran into Karl Ludwig Baron von Guttenberg. The Catholic Abwehr officer had introduced him to Count Moltke in 1941. "I gave him Holy Communion, which became his viaticum, on the day of his death, in a community mass, forbidden, of course, and celebrated in a hidden cellar room," Rösch recorded. "I last saw him on the night of 23 April 1945. A detachment of SS came to take him away." The guards led Guttenberg and thirty-six other inmates into the rubble of ruined buildings. About a hundred yards from the prison, the SS shot the prisoners in the backs of their heads.[12]

ON 23 APRIL, THE US ARMY ENTERED FLOSSENBÜRG. A JEWISH survivor in his early teens led the troops around.

"He showed us the path from the main buildings where the prisoners had to remove their clothes before walking down a number of steps into a small open area where they had placed the gallows," recalled Leslie A. Thompson, Protestant chaplain of the 97th Infantry Division. "Near this were buildings in which they stacked the bodies until they had time to burn them. There was a stack of many bodies here. Near this I observed a large cistern-like area. . . . Looking down, I saw that it was almost full of small bones."[13]

MÜLLER'S WIFE, MARIA, HAD STOPPED RECEIVING LETTERS. ON HER behalf, a local security official telephoned Kaltenbrunner in Berlin. "We have deleted the name of Josef Müller," the answer came back. "One may no longer mention that name. Müller is a dead man."[14]

Maria now hoped only to learn her husband's last words. His former secretary, Anni Haaser, lived near Dachau, and she visited the camp seeking news from transferees. Prisoners transferred between camps often carried news of executions, final messages or letters from the dead. From the reports of recent arrivals from Flossenbürg, Müller's Soviet friend Vassili Kokorin concluded that the SS had hanged him.[15]

In the third week of April, Kokorin heard that a new prisoner had arrived from Flossenbürg. Seeking Müller's last words, Kokorin went to the transferee's cell and tapped the grille. Someone stirred on the bunk and came over. The blue eyes that looked out through the bars belonged to Joey Ox.[16]

CHAPTER 26

THE EMERALD LAKE

Hans Rattenhuber left Hitler's bunker on Sunday, 8 April, to get some air. He unlocked three iron gates, climbed twelve spiral steps, and opened a gas-proofed steel door. It led out to the ruins of the chancellery garden. As Rattenhuber picked through smashed statues, he met Ernst Kaltenbrunner, head of the Reich Security Office. Kaltenbrunner had come up to smoke, and he had a story to tell.[1]

For nearly nine months, Kaltenbrunner had probed plots to kill Hitler. Because Rattenhuber had the job of protecting the Führer, he followed the findings with a kind of mortified rapture. In the last week, Kaltenbrunner said, the story had taken a wild turn. The finding of Canaris's diaries, at Zossen, had confirmed what Hitler long suspected: that many of the threats to his life and his power traced to "the Vatican, which Hitler . . . regarded as the greatest center of espionage in the world."[2]

The evidence had implicated Canaris and six of his colleagues. Their case file, originally opened by Heydrich, still carried the code name Black Chapel. The SS would hang them in secret. Where other conspirators had faced show trials, the Black Chapel plotters would vanish in night and fog. No one would know their punishments, crimes, or names. Hitler imposed absolute silence on the case. The true sources of the plot, Kaltenbrunner related, could not be revealed.[3]

Rattenhuber put a hand on Kaltenbrunner's elbow. "But you've crossed my friend Josef Müller off the list for me, haven't you?" Kaltenbrunner said he couldn't remember. One life less, or more, did not much matter in the "witch's sabbath" of those last days. The SS decided who died with a wave of the hand.[4]

Nazi court politics gave Rattenhuber an opening, however. He knew that Kaltenbrunner considered Himmler a cowardly crank and coveted his job as SS chief. Playing on those feelings, Rattenhuber recalled how Müller had told the Gestapo, in 1934, that he wanted to have Himmler shot. The Führer had vowed not to let Germany's internal enemies survive this war, as they had the last. But shouldn't "Joey Ox," who defied even Himmler, remain to rebuild from the ashes?[5]

When Kaltenbrunner did not demur, Rattenhuber pressed the point. Instead of killing Müller, the Nazis could use him as bait. Through Müller, they could ask Pius to seek a separate peace with the West. Reportedly, Himmler was making feelers through a Benedictine monk, Hermann Keller. Wouldn't a move through Müller stand a better chance? Especially since, as Kaltenbrunner had already told Hitler, "the pope personally" married Müller in Saint Peter's crypt?[6]

Kaltenbrunner said he would consider it. He would have his adjutant telephone Flossenbürg, to learn whether "the prisoner Müller was now, as instructed, in safety." Rattenhuber returned to the bunker and went down the spiral stairs.[7]

MÜLLER STOOD AT THE GALLOWS FOR NEARLY TWO HOURS. PLANES flew over Flossenbürg, deep-droning bombers. He heard distant detonations. Finally, one of the guards came up to him. "Something unforeseen" had happened. They sat him down in a blockhouse between the main building and the camp gate.[8]

A group of skeletal prisoners arrived. The travel warden argued with a camp officer. Müller heard someone yell, "They're not interested in names any more, just numbers!" The SS began beating a prisoner near the entrance. Stavitzki strode into the blockhouse. Seeing Müller, he started yelling, "That criminal is still walking around!"[9]

The guards led Müller back into the gallows yard. He awaited the order to mount the steps below the noose. Nothing happened. Gradually he wondered whether the SS meant only to play a game with him. Perhaps they wanted to prompt a "gallows confession." He clung to that straw and found fresh hope that he could survive, although he had no idea how.[10]

Twilight closed in. The commandant shouted that they'd have to continue "tomorrow." One of Müller's guards came over and said, "We're done for today." They took him back to his cell and shackled him to his pallet.[11]

That night Müller could not sleep. Someone yanked open his cell door and yelled, "Are you Bonhoeffer?" He hoped Dietrich was safe, that they couldn't find him in the chaos. Harsh light filled the cellblock; a strange unrest prevailed. Dogs kept barking. Toward dawn, the corridor began to bustle. Guards called cell numbers, two at a time, and the command, "Out, fast." Müller heard the familiar voice of Admiral Canaris. The hangmen called again, "Out!" Müller expected to hear his number, seven, called next. Instead, a silence fell.[12]

A guard removed Müller's leg shackles. "I don't know what's going on," the guard sighed. Berlin had branded Müller a "vile criminal," but now they didn't know what to do with him. The guard proffered a mug of broth and a piece of bread. Müller paced to circulate his blood.[13]

Around ten o'clock, white flecks drifted in through the barred window. They looked like snowflakes but smelled like fire. Abruptly the hatch in his cell door opened again. A captured British secret agent, Peter Churchill, said, "Your friends have been hanged already and are now being burned behind the ridge." Müller shook with grief and wept as he realized that the flakes whirling into his nose and mouth were all that remained of his friends.[14]

On 11 April, Müller heard the rumble of the approaching front. When Storm Leader Stavitzki entered his cell, Müller expected the beatings to resume. Instead, Stavitzki invited "Herr Doktor" to listen to the war news on a radio in the camp office. Hearing that the Americans had reached the Elbe, Müller asked what would happen to him now. "You'll be taken away from here, and then your fate will be decided," Stavitzki said. The SS man added that he worried about his own family. Müller said that he had a family, too, and hadn't heard anything about them for months. Yet, Müller recalled, "I did not have the courage to spit on him, which was my first impulse." Stavitzki began fussing with a backpack. Because he took an ice ax, like mountain climbers used, Müller inferred that the SS meant to make a last stand in the Alps.[15]

On 15 April, the SS loaded Müller and other special prisoners into a truck. Low-flying aircraft buzzed them as they crossed a long bridge. When they stopped for an air raid at Munich-Freising, Müller wanted to toss out a business card, so that friends in the cathedral chapter might know he still lived. But the guards seemed nervous, and Müller did not want to get shot if they misconstrued his move. The truck rattled southwest across the moors.[16]

The next day, Müller arrived at Dachau. The guards marched him over a bridge that spanned a twelve-foot-wide ditch, filled with water and fringed with barbed wire, into a special bunker for enemies of the regime. He could not leave the cell except during air raids. But an elderly SS officer, Edgar Stiller, told him, "Fräulein Anni Haaser will now be happy to know that you've arrived!" Soon afterward, Anni stood at the camp gate with a suitcase. "It was a moving reunion," Müller recalled, "overshadowed by the thought that it might be our last." On his way to meet her, Müller had seen train cars stacked with corpses.[17]

Vassili Kokorin kept close to Müller, treating him almost as a living totem. On 20 April, when Müller worried about making it home through the chaos, Kokorin wrote out a letter in Russian. He wanted his Catholic friend to have a communist safe-conduct pass. "The Red Army is in control out there! If anyone speaks Russian to you, show him that letter and you will be set free at once!"[18]

HITLER PINNED HIS HOPES ON A LAST GAMBLE TO PLUG THE BREACH in his front lines. On 21 April, he ordered SS General Felix Steiner to push his troops south during the night. If Steiner succeeded, he would cut off the Red Army north of Berlin; if he failed, the Reich would collapse.[19]

Steiner stalled. He had no troops to attack with, but he could not disobey a direct order. The next day, when Hitler learned that the counterattack had not begun, he turned purple and his eyes bulged. "That's it," he shouted. "The war's lost! But if you gentlemen imagine I'll leave Berlin now, then you've another thing coming. I'd sooner put a bullet in my brains!"[20]

On 23 April, Himmler's Lieutenant General Gottlob Berger arrived. Hitler ordered him to collect the prominent prisoners at Dachau and truck them to the Alps. Hitler's hands, legs, and head shook, and all that he kept saying, Berger remembered, was "Shoot them all! shoot them all!"[21]

THE GUARDS AT DACHAU LOADED THE SPECIAL PRISONERS INTO buses. As they passed through Munich, Müller barely recognized the bombed-out city. A direct hit had even demolished the figure of Christ the Savior at St. Michael's cathedral. Müller saw little chance that his own home on the Gedonstrasse had survived.[22]

They crossed into Austria. The buses wended the Tyrolean passes to Reichenau, a concentration camp near Innsbruck. The scene did not suggest that their path of sorrows had ended. Hoping for outside help, Müller gave one of his business cards to a guard and asked him to take it to Josef Rubner, general manager of the Innsbruck *Tiroler Graphik*, whom Müller himself had appointed as the newspaper's fiduciary trustee. The guard returned and reported that Rubner had said, "I don't know this man."[23]

FATHER RÖSCH WENT TO SEE THE WARDEN AT LEHRTERSTRASSE prison. After some consideration, Rösch chose four o'clock on the afternoon of 25 April, the octave of the protective feast day of the Holy Joseph and Mark, as the most sacrally auspicious moment. The warden's authority derived from a defunct regime, Rösch argued, and nobody cared about his decisions anymore, except the Russians, who would soon learn the wrong he had done. He should release the inmates and run for his life. After stalling a few minutes, the warden agreed. Rösch raced down the iron stairway into the cellar, shouting the news.[24] Berlin's last prisoners passed spectrally through the jail gates. In the street, they turned around and saw the building as their soul's eyes had longed to see it, from the outside. "Suddenly, the heaviest artillery-fire came down on us," Rösch recalled. He darted through explosions, ducking into doorways when the whistling came close. Just as the Russians arrived, Rösch found refuge in the Monastery of Saint Paul, where his Dominican co-plotter Odilo Braun kept an Orders Committee safe house.[25]

THE SS DROVE ITS SPECIAL PRISONERS TO THE BRENNER PASS. ON 28 April, they crossed the Alps into Italy. "We were evacuated in a group of about 150, in about six or seven buses with SS outriders, and a jeep taking up the rear with hand grenades and guns," recalled British prisoner Jimmy James. "We wound up to the Brenner [Pass], we stopped at midnight. We just stopped in the shadows and we didn't know what was going on. The SS had disappeared and we wondered what the score was." Müller suspected the Nazis would keep them hostage in a castle. Other rumors had it that, after the "final victory," Himmler would convict them in a show trial. "I found out years later," James said in 2000, "that the SS were going to machine gun the lot of us and say we had been killed by bombs."[26]

But their SS minders had split into factions. Obersturmführer Edgar Stiller led about thirty older conscripts. They "behaved decently," Müller recalled. Jailed Protestant Pastor Martin Niemöller buttonholed Stiller, trying to learn what would happen to them. "We got the impression that Niemöller treated the SS officer as his own adjutant, and, what was more, that Stiller had tacitly accepted this." A less friendly attitude prevailed among their SS escort detail: "twenty sinister characters, armed to the teeth." The group's leader, Untersturmführer Bader, had led a liquidation squad at Buchenwald.[27]

Müller sensed that Bader had something against him. Stiller had referred to an order from above: "Lawyer must not fall into the hands of the enemy alive." Had Stavitzki sent Bader out from Buchenwald, Müller wondered, to pull him back to the gallows? He decided to stay close to Colonel Bogislav von Bonin, who, despite retreating from Warsaw against Hitler's orders, remained an "honor prisoner" and carried a pistol.[28]

The SS returned in the early morning. They took the prisoners down the east side of the Brenner Pass, to the Tyrolean Valley. At a railway crossing, on the edge of the town of Villabassa, the caravan came to a sudden halt. The SS seemed uncertain what to do, but let the captives stretch their legs. One of the buses had a flat tire, fuel was running low, and no orders had arrived from Berlin. So the SS detachment got drunk.[29]

Some of the prisoners met in the railway hut to plan an escape. Two captured British Special Operations executive commandos formed a plan with captured Italian partisan General Sante Garibaldi, a descendant of the nineteenth-century Italian guerrilla hero. That night, with the help of locals loyal to their cause, Garibaldi and his chief of staff, Lieutenant Colonel Ferrero, slipped out of Villabassa, aiming to contact their compatriots in the surrounding mountains. They promised to return with guerrillas and attack the SS guards.[30]

"In the meantime the SS men in charge of the group had all got very tight on schnapps," James recounted. "One of them more or less passed out, and one of our chaps said, 'Well look, give him a bit more schnapps and then take his pocket book.' Which is what happened, and we found an order that the Allied officers and the various others were not to fall into Allied custody." Bader had by now told one of the prisoners that the SS had prepared a "special room."[31]

The hostages decided not to wait for Garibaldi's partisans. Some enterprising British prisoners hot-wired an old Volkswagen and drove over the mountains, hoping to reach an American headquarters and return with a rescue team. Colonel Bonin found a telephone in the town hall and asked the commanding general of the German 10th Army at Bolzano, about sixty miles southwest, to take the prisoners into protective custody. The general's chief of staff promised that a well-armed company would drive through the night and arrive by dawn the next day. "We went up and down the narrow streets with some trepidation, because the SS had originally planned to liquidate us in this isolated part of the Tyrol," Müller recalled. No one knew what final orders Himmler might have given, or when Allied forces might reach the area. Relatives of the Stauffenberg and Goerdeler families sought sanctuary with the local parish priest, who hid them in his rectory.[32]

The other prisoners bedded down on straw in the town hall. After midnight, the door flew open. An SS officer pointed to Müller: "You, come out here!" Colonel von Bonin jumped up and ordered the SS man to halt. The black shirt defiantly positioned himself in the threshold and repeated, "You, out!" Bonin drew his Luger and said, "I'll count to three. On two, you're a dead man!" The SS officer turned and fled.

But no one rested easily. James recalled an acute awareness of "SS men at each end with cocked Schmeisser [machine pistols]. That night was literally the Night of the Long Knives, because the SS were expecting something, possibly the [Italian] partisans to attack."[33]

On 29 April, Hitler called his commanders into conference. They told him that Russian troops had reached the nearby Potsdam station. The Wehrmacht had run out of bazookas and could no longer repair its tanks. The fighting would end within twenty-four hours. A long silence followed. With great effort, Hitler lifted himself from his chair and turned to go. His commanders asked what his troops should do when their ammunition ran out. He replied that he could not permit the surrender of Berlin. But whoever wished might try break out in small groups.[34]

At 3:00 p.m. the next day, Hitler's inner circle gathered in the lower bunker. Hitler had dressed in his usual olive-green shirt and black trousers. His mistress, Eva Braun, wore a blue dress with white trim and a favorite gold bracelet, set with a green jewel. Artillery shells crashed overhead. His eyes bleary, Hitler shook hands with Rattenhuber, Bormann, and Goebbels, and fewer than two dozen others. He spoke a few words in a low voice to each. Then, slowly, he walked with Eva Braun back to his study and closed the double doors.[35]

Eva Braun sat on a narrow couch. She kicked off her shoes and swung her legs up onto the blue-and-white fabric. Hitler sat next to her. They unscrewed brass casings that looked like lipstick containers and extracted thin glass vials filled with amber liquid. Eva bit the glass and rested her head on his shoulder. Her knees drew up sharply in agony. Controlling his trembling hand, Hitler raised the Walther to his right temple, clenched his teeth on the vial in his mouth, and squeezed the trigger.[36]

Rattenhuber heard no voices, and not even the sound of a shot. Hitler's butler, Heinz Linge, standing near Rattenhuber, remembered only the smell of gunpowder. When Hitler's entourage entered the room, they saw blood trickling down his cheek. His right temple had a red hole in it the size of a German silver mark. Eva sat with her head on Hitler's shoulder. In dying, she had flung her arm onto the table and overturned a vase of flowers.[37]

Hitler's guards carried the bodies up to the chancellery garden. His chauffer poured ten cans of gasoline on the corpses. Rattenhuber lit matches and tossed them onto Hitler and Eva where they lay. The matches kept going out. Rattenhuber pulled some sheets of paper from the cuff of his sleeve and twisted them into a torch. He lit the paper and threw the improvised kindling onto the cadavers. A tongue of flame leaped up. Rattenhuber stood at attention and raised his arm in the Hitler salute. Before he turned away, he saw the bodies curling and their limbs twitching in the fire.[38]

SNOW HAD FALLEN WHEN THE PRISONERS AT VILLABASSA AROSE ON 30 April. The SS guards at the town hall had all gone. In thanksgiving, French Bishop Gabriel Piquet, jailed for giving false papers to Jews, held a Mass in the local Catholic church. "Everybody went," British POW Jimmy James remembered. "Not only Catholics and Protestants, but Orthodox prisoners from Russia. It was very moving." During the service, the long-awaited Wehrmacht company arrived. The prisoners went to the town square. Brandishing a machine gun, Colonel von Bonin disarmed the few SS who had not already disappeared. The army company absorbed a few SS, identified by Stiller as "trustworthy and decent," and gave the others the chance to flee or try their luck with the Allies. "Bader and a few of them went down the valley," James recounted, "and I heard later that they had been stopped by the [Garibaldi] partisans and strung up."[39]

The Wehrmacht moved the prisoners to the Hotel Pragser Wildsee. One of the grand hotels of Europe's skiing nobles, it overlooked an emerald lake enclosed by white cliffs and dark woods. The Wehrmacht emplaced machine guns on the ridgelines, above the access road that snaked up the Pragser valley, creating a better defensive position against any SS Werewolf units. "It snowed continually and it was bitter cold in the hotel," Müller remembered.[40]

General Privalov held a May Day party in his room. As the liquor flowed, Vassili Kokorin began to weep. His "uncle," Stalin, would never trust him if he allowed himself to be liberated by "England, that whore." The Soviet security police would suspect the English secret service had turned him into a double agent. Kokorin had therefore decided to link up with Garibaldi's guerrillas at Cortina d'Ampezzo, about twenty-five miles south. Müller tried to dissuade him. The snow still stood three feet deep; frostbite had damaged Kokorin's feet when he parachuted behind German lines; the deprivations of a long custody had further weakened him. But Kokorin said that as a partisan officer, he must rejoin the "struggle." After a bear hug and Russian kisses, he vanished into the night.[41]

Hans Rattenhuber strapped on a steel helmet. In the predawn hours of 2 May, he broke through the bricked-up window of the Reich chancellery cellar with a crowbar. He clambered up and out onto the sidewalk of the Wilhelmstrasse under the Führer's balcony, cocked pistol in hand. Pausing and peering around, like an Indian scout, he gave a hand signal to the half-dozen Hitler henchmen behind him. They planned to bolt through subway tunnels and emerge northwest of the city, beyond the Russian zone.[42]

Rattenhuber crossed the Wilhelmsplatz, lit up by firelight. Hungry children sliced flesh from a dead horse. At the Kaiserhof subway station, Rattenhuber slid down the rubble-heaped chute of the stairwell and walked along the tracks, directly below the Soviet lines. By the beam of his flashlight, he picked his way over stiff corpses and half-wrecked staircases, past wounded troops and homeless families crowded against the tunnel walls. He surfaced at the Friedrichstrasse station. For another four hours, he crawled through cavernous connecting cellars, ran through burning buildings, and staggered down dark streets. In the morning a Soviet sniper's bullet finally claimed him, just a few yards from the Schultheiss brewery.[43]

"Two soldiers bring in the wounded Rattenhuber," Hitler's secretary Traudl Junge wrote in her diary. She huddled in the brewery's cellar, a prearranged meeting point for Hitler's fleeing entourage. "He has taken a shot in the leg, he is feverish and hallucinating. A doctor treats him and puts him on a camp bed. Rattenhuber gets out his pistol, takes off the safety catch and puts it down beside him. A general comes into the bunker. We discover that we are in the last bastion of resistance in the capital of the Reich. The Russians have now surrounded the brewery and are calling on everyone to surrender."[44]

On 4 May, a Ford jeep snaked up the road to the Hotel Pragser Wildsee. Spitting snow, spinning on patches of black ice, it finally rolled to a stop by the emerald lake. A crewcut lieutenant jumped out and identified himself as an advance man for General Leonard T. Gerow, Commander of the US Fifteenth Army. The German soldiers came down the ridgelines and turned in their weapons.[45]

General Gerow arrived with several companies of troops. He had earned the third star on his helmet as the first corps commander ashore at Normandy, and the German soldiers showed him "an almost religious deference," Müller recalled. Gerow congratulated the prisoners. Then he told them he could not grant their wishes to go home. He had orders to debrief and "clear" them in Naples.[46]

Gerow's troops drove them south. On 7 May, they stayed in a barracks at Verona. The next day, Müller boarded a Beechcraft C-45 transport and flew the remaining four hundred miles to Naples. As the plane crossed Rome he saw, far below, the green badge of the pope's gardens, and the united lines of St. Peter's, shaped like a key.[47]

EPILOGUE

"T̲he task of this hour is to rebuild the world," the pope said in a 9 May radio speech, as the guns fell silent in Europe. "On our knees in spirit before the tombs, before the ravines blackened by blood, before the countless corpses of inhuman massacres, it seems to us that they, the fallen, are warning us, the survivors: Let there arise from the earth, wherein we have been planted as grains of wheat, the molders and masters of a better universe."[1]

While the pope's words crackled on European radios, a boat sped to Capri. A tall, half-Jewish German economist stood in the stern. Gero von Gaevernitz had emigrated to the United States in 1924 but returned to Europe to help get rid of Hitler. As a case officer for OSS spymaster Allen Dulles in Berne, Gaevernitz had cultivated friendships with German resistance emissaries, including with Hans Bernd Gisevius, who had replaced Josef Müller as the plotters' liaison to the pope.[2]

Now, as he crossed the Bay of Naples, Gaevernitz began his final mission. Major General Lyman Lemnitzer had summoned him the day before, at theater HQ in Caserta, and given him a thin dossier on more than one hundred "Germans of a special brand." The Fifteenth Army had secured these political prisoners in the Italian Alps and flown them down to Naples. Some seemed ardent anti-Nazis, but the Allies knew little about them. The theater commander, Marshall Alexander, ordered them "isolated" in a specially evacuated hotel on Capri until Gaevernitz could give an opinion.[3]

At the Capri marina, Gaevernitz requisitioned a jeep. He rattled up a road to the Hotel Paradiso, on a cliff a thousand feet above the sea. The white helmets of military police ringed the grounds, enforcing security rules so tight that Gaevernitz had trouble getting in, even though Field Marshal Harold Alexander had signed his pass.[4]

"Once within the hotel, I was surrounded instantly by an agitated group of Germans," Gaevernitz remembered. "Many of these prisoners had gone through hell, and their nerves were still shaking from their experiences, the most recent of which had been escape from death at the hands of an SS murder squad."[5]

Josef Müller had received the suite normally reserved for King Farouk of Egypt. It had one of the most spectacular views Gaevernitz had seen in any European hotel, sweeping over the Bay of Naples, with Mount Vesuvius smoking majestically between the twin peninsulas of Ischia and Sorrento.[6]

"Gaevernitz interrogated me then for a long time," Müller recalled. They spent evenings together in the hotel garden. "Neither the monotonous steps of the guards nor the tropical [*sic*] moon could distract my attention from the extraordinary story of the barely known German Resistance [that] was disclosed to me," Gaevernitz wrote in 1946. "Here, I felt, was a man who could be of immeasurable help in the task that faced our occupation army in Germany." Finally Gaevernitz asked, "Would you be willing to work with us and give to our forces the benefit of your experience and knowledge?" This amounted to a recruitment pitch to return to Germany as an American secret agent.[7]

Müller agreed. But on the way back to Bavaria, he said, he would welcome the chance to stop in Rome. Gaevernitz promised to arrange a nice reunion there, if Müller first gave OSS interrogators ten days in Capri and told them his whole story.[8]

Gaevernitz returned to Caserta and typed up a report to General Lemnitzer. "Some of these prisoners should be decorated instead of being interned," Gaevernitz wrote on 13 May. Of the 60 million

Germans who roamed about freely, few had raised a hand against Hitler, even if they wanted to. Yet here was a group of men who had acted, risked their lives, lost their friends—and the Allies had locked them up. Gaevernitz advised theater HQ to send them home, where they would have "a good influence" on other Germans.[9]

On Capri, Müller came under the care of two American debriefers. One of them, Dale Clark, had studied at Harvard under former German chancellor Heinrich Brüning. Müller spoke about the Decent Germany, about Beck and Canaris, Oster and Dohnanyi, Stauffenberg and Moltke. He spoke about the holy Germany, about Kaas and Leiber, Preysing and Rösch, Bonhoeffer and Delp, the White Rose. But he spoke, too, about his own political ideas. Pacing with Clark on the roof of the Paradiso, looking out over the sea, Müller shared the vision of a European economic union he had developed with General Beck, and the new political movement he had discussed with his Kreisau and Italian friends. He wanted a Europe of Christian social democracies, linked by trade ties and united by a concept of the "dignity of the human person." Clark agreed to write a letter on Müller's behalf to General Lucien Truscott, commander of the occupying forces in Germany, who would have to approve Müller's plan for a new German political party, the Christian Democratic Union.[10]

On 26 May, agents of the US Army Counter Intelligence Corps captured SS officer Albert Hartl in Austria. British troops had arrested him earlier in the month, but released him as "uninteresting." The Americans sent Hartl to Dachau and then to other prison camps, where he implicated his SS superiors and subordinates in war crimes. He claimed never to have committed any atrocities himself.[11]

"I witnessed the execution of about 200 men, women and children of every age including babies," Hartl said. "The victims were forced to kneel in a large ditch and each one was shot separately in the back of the head, so that death was always instantaneous." To overcome moral depression, the mass executioners were kept well supplied with vodka. "An interesting medical phenomenon," as Hartl called it, was that "the

[SS] men, who had frequently taken part in the execution of women and girls, became sexually impotent for a certain period of time."[12]

Hartl wrote a long report on "The Vatican Intelligence Service." Among its great successes, he listed "contact with the German Military Intelligence of Admiral Canaris through the Munich lawyer and well-known Bavarian Catholic politician Dr Josef Müller." Hartl then offered to spy against the papacy for the United States. All he needed, he said, was a budget, a staff, and a multiyear contract. The final report on his interrogation attributed to Hartl "a definite emotional and psychological disturbance bordering on abnormality."[13]

Despite suspecting him of war crimes, the Allies set Hartl free. He soon became an apostle of yoga, environmentalism, and whole foods.[14]

FATHER RÖSCH MADE RECONNAISSANCE WALKS IN TORN CLOTHES and broken shoes. All Berlin seemed bedecked with red flags, even the Protestant churches. Drunken Soviet soldiers forced themselves into the Monastery of Saint Paul. Father Rösch later described them as "distinct Asian types," recalling that "one of them looked human." The Russians wanted watches, and one scrutinized a nun so closely that she held up the cross of her rosary in front of her. When asked if he "believed in Jesus Christ," Rösch prepared for martyrdom. The soldier, however, identified himself as a Uniate Ukrainian Catholic who only wanted to express his Christian convictions. The invaders withdrew. Others came later and took what they wanted. A Russian officer ordered the priests out when his men began to break down the doors to the nuns' quarters. A block commissar warned him that Jesuits might get sent to Siberia. When the commissar asked what he wanted, Rösch looked sadly at ruined Berlin and said, "I want to go back to Germany."[15]

On 8 May, he set out with a suitcase in a wheelbarrow. He planned to walk the 363 miles south to Munich. Five days later, he found himself trapped at night on the north bank of the Elbe, the barrier to the American Zone.[16]

In the moonlight, Rösch saw someone putting a canoe into the water. He called, shouted, whistled, clapped, until the man took notice. "I ran over and he admitted that the canoe didn't belong to him personally, he had 'borrowed' it. He said he would try to get help on the other side." By then a half-dozen other refugees had joined the Jesuit in beseeching the canoe man. He said he couldn't promise them anything, he was trying to get out of the Soviet zone just like they were. He paddled elegantly across the river and disappeared.[17]

Half an hour later, a barge appeared "from out of nowhere," Rösch recalled. The canoe man must have directed it to them. Rösch's wheelbarrow easily fit in. The ferryman said machine-gun fire had sunk other boats trying to cross, drowning the passengers. When their own barge reached the other side, the ferryman kept it against a bank of bushes for hours, in case a patrol appeared. Then he hurriedly tied up the barge and the refugees offloaded. Rösch pushed his wheelbarrow south on a dirt road, navigating by the stars.[18]

On 1 June 1945, a US Army jeep entered Vatican City. It turned onto an unmarked access road, barely wide enough for one vehicle, flanked by stone walls. The driveway opened out again into the interior court of Saint Damasso in the Apostolic Palace. Josef Müller strode from the jeep, followed by the US intelligence officers Dale Clark and Joe Cox. They entered one of the many doorways and took a small elevator to the third floor. In the warren of offices occupied by the Sacred Congregation for Extraordinary Affairs, bustling with papal guards and purple-sashed monsignors, they met the pope's *maestro di camera*. He led them along an outdoor colonnade, decorated by weather-beaten Rafael frescoes, and then down a back stairwell into a softly carpeted antechamber. As they genuflected just inside the door, the maestro said the Holy Father wished to speak with Müller alone. The two American spies waited patiently for three hours while Müller met with Pius the Twelfth.[19]

"I had hardly crossed the threshold into his study when the Holy Father approached me, and embraced me," Müller wrote in a detailed account of the audience. From Garibaldi and other freed Italians, Pius had heard of Müller's ordeal. He could not grasp how he had escaped.

Müller had worked wonders. The pope said he felt as if his own son had returned from terrible danger.[20]

"We were still standing at the door," Müller remembered. "He put his arm around my shoulder." Then, with his arm still around Müller's shoulder, the pope moved to a long table and sat Müller down, close to him, so they could hold hands. "Pius the Twelfth had often been accused of being a proud and detached Roman," Müller wrote afterward. "I saw nothing of that during my audience."[21]

The pope asked how he had survived it all. Müller said frankly that Catholic theology hadn't helped him because it raised too many options. "Instead, I relied on the prayers I learned as a boy." Hearing this, Pius "smiled and squeezed my hand heartily." His friends in Rome had prayed for him, too, the pope said. He himself had prayed for Müller every day.[22]

"This had not been an audience in the usual sense for quite some time," Müller recalled. "The Holy Father was still holding my hand, and I was able to speak quite frankly with him; it was, if I may say so, a type of common thinking." Müller said he had tried to follow the pope's teaching that "good and evil lived and worked in every human being." He thanked the pope for living that belief, by distinguishing between the Decent Germany and Hitler's Reich.[23]

"It was not easy," Müller quoted the pope as saying. "Yet just as you and your friends fought Hitler to the final consequence, I, too, felt compelled to try everything." He asked about the military officers who had plotted against Hitler. Müller spoke compassionately of Halder and Beck, the dilemmas they faced, the conflict of loyalties. They hated Hitler, but for a long time could not betray their fatherland.[24]

"Pius listened attentively, as I told him of the vow that Hans Oster and I had made," Müller recorded. "In that regard, we also came to speak of the Tresckow assassination plot, which failed through an unlikely coincidence to blow Hitler's plane out of the sky. The Holy Father had known about it." Pius expressed his approval, according to Müller, saying: "We had to wage war against the powers of evil. We contended with diabolical forces."[25]

At this point in the audience, Müller recalled, the pope became philosophical. For Christians, nothing in life lacked purpose. Therefore, he contended, the war must have had some meaning. Pius himself had struggled to find that meaning in his recent encyclical, *Interpreter of Universal Anguish*. Müller must have thought about it in his dungeons—his purpose on earth, on why people had to suffer so much. What did Müller think it all meant?[26]

He had learned a lot and unlearned a lot, Müller reflected. He had unlearned how to hate, because he had experienced hatred in all its forms. He had pondered the uniquely modern power to mobilize mass hatred. It all boiled down to "collectivism," he decided. The good of the group trumped the rights of the individual, regardless of the banners by which men marched. To guard against this, Europe must find renewal in a concept of personhood that elevated the individual above the herd. The spirit of early Christianity offered a base on which to build; for Christ had made his subjugated, discarded, rootless disciples feel as inherently good and worthy as the emperors who decided with their thumbs whether they lived or died. That concept of sacred selfhood, Müller vowed, would shape his own postwar political activities. "I told Pius of my plans to fashion a new bloc from strong Christians, regardless of denomination, in order to confront collectivism. That he agreed with this idea brought me great joy."[27]

ON 2 JUNE, PIUS CONVENED THE CARDINALS IN THE SISTINE Chapel. They gathered beneath the high windows, duplicating the Old Testament dimensions of Solomon's Temple. Tapestries by Raphael traced papal authority from Moses, via Christ, to Peter, and implicitly to Pius, who raised his hand in benediction.

"Today, after six years, the fratricidal struggle has ended, at least in one section of this war-torn world," he said. "The whole world today contemplates with stupefaction the ruins that it has left behind it." Expressing his sorrow for the victims of "the idolatry of race and blood," he spoke of "the hostility of National Socialism toward the church, a hostility which was manifest up to these last months, when National Socialists still flattered themselves with the idea that once they had secured victory in arms they could do away with the church forever.

Authoritative and absolutely trustworthy witnesses gave us intelligence of these plans." After that veiled reference to Müller, Pius alluded to the coup plots, obliquely referencing his own role:

> It was a tyranny for whose overthrow men planned. Would it then have been possible, by opportune and timely political action, to block once and for all the outbreak of brutal violence and to put the German people in the position to shake off the tentacles that were strangling it? Would it have been possible thus to have saved Europe and the world from this immense inundation of blood? No one would dare to give an unqualified judgment. But We cherished the hope that Germany would rise to new dignity and new life when once she had put to rest the satanic specter raised by National Socialism. For the situation suggested these words of warning to us, as Our Divine Master said: Those who put the sword to others shall die by the sword.

Those words caused murmurs in diplomatic Rome—not because of their meaning, but because of their timing. American chargé d'affaires Harold Tittmann recorded "rather widespread criticism of the Pope in connection with his latest speech, because he had waited until Germany had been defeated before attacking the Nazis in public."[28]

JOSEF MÜLLER RETURNED TO MUNICH TO HELP REBUILD HIS RUINED country. While working as a US intelligence agent, code-named "Robot," he cofounded the Bavarian wing of the Christian Democratic Party, which dominated West German politics. As Bavarian minister of justice, still on the CIA's agent list, Müller led the prosecution of Nazi war criminals not sentenced at Nuremberg. Perry Miller, the authority on American Puritanism on loan to OSS from Harvard, recorded that "Mueller's importance is such that for a time he was considered a possible successor to [Bavarian Prime Minister Fritz] Schaeffer, but his allegedly leftist sentiments have aroused the animosity of the older Catholic leadership in Bavaria." He had many faults in the eyes of the conservatives: he seemed "insufficiently federalist," as well as "too casual," and even "not Catholic enough." By his own account, Müller felt most comfortable on the political left, because, as he liked to say, Christ had always taken the side of the oppressed.[29]

In the end he was a quiet maker of the postwar Church and world. His wartime interfaith efforts, which brought Dietrich Bonhoeffer to the Vatican crypt, helped spark the reforms of the Second Vatican Council, which hailed the spiritual authenticity of Judaism. As a champion of papal transnationalism, Müller wove Catholic ideas from the German resistance into broader discourses about Christian Democracy, NATO, European unity, and human rights. As Germany's leading advocate of a European Common Market, he earned a reputation as the "godfather of the Euro." He died in 1979, with his dream of a United Europe unrealized but within reach. His home town of Steinwassen put up a granite monument, depicting oxen pulling a cart, to remember Joey Ox.[30]

When Pius the Twelfth came under attack for his wartime silence, Müller defended him. Even before returning to Germany in 1945, Müller laid down the line he followed in later years. Lingering in Rome after his audience with Pius, Müller found himself at a dinner party with Tittmann, who asked why Pius had not spoken out earlier. The American diplomat detailed Müller's reply.

"Dr. Mueller [*sic*] said that during the war his anti-Nazi organization in Germany had always been very insistent that the Pope should refrain from making any public statement singling out the Nazis and specifically condemning them and had recommended that the Pope's remarks should be confined to generalities only," wrote Tittmann. Further, Müller "said that he was obliged to give this advice, since, if the Pope had been specific, Germans would have accused him of yielding to the prompting of foreign powers and this would have made the German Catholics even more suspected than they were and would have greatly restricted their freedom of action in their work of resistance to the Nazis. Dr. Mueller said the policy of the Catholic resistance inside Germany was that the Pope should stand aside while the German hierarchy carried out the struggle against the Nazis inside Germany. Dr. Mueller said the pope had followed this advice throughout the war."[31]

Tittmann forwarded the explanation to Washington without comment. He had already reported that Pius had pursued "an ostrichlike policy toward atrocities that were obvious to everyone." But the pope, Tittmann reflected, had not merely buried his head in the sand; he had pursued his whole policy underground, in search of "the opportune moment to play the part of mediator." Since no one knew "what the Nazis would have done in their ruthless furor had they been further inflamed by public denunciations coming from the Holy See," as Tittmann wrote, he hesitated to blame Pius—especially since the Allies sometimes asked him not to appeal for the Jews. "Sir D'Arcy [Osborne] called "and said he feared the Holy Father may make an appeal on behalf of Jews in Hungary," US diplomat Francis C. Gowen recorded on 7 November 1944. "Sir D'Arcy said something should be done to prevail upon the Pope not to do this as it would have very serious political repercussions." The British worried about upsetting Stalin, because condemnation of specific atrocities might expose the Soviet murder of 22,000 captured Polish officers in the Katyn Forest. Buffeted by shifting pressures from all sides, Pius did not so much keep above the fray as work below it.[32]

About Müller himself, one mystery lingered for a time. "Why wasn't Mueller [*sic*] executed?" the London Station of the US Strategic Services Unit asked after the war. "Everyone else taking part in the July 20 conspiracy was [killed] and Mueller, while admittedly having good connections, wasn't any more important or presumably better protected than Oster, Canaris, and various others. . . . Was he just plain lucky or did he at one time or another talk?" After a two-month inquiry, however, James Angleton's Roman counterspy unit deemed Müller's story "well corroborated from outside checks." Any remaining questions about Müller were answered to the CIA's satisfaction on 30 October 1955, after Hans Rattenhuber returned from Soviet captivity, and a British spy turned Cambridge don rang his doorbell at No. 10 Schaflachstrasse, Munich.[33]

Rattenhuber told how he intervened to spare Müller's life. An SS adjutant telephoned the death camp as Müller stood at the gallows: "The call saved him literally at the very last moment." But why had the message come at all? Müller called it a "miracle," the result of the pope's prayers; SS officer Walter Huppenkothen said that Müller was just "lucky." In fact, Müller's character set his fate. He owed his rescue to his friendship with Hitler's chief bodyguard—a friendship based on Müller's 9 February 1934 confession, in Gestapo custody, that he sought to have Himmler put up against the wall and shot. Joey Ox won his life because he had once been ready to lose it.[34]

ACKNOWLEDGMENTS

Many archivists and librarians helped me build this book. Maciej Siek-ierski, senior curator and research fellow at the Hoover Institution, un-sealed Father Robert Leiber's papers. Susan Vincent Molinaro of the New York Society Library procured hard-to-find journal articles. For access to the Harold C. Deutsch Papers, in the US Military History In-stitute at Carlisle Barracks, Pennsylvania, I thank Clifton P. Hyatt and Archives Technician Carol S. Funck. At the US National Archives and Records Administration, I benefited like so many from the late John E. Taylor's encyclopedic knowledge of wartime intelligence records.

In Vatican City, Father Peter Gumpel, SJ, was unsparing with his time and meticulous in his responses to my queries. Walter Patrick Lang, Knight Commander in the Papal Order of the Holy Sepulcher, has been my patient mentor in secret intelligence matters.

I owe much to a larger community of interest. For more than a de-cade, William Doino and Dimitri Cavalli have run a kind of email salon on the "Pius Wars." Thanks to them, my in-box has filled with the insights of many others: Joseph Bottum, John Conway, Rabbi David G. Dalin, Kevin Doyle, Michael Feldkamp, Eugene Fisher, Gerald Fogarty, Patrick J. Gallo, John Jay Hughes, Michael Hesemann, Gary Krupp, Vincent Lapomarda, Bill Moynihan, Matteo Luigi Napolitano, Ronald J. Rychlak, and Andrea Tornielli.

Others generously gave feedback and encouraged me. I received valuable suggestions and support from Michael Burleigh, Tim Duggan, the late Sir Martin Gilbert, Sam Harris, Howard Kaminsky, Roger Labrie, Paul D. McCarthy, Andrew Miller, Aaron Haspel, Gerald Posner, Richard Eisner, Deborah Stern, George Weigel, David I. Kertzer, and David Thomas Murphy.

To specialists in several fields abutting this book I owe a great debt. The works of Harold C. Deutsch, Roman Bleistein, Robert A. Graham, Peter Hoffmann, Antonia Leugers, Owen Chadwick, Beate Ruhm von Oppen, David Alvarez, John Lukacs and Sir Ian Kershaw have proved invaluable to me.

I've learned much from those who take a more severely critical approach to Pius than I do. James Carroll, Hubert Wolf, John Cornwell, Susan Zuccotti, Daniel Goldhagen, and Garry Wills are always at the dinner party in my head. Where I do not share their conclusions, I respect their intentions and admire their work.

A great team of book professionals had my back. I thank especially Lara Heimert of Basic Books, and Sloan Harris of International Creative Management, for their patient interest in my work. I received great support also from Liz Farrell and Heather Karpas at ICM; and, at Basic, from Michelle Welsh-Horst, Melissa Raymond, Jennifer Thompson, Clay Farr, Cassie Nelson, Allison Finkel, Dan Gerstle, Katy O'Donnell, and Leah Stecher. Copy editor Katherine Streckfus was everything a writer could ask for.

My father, Robert W. Riebling, generously helped me in a range of places and ways—from the Ronald Reagan Presidential Library, in California, to the Hotel Pragser Wildsee in Italy. His spirit and his effort never flagged. Dad, thanks.

Joyce Riebling, my mother, sent me good books bearing on this project. No child could ever receive more intellectual encouragement from a parent than she gave me.

Nan and Stephen, thank you for everything you have done for our family through all these years. I love you more than I can say.

Eden and Freya—it's finally done! I'm home.

Robin, you carried me all the way. I owe my greatest thanks and all my love to you.

ABBREVIATIONS

AAW	Archiwum Archiediecezjalne We Wroclawiu [Archive of the Archdiocese of Wroclaw].
AB	Siemer, Laurentius. *Aufzeichnungen und Briefe*. Frankfurt am Main: Knecht, 1957.
ACDP	Archiv fur Christlich-Demokratische Politik der Konrad-Adenauer-Stiftung [Archive for Christian Democratic Policy of the Konrad Adenauer Foundation], Berlin.
AD	Bleistein, Roman. *Alfred Delp: Geschichte eines Zeugen*. Frankfurt am Main: Knecht, 1989.
ADB	Volk, Ludwig, ed. *Akten deutscher Bischöfe über die Lage der Kirche, 1933–1945*. 6 vols. Mainz: Matthias Grünewald, 1965–1979.
ADG	Neitzel, Sönke. *Abgehört: Deutsche Generäle in britischer Kriegsgefangenschaft, 1942–1945*. Berlin: Ullstein Buchverlage, 2005. In English: *Tapping Hitler's Generals: Transcripts of Secret Conversations, 1942–45*. Tr. Geoffrey Brooks. St. Paul: MBI, 2007.
ADOPSJ	Archiv der Oberdeutschen Provinz SJ München [Archives of the Upper German Province of the Society of Jesus, Munich; now Deutschen Provinz der Jesuiten].
ADSS	*Actes et Documents du Saint-Siège relatifs à la seconde guerre mondiale*. Ed. Pierre Blet et al. 11 vols. Vatican City: Libreria Editrice Vaticana, 1965–1981. In English: Vol. 1 (only), *The Holy See and the War in Europe, March 1939–August 1940*. Ed. Gerard Noel. Dublin: Clonmore and Reynolds, 1968.
AEM	Archiv des Erzbischofes München und Freising [Archive of the Archdiocese of Munich].

AES	Archivio della Congregazione degli Affari Ecclesiastici Straordinari [Archive of the Congregation for Extraordinary Ecclesiastical Affairs].
AH	Neuhäusler, Johannes. *Amboss und Hammer: Erlebnisse im Kirchenkampf des Dritten Reiches*. Munich: Manz, 1967.
AIGRH	Heideking, Jürgen, and Christof Mauch, eds. *American Intelligence and the German Resistance to Hitler: A Documentary History*. Boulder: Westview, 1996.
AKMF	*Akten Kardinal Michael von Faulhabers, 1917–1945*. 2 vols. Mainz: Matthias Grünewald, 1975, 1978.
AR	Bleistein, Roman. *Augustinus Rösch: Leben im Widerstrand: Biographie und Dokumente*. Frankfurt am Main: Knecht, 1998.
ASD	Archiv der sozialen Demokratie [Social Democracy Archive, Bonn].
ASV	Archivio Segreto Vaticano [Vatican Secret Archive], Vatican City.
AWDP	Allen W. Dulles Papers, Mudd Manuscript Library, Princeton University.
BA	Bundesarchiv [German Federal Archives], Berlin.
BF	Moltke, Helmuth James von. *Briefe an Freya, 1939–1945*. Munich: C. H. Beck'sche Verlagsbuchhandlung, 1988.
BPDB	Schneider, Burkhart, ed., with Pierre Blet and Angelo Martini. *Die Briefe Pius' XII an die Deutschen Bischöfe, 1939–1944*. Mainz: Matthias Grünewald, 1966.
BV	Hoffmann, Peter, ed. *Beyond Valkyrie: German Resistance to Hitler: Documents*. Montréal: McGill-Queen's University Press, 2011.
CE	*The Catholic Encyclopedia*. 15 vols. New York: Robert Appleton, 1912.
CI-FIR/123	"Counterintelligence Final Interrogation Report no. 123. Prisoner: Hartl, Albert." US Army, HQ 7707 MI Service Center, 9 Jan. 1947. Author's collection.
CSI/SI	US Central Intelligence Agency, Center for the Study of Intelligence, *Studies in Intelligence* (Unclassified Extracts from Classified Studies) [periodical series].
DBW	*Dietrich Bonhoeffer Werke*. Individual titles in series cited by title and volume.
DGFP	*Documents on German Foreign Policy, 1918–1945*. London, Her Majesty's Stationery Office, 1957–1966.
DJ-38	Hugh Trevor-Roper (Lord Dacre) Papers. Selected files from records and documents relating to the Third Reich, Group 14: Additional Material, Microfilm no. DJ 38, Microform Academic Publishers, East Ardsley, UK.
DKK	*Dossier: Kreisauer Kreis: Dokumente aus dem Widerstand gegen den Nationalsozialismus: Aus dem Nachlass von Lothar König SJ*. Ed. Roman Bleistein. Frankfurt am Main: Knecht, 1987.

DNTC   Donovan Nuremberg Trials Collection, Cornell University Law Library, Ithaca, New York.

EGR   Benz, Wolfgang, and Walter H. Pehle, eds. *Encyclopedia of German Resistance to the Nazi Movement.* Tr. Lance W. Garner. New York: Continuum, 1997.

EPV   Stehle, Hansjakob. *Eastern Politics of the Vatican, 1917–1979.* Athens: Ohio University Press, 1981.

FDRL   Franklin D. Roosevelt Presidential Library, Hyde Park, New York.

FO   Archives of the British Foreign Office, National Archives (UK), Kew.

FRUS   *Foreign Relations of the United States.* Washington, DC: US Government Printing Office. Cited by volume and publication date.

GM   Leugers, Antonia. *Gegen eine Mauer bischöflichen Schweigens: Der Ausschuss für Ordensangelegenheiten und seine Widerstandskonzeption, 1941 bis 1945.* Frankfurt am Main: Knecht, 1996.

GRGG   General Reports on German Generals, National Archives, UK, Kew.

GS   Delp, Alfred. *Gesammelte Schriften.* Ed. Roman Bleistein. 5 vols. Frankfurt am Main: Knecht, 1982–1984, 1988.

GSA   Geheimes Staatsarchiv, Munich [Secret State Archive, Munich].

HDP   Harold C. Deutsch Papers. Boxes 1, 2, 4, 20. CD-R, hand-labeled "02-25-2011." US Army War College, Carlisle Barracks, Pennsylvania. Documents cited, where possible, by series, box, and folder: e.g., III, 1/7 (Series III, Box 1, Folder 7). The archive could not provide this information for all of the documents, and, in some cases, the identifying information in the CD conflicted with that in the War College finding aid. Where the army archivists were unable to resolve such discrepancies, I have omitted reference to series, box, and folder. Copies of some of Deutsch's papers are held in the Insitut für Zeitgeschichte (IFZ), Munich.

HGR   Hoffmann, Peter. *The History of the German Resistance 1939–1945, 3rd ed.* Cambridge, MA: MIT Press, 1996.

HPS   Hoffmann, Peter. *Hitler's Personal Security.* New York: Da Capo, 2000.

IfZ   Institut für Zeitgeschichte [Institute for Contemporary History, Munich].

IMT   International Military Tribunal, Nuremberg.

JFKL   John F. Kennedy Presidential Library, Boston, MA.

KB   Kaltenbrunner Berichte [Kaltenbrunner Reports]. Published in *Spiegelbild einer Verschwörung: Die Kaltenbrunner-Berichte an Bormann und Hitler über das Attentat vom 20 Juli 1944. Herausgegeben vom Archiv Peter für historische und zeitgeschichtliche Dokumentation.* Stuttgart: Seewald, 1961.

KGN	Rösch, Augustin. *Kampf gegen den Nationalsozialismus.* Ed. Roman Bleistein. Frankfurt am Main: Knecht, 1985.
KLB	Wietschek, Helmut, et al., eds. *Die kirchliche Lage in Bayern nach den Regierungs-präsidentenberichten, 1933–1943.* 7 vols. Mainz: Matthias Grünewald, 1966–1981.
KV	Kartellverband der katholischen Studentenvereine Deutschlands [Association of German Student Societies].
LF	Moltke, Helmuth James von. *Letters to Freya.* New York: Knopf, 1990.
LK	Müller, Josef. *Bis zur letzten Konsequenz: Ein Leben für Frieden and Freiheit.* Munich: Süddeutscher, 1975.
LPP	Bonhoeffer, Dietrich. *Letters and Papers from Prison.* Enl. ed. Tr. R. H. Fuller and John Bowden et al. New York: Simon and Schuster, 1997.
MBM/155	Miscellanea Bavarica Monacensia. Dissertationen zur Bayerischen Landes- und Münchner Stadtgeschichte herausgegeben von Karl Bosl und Richard Bauer, Band 55: "Josef Müller (Ochsensepp). Mann des Widerstandes und erster CSU-Vorsitzender" (Friedrich Hermann Hettler), Kommissionsverlag UNI-Druck München, Neue Schriftenreihe des Stadtarchivs München, 1991.
NARA	US National Archives and Records Administration, College Park, Maryland.
NCA	*Nazi Conspiracy and Aggression.* Nuremberg Trial materials. Red Series. 10 vols. Washington, DC: US Government Printing Office, 1946–1948; /B = Supplement B.
OAM	Ordensarchiv Münsterschwarznach [Order Archives, Münster].
OUSCC	Office of US Chief of Counsel for the Prosecution of Axis Criminality [International Military Tribunal, Nuremberg].
PCCTR	*The Persecution of the Catholic Church in the Third Reich: Facts and Documents Translated from the German.* Ed. Walter Mariaux. London: Catholic Book Club, 1942 [1940]. Reports to the Vatican by Josef Müller and Johannes Neuhäusler, 1933–1940.
PP	Ludlow, Peter. "Papst Pius XII., die britische Regierung und die deutsche Opposition im Winter 1939/40." *Vierteljahrshefte für Zeitgeschichte* 3 (1974): 299–341.
PWF	Pave the Way Foundation, New York, New York.
RV	Rerum Variarum (Archivio Segreto Vaticano) [Miscellany, Vatican Secret Archive].
SFH	Hoffmann, Peter. *Stauffenberg: A Family History.* New York: Cambridge University Press, 1995.
SO	Sanctum Officium (Archivio Segreto Vaticano) [Holy Office, Vatican Secret Archive].
SVC	Constantini, Celso. *The Secrets of a Vatican Cardinal: Celso Constantini's Wartime Diaries, 1938–1947.* Ed. Bruno Fabio Pighin. Tr. Laurence

B. Mussio. Montréal: McGill-Queen's University Press, 2014. Originally in Italian: *Ai margini della Guerra (1838–1947): Diario inedito del Cardinale Celso Constantini*. Venice: Marcianum, 2010.

TRP Guiducci, Pier Luigi. *Il Terzo Reich Contro Pio XII: Papa Pacelli nei documenti nazisti*. Milan: Edizioni San Paolo, 2013.

TT Hitler, Adolf. *Hitlers Tischgespräche*. Ed. Henry Picker. Wiesbaden: VMA-Verlag, 1983. In English (variant ed.): *Hitler's Table Talk: His Private Conversations*. Tr. Norman Cameron and R. H. Stevens. New York: Enigma, 2000.

UKNA National Archives, UK, Kew Gardens.

VfZ Vierteljahrshefte für Zeitgeschichte.

VKZ Veröffentlichungen der Kommission für Zeitgeschichte [Publications of the Commission for Contemporary History].

VS Kessel, Albrecht von. *Verborgene Saat: Aufzeichnungen aus dem Widerstand 1933 bis 1945*. Ed. Peter Steinbach. Berlin: Ullstein, 1992.

VW Buchstab, Günter, et al., eds. *Verfolgung und Widerstand, 1933–1935: Christliche Demokraten gegen Hitler*. Düsseldorf: Droste, 1990.

WP Weizsäcker, Ernst von. *Die Weizsäcker-Papiere, 1933–1950*. Ed. Leonidas E. Hill. Frankfurt am Main: Propyläen, 1974.

NOTES

Prologue

1. "Best agent": Hartl, "The Vatican Intelligence Service," 9 Jan. 1947, CI-FIR/123. Giving Jews false papers and money: Kaiser, diary, 6 April 1943, NARA, RG 338, MS B-285; Hoffmann, *Stauffenberg*, 185. Sensational significance: CSDIC report, "Kopkow's Account of the Plot," 9 April 1946, Lord Dacre Papers, DJ 38, Fol. 25. "Spy service . . . Catholic clergy": Kaltenbrunner to Bormann, 29 Nov. 1944, KB, 508 ("*Durch die internationalen Verbindungen... der katholischen Geistlichkeit ist hier ein besonderer Nachrichtendienst aufgezogen worden*").

2. "Refused to confess": Huppenkothen, deposition, 24 April 1948; Müller, "Lebenslauf," 7 Nov. 1945, DNTC. "Nerves like ropes": Schmäing, "Aussage," Verfahren Roeder, MB 6/6, 787. Jujitsu: Müller, transcript, Sept. 1966, HDP, III, 1/7. "To look at": Best, *Venlo Incident*, 181.

3. Behind his back: Gaevernitz, "From Caserta to Capri," 5.

4. Tore them up: Müller, "Flossenbürg," LK, 246.

5. Plans recorded: Kaltenbrunner to Bormann, 29 Nov. 1944, KB, 508–510.

6. "Talk or die!": Huppenkothen, transcript, 5 Feb. 1951, HDP, 2/10.

7. "Execution yard?": Müller, "Flossenbürg," LK, 248.

8. "He died": US 3rd Army JAG, War Crimes Branch, "Report of Investigation," 21 June 1945, NCA, IV, 2309-PS.

9. Privalov's view: Müller, "Flossenbürg," LK, 248, 250; Müller, "Befreiung und Abschied," LK, 274.

CHAPTER 1: DARKNESS OVER THE EARTH

1. "Whole world": Hoek, *Pius XII*, quoting Duff Cooper, who resigned as first Lord of the British Admiralty the day after the 1938 Munich Agreement with Adolf Hitler.

2. "Name Pius": Hatch and Walshe, *Crown*, 19–20; cf. Lavelle, *Man Who Was Chosen*, 94–100; Walpole, "The Watch."

3. Disappeared into St. Peter's: Doyle, *Life*, 181; Cianfarra, "Hailed by Throngs," *New York Times*, 3 March 1939.

4. "Responsible cares": Pius XII, *Summi Pontificatus*, 20 Oct. 1939.

5. Touch the cake: Lehnert, *Servant*, 64. Two in the morning: Ibid, 66.

6. Described what followed: On Pacelli's descent to the crypt, in accordance with a tradition observed by most newly elected popes, see Doyle, *Life*, 182: "An hour or so later that night, the newly elected Vicar of Christ . . . descended the marble stairs to St. Peter's Basilica. He walked the whole length of the building and made his way to the grotto under the main altar to kneel at the tomb of Saint Peter, the Prince of Apostles. After praying some time there, he proceeded to the tomb of his beloved predecessor, Pius XI." On the route through the back passages, see Cousins, *Triumvirate*, 27–28.

7. Earthen hole: The most likely chronology is (1) decision, c. 2–3 March 1939; (2) announcement, 28 June 1939; (3) excavation, 1940. Tardini wrote in 1960 that Pacelli had "formulated [this decision] for me shortly after his selection" (*Memories*, 80). Guardacci, who helped execute the decision, asserted that "the real impulse came to him just before he was elected to the papacy" and took form in a formal order on 28 June 1939, during the vigil of the feast of the Apostles Peter and Paul ("Necropolis," in Guardacci, *Crypt*). Jesuit Father Peter Gumpel, the former relator in Pacelli's beatification, reports that in Guarducci's deposition for 6 Nov. 1970 (still sealed at time this book went to press), "[Guarducci] says—and this results also from other sources—the excavations under Saint Peter's started in 1940, not in 1939." Gumpel, interview, 17 May 2014. "His pontificate": Tardini, *Memories*, 80.

8. Big snakes: Tacitus, *Histories*, Book 2, 93; Pliny, *Historia Naturalis*, Book 16, 201. His grave: "The infant Church was obviously surrounded by a hostile world, by a hostile Jewish world in particular; and it has been suggested . . . that the absence of any mention of St. Peter in the Pauline salutations to and from Rome may have been due to security-reasons. It might well have been held prudent to keep the whereabouts of this Jewish-Christian leader secret." Toynbee and Perkins, *Shrine*, 133–134 n 3. Mysterious core: Walsh, "Beneath the High Altar," *Bones*, 33. Gold and silver: Sheridan, *Romans*, 99. Bronze casket: Wilpert, "La tomba di S. Pietro," *Rivista di archeologia cristiana*, 13 (1936), 27–41; Kirschbaum, *Tombs*, 52. Expedition: Poole, "Crypt," in CE, vol. 4; Guarducci, *Cristo e San Pietro in un documento precostantiniano della necropoli vaticana*. Old curse: Frale, "Petrusgrab," Radio Vatican (de), 2 Feb. 2012. Possible misfortune: Bartoloni, "St. Peter's Tomb," *L'Osservatore Romano*, 29 Aug. 2012, 6.

9. Untouched since imperial times: Toynbee and Perkins, *Shrine*, xv–xvi, 44, 61 n 3; 133–134 n 3; Burton, *Witness*, 93.

10. Adventures of reason: "Pius XII was very careful not to close any doors [to science] prematurely. He was energetic on this point and regretted the case of Galileo." Leiber, "Pius XII," *Stimmen der Zeit*, Nov. 1958. "Nebulae": Pius XII, Address to Pontifical Academy of Sciences, 30 Nov. 1941. Outtakes: Pius XII, Address to Pontifical Academy of Sciences, 3 Dec. 1939; Monti, *La Bellezza dell'Universo*. "The risks": Pius XII, address to Pontifical Academy of Sciences, 3 Dec. 1939. Full exploration: Toynbee and Perkins, *Shrine*, xvi.

11. Newly elected pope: 8 Prinz-Albrecht Strasse: Rürup, ed. *Topographie des Terrors*, 70–80; Bleistein, "Josef Roth und Albert Hartl," *Beiträge zur altbayerischen Kirchengeschichte* 42 (1996), 98; Ladd, *Ghosts of Berlin*, 157; Moorhouse, *Berlin at War*, 230; Gisevius, *Bitter End*, 43; Reitlinger, SS, 46; Dederichs, *Heydrich*, 66–67; Müller, "Aussage," 10 Oct. 1947, IfZ, ED 92, 59; Hapig, diary, 28 Aug. 1944, *Tagebuch*, 39, and diary, 23 Sept. 1944, ibid., 42.

12. "Very moody"; Hartl, interrogation, 9 Jan. 1947, CI-FIR/123. "Unsuitable": Neuhäusler, "2. Mit Staatsminister Esser," AH, 42–46. Best friend: Kochendörfer, "Freising unter dem Hakenkreuz," 680.

13. "Woke up": Hartl, interrogation, 9 Jan. 1947, CI-FIR/123. "Fallen angel": Höttl, *Secret Front*, 32. "Beaten and poisoned": Hartl, interrogation, 9 Jan. 1947, CI-FIR/123.

14. "Hem them in": Gestapo conference notes, July 1937, in Neuhäusler, *Kreuz und Hakenkreuz*, I, 371–382. "Any other God but Germany": Heiden, *History of National Socialism*, 100. "Hatred of a renegade": SSU/X-2 London, "Statement by Dr. Höttl," 19 Dec. 1945, NARA, RG 223, 174/116/880; "Personalakt Hartl: Lebenslauf des SS-Obersturmführers Albert Hartl vom 3. Oktober 1936," BA/Zld.

15. Senior leaders: "Such material would then be evaluated and sent as a report either to Ribbentrop, Himmler, Hitler, or Göring, etc.," Hartl, interrogation, 9 Jan. 1947, CI-FIR/123. Secret and public: The dossier went through at least four stages: (1) A basic précis by the Reich Foreign Ministry via Moulin Eckart, "Papst Pius XII," 3 March 1939, TRP, 89–91; (2) SD [Hartl], "Lage-Bericht," 1st quarter [March] 1939, dossier R 58/717, BK (TRP, 91–92); (3) Hartl, "Papst Pius XII," 1939 [c. 12 March]; (4) Patin [Hartl], "Beiträge." Hartl fleshed out his assessment in briefings to Himmler and Heydrich, in SS reports, in lectures to SS trainees, and in propaganda directives to SS officials. For the substance of Hartl's assessments, which show a doctrinaire consistency, see Hartl, "Priestermacht," 1939; idem, "The Vatican Intelligence Service," 9 Jan. 1947, CI-FIR/123, Annex I; idem, "Vatican Politics," ibid., Annex II; "Aufklärungs- und Redner-Informationsmaterial der Reichspropagandaleitung der NSDAP," *Lieferung* 20 (Aug. 1935): 1–7 (Kirche: Polit. Katholizismus), GPA; and Höttl, "Vatican Policy and the Third Reich," 26 Nov. 1945, NARA, RG 226, Entry 174, Box 104, Folder 799. My account of how the SS "Vatican expert" portrayed Pacelli draws on those sources, and on three that Hartl's dossier cites: Kaas, "Pacelli,"

12 Dec. 1929, *Reden*, 7–24; Pacelli, "Wesen und Aufgabe der Katholischen Aktion," Magdeburg, 5 Sept. 1928, GR, no. 36; and Bierbaum, "Pius XII: Ein Lebensbild," 1939.

16. Biography: Eckart [for Hartl], "Papst Pius XII," 3 March 1939, TRP, 89–91.

17. Praised Hitler: On 13 March 1933, Pius XI had convened a secret consistory. Cardinal Faulhaber was present. "Cardinal Faulhaber had previously had an audience with Pius XI the day before. And in the consistory, the pope had spoken a brief word in praise of Hitler, in fact commending him for having fiercely opposed Communism. I cannot remember whether these words by Pius XI had been the talk of Rome at the time. I learned only later that the pope is alleged to have said that. There was nothing about it mentioned in the official transcript of his speech, which appeared in *Acta Apostolicae Sedis*, nor was there any mention of it in the *Osservatore Romano*. Nevertheless, Pius XI must have spoken these words, these laudatory words about Hitler, because von Bergen, the German ambassador in Rome, traveled directly to Berlin right after these remarks by Pius XI. And the German bishops made mention of the pope's words in their 1935 report to Hitler." Leiber, "Bandaufnahme," 5. Tax revenues of 500 million marks: Hitler, *Reden*, 397–398. "Aloof Catholics": Hartl, "National Socialism and the Church," 9 Jan. 1947, CI-FIR/123, Annex IV. Fifty-five notes: Leiber, "Mit brennender Sorge," 419. "Absurd": Höttl, "Vatican Policy and the Third Reich," 26 Nov. 1945, NARA, RG 226, Entry 174, Box 104, Folder 799.

18. Cutting words: Guiducci, "Il Papa," TRP, 50; Wolf, *Pope and Devil*, 266; God-man, *Hitler and the Vatican*, 145. "Struggles to death," etc.: Pius XI, *Mit Brennender Sorge*, 14 March 1937. "Summoned the whole world": "Bericht über die Arbeitstagung der Kirchen Sachbearbeiter beim Reichssicherheitshauptamt am 22. und 23. September 1941," IfZ, 4920/72, 218; Graham and Alvarez, *Nothing Sacred*, 59.

19. "Big family of God": Hartl [Heydrich], *Angriff*, 26. Hartl later said that he helped write this and other works by Heydrich, who published under the pen name Dieter Schwarz. Hartl, "National Socialism and the Church," 9 Jan. 1947, CI-FIR/123, Annex IV. "Race and blood": Hartl, "Pius XII," 16. Jesse Owens and rabbis: "Innuendo by Nazis Arouses Catholics," *New York Times*, 17 Dec. 1936, 14. "Judaized USA press": Hartl, "Pius XII," 17.

20. "Ideologically un-teachable": Gestapo Munich, 1 Jan. 1937, GSA, MA, 106889; 106411, fols. 103f. "Deaf to any discussion": Gestapo Munich, 1 Aug. 1937, 42, GSA, MA 106689. "Wanted here": Gendarmerie-Station Hohenwart, 3 June 1935, Landrat 72055; Kershaw, *Opinion*, 244–245.

21. Birkner: He obtained a scholarship in Rome that allowed him to work for a decade (1930–1940) at the Vatican Apostolic Library, researching Cardinal Giovanni Morone, *spiritus movens* of the Council of Trent. Until 1939, Birkner worked also for the German Historical Institute in Rome, researching sixteenth-century nunciature reports. Guiducci, "La figura Birkner," TRP, 133. On Birkner, see also *Zeitschrift der Savigny Stiftung für Rechtsgeschichte: Kanonistische Abteilung 42* (1956), 555ff.; *Historisches Jahrbuch 76* (1957), 623–625; Jedin, *Lebensbericht*, 66, 102. "Evil spirit":

Mackensen to Ribbentrop, 28 July 1941, Politisches Archiv, Federal Foreign Office, Nachlass Mackensen, Bd. 4, fol. 47 (TRP, 290).

22. "Death of the Führer": O. A. Donau (SS-Oberabschnitt Donau), Austria (Department SS Upper Danube), report from Rome, 1938 [no day/month], MfS HA IX/11, 11 PV 270/68, vol. 23, pp. 2–4 (Birkner), reprinted in TRP, 130–132. "Save the world": Hartl, "Pius XII," 16.

23. "So long": Patin, "Beiträge," 135.

24. "First hostile act": Goebbels, diary, tr. Taylor, 4 March 1939, 10.

25. "Little asthmatic": Rösch to Brust, Feb. 1943, KGN, Doc. 17, 203ff. "Agent for German questions": Leiber, "Unterredung," 26–27 Aug. 1960, IfZ, ZS 660, 2. "Sort of scientific secretary": Poole to Dulles, 10 Oct. 1944, Annex E, OSS, NARA 226/16/1131. For other versions of Leiber's titles, see Hollen, *Heinrich Wienken, der 'Unpolitische' Kirchenpolitiker*, 119 and n. 654; Hudal, *Römische Tagebücher*, 301–302; Leiber, interview, OSS 2677th Regiment, 18 Aug. 1944, NARA, RG 226, Entry 136, Box 14; OSS to OWI-London, 24 July 1944, NARA, 226/16/1015.

26. "Never a Vatican official": Gumpel, interview, 1 June 2014.

27. "It is evident": Father Felix Morlion, OP, to Ronald Reagan, undated enclosure to National Security Council memorandum, Rodney B. McDaniel to Thomas C. Dawson, "Subject: Reply to Ambassador Wilson," 23 May 1986, Reagan Library, Wilson Files, NSC 8604016.

28. Mouth shut: Gumpel, interview, 1 June 2014. "Absolute secrecy": Mackensen to Ribbentrop, 28 July 1941, Politisches Archiv, Federal Foreign Office, Nachlass Mackensen, Bd. 4, fol. 43–45 (TRP, 291). Must know everything: Hoek, *Pius XII*, 60.

29. Straightforward: Leiber showed a "decisiveness of an expression and [a] readiness to label a spade a spade." Deutsch, "Pius XII," Jan. 1966, HDP, VII, 4/8, 9 n 19. "Polished steel": Mackensen to Ribbentrop, 28 July 1941, Politisches Archiv, Federal Foreign Office, Nachlass Mackensen, Bd. 4, fol. 43–45 (TRP, 291). "Riding dress": Lehnert, *Servant*, 26. "No, no, no": Gumpel, interview, 17 May 2014.

30. "Little bit strange": Gumpel, interview, 17 May 2014. Slaughtered lambs: Gumpel, interview, 1 June 2014: "It was a practice done by a Swiss university professor, [Paul] Niehans [1882–1971]. The man was famous, and, for example, the German Chancellor Adenauer received the treatment; so did many other high-ranking personalities—not only here in Europe, but also in the Americas. A number of more traditional-minded doctors contested his methods, saying it was a useless kind of thing. . . . Niehans came to the Vatican, and practiced this injection on Pius the Twelfth [and] also on Father Leiber." "I do not fear Peter": Rafferty, "Power Brokers in the Vatican," *Financial Times*, 27 Aug. 1988.

31. Break . . . away: Faulhaber, "Denkschrift," 5 March 1939, BPDB, An. 4. "Believed in" the Führer: "We must recognize that at that time, even a large majority of Catholics believed in, and supported, Hitler. This was because they believed he would end unemployment. That had worked." Leiber, "Bandaufnahme," 1963, 11.

"Hatred for the Church": ASV, AES, Germania 1936–1939, Pos. 719, fasc. 316, 34. "National church": Faulhaber may have been influenced by the widely read Hermann Rauschning, who had written about six months before: "A schismatic separation of German Catholicism from Rome, inevitable as it seems today . . . will be a brief episode on the way to the comprehensive aim of destroying the Christian faith as the most deepseated root of Western civilization and of the social order. . . . The schismatic creation of a national Catholic church is only a question of time." Rauschning, *Revolution of Nihilism and Warning to the West*, 22, 118–119.

32. Thor's Hammer: Per intelligence reports Faulhaber received by 1939: "The Ersatz Religion," PCCTR, 3/VIII, 483–484; "The Neo-Pagan Cult," PCCTR, 3/VIII/2, 490–491; "Occupational Organizations and Their Publications," PCCTR, 3/II, 355. With a Swastika: As reported to Faulhaber: "The Neo-Pagan Cult," PCCTR, 3/VIII/2, 489.

33. Retraction: "The solemn declaration made by the Austrian episcopate on 18 March was, of course, not an approbation of anything incompatible with the laws of God and the liberty of the Catholic Church." PCCTR, 1/I, 10 (6 April 1938). Unsure about Innitzer: "Pacelli at that moment definitely did not trust him." Gumpel, interview, 1 June 2014. Vulnerable to pressure: According to the agent Pacelli sent to the scene, the Nazi delegation to Innitzer included a low-ranking official, the son-in-law of a Catholic church painter, "who knelt down before the cardinal, and said: 'I beg Your Eminence to bless, not only me and my family personally, but also the task which I must carry out in service to the Church and the state.' Innitzer was . . . far too credulous—and that had softened him up . . . and after they had talked some more he signed it and even wrote 'Heil Hitler' because they had manipulated him. That's what he told me." Müller, transcript, July 1963, HDP, III, 1/7. Do so for him: Gumpel, interview, 1 June 2014. True to form, only Innitzer returned to the Reich with a news-making statement from the pope: "My whole affection and concern belong to the German nation." See the unbylined wireless story, "Pope Pius Sends Blessing to Dear German Children," *New York Times*, 14 March 1939, n.p. (archival PDF).

34. Audio spying system: Leiber, transcript, 17 May 1966, 37. The precise dates of Pius's decision and of the installation remain unknown, and the existence of an audio surveillance system under the previous pope cannot be excluded, especially since Pius followed his predecessor's example in using other covert methods, such as funding clandestine couriers through the Peter's Pence. Although Father Gumpel asserts that the eavesdropping system was installed just before German Foreign Minister Joachim von Ribbentrop's 11 March 1940 visit (interview, 17 May 2014), the making of verbatim transcripts from papal meetings on 6 and 9 March 1939 suggests that a surveillance/recording system existed by then.

35. "Environment of the pope": Gumpel, interview, 17 May 2014.

36. Came of age: A 1959 CIA study found "abundant evidence that even in World War I intelligence made extensive use of microphones along with other forms of clandestine eavesdropping" (CIA, "Early Development of Communications Intelligence,"

1959, CSI/SI, 3). One much-feared technique of the time, hot miking, "convert[ed] the telephone into a microphone for general eavesdropping when it is not being used to make a call" (CIA, "Audiosurveillance," 1960, CSI/SI, 14:3). Thus, US Berne spymaster Allen W. Dulles advised his operatives to "always unplug during confidential conversations" (Dulles, "Some Elements of Intelligence Work," n.d., AWDP, Reports, Subseries 15a). Likewise, Cardinal Celso Constantini, prefect of the Vatican's Sacred Congregation for the Propagation of the Faith, noted that before Bishop Antonio Giordani began speaking, "he took the precaution of switching off the telephone line" (Constantini, diary, 31 Jan. 1941, SVC, 71). Covert recordings: British intelligence in German POW centers secretly recorded 64,427 conversations on gramophone discs (UKNA, WO 208/3451; UKNA, WO 208/4136–4140; cf. Neitzel, *Abgehört*, 19). When US Undersecretary of State Sumner Welles visited Berlin in 1940, he "assumed that the omnipresent German Secret Police dictaphones must be installed in the walls" (Welles, "Report," 29 March 1940, FRUS, 1940, I). In 1940, Franklin Roosevelt bugged meetings in his office using 35 mm scribed acetate sound film and a microphone concealed in a lampshade (Powers, "The History of Presidential Audio Recordings," CIDS Paper, NARA, 12 July 1996). "There is no question that Roosevelt was bugged [by Soviet intelligence] at Teheran and Yalta" (CIA, "A Different Take on FDR at Teheran," 2005, CSI/SI, 49:3). The FBI hid microphones in a Charleston, South Carolina, hotel room that John F. Kennedy shared with a suspected Nazi spy, Mrs. Inga Fejos, and heard "Kennedy and Mrs. Fejos engaged in sexual intercourse" (FBI, "Mrs. Paul Fejos," 9 Feb. 1942, file no. 100-3816, Hoover Confidential Files, Arvad). Dictaphone: Kennedy, diary, 13 March 1939, Joseph P. Kennedy Papers, 8.2.2, Ambassador's Correspondence, Subject File: Pope Pius XII—Coronation, Box 130, JFKL; Ventresca, *Soldier of Christ*, 134, 348 n 24; cf. Cabasés, "Cronistoria": "For the first time, an employee of the Vatican Radio was locked as a 'conclavist' inside the perimeter of a confidential meeting, to cope with any electronic problems that might occur." Inventor of the radio: Marconi, correspondence, 1933 (reporting the opening of the microwave radio telephone service for the Vatican), and photographs of the equipment and aerial, 1933, in "Papers Concerning Microwave Experiments, 1930–4," MS, Marconi 377, Marconi Archives, Bodleian Library, Oxford; Cabasés, "Cronistoria"; Radio Vaticana, "The Founding of Vatican Radio," 1 April 2014; Baker, *A History of the Marconi Company, 1874–1965*, 202.

37. Summer villa: G.A. Mathieu, "Papers Concerning Microwave Experiments, 1930–4," MS, Marconi 377, Marconi Archives, Bodleian Library, Oxford; Ambrose Fleming, "Guglielmo Marconi and the Development of Radio-Communication," *Journal of the Royal Society of Arts* 86, no. 4436 (1937): 62. "Electra": Radio Vaticana, "The Founding of Vatican Radio," 1 April 2014. "Institutional tasks": "Activities of Radio Station from the Vatican, February 12, 1931–October 2, 1934," in Cabasés, "Cronistoria." Pope's speeches: Transcript, "Niederschrift über die zweite Konferenz," 9 March 1939, BPDB, Anhang 9. "Extraordinary services": Cabasés, "Cronistoria." Bugging his visitors: Cf. Conway, "The Meeting Between Pope Pius XII

and Ribbentrop," *CCHA Study Sessions* 35 (1968): 116 ("Vatican Radio technicians installed a listening device in the meeting room").

38. Access to it: In addition to several Sampietrini, the Vatican's hereditary workmen, the team likely included a British Marconi engineer, Gerald Isted, known for rolling up his sleeves and using a screwdriver and pliers. The Vatican's chief engineer, Enrico Galeazzi, almost certainly knew of the operation, as did Jesuit Father Leiber. Radio Vatican operator Mario Mornese likely tested the equipment and ran the recorder. Cabasés, "Cronistoria"; Radio Vaticana, "Summario," 1 April 2014. Papal Library: The library contains two rooms. The larger, more formal *bibliothèque pontificale* is a corner room. Through it one passes to the cozier and less formal *bibliothèque secrète*. The available records do not indicate in which room Pius met the cardinals (Gumpel, interview, 1 June 2014). Both library rooms shared a wall with anterooms, which, however, could only be reached by separate entrances ("Ground Plan of the Vatican Palace," image file, author's collection). Test the system: The classical installation techniques described here receive exegesis in Wallace et al., *Spycraft*, 175, 177, 180–181, 185, 187, 201–204, 396, 412–413, 416, 496 n 9. As of 1960, the CIA judged audio installations to share universal features: "There is no mystery about any of these methods; the principles involved are common knowledge among communications and electronic engineers, and they are employed in practice to a greater or less extent by all intelligence and policing agencies and by private investigators. . . . In every case the plan will contain the following elements: Cover and method for approaching and entering the target to be bugged or the place where a line is to be tapped. Preparation of the required tools and equipment and method of packaging and delivering. Protective surveillance prior to and during the operation, with a primary and an alternate means of communication between the surveillance team and those inside the target. Membership of the team assigned to the job, its chain of command and distribution of responsibility" (CIA, "Audio-surveillance," 1960, CSI/SI, 14:3).

39. "Room next door": Leiber, transcript, 17 May 1966, unpublished portion, n.p.; cf. Safire, "Essay: Happy to Watergate You," *New York Times*, 14 June 1982.

40. Set to work: G. Raymond Rocca, interview, Jan. 1992. Rocca served with X-2, the counterintelligence branch of the US Office of Strategic Services in Rome, which obtained at least forty-two purported papal transcripts (NARA, RG 226, Entry 174, Box 1, Folder 2). Fried food: Wallace et al., *Spycraft*, 177 (similiar episode in secular lore). Parrot: The anterooms, which shared a connecting door, could be reached by two entrances unconnected with the library—a stairwell, and a door opening onto the courtyard ("Ground Plan of the Vatican Palace," image file, author's collection).

41. Father Leiber possessed: Father Leiber kept a box disguised as a red book in Pacelli's library. Neuhäusler, "Ein altes Buch," AH, 133–134. Condenser microphone: Radio Vaticana Museum, Exhibit MI012. Although the use of other devices cannot be excluded, the other known models of the period appear too large for easily concealment. Leather briefcase: Radio Vaticana Museum, Exhibit AA 003.

42. Dragon-toothed tower: Cabasés, "Cronistoria"; Radio Vaticana, "Summario," 1 April 2014. Separate room: Pawley, *BBC Engineering*, 178–182. Spooled steel: Marconi, research files on Marconi-Stille equipment: correspondence regarding Blattnerphone, 1933–1935; draft operating instructions for Marconi-Stille recorder-reproducer equipment type MSR3, c. 1934; and file for job no. 1556, Marconi-Stille equipment, 1935–1938 (MS, Marconi 772/773, Marconi Archives, Bodleian Library, Oxford). Marconi-Stille designates not the model but the machine's makers.

43. "Record" position: "Marconi-Stille Technical Instructions," Jan. 1937, research files on Marconi-Stille equipment, c. 1934–1938, MS, Marconi 773, Marconi Archives, Bodleian Library, Oxford.

44. Six minutes to nine: Lehnert, *Servant*, 93–94. Pectoral cross: Charles-Roux, *Huit ans*, 74.

45. Corner room: This description of the papal library and the approach to it builds on photographs in the author's collection and on Alvarez, *The Pope's Soldiers*, 311; Baumgarten, "Vatican," CE, vol. 15 (1912); Boothe, *Europe in the Spring*, 43 (describing an audience in March 1940); Cianfarra, "German Cardinals Confer with Pope," *New York Times*, 7 March 1939; idem, "Vatican Machinery Runs Smoothly," *New York Times*, 12 March 1939; idem, *Vatican and the War*, 167; Gumpel, interview, 1 June 2014; Hatch and Walshe, *Crown*, 206; Kertzer, *The Pope and Mussolini*, 41–42, citing Confalonieri, *Pio XI visto da vicino*, 173, 270–271 (describing the room as used by Pius the Eleventh, presumably little changed before the remodeling in the summer of 1939); Lehnert, *Servant*, 86; Wall, *Vatican Story*, 72–76 (recalled from a visit in 1944–1945).

46. "Present time": Unless otherwise noted, all direct quotations given in the reconstruction of this meeting are from "Niederschrift," 6 March 1939, BPDB, An. 6. Where the participants read from prepared memoranda, or where other documents bear on the topics discussed, reference is made to these in the notes below. "Honorable sir": Pius XII to Hitler, 6 March 1939, BPDB, An. 7.

47. Closed its schools: Bertram, "Denkschrift," 4 March 1939, BPDB, An. 2.

48. "Won't go away": Faulhaber, "Denkschrift," 5 March 1939, BPDB, An. 4. "Shall destroy": Hitler, 30 Jan. 1939, *Reden*, 401–402. Building on fire: Müller, "The Refusal of Legal Protection," PCCTR, 2/IX, 258.

49. Sharpened it: Faulhaber's draft and Pacelli's rewrite in Albrecht, *Notenwechsel*, I, 404ff.

50. "Hostile to the Christian cross": Pacelli used similar words in a letter to Cardinal Schulte: "false prophets arise, proclaiming themselves with satanic pride to be the bearers of a new faith and a new gospel that is not the Gospel of Christ . . . [T]he bishop who fulfils his apostolic duty of making known the truth and exposing those who in the stubborn blindness of their neo-paganism would erase the Cross of Christ from the Credo of their people contributes to the true exaltation and real greatness of his country and nation." Pacelli to Schulte, 12 March 1935, PCCTR, 1/I, 3–4.

51. "Timely and exact intelligence": Faulhaber, "Denkschrift," 5 March 1939, BPDB, An. 4.

52. "Handling to myself": Leiber, "Bandaufnahme," 1963, II.

53. "Must fight": Niederschrift, 6 March 1939, BPDB, An. 6.

54. Shrewd perceiver: Hartl, "Pius XII," 7. "What he does": Ibid. Measured: Hartl, ibid., 5. Pedantic, or fussy: Hartl, ibid., 7. Voice rise: Ibid.

55. "Outdated, slack": Hartl, "Priestermacht," 20. Deep divisions: Hartl, "Pius XII," 23.

56. "Sly methods": Hartl, "Priestermacht," 20.

57. "Strictly speaking": Hartl, "The Vatican Intelligence Service," 9 Jan. 1947, CI-FIR/123, Annex I.

58. "Main altar": Hartl, interrogation, 9 Jan. 1947, CI-FIR/123.

59. "Depose heads of state": Hartl, "Priestermacht," 20. Jesuit agents: Ranke, *Popes*, 215–216; Cormenin, *Popes*, 2:274, 261. "Fighting stance": Kaltefleiter and Oschwald, *Spione im Vatikan*, 43.

60. "Extremely difficult": Hartl, "The Vatican Intelligence Service," 9 Jan. 1947, CI-FIR/123, Annex I. Inner circle: Reportedly, only four people had full knowledge of Vatican secret operations: the pope, the Jesuit general, the cardinal secretary of state, and the undersecretary for extraordinary affairs. Hartl, "The Vatican Intelligence Service," 9 Jan. 1947, CI-FIR/123, Annex I. "Meager": Ibid.

61. Gröber: Hartl, interrogation, 9 Jan. 1947, CI-FIR/123. Gay nightclubs: Hartl, "National Socialism and the Church," 9 Jan. 1947, CI-FIR/123, Annex IV. "Two married women": Patin, testimony, OUSCC, 24 Sept. and 3 Nov. 1945.

62. "Cutouts": McGargar, *Short Course*, 116. "Break the courier system": Gestapo conference notes, July 1937, in Neuhäusler, *Kreuz und Hakenkreuz*, 1:371–382.

63. "Ran a courier station": Hartl, "The Vatican Intelligence Service," 9 Jan. 1947, CI-FIR/123, Annex I.

64. Bantered: Unless otherwise noted, all quotations in this account of the 9 March conference are from Niederschrift, 9 March 1939, BPDB, An. 9. Sainthood: "Card. Faulhaber: If only they let us keep the buildings! They want to make Scheyern [a Benedictine abbey in Upper Bavaria] into a Hitler Youth hostel. I've immediately turned it into a devotional center. Card. Bertram: That will assure your sainthood: We'd rather have no seminary become a National Socialist facility." Niederschrift, 9 March 1939. Bertram laughed: The transcript contains this exchange:

> CARDINAL INNITZER: I think use [the formal] "Sie" instead of the [familiar] "Du" when addressing Hitler.
> BERTRAM: One can also interpret it as: we don't consider ourselves to be so intimate with you!
> HOLY FATHER: In Italy they say now, "Tu" or "Voi." I say "Lei," but as noted in Italy will be the other way.

BERTRAM: I would say "Sie." Otherwise, the letter is good.
HOLY FATHER: Otherwise, everything is in order?
ALL CARDINALS: Yes!
INNITZER: It has to make such a good impression.
BERTRAM: It should not say *Dilecte fili* [beloved son] in there. He [Hitler] would not like to hear that. (Joking [*Scherzend*]) The Holy Father also says Heil, Heil!

65. "Big evil": Niederschrift, 6 March 1939, BPDB, An. 6.

66. Damascus in a basket: cf. Acts 9:24f. and 2 Corinthians 11:32f.

67. Europäische Hof: A hostel run by the Sisters of the Holy Family, near the main railroad station in Munich.

68. "Danger is great": Niederschrift, 9 March 1939, BPDB, An. 9.

69. "Ruler of the world": Hesemann, *Papst*, 123. Coronation details are from Burton, *Witness*, 123; Chadwick, *Britain and the Vatican*, 43; Cianfarra, "Weather Perfect," *New York Times*, 13 March 1939; idem, *Vatican and the War*, 52; Cornwell, *Hitler's Pope*, 210, 220–221; Doyle, *Life*, 176, 179; Greene, "The Pope," 263; Hartl, "Pius XII," 25; Hatch and Walshe, *Crown*, 135–138; Hesemann, *Papst*, 120–123; Hoek, *Pius XII*, 15, 81–83; Padellaro, *Portrait*, 154; Sheridan, *Romans*, 99; Hebblethwaite, *In the Vatican*, 2; Hofman, *O Vatican!*, 10; Lehnert, *Servant*, 70–72; Sharkey, *White Smoke Over the Vatican*, 20, 22n.

70. "Very moving": Graham Greene, "The Pope Who Remains a Priest" (Sweeney, 263).

71. "Swiftly and strongly!" Domarus, *Reden*, 1485–1486. Orders: Kershaw, *Nemesis*, 169 n 81.

72. Snow and mist: Kershaw, *Nemesis*, 171 n 100. Mercedes: Linge, "Kronzeuge," 2. Folge, 40; Baur, *Ich flog Mächtige der Erde*, 168; NARA, RG 242-HL ML 941, 942; BA, NS 10/124. Gang of 800: Shirer, transcript [telephoned to Murrow], 17 March 1939, *Berlin Diary*, 38. "Obtained confidentially": Orsenigo to Maglione, 18 March 1939, Report 26.724, AES 1283/39, ADSS, I, no. 3. Soon 487 . . . Jesuits . . . "a common sight": Study published by the Department of Information of the Czechoslovak Ministry of Foreign Affairs, *Two Years of German Oppression in Czechoslovakia* (Woking: Unwin. Brothers Limited, 1941), 72: "German Crimes Against Czechoslovakia," 5 Aug. 1945, Edmund A. Walsh Papers, Georgetown, "The Churches and Nazi Germany," Box 10.

73. "All countries to resist": Kershaw, *Nemesis*, 174 n 115. "Serious consequences": Cortesi to Maglione, 18 March 1939, Report 202, AES 1528/39, ADSS, I, no. 4. "Grave": Ready to Cicognani, 15 April 1939, ADSS, I, no. 19.

74. "Shadow of the Swastika": Ley, "Wir oder die Juden," *Die Hoheitsträger* 3 (May 1939), 4–6, GPA.

75. High extreme: Leiber, "Pius XII"; Pacelli, most agreed, would be a "political pope" (Leon Poliakov, "Pius XII and the Nazis," *Jewish Frontier*, April 1964). The

Berlin paper *Lokal Anzeiger* noted that "the Cardinal with the greatest political experience has been elected" (Doyle, *Life*, 10).

76. Pacellis lost: Alvarez, *Pope's Soldiers*, 207–252. On Pacelli's youth, see also Giordano, *Pio XII*; Konopatzki, *Eugenio Pacelli*; Padellaro, *Portrait*; Cornwell, *Hitler's Pope*, 31; Hatch and Walshe, *Crown*, 51; Doyle, *Life*, 33. For the expectations placed upon Pacelli from an early age, see Wall, *Vatican Story*, 78.

77. Contradiction: OSS Black Report #28, c. July 1944, NARA, RG 226; d'Ormesson, *De Saint Pétersbourg à Rome*, 196; Kessel, "The Pope and the Jews," ed. Bentley, *The Storm Over the Deputy*, 71–75; Osborne to *The Times* (London), 20 May 1963, 7; Hebblethwaite, *In the Vatican*, 31–32; Macmillan, *Blast of War*, 460; Rhodes, *Power*, 37; Wall, *Vatican Story*, 72, 77; Heer, "The Need for Confession," *Commonweal*, 20 Feb. 1964,

78. "Ray of light": Schneider, *Verhüllter Tag*, 174; EPV, 212, 214. Vatican Foreign Office: Quigley, *Peace*, 55; "Useful means": Leiber, "Pius XII."

79. "One is tempted": "Cahiers Jacques Maritain," 4, L'Ambassade au Vatican (1945–1948), File Ambassade I, Le Centre d'Archives Maritain de Kolbsheim. On conditions under which souls can be saved, the traditional Catholic dictum is *salus animarmum suprema lex* (the salvation of the individual soul is the Supreme Law)—with the vital caveat that there can be no salvation *extra muros ecclesiae* (outside the walls of the Church).

80. Political world: Popes who led armies include, most notably, Pope Julius the Second, fl. 1502.

81. Surged into Poland: Hatch and Walshe, *Crown*, 147, 187.

82. "Pontificate of war": Cianfarra, *Vatican and the War*, 187; Tardini, *Memories*, 40.

83. Others their faith: Graham, *Vatican and Communism*, 46; Hollis, *Jesuits*, 101.

84. "Cannot say so": OSS, SAINT London to SAINT Washington, 26 Nov. 1945, NARA, RG 226, Entry 174, Box 104, Folder 799; Charles-Roux to Bonnet, 6 Oct. 1939, QO, Vatican, no. 30, 105.

85. Way for what followed: Hassell, diary, 19 Oct. 1939, 79; Kershaw, *Nemesis*, 243 n 71, and Cianfarra, *Vatican and the War*, 207; Weigel, *Witness*, 52 n 27; Wytwycky, *Other Holocaust*, 51, calculates 2.4 million Gentile Polish victims; Wistrich, *Hitler and the Holocaust*, 3, credits the figure of 3 million.

86. "Gentile nor Jew": Pius XII, *Summi Pontificatus*, 20 Oct. 1939.

87. "Pope Condemns": *New York Times*, 28 Oct. 1939, 1, 4. "Outspoken a document": Cavalli, "Jewish Praise for Pius XII," *Inside the Vatican*, Oct. 2000, 72–77; Osborne to Halifax, 3 Nov. 1939, UKNA, FO 371/23791/37-39; Chadwick, *Britain and the Vatican*, 85; Graham, "Summi Pontificatus," *Civiltà Cattolica*, Oct. 1984, 139–140.

88. Help kill Adolf Hitler: Groscurth, "Diensttagebuch," 20 Oct. 1939, *Tagebücher*, 299.

CHAPTER 2: THE END OF GERMANY

1. Left hand: Heydecker and Leeb, *Nuremberg Trials*, 192.

2. Military briefings: Gisevius, *Bitter End*, 361. War crimes tribunal: Baumgart, "Ansprache," VfZ 19 (1971); cf. Kershaw, *Nemesis*, 207.

3. "Plan for mediation": Canaris, "Notizen," 22 Aug. 1939, DGFP, D, VII, 204, no. 192.

4. "Hearts to pity!": Baumgart, "Ansprache," VfZ 16 (1978): 143, 148.

5. "Polish clergy": Schlabrendorff, "Events," 1945, DNTC, 31.

6. "Now do yours": Albrecht, Kriegstagbuch, 22 Aug. 1939, VfZ 16 (1978): 149.

7. "Icy silence": IMT, Doc. 798-PS. Down the mountain: Liepmann, "Persönliche Erlebnisse," IFZ, ED 1/3, 30.

8. "Bloody war": Below, *At Hitler's Side*, 28; cf. Speer, *Inside*, 224.

9. "Any time": Canaris, "Notizen," 22 Aug. 1939, DGFP, D, VII, 204, Doc. 192. "Telescopic-sighted firearm": Hitler, "Tischgespräche," 3 May 1942, HT, no. 98.

10. "Spiritual factors": Canaris, "Notizen," 22 Aug. 1939, DGFP, D, VII, 205–206, Doc. 193. "Black crows": Hitler, "Tischgespräche," 3 May 1942, HT, no. 98. "Dunderheads": Hitler, "Tischgespräche," 3 May 1942, HT, no. 97. "Round up": Hitler, "Tischgespräche," 3 May 1942, HT, no. 97.

11. Canaris read out: Groscurth, "Privattagebuch," 24 Aug. 1939, *Tagebücher*, 179. "Monstrous scene": Gisevius, *Bitter End*, 361.

12. Old ideals: Hassell, diary, and Reck, diary, passim; cf. Trevor-Roper, "Canaris," 102; Kershaw, *Nemesis*, 401, 406; Mommsen, *Alternatives*, 60–61. Sexual honor: Schlabrendorff, "Events," c. July 1945, DNTC/93, 25; Buchheit, *Geheimdienst*, 307–308. Helped create: Weizsäcker, *Memoirs*, 142. Damage the Nazis: OSS, Special Report 81, "Ecclesiastical Contact with Allied Intelligence," 6 March 1945, Appendix IV, NARA, RG 226, Entry 180, Box 1, vol. 1, Roll 5, A 3303. From within: US Army, CIC, "Dr. Mueller, a Good German," 9 June 1945, NARA, RG 226, Entry 125, Box 29.

13. "With an ax": Fest, *Plotting Hitler's Death*, 109.

14. "Get involved": Testimony of Louis P. Lochner, taken at Berlin, 25 July 1945, by Colonel John A. Amen, NARA, RG 238; Lochner, *What About Germany?*, 1–5 (includes extracts from the document).

15. "Appalling idea": Weizsäcker, diary, 25 Aug. 1939, WP, 161. Left in a sweat: Gundalena von Weizsäcker, affidavit, IMT, Case 11, Tribunal IV, vol. 28 (1948). "Kill a man": Kordt, *Nicht aus den Akten*, 370.

16. "End of Germany": Gisevius, *Bitter End*, 374–375.

17. Poured into Poland: Kershaw, *Nemesis*, 222. "All be killed": Groscurth, "Privattagebuch," 8 Sept. 1939, *Tagebücher*, 201.

18. Train had stopped: "Hitler's Itinerary," HPS, xxi. "Settled by the Führer": Canaris, diary, 12 Sept. 1939, IMT, NCA 3047-PS, V, 769.

19. Entered the meeting: Breitman, *Architect*, 70–71. "Meant 'kill'": Lahousen, interrogation, 19 Sept. 1945, NARA, RG 238, M-1270/R. "Destroy?": Halder, testimony, 26 Feb. 1946, IMT, NCA, B/20.

20. Sun red: Mueller, *Canaris*, 169; Schellenberg, *Labyrinth*, 58; Tolischus, "Last Warsaw Fort Yields to the Germans," *New York Times*, 29 Sept. 1939. "In the world!": Imperial War Museum, 08.131/1, Adam Kruczkiewitz manuscript, 168; Hastings, *Inferno*, 21. "Lust for blood": CSDIC, "Halder on Hitler," Report GRGG 8-13 Aug. 1945, Lord Dacre Papers, DJ 38, Folder 6. Vomited: Deutsch, "The Opposition Regroups," CHTW, 57. "Entirely broken": Hassell, diary, 10 Oct. 1939, 48–50.

21. "Continuation of the war": Kessel, "Verborgene Saat," 12 April 1945, VS, 191. "French campaign": Surveillance transcript, GRGG 210, 11–12 Oct. 44, UKNA, WO 208/4364, ADG, Doc. 111. Coup in Berlin: Keitel, *Memoirs*, 97–98; Buchheit, *Geheimdienst*, 313; Kessel, "Verborgene Saat," 12 April 1945, VS, 186.

22. "Innocuous": Weizsäcker, *Memoirs*, 142. Mad dog: Heinz, "Von Wilhelm Canaris zum NKVD," c. 1949, NARA, Microfilm R 60.6.7, 82. All over Germany: Heinz, testimony, 7 Feb. 1951, HDP; Huppenkothen, trial transcript, 245, HDP.

23. Mute awe: Trevor-Roper, "Admiral Canaris," 113. "Influence": Schellenberg, *Labyrinth*, 347. Company of a priest: Bartz, *Tragödie*, 12; Abshagen, *Canaris*, 45ff. Cassock: Abshagen, *Canaris*, 34; Höhne, *Canaris*, 41. Calculation: Deutsch, "Pius XII," HDP, VII, 4/8, 5, 2 Dec. 1965.

24. "Diplomat in Berlin": Burton, *Witness*, 68. Change the regime: Leiber, "Aussage," 7 April 1966; Müller, "Aussage," 22 Sept. 1966, HDP, III, 1/7; Lehnert, "Aussage," 19 Feb. 1967, HDP.

25. Born for the mission: Hesemann, "Defensor civitatis," *Der Papst, der Hitler trotze*, 136.

CHAPTER 3: JOEY OX

1. Bad and good fortune: Müller, transcript, 24 March 1966, HDP, III, 1/7; Müller, "Ochsensepp," LK, 19–20, 22.

2. "Worked wonders": Müller, "Aussage," 31 March 1958, HDP. "Twenty-one": Müller, "Sturm auf die Kaserne," LK, 33. "Adventurer": Schwarz, *Adenauer*, 427. "Good man": *Süddeutsche Zeitung* obituary, in Pross, *Paying for the Past*, 8.

3. Godfather figure: MBM/155, 3.3 (Koch to Hettler, 3 Nov. 1988; Hettler, "Gespräch mit Josef Feulner," 17 Oct. 1989; Christa Müller to Hettler, 31 Oct. 1989); Gumpel, interviews, 17 May and 1 June 2014.

4. "Popular comrade": Roeder, "Anklageverfügung," Sept. 1943, LK, 184. "Conviviality": Deutsch, *Conspiracy*, 113. Drinking bet: Müller, "Neuer Anfang," LK, 326. Kaiserhof: Müller, "Drohungen und Geschrei," LK, 190. "Hanged correctly": Müller, "Hart auf Hart," LK, 175.

5. "Nameless mass," "unleashed here": Müller, "Hitler wird Reichskanzler," LK, 37.

6. Müller quit: Müller, "Machtübernahme," LK, 40.

7. Inflame the situation: Ibid., 41.

8. "People's will": Ibid., 42.

9. Firing squad: Ibid., 44.

10. Switzerland: Ibid., 45; but cf. Hettler, "Gespräch mit Dr. Philipp Held," 7 Dec. 1988, MBM/155.

11. Dachau: Broszat, "Concentration Camps 1933–35," in Krausnick, ed., *Anatomy*, 404. Convict's stripes: Müller, "Machtübernahme," LK, 47. Close Dachau: Ibid., 48. Kept it open: IMT, XX, 471, 455–456.

12. "Punishable by death": Müller, "Kampf gegen die Kirche," LK, 54.

13. Transcript made of the interview: Except where noted, direct quotes are from "Reichsverband der deutschen Zeitungsverleger an die Polizeidirektion München," 16 Oct. 1934, IfZ, ED 120/331; cf. "Dr. Josef Müller—Koalitionspartner Hitlers," *Süddeutsche Zeitung*, no. 92, 12 Nov. 1946; Schattenhofer, Chronik, 211; "Diskussion um Dr. Müller," ACDP, Nachlass Zwicknagl; Hettler, "Schlusszusammenfassung," MBM/155.6. Müller agreed: Cf. Moltke to Freya, 11 Jan. 1945, LF, 412. Practicing law: "Reichsverband der deutschen Zeitungsverleger an die Polizeidirektion München," 16 Oct. 1934, IfZ, ED 120/331; "Dr. Josef Müller—Koalitionspartner Hitlers," *Süddeutsche Zeitung*, no. 92, 12 Nov. 1946; Schattenhofer, *Chronik*, 211.

14. Müller's position?: Müller, "Befragung," 21 May 1970, IfZ, ZS 659/4, 163.

15. "Compromise there?": Müller, "Die Vernehmung," LK, 59; cf. Reichsverband der deutschen Zeitungsverleger an die Polizeidirektion München, 16 Oct. 1934, IfZ, ED 120/331; "Dr. Josef Müller—Koalitionspartner Hitlers," *Süddeutsche Zeitung*, no. 92, 12 Nov. 1946; Schattenhofer, Chronik, 211. Let him go: Müller, "Die Vernehmung," LK, 62; cf. Müller, "Befragung," 21 May 1970, IfZ, ZS 659/4, 169; Müller, "Lebenslauf," 7 Nov. 1945, DNTC, vol. XVII, Sub. 53, Pt. 2, Sec. 53.041.

16. Beer brotherhood: Müller, transcript, 31 June 1958, HDP, III, 1/7. Against the Church: Müller, "Vernehmung," LK, 63.

17. Müller and Faulhaber: Müller "Vernehmung," LK, 61; Müller, "Lebenslauf," 7 Nov. 1945, DNTC, Vol. XVII, Sub. 53, Pt. 2, Sec. 53.041. "Trusted collaborator": Gumpel, interview, 1 June 2014. "Sacrilegious": Müller, "Der Papst bleibt unbeirrt," LK, 116.

18. Uninitiated: The Mark Gospel contains many secrecy injunctions. "He [Jesus] was preaching in Galilee. When he had spoken, he strictly charged: See thou tell no one" (1: 39–44). "Going out of the coasts of Tyre, he came by Sidon to the sea of Galilee. And he charged them that they should tell no man" (7:36). "Then he saith to them: But whom do you say that I am? Peter answering said to him: Thou art the Christ. And he strictly charged them that they should not tell any man of him" (8:30). "And as they came down from the mountain, he charged them not to tell any man what things they had seen" (9:8). "And departing from thence, they passed through Galilee, and he would not that any man should know it" (9:29). With one exception, Matthew and Luke record the secrecy commands only in passages that parallel Mark, and they sometimes omit Mark's secrecy material; the exception is the famous dictum in Matthew: "Give not that which is holy to dogs; neither cast your pearls before swine; lest perhaps they trample them under their feet, and turning

upon you, they tear you" (7:6). The John Gospel records that "Jesus hid himself . . ." (8:59) and "Jesus therefore walked no more openly among the Jews. . . ." (11:54). Sons of Thunder: "Going up into a mountain, he called unto him whom he would. And he made that twelve should be with him, and that he might send them to preach. He named them The Sons of Thunder. And he strictly charged them that they should not make him known" (Mark 3:13 ff.). In Mark (6:07ff) Jesus dispatched his elite twelve cadre out on missions of unstated nature, in pairs, instructing them even in a sort of safe house system: "stay there [in each house] until you leave those parts." When they returned, they reported "whatsoever they had done." Separate entrances: "But when his brethren were gone up unto the feast, then went he also up, not publicly, but as it were in secret" (John 7:10). Coded signals: In response to his disciples' question about the Passover, Jesus told two of them, "Go into the city, and a man carrying a jar of water will meet you. Follow him, and wherever he enters, say to the master of the house, 'The Teacher says, Where is my guest room, where I may eat the Passover with my disciples?' And he will show you a large upper room furnished and ready; there prepare for us." The disciples set out and went to the city and found it just as he had told them (Mark 14:12–16). "House of Annas": Keller, *Bible as History*, 345.

19. "Might betray": Barnes, "The Discipline of the Secret," CE. To protect the holiest part of the Eucharist from spies, a custom developed of dismissing the "catechumens" (those preparing for Baptism) before consecration of the Eucharist. St. Gregory of Nazianus speaks of a difference of knowledge between those who are without and those who are within (*Oratio*, xi.) The *Catechetical Discourses* of St. Cyril of Jerusalem are entirely built upon this principle; in his first discourse, he cautions his hearers not to tell what they have heard. "Should a catechumen ask what the teachers have said, tell nothing to a stranger; for we deliver to thee a mystery . . . see thou let out nothing, not that what is said is not worth telling, but because the ear that hears does not deserve to receive it." (*Cat.*, Lect. i, 12). Thus also Pope Innocent I: "I dare not speak the words, but I should seem rather to betray a trust than to respond to a request for information" (*Epist.* i, 3). Thus too Saint Basil: "These things must not be told to the uninitiated" (*De Spir. Sanct.*, xxvii); "One must not circulate in writing the doctrine of mysteries which none but the initiated are allowed to see" (*ad Amphilochium*, xxvii).

20. "Nailed on crosses": Tacitus, *Annals*, Vol. XV, Ch. 44. Sardinia: Packard, *Peter's Kingdom*, 18. One hundred seventy . . . thirty-three times killed: Doyle, *Life*, 207. For partial lists of murdered or martyred popes, see Bunson, *Pope Encyclopedia*, 29, 236.

21. Defend themselves: By one account, St. Augustine of Hippo informed on the Manicheans to Pope Leo the First—even pretending to defect to their ranks, the better to betray them. Cormenin, *History*, I, 84, 117. Spies: Papal informants uncovered the planned kidnappings of Gregory the Second (720), Adrian the First (780), and Nicholas the Fifth (1453); enabled the rescue of Leo the Third (795); warned Gelasius that the Holy Roman Emperor Henry the Fifth was descending on Rome (1118); tipped Innocent the Fourth that Emperor Frederick the Second planned to assassinate him

(1248) and told Julius the Second that the French King Louis planned to depose him (1507). Cormenin, *History*, I, 148, 178, 201, 208, 400–401, 476; Cheetham, *History*, 180; Shaw, *Julius II*, 213. Ambushes: Aquinas, *Summa Theologica*, Part II, Question 40. Protestant kings: Hogge, *God's Secret Agents*, passim, and Gerard, *Hunted Priest*, passim. Beheaded: Rhodes, *Power*, 35.

22. "Dangerous job": Neuhäusler, "Ein schwerer Auftrag," AH, 14–15.

23. "Help you": Neuhäusler, "Gespräche in Rom," AH, 21–23.

24. "For anything," ten priority targets: Ibid. Neuhäusler, "Augen und Ohren auf für alles!", AH, 15-16.

25. Evaluating: Neuhäusler, "Augen und Ohren auf für alles!", AH, 15–16. "Likely": Müller, "Mit dem 'Abbas' auf Reisen," LK, 73.

26. "A panty": "[B]etr: Besprechnung mit Dr. Jos Müller," 23 Feb. 1952, IfZ, ZS A-49, 45: "Bei der Unterredung über Dr Panholzer springt die Pia auf und hob den Rock und zeigte auf Ihrem nacktem Arsch eine Narbe die sie für den Führer erhalten hatte. M: sie trug nicht einmal ein Höschen um ihr Ehrenmal bei passender Gelegenheit leichter vorzeigen zu können."

27. "Full freedom": Müller, "Interference with the Teaching of the Church," PCCTR, 2/II, 59. Mail, phones: OSS, "Persecution of the Christian Churches," 6 July 1945, DNTC, XVIII/3. Wider world: Müller, "Evidence from the German Hierarchy," PCCTR, 1/II, 13ff. Orsenigo: Müller, transcript, 8 Aug. 1963, Tape VI, HDP, III, I/7. "Peculiarly dependent": OSS, "Persecution of the Christian Churches," 6 July 1945, DNTC, XVIII/3. Mnemonic key: Kahn, *The Codebreakers*, 112ff. Semaphore: Wynn, *Keepers of the Keys*, 120–121. "Pope's Finger": Cabasés, "Cronistoria Documentata e Contestualizzata della Radio Vaticana."

28. Schneidhuber: DBW, 16, "Index of Names," 819. "A Lesbian": Confidential information; but cf. the description of her as the girlfriend, housemate, and traveling companion of "Mrs. Anna Jenny Meyer, born Liepmann," in Marga Schindele to Munich Central Collecting Point, 20 Dec. 1945, NARA, Ardelia Hall Collection: Munich Administrative Records, Restitution Claim Records, Jewish Claims, 0164-0174 (J-0173), and Gudrun Wedel, *Autobiographien von Frauen: ein Lexikon* (Böhlau Verlag Köln Weimar, 2010), 287 ("with a girlfriend since about 1903"). "Quickly and well": Neuhäusler, "Papstbitte," AH, 130. Theresienstadt: Isarflösse.de, "'Sie lebten mitten unter uns,'" accessed 12 July 2014 at: http://www.isarfloesser.de/nachrichtenleser/items/sie-lebten-mitten-unter-uns-aktion-gehdenksteine-9.html.

29. "Dangerous things": Gumpel, interview, 1 June 2014. "Our heads": Neuhäusler, "Meine Briefträger ins Ausland," AH, 131.

30. Crypt: Neuhäusler, "Aussage," 25 March 1966, HDP. A later SS memo reported that the pope personally officiated at the wedding (Kaltenbrunner to Bormann, 26 Nov. 1944, KB, 509). In fact, he merely interceded so that Müller could marry on Holy Thursday (the Church did not normally allow weddings during Lent). Müller, "Trauung in Rom," LK, 63–66.

31. Red book: Neuhäusler, "Ein altes Buch verbirgt viel Neues," AH, 133–134.

32. Suspected traitors: Müller, transcript, July 1963, HDP, III, 1/7; cf. Groppe, *Ein Kampf um Recht und Sitte*, 2:10, 56; Groppe, "The Church's Struggle in the Third Reich," *Fidelity*, Oct. 1983, 13; Müller, "Mit dem 'Abbas' auf Reisen," LK, 71; Müller, "Training in the Ordensburgen," PCCTR, 3/III/5, 348, 350.

33. Night of Broken Glass: Müller, "Letzte Hilfe für Cossmann," LK, 155.

34. Stay and fight: Müller, "Meine Rettung," LK, 278. Pact with Pacelli: Ibid., 228.

35. Schmidhuber . . . Canaris: Müller, transcript, 3 Aug. 1963, Tape I, HDP, III, 1/7.

36. Foreign accents: Sonderegger, "Mitteilungen," c. 1954, Bartz, *Tragödie*, 154–155.

37. "We know": Müller, transcript, April 1958, HDP, III, 1/7.

38. "Business matters": Müller, "Geheimnisvolle," LK, 13. Legal chess: Deutsch, *Conspiracy*, 112.

39. "Certain matters": Müller, transcript, April 1958, HDP, III, 1/7.

40. "Now, Dr. Müller": Müller, transcript, 31 June 1958, HDP, III, 1/7.

41. "After this prologue": Ibid. "Assassination": Müller, "Geheimnisvolle Einladung," LK, 17.

42. Couldn't sleep: Müller, transcript, Aug. 1960, HDP, III, 1/7.

43. "Dice had fallen," "exterminate the Jews": Müller, transcript, 22 Sept. 1966, HDP, III, 1/7.

44. Jews in Poland: Müller, transcript, 2 Sept. 1954, IfZ, ZS 659 /1, 60. Dossier: Gisevius, *Wo ist Nebe?* 222. Vatican should know: Müller, transcript, 5 Aug. 1963, Tape IV, HDP, III, 1/7. Proof to Pius: Müller, transcript, 8 Aug. 1963, Tape VI, HDP, III, 1/7; cf. Höttl, "Vatican Policy and the Third Reich," 26 Nov. 1945, NARA, RG 226, Entry 174, Box 104, Folder 799.

45. "A criminal like Hitler": Müller, transcript, 31 June 1958, HDP, III, 1/7.

46. Above party pressures: Rothfels, *German Opposition*, 100. One trusted power: Cf. Macaulay, "Lord Clive," *Essays*. "Hippogriff": Trevor-Roper, *Last Days*, 238. Their behalf: Müller, "Aussage," 11 June 1952, IfZ, ZS 659/2, 22.

47. Gallows alone: Müller, transcripts (5 Aug. 1963, Tape II; 3 Aug. 1963, Tape I; 22 Sept. 1966, 31 June 1958), HDP, III, 1/7.

48. "Diabolical powers": Müller, transcript, 22 Sept. 1966, HDP, III, 1/7.

49. Vatican crypt: Gumpel, interview, 1 June 2014.

50. Behind its name: Müller, "Meine Römischen Gespräche," LK, 82–83.

51. Like Jesus: Müller, "Quo Vadis," LK, 18; cf. "Acts of Peter," Apocryphal New Testament. The legend of Peter's return to the cross built on a pagan theme. In pre-Christian times, the site of the Quo Vadis chapel was a shrine to the god of the return where travelers offered devotions before dangerous journeys. Stagnaro, "Where Peter Saw the Risen Christ," *National Catholic Register*, 1 April 2010.

52. Max Weber: "Gespräch mit Dr. Philipp Held," 7 Dec. 1988, MBM/155; Josef Held to Fr. W. Braunmiller, 12 Nov. 1946, NL Ehard, 884; Müller, "Die Dolchstosslegende entsteht," LK, 34. "In God's Name": Müller, "Der 'Ochsensepp,'" LK, 19.

53."I'll bite off my tongue": Müller, "Wer ist dieser X?", LK, 215. Relay his response: Müller, transcript, 3 Aug. 1963, Tape I, HDP, III, 1/7.

CHAPTER 4: TYRANNICIDE

1. No later than 16 October: Müller returned to Germany from Rome on 18 Oct. after being told of Pius's decision by Kaas. Huppenkothen testimony, 5 Feb. 1951, 222, HDP.

2. Resolute form: Leiber, "Pius XII." Thus too Myron Taylor: "by temperament important decisions do not come easy to Pius" ("Vatican Matters, 1945," NARA, RG 59, Box 34). Cardinal Roncalli likewise noted Pius the Twelfth's inability to act decisively unless he was absolutely sure of himself, wholly "at peace with his conscience." Memorandum to the State Department, Paris, 19 July 1949, Myron C. Taylor Papers, Truman Library, Box 49. "Out of character": CHTW, 111.

3. Pledge of secrecy: Details of Pacelli's recruitment into the Congregation were related during the first year of his papacy by his earliest secular biographer (Hoek, *Pius XII*, 30). Hoek's version was followed (and embellished) by later biographers, who seldom credited Hoek as their source. On Gasparri see Cianfarra, *Vatican and the War*, 74–75; Hebblethwaite, *Paul VI*, 9 ("charming but slippery"); Howard, diary, 15 April 1917, in CHTW, 109 ("portly, dwarflike").

4. Groomed him for power: Quigley, *Peace*, 54. Buckled shoes: Cianfarra, *Vatican and the War*, 76.

5. Beekeeping: Hales, *Church*, 232; Rhodes, *Power*, 208.

6. Sharpened sticks: Rhodes, *Power*, 207. Paying bribes: The politician was reportedly Jacques Piou, the leader of the Action Libérale political party. Alvarez, *Spies*, 58.

7. Papal intelligence system: Padellaro, *Portrait*, 24. Religious issues: On the role of the nuncios, see Segreteria di stato, "Exposito," 11 May 1862 (Graham, *Vatican Diplomacy*, 235); Blet, "Response," *L'Osservatore Romano*, 29 April 1998; Graham, *Vatican Diplomacy*, 125; Graham and Alvarez, *Nothing Sacred*, 62; Reese, *Inside the Vatican*, 266. Political sources: ADSS, IV, 162–163. "Catholic Action": On Catholic Action and the new alliance with the laity, see ADSS IV, 121–123, 140–142; Graham, *Vatican and Communism*, 2; Alvarez (1991), 594–595; Alvarez, *Spies*, 60 n 19; Pius X, *Il Fermo Proposito*, 11 June 1905; Benigni, "Leo XIII"; Doyle, *Life*, 123.

8. On Benigni, see Alvarez, *Spies*, 74–77; Aveling, *Jesuits*, 334; Cornwell, *Hitler's Pope*, 36–37; Peters, *Benedict*, 46, 51; Godman, *Hitler and the Vatican*, 24; Chadwick, *History of the Popes*, 357; Lernoux, *People of God*, 54.

9. Catholic cause: Graham, *Vatican Diplomacy*, 136; Alvarez, "Vatican Intelligence," INS 6, no. 3 (1991): 605; Poulat, *Intégrisme et Catholicisme intégral*, 524–528; Alvarez, *Spies*, 84.

10. Italian battleships: Bertini to Questore di Roma, 25 Nov. 1914, A4, Spionaggio: Gerlach, busta 144, DCPS, ACS; Questore di Roma to Direttore Generale

di Pubblica Sicurezza, 27 Feb. 1917, DGPS, ACS; Gerlach to Benedict XV, 30 June 1917, Italia, 480, Affare Gerlach, SCAES; Gerlach to Erzberger, 9 May 1916, Erzberger Papers, Bundesarchiv, File 33; Rennell Rodd to A. J. Balfour, 9 March 1917, UKNA, FO 371/2946; Henry Howard memorandum, 27 May 1915, UKNA, FO 371/2377; Count de Salis, "Report on the Mission to the Holy See," 22 Oct. 1922, UKNA, FO 371/7671; unsigned memorandum, 24 March 1917, Ufficio Centrale d'Investigazione, busta 3, f. 39, DGPS, ACS; Alvarez, *Spies*, 99, 100, 102–103.

11. Parliament and people: Kaas, "Pacelli," 12 Dec. 1929, *Reden*, 7.

12. Operations in Germany: Leiber, "Pius XII" and 7 April 1966, transcript (Deutsch, *Conspiracy*, 108); Alvarez, *Spies*, 116; Howard to Franz von Recum, 10 Dec.1950 (Deutsch, *Conspiracy*, 109–110); Howard, diary, 15 April 1917, 118 (Deutsch, *Conspiracy*, 109); Peters, *Benedict*, 199; Cianfarra, *Vatican and the War*, 85; Erzberger to Hertling, 8 Jan.1917, Hertling Papers (Epstein, *Erzberger*, 150); Doyle, *Life*, 40; Hatch and Walshe, *Crown*, 72.

13. "Steps of a cat": Griesinger, *Jesuits*, 2:227. Anti-Jesuit laws: For the Bavarian backstory, see Cheetham, *History*, 283; Cormenin, *History*, 2:213; Kampers and Spahn, "Germany," in CE, vol. 6 (1909); Graham, *Vatican Diplomacy*, 119; Griesinger, *Jesuits*, 2:219, 227, 239; Hales, *Church*, 20; Leo XIII, *Officio Sanctissimo*, 22 Dec. 1887, and *Militantis Ecclesiae*, 1 Aug. 1897; Hollis, *Jesuits*, 24; Kahn, *Codebreakers*, 89, 112ff.; Leiber, "Pius XII"; Padellaro, *Portrait*, 53; Rhodes, *Power*, 77–78; Schnürer, "Papal States," in CE, vol. 14 (1912); Tardini, *Memories*, 51; Wittmann, "Bavaria," in CE, vol. 2 (1907).

14. Superior-general in Switzerland: On Erzberger, see especially Alvarez, *Spies*, 91–93, 95, 97–98, 104; A4, Spionaggio: Gerlach, busta 144, Direzione Generale della Pubblica Sicurezza (DGPS), Ministero dell'Interno, Archivo Centrale dello Stato (ACS), Rome; Howard, diary, 28 Jan. 1915, Vigliani to Questura di Roma, 27 Feb. 1915, A4, Spionaggio: Gerlach, busta 144, DCPS, ACS; Erzberger Papers, Files 41 and 42; Erzberger, "Memorandum Concerning the Future Position of the Holy See," 11 Nov. 1915, F.O., File 1498; Erzberger, Report to Bethmann, n.d. [c. March 1915], Erzberger Papers, File 34; Erzberger, *Third Report*, 1; Farnesina, Serie Politici P., Pacco 30, Stamped letter 050580, 14 Sept. 1891. Ending the war: For Erzberger's evolution from German loyalist to an agent of the papal peace plan, see Erzberger memorandum, 15 July 1917, Erzberger Papers, File 18; Erzberger to Gerlach, 28 July 1915 (Erzberger Papers, File 6); Erzberger to Hertling, 8 Jan. 1917 (Erzberger Papers, File 32); Erzberger to Ludendorff, 7 June 1917 (Erzberger Papers, File 6); Erzberger to Gerlach, 6 May 1916 (Erzberger Papers, File 6); Gerlach to Erzberger, 17 Aug. 1915 (Erzberger Papers, File 6); Bell to Bachem, 5 and 22 Feb. 1932, Bachem Papers, File 90; Vatican SRS, Guerra Europa, 1914–1918, 1, viii, 17, vol. 3, folios 5051.

15. Storm that followed: On the revolutionary mood in postwar Germany and Munich, see Evans, *Coming*, preface; Steigmann-Gall, *Holy Reich*, 13; Gallagher, "Personal, Private Views," *America*, 1 Sept. 2003; Erzberger to Pacelli, 31 Oct. 1918, Erzberger Papers, File 56; Padellaro, *Portrait*, 44; Payne, *Life and Death*, 122; Rhodes,

Power, 69; Stromberg, *Intellectual History*, 367. Soviet republic: Kessler, diary, 21 Aug. 1919, cited in Kaes et al., *Weimar Republic Sourcebook*, 52; Murphy, *Popessa*, 48; SRS, *Baviera*, Fasc. 40, folio 37 (the first letter extant in the files from Pacelli in Munich in 1919 is dated 3 Feb.); Pacelli to Gasparri, 18 April 1919, SRS, Baviera. Sparing his life: Feldkamp, "A Future Pope in Germany"; Hatch and Walshe, *Crown*, 83; Hoek, *Pius XII*, 49; Brusher, "Pope Pius XII," CE; Lehnert, *Ich durfte*, 15f.; Stehle, *Eastern Politics*, 18. Nunciature with gunfire: Burton, *Witness*, 50–51; Burleigh, *Third Reich*, 40; Doyle, *Life*, 52; Feldkamp, "Future Pope"; Hatch and Walshe, *Crown*, 83; Brusher, "Pius XII," in CE; SRS, *Baviera*, folios 4647 RV; Toland, *Hitler*, 81. Demurred: Murphy, *Popessa*, 49, 51. Surrender: Weisbrod, "Assassinations of Walther Rathenau and Hanns-Martin Schleyer," in *Control of Violence*, 365–394.

16. Torn from his hand: On the last days and assassination of Erzberger, see Epstein, *Erzberger*, 149n, 373, 384, 286; Mommsen, *Alternatives*, 210, and 298 n 15; Alvarez, *Spies*, 128; Padellaro, *Portrait*, 49; Kohler, diary, *Kölnische Volkszeitung*, 27 Aug. 1921, at Erzberger Papers, File 43; *Badische Zeitung*, 29 Nov. and 3 Dec.1946.

17. New government: On Pacelli and Faulhaber, see Burton, *Witness*, 116; Padellaro, *Portrait*, 152; Mommsen, *Alternatives*, 289 n 9; GSA, Ges. Papstl. Stuhl 996, Ritter to BFM, 9 Nov. 1923 (Stehlin, *Weimar and the Vatican*, 285); Leugers, *Mauer*, 139; Hamerow, *Road*, 60; Pridham, *Hitler's Rise*, 154. "Mystery play": Kaas, "Pacelli," 13.

18. Little about Hitler: On Pacelli's ignorance about Hitler, see Lapide, *Three Popes*, 118; Payne, *Life and Death*, 165; Doyle, *Life*, 97. Anti-Christian rhetoric: For Mayer and Hitler, see Renshaw, "Apostle of Munich"; Müller, "Sturm auf die Kaserne," LK, 31; Dornberg, *Munich*, 251; Steigmann-Gall, *Holy Reich*, 50; Lapomarda, *Jesuits*, 1 n 6. "Closely watched": Ritter to BFM, 9 Nov. 1923, GSA, Ges. Papstl. Stuhl 996.

19. "BVP": On the Vatican's putsch-related apprehension about Ludendorff, the French, and the prospects for a Bavarian concordat, see Stehlin, *Weimar and the Vatican*, 285–286; GSA, Ges. Päpstl. Stuhl 996, Ritter to BFM, 9 Nov. 1923; Stehlin, *Weimar and the Vatican*, 285.

20. "Traitor": For denunciations by the lower clergy, see Gordon, *Putsch*, 448. Impact: For the Vatican's decision to leave direct action to the BVP, see Stehlin, *Weimar and the Vatican*, 286; Gordon, *Putsch*, 448. Matt's counter-putsch is detailed in Dornberg, *Munich*, 148–149. Military against Hitler: On Mayer's break with Hitler, see Holmes, *Papacy*, 146–147. The Nazis also blamed Cardinal Faulhaber's maneuverings and sermons for undermining their popular support: Gordon, *Putsch*, 448; Stehlin, *Weimar*, 286, 289, Pridham, *Hitler's Rise*, 152.

21. Grudge: On Catholic denunciations of popular nationalism before the putsch, see Biesinger, *Concordats*, 122; Pridham, *Hitler's Rise*, 153; Rychlak, *Hitler, the War, and the Pope*, 18, citing Pacelli in *Bayerischer Kurier*, 21 Oct. 1921; Holmes, *Papacy*, 101. On the nationalists' disdain for Rome, see especially Rhodes, *Power*, 82. For Father Schlund, see his *Neugermanisches Heidentum im heutigen Deutschland*; Stehlin, *Weimar and the Vatican*, 286; *L'Osservatore Romano*, "Manifestazioni neopagane," 28 Feb. 1924. Real power: Murphy, *Diplomat*, 204–205; Cheetham, *Popes*, 283.

22. Military personalities: Hesemann, *Der Papst*, 72.

23. Reached his goal: Ibid., 84.

24. "Criminals and fools": Ibid., 85.

25. Killed lay-Catholic leaders: Schellenberg, *Labyrinth*, 5. Ashes in the mail: Conway, *Nazi Persecution*, 92–93; Burleigh, *Third Reich*, 678; Payne, *Life and Death*, 275; Forschback, *Edgar J. Jung*; Payne, *Rise and Fall*, 278.

26. "Symbols of superstition": Prittie, *Germans*, 80. Three years before: Holmes, *Papacy*, 108. Bedroom window: Cianfarra, *Vatican and the War*, 100.

27. Cardinals to Rome: Cardinals Faulhaber from Munich, Bertram from Breslau, Schulte from Cologne, and Bishops Preysing from Berlin and Galen from Münster (Godman, *Hitler and the Vatican*, 124). "Abyss": AES, Germania 1936–1938, Pos. 719, fasc. 312, 5ff.

28. Nazism by name: Volk, *Akten Faulhaber*, 2:28.

29. Every parish: Blet, *Pius XII*, 52. Along the Rhine: Benz and Pehle, *Encyclopedia*, 94. Remote villages: Prittie, *Germans Against Hitler*, 77. Tabernacles: Rychlak, *Hitler, the War, and the Pope*, 93; Chadwick, *Britain and the Vatican*, 20.

30. Second-floor window: Müller and Neuhäusler, "Attacks on Catholic Bishops," PCCTR, 259.

31. "Hostile to National Socialism": Cornwell, *Hitler's Pope*, 217, quoting *Berliner Morgenpost*, 3 March 1939. "Weapons": Ley, "Wir oder die Juden," *Die Hoheitsträger* 3 (May 1939): 4–6.

32. Emperor Domitian: Lehnert, *Servant*, 115–116, 128–129, 132–133. Young pontificate: Müller, transcript, Aug. 1960, HDP, III, 1/7; Leiber to Deutsch, 26 Aug. 1960 and 21 May 1965, HDP, VII, 4/8, "Pius XII," 10; Leiber to Müller, 28 Oct. 1953, IfZ, ZS 660, 11; Leiber, 26–27 Aug. 1960, IfZ, ZS 660, 8.

33. Could kill: Aquinas, *Summa Theologica*, 1a 2ae, q. 21, art. 4, ad 3.

34. Removing the tyrant: Bride, "Tyrannicide," *Dictionnaire de Théologie Catholique*, vol. 15 (1950), 2011; Lewy, "Secret Papal Brief on Tyrannicide," *Church History* 26, no. 4 (1957); Mariana, *De rege et regis institutione*, Lib. I, c. vi; Pastor, *History of the Popes*, 26:27–28; Rance, "L'Arret contra Suárez (26 June 1614)," *Revue des Questions Historiques* 37 (1885): 603–606; Suárez, *Defensio fidei Catholieae et Apostolicae adversus Anglicanae sectae errores*, Lib. VI, c. iv, secs. 14–18.

35. "Never let go": Müller, "Attacks on the Honor of the Church," PCCTR, 2/X, 282, quoting Rosenberg, remarks at Troppau, 31 March 1939.

36. "Hundreds of priests": ADSS, III, p. 12-13. "Extermination of the Jews": Müller, "Meine Römischen Gespräche," LK, 82–83. "His knees": Müller, statement, 2 Sept. 1954, IfZ, ZS 659 /1, 60.

37. Defender of Christian values: Kershaw, *Hitler Myth*, 106; cf. Pius XII, Address to College of Cardinals, 2 June 1945. Tribal traditions: Höhne, *Death's Head*, 48. "Flabbiness?": Speer, *Inside*, 142. "Suicidal tolerance": Ludecke, *I Knew Hitler*, 46–56. Soccer stadium: Begsen, *Der stille Befehl*, 77. "Mistake of some subordinate," "systematic and calculated": PCCTR, "Preface," vii. "The Party": Pius XII to Schulte,

18 Jan. 1940, BPDB, no. 33. "Wicked person": Gallagher, *Vatican Secret Diplomacy*, 88, quoting Alfred W. Klieforth to Jay Pierrepont Moffat, 3 March 1939, Moffat Papers, MS Am 1407, vol. 16, Houghton Library, Harvard University.

38. Removing Hitler: Müller, "Befragung des Staatsministers," 2 Sept. 1954, IfZ, ZS 659/1, 50; Müller, "Unkorr. NS üb. Gespräch," 1963, IfZ, ZS 659/3, 23, 25; Müller, transcripts, 31 June 1958, 24 March and 22 Sept. 1966, HDP, III, 1/7.

39. Learned of it: Leiber, transcript, 21 May 1965, HDP. "Tyrant by force": Chadwick, *Britain and the Vatican*, 91. "History of the Papacy": Deutsch, "Pius XII," 2 Dec. 1965, HDP, VII, 4/8. "Much too far": Leiber, "Unterredung," 26–27 Aug. 1960, IfZ, ZS 660, 2. Kill the pope: Leiber, transcript, 21 May 1965; Deutsch, "Pius XII," 12–13, HDP, VII, 4/8.

40. "Heard in Britain": Leiber to Deutsch, 26 Aug. 1960 and 21 May 1965, HDP, VII, 4/8, "Pius XII," 10. Words of the pope: Leiber, "Unterredung," 26–27 Aug. 1960, IfZ, ZS 660, 3; Christine von Dohnanyi to Deutsch, 26 June 1958, "Pius XII," HDP, VII, 4/8; Müller, transcript, 24 March 1966, HDP, III, 1/7; Müller, transcript, 22 Sept. 1966, HDP, III, 1/7; Müller, "Befragungen [Widerstand II]," 26 March 1963, IfZ, ZS 659/4, 208. "Without Hitler": Huppenkothen, trial transcript, 5 Feb. 1952, 225; Huppenkothen, transcript, 5 Feb. 1951, HDP, 2/10; Müller, "Gefährliche Reise," LK, 106; cf. "Informations sur les Antécédents et le Sujet de la Mission de Mr. Myron Taylor," ADSS, V, no. 500, 15 Oct. 1942.

Chapter 5: Someone to Kill Him

1. Pius's villa: Müller, transcript, 24 March 1966, HDP, III, 1/7. Next day: Huppenkothen, transcript, 5 Feb. 1951, 222, HDP, 2/10. Almost no one: Müller, "Meine Römischen Gespräche," LK, 85.

2. Play tricks: Dulles, "Elements of Intelligence Work," n.d. [1943–1945], AWDP, Series 15a. Way to win: Müller, "Unschätzbar wertvolle Dokumente," LK, 108.

3. "Removal of Hitler": Groscurth, *Tagebücher*, 20 Oct. 1939. Hoffmann suggests that Groscurth was describing efforts to secure a peace settlement "through *Swedish or Vatican* intermediaries" (*History*, 128; emphasis added). But when quoting Groscurth, Hoffmann omits the words alluding to the Vatican: "The Pope is very interested." Later in the same work (158, 585 n 46), Hoffmann avers that Groscurth was indeed citing the Vatican connection, and he links Groscurth's words to Müller's return from Rome on 18 Oct. (the date given by former SS investigator Walther Huppenkothen, trial transcript, 5 Feb. 1951, 222). Groscurth's diary entry in fact fits the chronology of the Vatican contacts, rather than any peace feelers through Sweden, which occurred later in the month (Groscurth cites them in his diary entry for 27 Oct.). Deutsch (*Conspiracy*, 120) retains Groscurth's reference to the pope and thus infers the "Vatican connection." The phrase "categorical demand for the removal of

Hitler," echoing Pius's phrase, "any government without Hitler," reappeared in the X-Report of March 1940.

4. Coup planners: Chadwick, *Britain and the Vatican*, 83–84, catalogs *Times* reports on the writing of the encyclical. As noted above, Pius likely conveyed his response on or by 17 October, since Müller returned to Berlin with the answer the next day. Huppenkothen, transcript, 5 Feb. 1951, 222, HDP, 2/10. "Work of resistance": Tittmann to Taylor, 4 June 1945, Taylor Papers, FDRL.

5. "Gentile nor Jew": Pius XII, *Summi Pontificatus*, 20 Oct. 1939.

6. Consent of the government: Ruffner, "Eagle and Swastika," CIA Draft Working Paper, April 2003, II, 30. "German intelligence agencies ran across various leads to Mueller's clandestine role, but Adm. Wilhelm Canaris, the head of the Abwehr, was able to divert the SD from arresting Mueller." Ibid.

7. Müller met Canaris: The account in "Geheimnisvolle Einladung," LK, 17, places the initial meeting with Canaris on the day after Müller's meeting with Oster, that is, to a day after c. 28–29 Sept.; but in Müller's HDP debriefings he spoke as if the meeting came later (transcript, 29 May 1958, HDP, III, 1/7). The meeting most likely occurred in connection with the establishment of Müller's cover and his formal commission with the Abwehr, which did not occur until after his first wartime trip to Rome, as indicated by Müller's own recounting. Thus the meeting presumably occurred *after* 18–20 Oct., when the Abwehr learned that Pius "greenlighted" the operation, but *before* Müller's 23 Oct. efforts to establish cover by "showing" his Roman mission to Abbott Corbinian Hofmeister, whom he leveraged to develop the Italian contacts that made his mission plausible (Maier to Deutsch, 17 July 1967, CHTW, 127). It would seem most likely that Müller and Canaris met on 21–22 Oct., just after the results of Müller's first mission had the impact that Groscurth recorded (*Tagebücher*, 20 Oct. 1939). Have a seat: Lina Heydrich, "Aussage," c. 1953–1954, Bartz, *Tragödie*, 82; Gutterer, "Mitteilungen," c. 1953, Bartz, *Tragödie*, 95.

8. Started the war anyway: Müller, "Geheimnisvolle Einladung," LK, 16.

9. Negligence: Müller, transcript, July 1963, HDP, III, 1/7.

10. Went on in Poland: The phrase "Polish atrocities" appears by c. 13 Nov. 1939, in the summary of a talk with Leiber (Müller, "Besprechung in Rom beim Vatikan," IfZ, ZS 659); cf. Halder, transcript, 7 Aug. 1945, CSDIC, TRP, DJ 38, Folder 6. Sponsored them: Halder, transcript, 26 Feb. 1946, NCA, B/20; cf. Hassell, diary, 19 March 1940, 82.

11. Arthur Nebe: Schlabrendorff, "Events," 1945, DNTC/93, 46.

12. Diplomatic codes: Müller, "Unkorr. NS üb. Gespräch," 1963, IfZ, ZS 659/3, 23–24; Gisevius, *Wo ist Nebe?* 227. Swarmed with informants: Müller, transcript, 5 Aug. 1963, Tape IV, HDP, III, 1/7. To help the pope: "Besprechung mit Dr. Jos Müller," 23 Feb. 1952, IfZ, ZS A-49, 45; Müller, transcript, 8 Aug. 1963, Tape V,

HDP, III, 1/7; Müller, "Befragung [Fritschkrise]," 11 Oct. 1969, IfZ, ZS 649/4, 154; Müller, "Geheimberichte und Planspiele," LK, 103; Müller, "Befragungen [Widerstand II]," 26 March 1963, IfZ, ZS 659/4, 200; cf. Müller and Hofmeister, 8 Aug. 1963, HDP, III, 1/7.

13. Volunteered for a task: Müller, transcript, 24 March 1966, HDP, III, 1/7.

14. Kept their word: Müller, "Der Papst bleibt unbeirrt," LK, 116.

15. Wrong hands: Müller, transcript, April 1958, HDP, III, 1/7; CHTW, 117.

16. Reverently: Müller, "Befragung," 2 Sept. 1954, IfZ, ZS 659/1, 56. Pleased Müller: Müller, "Geheimnisvolle Einladung," LK, 16. Solace and hope: Müller, "Meine Römischen Gespräche," LK, 83. "Wish this to be so": Pius XII, radio message, 24 Aug. 1939, ADSS, I, no. 113; cf. Blet, *Pius XII*, 21. "Rid of him!": Müller, transcript, 31 May 1958, HDP, III, 1/7; CHTW, 62.

17. "Someone to kill him": Müller, "Geheimberichete und Planspiele," LK, 102.

18. Arguments swirled: Müller, "In der zweiten Heimat," LK, 89. "Obedience": Müller, "Fehlgeschlagen," LK, 158. Resistance to rulers: "Let every person be subordinate to the higher authorities, for there is no authority except from God, and those that exist have been established by God." Romans 13:1 (US Conference of Catholic Bishops, 2011). "Doing right": Smith, *Age of the Reformation*, 594–595. "Murder": Luther, *Selected Letters*, Lulu.com, 223; Luther, *Works* (1915 Muhlenberg ed.), 1:242–248.

19. Even necessary: British Jesuit Cardinal William Allen pronounced it "not only the right, but the duty" of the people to slay a tyrant (*Ad persecutores Anglos pro Christianis responsio*, 1582). British Jesuit Robert Parsons argued that "much rather would his subjects be bound in such a case to expel him from the throne" than to accept injustice (*Andreae Philopatri ad Elizabethae reginae edictum responsio*, no. 162). The Spanish Jesuit Immanuel Sa wrote in 1595: "Equally right is the principle that anyone among the people may kill an illegitimate prince; to murder a tyrant, however, is considered, indeed, to be a duty." Griesinger, *Jesuits*, 2:69. "Heretic king": Ranke, *History*, 216n. "Libation to God": Cormenin, *History*, 2:288. Feared to tread: Later Catholics volunteering to kill Hitler included Axel von dem Bussche and Claus von Stauffenberg. Earlier, a Swiss Catholic theology student, Maurice Bavaud, had tried to kill Hitler. Hoffmann, "Maurice Bavaud's Attempt to Assassinate Hitler in 1938," *Police Forces in History* 2 (1975): 173–204.

20. "Position": Müller, "Gefährliche Reise," LK, 107. Rest there: Müller, n.d., in Deutsch, *Conspiracy*, 196.

21. "Desired conclusion": Leeb to Brauchitsch and Halder, 11 Oct. 1939, and 31 Oct . 1939, in Kosthorst, *Die Deutsche Opposition*, 160–168. Into their plans: Ibid., 51.

22. Country of Hitler: Maier, transcript, 27 July 1967, HDP. Hitler's life: Hoffmann, *History*, 136.

23. Oath: Kordt, "Denkschrift der Vortagenden Legationsräte im Auswärtigen Amt Dr. Hasso von Etzdorf unter Dr. Erich Kordt," Oct. 1939, Groscurth, *Tagebücher*, Anhang II, no. 70; Halder, "Erklärung," 8 March 1952, IfZ, ZS 240; Groscurth,

Tagebücher, 219 n 566. Perplexities about tyrannicide: Kaltefleiter and Oschwald, *Spione im Vatikan*, 133. "Highest praise": Kordt, *Nicht aus den Akten*, 370–371.

24. Give orders: Lahousen, "Zur Vorgeschichte des Anschlages vom 20. Juli 1944," IfZ, ZS 658.

25. Guards to his presence: Kordt, *Nicht aus den Akten*, 371, 373.

Chapter 6: Luck of the Devil

1. "Another word": Deutsch, *Conspiracy*, 34.

2. Attack plan: Wheeler-Bennett, *Nemesis*, 470–472. Troop trains: Keitel, "Erinnerungen," 226. "Mutinies": Groscurth, diary, 5 Nov. 1939.

3. "Stupidest recruit": As related by Brauchitsch after the war, in the Bridgend prisoner of war camp: John, *Twice*, 61. "Victory in Poland!": Keitel, "Erinnerungen," 226.

4. "Spirit of Zossen": Hoffmann, *History*, 137. Echo in the great hall: Höhne, *Canaris*, 391; Klaus-Jürgen Müller, *Der deutsche Widerstand*, 521; Deutsch, *Conspiracy*, 226ff.

5. Clenched teeth: Engel, "Aussprache Hitler-Oberbefehlshaber des Heeres Am 5 November 1939 im grossen Kongressaal der alten Reichskanzlerei," May 1966, HDP. "Convulsed": According to Hitler's adjutant: Höhne, *Canaris*, 392; Deutsch, *Conspiracy*, 226. Crush defeatists: Halder, statement, CSDIC, 7 Aug. 1945, TRP, DJ 38, Folder 6. Night of the Long Knives: Kosthorst, *Die Deutsche Opposition*, 98–99.

6. Nothing of the plot: Kessel, "Verborgene Saat," 12 April 1945, VS, 190. Military at the Vatican: Müller, "In der Zweiten Heimat," LK, 90.

7. Tolentino: Müller, transcript, Aug. 1963, HDP, III, 1/7. Rules of the game: Deutsch, "Pius XII," Jan. 1966, HDP, VII, 4/8, 9 n 19.

8. Never met Müller: Müller, transcript, 31 June 1958, HDP, III, 1/7. "Common mouth": Müller, "Unkorr. NS üb. Gespräch," 1963, IfZ, ZS 659/3, 17; Müller, "Der X-Bericht entsteht," LK, 125. "Well-reasoned command": Müller, "Meine Römischen Gespräche," LK, 85.

9. "Gregor": Müller, report, c. 13 Nov. 1939, HDP, II, 3/7. Seemed pleased: Müller, "Der Papst bleibt unbeirrt," LK, 116. Placed in him: Müller, transcript, 31 June 1958, HDP, III, 1/7.

10. On 8 November: Regie-Programm für den 8/9 November 1939 in München, Gesamtleitung: Gau-propagandaleiter Pg. Karl Wenzl, BA, NS 10/126.

11. Hidden a bomb there: Hoch, "Das Attentat auf Hitler im Münchner Bürgerbräukeller 1939," VfZ, 17, 1969, passim; NARA, RG 242-HL ML 941, 942. Ticking: Duffy, *Target Hitler*, 26f.

12. Filed out of the hall: Hitler, speech, 8 Nov. 1939, ed. Domarus, *Reden* 3:1865ff.; Hitler, Koeppen, Bericht no. 28, 7 Sept. 1941; Hitler, remarks, 3 May 1942, BV, no. 204.

13. "Find a way out": The *New York Times* reported "indications" that the Gestapo and SS "were starting on a far-flung spy hunt and a drive to remove agitators opposing

the Reich in politics or war." "Hitler Escapes Bomb Explosion by 15 Minutes," *New York Times*, 9 Nov. 1939.

14. "Get rid of him": Below, *At Hitler's Side*, 44.

15. Planted the bomb: Müller, "In der zweiten Heimat," LK, 91.

16. "Luck of the Devil": Müller, "Der 20 Juli 1944," LK, 197.

17. Kordt's plan: Ueberschär, *Generaloberst Halder*, 28; Müller, "Aussage," 4 June 1952, IfZ, ZS 659/2, 11. "Chance to shoot": Kordt, *Nicht aus den Akten*, 374.

18. "No friend of mine": Frank, *Im Angesicht des Galgens*, 408.

19. "Good faith": Cadogan, diary, 29 Sept. 1939, 220. End the war: Huppen-kothen, "Verhältnis Wehrmacht Sicherheitspolizei," HDP, 2/10.

20. All-well: Best, *Venlo Incident*, 16–17.

21. Marched them into Germany: Schellenberg, *Labyrinth*, 79–80.

22. Skeptical: MI6, "Final Report [Schellenberg]," 29 Nov. 1945, NARA, RG 319, IRR, IS, Box 5, ed. Doerries, 69–70; Gisevius to Dulles, "Political Background," 1945–1946, AWD, Box 29, Folder 2; Müller, "Befragungen [Widerstand II]," 26 March 1963, IfZ, ZS 659/4, 202; Müller, transcript, 5 Aug. 1963, Tape IV, HDP, III, 1/7; Hettler, "Der Venlo Zwischenfall," MBM/155, 4.3.1.

23. "Friendly as ever," "on no account": Osborne to Halifax, 21 Nov. 1939, UKNA, FO C 197497/13005/18 (1939): PP, Doc. III, 326–328. "Venloo [*sic*]": Cadogan, minutes, 24 Jan. 1940, UKNA, FO 371/24363/C/267/62.

24. Hitler's rooms: Rattenhuber, circular, 22 Feb. 1940, BA, NS 10/137. "Numbed fatalism": Dispatch, "Mr. Osborne to Viscount Halifax (Received November 26) (No. 221. Confidential.), Rome, November 21, 1939," FO C 197497/13005/18 (1939): PP, Doc. III, 326–328.

CHAPTER 7: THE BLACK CHAPEL

1. Too many: Deutsch: *Conspiracy*, 129. Secret Jesuit: Müller, transcript, 8 Aug. 1963, HDP, III, 1/7.

2. Hole in the heart: Burns, *Papa Spy*, 191, citing research by Jesuit historian Robert Graham. "One of the best": Hartl, interrogation, 9 Jan. 1947, CI-FIR/123.

3. Keller and Walzer: Müller and Hofmeister, transcript, 8 Aug. 1963, HDP, III, 1/7. "Is not the campaign": Stein to Pius XI, 12 April 1933, AES, Germania, Pos. 643, PO fasc. 158, 16r–17r; Besier, *Holy See*, 126; Wolf, *Papst und Teufel*, 210, 214–216; Godman, *Hitler and the Vatican*, 34–35. In charge of Beuron: Keller, "Zeugenschrift-tum," 4 July 1967, IfZ, ZS 2424.

4. Mount Zion: Keller, "Zeugenschrifttum," 4 July 1967, IfZ, ZS 2424.

5. "Out for revenge": Müller, "Die Affäre Keller," LK, 96.

6. Grand Mufti; Stuttgart Abwehr: Keller, "Zeugenschrifttum," 4 July 1967, IfZ, ZS 2424. "Manuscripts": "It was his custom to disguise his intelligence activity, whenever he found it impossible to work openly for the SD, by posing as a collector

of photostats of medieval manuscripts located in French monasteries and libraries, claiming that such a collection was for the use of his own monastery in Beuron." Hartl, interrogation, 9 Jan. 1947, CI-FIR/123.

7. Etscheit: Müller, "Die Affäre Keller," LK, 95. Commission to buy milk: Keller, "Zeugenschriftum," 4 July 1967, IfZ, ZS 2424.

8. In Rome: Maier, transcript, 17 July 1967, HDP. Pen of Evelyn Waugh: Lukacs, "Diplomacy of the Holy See during World War II," *Catholic Historical Review* 60, no. 2 (1974): 271ff. "With great circumpsection": Bernardini to Maglione, 22 Nov. 1939, rec. 23 Nov., Telegram 52, AES 8790/39, ADSS, I, no. 221.

9. "We reckoned": Müller, "Die Affäre Keller," LK, 97. Intelligence courier: Müller and Hofmeister, transcript, 9 Aug. 1963, HDP, III, 1/7. Within days: Keller, "Zeugenschrifttum," 4 July 1967, IfZ, ZS 2424.

10. "Secret intelligence," "shortly before the war": Müller, transcripts, Aug. 1958 and 8 Aug. 1963 HDP, III, 1/7.

11. "*Schmarren*": Ibid.

12. Swiss newspaper: Halder, transcript, 9 Aug. 1960, HDP.

13. Could say nothing: Lehnert, transcript, 19 Feb. 1967, HDP.

14. Ascher: Müller, transcript, Aug. 1958, HDP, III, 1/7; Leiber, transcript, 9 April 1966, HDP.

15. Birreria Dreher: Müller, transcripts, 8 Aug. 1958, and 8 Aug. 1963, HDP, III, 1/7. Paris: Keller, "Zeugenschriftum," 4 July 1967, IfZ, ZS 2424.

16. "For almost a minute": Schellenberg, *Labyrinth*, 348. All other quotations from this conversation are from that source.

17. *Schwarze Kapelle*: Schellenberg, *Labyrinth*, 347. "Ammunition pack": Schellenberg, *Memorien*, 322 (not in English translation).

CHAPTER 8: ABSOLUTE SECRECY

1. "Carefully guarded": Osborne to London, 1 Dec. 1939, UKNA, FO C 19745/13005/18 (1939); PP, Doc. IV, 528–529.

2. "From any German": Müller, transcripts of 29 May 1958 and 6 Aug. 1963, HDP, III, 1/7.

3. Know too much: Krieg, transcript, 22 Feb. 1967, HDP, III, 1/7. Ciano's distrust: Weizsäcker, *Memoirs*, 222.

4. "Secret agent": Hofmeister, transcript, 6 Aug. 1963, HDP, III, 1/7. Swiss plan: Kurz, transcript, 22 Aug. 1958, HDP.

5. Great attack: Osborne to Halifax, 9 Jan. 1940, UKNA, FO C 770/89/18 (1940); PP, Doc. V, 529–530.

6. Keep no copy: Osborne to Halifax, "12th January 1940 Secret," Halifax Papers, FO 800/318, copy in FO C 1137/89/18 (1940): PP, Doc. VI, 330–332.

7. On the 10th: Deutsch, *Conspiracy*, 140.

8. German source: Charles-Roux to Ministère des Affaires Etrangères, 17 Jan. 1940, HDP.

9. Spring or even before: Charles-Roux to Ministère des Affaires Etrangères, 16 Jan. 1940, HDP. Cell in Germany: "At first I naturally assumed this intelligence came from the Italian Gouvernment, but now I am inclined rather to believe it was a German source. I know that in fact the Vatican has sources of intelligence on German affairs beyond the Nunciature in Berlin." Charles-Roux to Ministère des Affaires Etrangères, 17 Jan. 1940, HDP.

10. Coming German attack: Maglione to Micara, 9 Jan. 1940, ADSS, I, no. 241. Warn the Dutch: Giobbe to Maglione, 14 Jan. 1940, and Maglione to Giobbe, 15 Jan. 1940, ADDS, I, nos. 243/244.

11. Radio Vatican bulletins: Leiber to Deutsch, 26 Aug. 1960, HDP; cf. Attolico to Maglione, AES 1752/40, 20 Feb. 1940, ADSS, III, no. 116. Secret action: Gumpel, interview, 17 May 2014.

12. Low Countries: Cf. Jacobsen, "10. January 40—*Die Affäre* Mechlin," *Wehrwissenschaftliche Rundschau* 4 (1954): 497–515.

13. Cologne, and Vienna: Osborne mentioned only that the coup would not begin in Berlin; the plotters' captured papers and Gestapo inquiry (KB, passim) revealed the other key centers as Cologne, Munich, and Vienna (later, also Paris). Basis for talks: The plotters sought assurance that France would not occupy the Rhineland. They would combine the Rhineland and Westphalia into a West German State; Austria would stay in the Reich; Poland and non-German Czechoslovakia would become independent. "I asked if there was any reparation for the monstrous suffering inflicted on these countries, but there was not." Osborne to Halifax, 7 Feb. 1940, Halifax Papers, UKNA, FO 800/318; PP, Doc. IX, 333–335.

14. Have to respond: Osborne to Halifax, "Personal and Secret," 7 Feb. 1940, Halifax Papers, UKNA, FO 800/318, copy in FO C 2522/89/18 (1940): PP, Doc. IX, 333–335.

15. "Bump off": Ibid. "Was meant": Chamberlain, notation, c. 15 Feb. 1940, UKNA, FO C 2522/89/18 (1940): PP, Doc. X, 335.

16. Pius told him: Osborne to Halifax, 19 Feb. 1940, Halifax Papers, UKNA, FO 800/518: PP, Doc. XIII, 337.

17. Resistance through the pope: Halifax to Osborne, 17 Feb. 1940, UKNA, C 2522/89/18 (1940): PP, Doc. XII, 336–337.

18. British answer: Halifax to Osborne, 17 Feb. 1940, UKNA, FO C 2522/89/18. (1940): PP, Doc. XII, 336–337. Chadwick, *Britain and the Vatican*, 94, states that the message arrived on 26 Feb. 1940; Meehan, *Unnecessary War*, gives the date as the 23rd; neither cites an archival source. "Yet today": Müller, testimony, Huppenkothen trial, 9 Feb. 1951, 222, HDP. "Going ahead": Müller, "Der X-Bericht entsteht," LK, 124; cf. Leiber to Deutsch, 26 Aug. 1960, in "Pius XII," HDP, VII, 4/8; Müller, transcript, 22 Sept. 1966, HDP, III, 1/7; Müller, "Befragungen [Widerstand II]," 26 March

1963, IfZ, ZS 659/4, 218–219; Leiber, "Unterredung," 26–27 Aug. 1960, IfZ, ZS 660, 9; Leiber to Müller, 28 Oct. 1953, IfZ, ZS, 660, 12.

Chapter 9: The X-Report

1. Seven statements: Leiber, debriefing, 26 Aug. 1960, HDP. At any moment: Leiber to Deutsch, 21 May 1965, "Pius XII," HDP, VII, 4/8.

2. Fountains on St. Peter's Square: Leiber, "Unterredung," 26–27 Aug. 1960, IfZ, ZS 660, 2–3, 9; Müller, 5 Aug. 1963, Tape II, HDP, III, 1/7.

3. Meeting with Müller: Müller, "Unkorr. NS üb. Gespräch," 1963, IfZ, ZS 659/3, 17; Müller, "In der zweiten Heimat," LK, 88. Müller's hotel: Müller, transcript, 9 April 1966, HDP, III, 1/7. Reading them: Müller, transcripts, 8 Aug. 1963 and 24 March 1966, HDP, III, 1/7.

4. Aggression and war: Osborne to Halifax, 23 Feb. 1940, UKNA, FO C 3044/89/18 (1940): PP, Doc. XIV, 337–338.

5. Heard that story: Cadogan, diary, 28 Feb. 1940, ed. Dilks, 256–257. "Mgr. Kaas": Foreign Office (London) telegram to Osborne, 4 March 1940, PP, Doc. XVI, 339 n 48. German seminarians: Cited in Osborne to Nichols, 21 March 1940, UKNA, FO R 3781/3237/22 (1940): PP, Doc. XV, 338–339.

6. "Secret agents": Osborne to Nichols, 21 March 1940, UKNA, FO R 3781/3237/22 (1940): PP, Doc. XV, 338–339.

7. 10–11 March: The date and text of this Halifax letter, mentioned in Osborne's 27 March note, remain uncertain. Osborne wrote up a summary for Pius, but could not "give its date or any reference," he told London, "as I destroyed it in deference to the Pope's request for absolute secrecy." Osborne does, however, give a clue to the note's date and content: "If I remember rightly [it] was mentioned in your letter [that] other similar approaches had reached His Majesty's Government through other channels." Osborne here apparently refers to Ulrich von Hassell's 22/23 Feb. meetings with unofficial British emissary J. Lonsdale Bryans in Arosa Switzerland, of which Cadogan had news by 28 Feb. (diary, ed. Dilks, 256–257). Thus Halifax probably sent this final communication to the plotters around 28 Feb. or in early March. Allowing up to ten days for the arrival of the message by diplomatic pouch through Axis-aligned Italy (Halifax's 17 Feb. letter reached Osborne only on 26 Feb.), this Halifax letter would have reached the Vatican around 9–10 March. Müller was in Rome on 11 March ("Unkorr. NS üb. Gespräch," IfZ, ZS 659/3, 24) and he likely received the final British terms then. Müller would then have had five days to fly back to Berlin and work up Halifax's terms into the X-Report material, which Hassell saw on the 16th (diary, 83). That general rhythm of events would accord with the surviving witnesses' memories of a rushed process (Christine von Dohnanyi to Deutsch, 26 June 1958, "Pius XII," HDP, VII, 4/8). Hassell's diary described the British terms: "Halifax, speaking expressly for the British government, was . . . cagey in framing his statements and touched on points

like 'decentralization of Germany' and 'a referendum on Austria.'" That language, echoing Halifax's 17 Feb. greenlighting note to Osborne (UKNA, C 2522/89/18 1940; PP, Doc. XII, 336–337), perhaps occurred in a papal summary that formed a top-sheet of the X-packet. "Regime": Leiber, "Unterredung," 26–27 Aug. 1960, IfZ, ZS 660. Fisherman: Leiber, debriefing, 26 Aug. 1960, HDP.

8. Rejoiced: Müller, testimony, Huppenkothen trial, 9 Feb. 1951, 222, HDP. Intrigues: Müller, "Diskussionen," LK, 133.

9. Down to wait: Leiber, debriefing, 26 Aug. 1960, HDP.

10. Typed pages: Müller, transcript, 9 Feb. 1967, HDP.

11. "Decent Germany": Müller, testimony, Huppenkothen trial, 5 Feb. 1951, transcript, 178. Armistice through the pope: Deutsch, "British Territorial Terms as Reportedly Stated in the X-Report" (chart), CH, 302; Leiber to Müller, 28 Oct. 1953, IfZ, ZS, 660, 13–14. Attack on the Soviet Union: Responding to such an accusation in the Prague journal *Prace*, Pius XII dictated and corrected in his own hand a démenti that appeared in *L'Osservatore Romano*, 11–12 Feb. 1946: ADSS, I, 514–515. Help the conspirators: Hassell, diary, 19 March 1940, 83.

12. Organize a revolt: Osborne to London, 27 March 1940, UKNA, FO C 4743/5/18 (1940): PP, Doc. XVI, 339–340.

13. "Disillusioned": Osborne to Halifax, 3 April 1940, Halifax Papers, FO 800/318: PP, Doc. XVIII, 340–341.

14. Wishes and thanks: Osborne to Halifax, 3 April 1940, Halifax Papers, FO 800/318: PP, Doc. XVIII, 340–341. Plotters through Müller: Hassell, diary, 6 April 1940, 87–88 ("I met with Oster and Dohnanyi at Oster's [on the evening of 3 April]. . . . They then showed me the notes of a go-between, Dr. Josef Müller, from which it would appear that the Pope and the British hold fast to their viewpoint").

15. Unarmed man: Halder, transcript, 9 Aug. 1960, HDP; Groscurth, diary, 1 Nov. 1939. X-Report: Müller, transcript, 27 May 1970, IfZ, ZS 659/4, 180; Müller, transcript, 22 Sept. 1966, HDP, III, 1/7.

16. "Christian morality": Hassell, diary, 19 March 1940, 83. Put him aside: Hassell, diary, 6 April 1940, 86. Halder said that he turned down Hassell for "reasons of caution." Halder, transcript, 9 Aug. 1960, HDP.

17. Documents to Halder: Hassell, diary, 6 April 1940, 88. SS crimes: Bethge, *Bonhoeffer*, 674.

18. Vatican cutout: Halder, transcript, 9 Aug. 1960, HDP.

19. "Arrest me": Sendtner in E.P., *Die Vollmacht des Gewissens*, 1:473.

20. "Signature?": Halder, transcript, 9 Aug. 1960, HDP. Ten days: Thomas, "Mein Beitrag zum Kampf gegen Hitler," 4.

21. New opportunity: Hassell, *Diaries*, 129; Liedig, transcript, 9 Aug. 1960, HDP. Schönhöffer: Müller, transcript, 22 Sept. 1966, HDP, III, 1/7. Information to London: Osborne to London, 27 March 1940, UKNA, FO C 4743/5/18 (1940); PP, Doc. XVI, 339–340.

22. React in force: Müller, transcript, 22 Sept. 1966, HDP.

23. "None came": Leiber to Deutsch, 26 Aug. 1960, "Pius XII," HDP, VII, 4/8.

24. Produced nothing: Leiber, "Unterredung," 26–27 Aug. 1960, IfZ, ZS 660, 5.

CHAPTER 10: WARNINGS TO THE WEST

1. Again felt obliged: Christine von Dohnanyi, "Vollmacht des Gewissens," Publikation e.V 1956, 487, IfZ, ZS/A 28., Bd. 13.

2. "Clean hands": Müller and Christine von Dohnanyi, testimony, E.P., 1 Dec. 1958, IfZ, ZS 659.

3. Church business: Rohleder, testimony, E.P., 25 Feb. 1952, HDP; Müller and Hofmeister, transcript, 9 Aug. 1963, HDP, III, 1/7. "Just ahead": Deutsch, *Conspiracy*, 336 n 17, citing "conversations with Dr. Müller."

4. Rubber stamp: Müller, transcript, 23 Feb. 1967, HDP, III, 1/7.

5. Eighth: Jacobsen, *Fall Gelb*, 141; Sas, "Het begon in Mai 1940," Part II, 16. Attack dates: Müller, transcript, 22 Sept. 1966, HDP, III, 1/7.

6. "Board meeting": Schmidhuber, transcript, 6 Aug. 1958, HDP; Leiber, transcript, 26 Aug. 1960, HDP; Müller, transcript, 28 Feb. 1967, HDP, III, 1/7. Briefed the pope: Leiber, transcripts, 26 Aug. 1960 and 9 April 1966, HDP.

7. Intelligence at once: Tardini, notation, 9 May 1940, HDP. Brussels: ADSS, I, 436. Marie José: Tardini, *Memories*, 118–119.

8. Sabotage: Charles-Roux, report summary 7 May 1940, HDP; Charles-Roux, *Huit ans au Vatican*, 384.

9. Adrien Nieuwenhuys: Leiber, transcript, 26 Aug. 1960, HDP.

10. "Development is near": Nieuwenhuys to Brussels, telegram no. 7, 4 May 1940, Service Historique, Belgian Ministry of Foreign Affairs.

11. Vatican warnings: The warnings were ample. See Maglione to Micara and Giobbe, Telegram no. 30 (A. E. S. 3994/40), and Telegram no. 18 (A.E.S. 3993/40), 3 May 1940, ADSS, I, no. 293; Maglione, note, AES 2895/40, ADSS, I, no. 295, n. 1; minutes, War Cabinet meeting, 7 May 1940, UKNA, FO, WM 114 (40), 5 (PP, Doc. XVIII, n. 57); Osborne to London, 6 May 1940, UKNA, FO C 6584/5/18 (1940): PP, Doc. XVIII, 54. "Expectations before": Osborne to London, 6 May 1940, UKNA, FO C 6584/5/18 (1940): PP, Doc. XVIII, 541. Mid-April: Osborne to London, 19 March 1940, UKNA, FO, R 3546/57/22, PP, Doc. XVI, n. 51.

12. Counter-signature: Tardini, *Memories*, 116–119; ADSS, I, 444–447.

13. Spurred on by Berlin: Müller, "Attacken auf den Papst," LK, 142.

14. "Even worse": Montini, note, 13 May 1940, A.S.S. no. 13628, ADSS, I.

15. "Trapped animal": Osborne, diary, 5 Jan. 1941, in Chadwick, *Britain and the Vatican*, 140. "Cave of Spies": Ibid., 174, citing Italian Embassy to the Holy See, memorandum, 10 May 1943, AE, Santa Sede, 1943, Busta 66. Trevi Fountain: Osborne to Halifax, 3 May 1940, UKNA, FO 371/24935/69; Maglione to

Alfieri, 8–10 May 1940, AE, Sante Sede, 1940, Busta 49. "Death to the pope!": *Tablet* (London), 30 Aug. 1941.

16. Manuscripts: Padellaro, *Portrait*, 188; Hatch and Walshe, *Crown*, 155.

17. "Dubious intrigue": Osborne to Halifax, 9 Jan. 1940, UKNA, FO, C 770/89/18 (1940) (PP, Doc. V, 529–530). Suburban rectory: Müller, transcripts, 31 June 1958, 24 March 1966, 5 Aug. 1963, Tape II, HDP, III, 1/7. Their papers: Noots, transcript, 9 Sept. 1960, HDP.

18. How perilous: Gasbarri, *Quando il Vaticano confinava con il Terzo Reich*, 1217; Hofmann, *O Vatican!* 28; Graham and Alvarez, *Nothing Sacred*, 92–93; Holmes, *Papacy*, 152.

Chapter 11: The Brown Birds

1. "High treason": Höttl, "The Jesuit Intelligence Service (General Commando Munich)," 26 Nov. 1945, NARA, RG 226, 174/104/799. His movements: Müller, transcript, 21 Feb. 1967, HDP.

2. "Giovanni": Müller, "Die Braunen Vögel," LK, 148.

3. "God help us": Ibid.

4. Turned away: Ibid., 148–149.

5. "Rome 1 May": Nieuwenhuys to Brussels, telegram no. 7, 4 May 1940, Service Historique, Belgian Ministry of Foreign Affairs.

6. Vatican connections: Neuhäusler, transcript, 25 March 1966, HDP. "Leader of the investigation": Müller, "Die Braunen Vögel," LK, 150: "Der Admiral hatte mich zu meinem eigenen Untersuchungsführer gemacht."

7. Next Müller called: Deutsch, *Conspiracy*, 345. A "satisfactory conversation": "Landsmann, wird gesucht," LK, 152.

8. Ascher: Müller, transcript, Aug. 1958, HDP, III, 1/7; Leiber, transcript, 9 April 1966, HDP.

9. "I have had an inspiration": Deutsch, *Conspiracy*, 346.

10. Gymnastics coach: Weitz, *Hitler's Diplomat*, 234–235.

11. Müller's name: Rohleder, testimony, E.P., 25 Feb. 1952.

12. Ascher: Müller, transcript, 25 Feb. 1967, HDP, III, 1/7.

13. "Logically convincing," "inconclusive": Deutsch, *Conspiracy*, 348.

14. Accusation: Huppenkothen, "Verhältnis Wehrmacht-Sicherheitspolizei," HDP. Delivery to Canaris: Müller, transcript, 25 Feb. 1967, HDP, III, 1/7.

15. Word of honor: Müller, "Unkorr. NS üb. Gespräch," 1963, IfZ, ZS 659/3, 20.

16. "Absolute silence": UKNA, FO 371/26542/C 610/324/P.

17. German plotters: Leiber, transcript, 26 Aug. 1960, HDP. Fortune's wheel: Müller, "Fehlgeschlagen," LK, 161. Basics of the plot: Müller, "Italien nach Befreiung," LK, 284.

18. "Here within": Curran, "Bones," in *Classics Ireland* 3 (1996).

19. Beck: Müller, transcript, 4 Aug. 1960, HDP. "Impossible": Müller, "Der X-Bericht entsteht," LK, 124. Integral to plans: Müller, testimony to E.P., 31 Aug. 1953, IfZ.

20. On Müller and Bonhoeffer see: Bonhoeffer to Bethge, 18 Nov. 1940, DBW, 16, 1/29; Bonhoeffer to Bethge, from Ettal, postmarked "Munich, 10-31-40," DBW, 16, 1/24; Müller, transcript, 8 Aug. 1963, Tape III, HDP, III, 1/7.

21. Key to the library: "Die Benediktinerabtei Ettal," 405; "Festschrift Dr. Josef Müller-zum 80. Geburtstag-27. März 1978," Munich, 1978.

22. "Unity of Christendom": Bonhoeffer, "Sketch," c. 2 Dec. 1940, DBW, 16:498. "Boldness": Bonhoeffer to Bethge, 29 Nov. 1940, ibid., 96. Become treason: Editor's Afterword, ibid., 652 n 26, citing Bethge, 14 Feb. 1987.

23. Christmas 1940: Bonhoeffer to Bethge, 16 Nov. 1940, DBW, 16, 1/27; Bonhoeffer to Hans-Werner Jensen, 26 Dec. 1940, DBW, 16, 1/52; Bonhoeffer to Paula Bonhoeffer, from Ettal, 28 Dec. 1940, DBW, 16, 1/53; Bethge, *Bonhoeffer*, 725, and 1003 n 129; "Vernehmung von Pater Zeiger," 9 July 1948, IfZ, ZS A-49, 25ff.; Dulles, *Germany's Underground*, 118; Lange, "Der Pfarrer in der Gemeinde Heute," *Monatsschrift für Pastoraltheologie* 6 (1966): 199–229; Schlabrendorff, "Betrifft: Haltung dar Kirchen Deutschlands zu Hitler," 25 Oct. 1945, DNTC, vol. X, 18:4; Schlabrendorff, "Events," 8.

24. Bells for bullets: Rösch, "Aufzeichnung," 31 Aug. 1941, KGN, 91; Lang, *Der Sekretär*, 193ff.; Bormann to Gauleiters, 13 Jan. 1941, Volk, *Akten*, V, 314 n 2, 543; AD, 191; Volk, *Akten*, V, 543; Ditscheid, "Pater Laurentius Siemer—Widerstandskämpfer im Dritten Reich," Radio Vatican, 21 July 2006. "Church in Germany": As Pius wrote the Bishop of Limburg on 20 Feb. 1941 (BPDB, no. 65). Later that year, Pius told a French cardinal: "If Germany wins the war, I believe it will be the greatest catastrophe to strike the Church in many centuries." Graham, *Vatican and Communism*, 185.

25. Militant popular front: Schlabrendorff, "Events," 8.

26. Classroom keys: Landrat Parsberg 939, 26 Sept. 1941; GP Velsburg, 21 Sept. 1941; KLB, IV, 294; Kershaw, *Popular Opinion and Political Dissent*, 346. Pitchforks: BDSG, 655 n 2. Restored the crosses: Epp to Lammers, 23 Dec. 1941, GSA, Reichsstaathalder 157; Siebert to Wagner, 29 Jan. 1942, GSA, MA 105248.

27. "Prepared to die": Duschl to Bertram, 1 Dec. 1940, AAW, IA25c57. Second plot against Hitler: Lapomarda, *Jesuits*, 13.

CHAPTER 12: FORGING THE IRON

1. "Deserve no better": Moltke, 11 Aug. 1940, LF, 104–106.

2. "Cover in the fields": Moltke, 13 Aug. 1940, LF, 97–98.

3. "Renewing themselves": Moltke, 8 Aug. 1940, LF, 86–87.

4. "Countrymen": Moltke to Curtis, [15?] April 1942; Balfour and Frisby, *Moltke*, 185 (not in BF or LF).

5. Along Catholic lines: Moltke, 28 Sept. 1941, LF, 166.

6. Headquarters in Berlin: Moltke, 13 Oct. 1941, BF, 303. "Strongest man in Germany": Moltke, 10 April 1943, LF.

7. Oster's resistance group: Korherr, "Guttenberg," *Deutsche Tagenpost*, 28 April 1965. Another member: Moltke to Freya, LF, 16.

8. Upstairs and rang: Rösch, "Delp †," 22 Jan. 1956, AR, 308.

9. "Splendid library": Rösch, "Kirchenkampf 1937–1945," 22 Oct. 1945, AR, 220–222. "Listening": Roon, *German Resistance*, 108.

10. "Hands of Hitler": Rösch, "Kirchenkampf 1937–1945," 22 Oct. 1945, AR, 220–222.

11. "Germany is lost": Balfour and Frisby, *Moltke*, 165.

12. Affiliated themselves with Nazism: Protestant tradition, nurtured in nationalist states seeking cultural homogeneity, had made more room for racism than did the Roman Catholic tradition, with its transnational perspective and its universalist claims on all souls. "Completing the Reformation: The Protestant Reich Church," Steigmann-Gall, *Holy Reich*, 185–189. Christian resistance to Hitler: "Because of its more consistent stance, the Catholic Church was able to assert its position more successfully within its domain than was the Protestant Church." Norden, "Opposition by Churches and Christians," EGR, 49. "Bishops and the pope": Balfour and Frisby, *Moltke*, 165.

13. "Will you cooperate?": Rösch, "Delp †," 22 Jan. 1956, AR, 308.

14. "Help from the Catholic Church": Bleistein, Rösch, "Kampf," KGN, Doc. 26, 263f. Talks there: Rösch, Jan. 1956. *"Grüss Gott"*: Rösch, "Delp †," 22 Jan. 1956, AR, 306.

15. From Canaris: Leiber, transcript, 9 April 1966, HDP. For the Vatican's advance intelligence on Operation Barbarossa, see also: Appunto Tardini, ADSS, IV, 60, n. 2; Muckermann, *Im Kampf zwischen zwei Epochen*, 643; Bernardini to Maglione, 28 April 1941, ADSSS, IV, no. 331; Count Dalla Torre, 15 May 1941, ADSS, IV, 474, n 4; CSDIC, GG Report 346, 24 Aug. 1945, Lord Dacre Papers, DJ 38, Folder 7(d); Dippel, *Two Against Hitler*, 103, 106; Gisevius, "Information given [to Dulles] under date of December 19, 1946," AWDP, Subseries 15c; Höttl, "Miscellaneous notes on the activities of the Japanese intelligence service in Europe," 7 July 1945, NARA, RG 226, 174/104/799; Höttl, The Secret Front, 289; Hudal, *Römische Tagebücher*, 213; Müller, "Aussagen," 4 June 1952, IfZ, ZS 659/2, 31-32; Müller, transcript, 24 March 1966, HDP, III, I/7; Müller, transcript, 31 Aug. 1955, IfZ, ZS 659/1, 41.

16. On the spot: Eidenschink, interrogation (with Müller), 6 Nov. 1945, DNTC, vol. XVII, Sec. 53.015; Schlabrendorff, "Events," 93, 42; CSDIC, GG Report 346, 24 Aug. 1945, TRP, DJ 38, Folder 7(d); surveillance transcript, 20–21 Nov. 1944, GRGG 226, UKNA, WO 208/4364 (ADG, Doc. 115).

17. Army's honor: Canaris, "Betr.: Anordnung für die Behandlung sowjetischer Kriegsgefangener, Berlin, 15.9.1941," Überschär and Wette, *Überfall*, 301–305.

18. "Old formulations": [B]etr: Besprechung mit Dr. Jos Müller, 23 Feb. 1952, IfZ, ZS A-49, 44. "The dreamers": Müller, transcript, 31 Aug. 1955, IfZ, ZS 659/1, 37.

19. Only his travel: Hoffmann, *Hitler's Personal Security*, 226–227.

20. Victory parade: "Protokoll aus der Verhandlung Halder [vor der] Spruchkammer X München," 124 (Schacht's evidence at hearing on Halder before Denazification Court); Marianne Grafin Schwerin von Schwanenfeld, "Ulrich-Wilhelm Graf Schwerin von Schwanenfeld," typescript, n.d.; Pechel, *Deutscher Widerstand*, 156; Hassell, diary, 19 Jan. 1941, 108–109; Ritter, *Goerdeler*, 274; Hoffmann, *History*, 229. Plan his Russian war: Goebbels, diary, 13 May 1941, 362. Younger military staffers: Hassell, diary, 4 Oct. 1941, 143; Schlabrendorff, "Events," 93, 48; Schwerin, "Von Moskau bis Stalingrad," *Köpfe*, 229–246; Vollmer, *Doppelleben*, 155; Fest, *Hitler's Death*, 179–186.

21. "Vast Russian steppes": Hoffmann, *Stauffenberg*, 137 (without source). "Amen in church": Burleigh, *Third Reich*, 712, citing Hoffmann, *Stauffenberg*, 137, where the quote does not, however, appear; but cf. Scheurig, *Tresckow*, 112–113. "Ball over there": Scheurig, *Tresckow*, 115. Emissary to Beck's group: Hassell, diary, 4 Oct. 1941, 142–144.

22. "Navigates a whirlpool": Kaltenbrunner to Bormann, 15 Sept. 1944, KB, 390–391. "Nuclei": Hassell, diary, 4 Oct. 1941; Zeller, *Flame*, 159.

CHAPTER 13: THE COMMITTEE

1. Depository: Müller, transcript, 8 Aug. 1963, Tape VI, HDP, III, 1/7. Reports to Rome: Rösch, report on anticlerical graffiti in Sept. 1935, OSS, "Persecution," 6 July 1945, DNTC, vol. XVIII, 3. From Rome to Germany: "Independent of the Roman conversations, it was also possible for me to maintain contact, with the pope on the one hand and with [Dominican Provincial] Fr. Laurentius Siemer, [and with Jesuit Provincial] Fr. Rösch . . . on the other hand." Müller, "Befragung des Staatsministers," 2 Sept. 1954, IfZ, ZS 659/1, 51.

2. Fulda: Hartl, "Vatican Intelligence Service," 9 Jan. 1947, CI-FIR/123, Annex I; Leiber, transcript, 17 May 1966, 40; Hartl, interrogation, 9 Jan. 1947, CI-FIR/123; cf. Höttl, *Secret Front*, 40.

3. Only to the pope: Ahaus, "Holy Orders," in CE, vol. 11 (1911); in Nazi-occupied Europe, Kwitny, *Man of the Century*, 60; thus, "if someone wanted to deal with the pope, he didn't first have to ask the bishops' permission, or [ask] how they would behave if the pope made a peace overture." Müller, "Unkorr. NS üb. Gespräch," 1963, IfZ, ZS 659/3, 14. Martial spirit: "No other group of Catholic people resisted Hitler as much as the Munich Jesuits. Their importance lies in the extent of their activity. The Jesuits sought to push the bishops into confrontation with Hitler; they worked with the Kreisau Circle in planning for a post-Nazi government of Germany; some of them involved themselves in the moral question about assassinating Hitler, and some rescued or attempted to rescue Jews." Phayer, "Questions about Catholic Resistance," *Church History* 70, no. 2 (2001): 339. Heroism: Pius XI, *Inviti All'eroismo. Discorsi di S.S.Pio XI nell'occasione della lettura dei Brevi per le Canonizzazioni, le Beatificazioni, le*

proclamazioni dell'eroicità delle virtù dei Santi, Beati e Servi di Dio, 3 vols.; Godman, *Hitler and the Vatican*, 167.

4. "Lord God": Rösch, "Bericht über die Tagung der Superioren-Vereinigung in Berlin am 26. und 27. Mai 1941," 1 June 1941, KGN, Doc. 2, 63–66. "Intelligence service": "Vorschläge fur einen kirchlichen Informationsdienst, Mitte Juni 1941," ADB, V, no. 664 (AAW, lAz5b57, with heading, "Das Kirchliche Nachrichtenwesen. 7 Tatsachen–Vorschläge, Juni 1941," inscribed by hand: "Antrag Würzburg"); Rösch, "Denkschrift," c. 20 June 1941, ADB, VI, no. 665; Rösch, "Aufzeichnung," 31 Aug. 1941, KGN, Doc. 6, 89ff.; transcript, "Diözesan-Intelligences-Dienst [Diocesan Intelligence Service]," 14 Sept. 1941, OAM, GAI2p; Rösch, "Lagebericht aus dem Ausschuss für Ordensangelegenheiten," 28 Sept. 1941, KGN, Doc. 7, 98ff.; Conference of Bavarian Ordinariat Representatives, 14 Oct. 1941, ADB, V, 570f.; Angermaier to Faulhaber, 2 Feb. 1942, ADB, V, II, 865; Siemer, *Erinnerungen*, vol. 2, 415–441. Just the Committee: Rösch, "Lagebericht aus dem Ausschuss für Ordensangelegenheiten," 28 Sept. 1941, KGN, Doc. 7, 98ff.; Rösch, report, 23 April 1942, ADB, II, 915; Siemer, "Erinnerungen," vol. 2, 415, ACDP, I, 096; Bleistein, "Lothar König," DKK," 16–19; Höllen, *Heinrich Wienken*, 101; Ordensangelegenheiten, 17 Aug. 1941, AEM, Faulhaber papers, 8189; Bauer, statement, c. Nov. 1979, NLB; Leugers, "Besprechungen," GM, 180.

5. Like-minded men: König to Rösch, 31 Jan. and 6 Feb. 1941; note re: telephone call from Munich, 18 April 1941; Leugers, "Gruppenprofil," GM, 136–140; Orders Committee report, 14 June 1942, ADB, II, no. 893; Rösch to Brust, 22 April 1942, KGN, Doc. 12, 160ff.; Rösch, "Aus meinem Kriegstagebuch," *Mitteilungen aus der Deutschen Provinz* 8 (1918–1920), 284; Rösch, "Bericht und Stellungnahme aus dem Ausschuss für Ordensangelegenheiten," 14 June 1942, KGN, Doc. 14, 181ff.; Superiors Association report, 1 June 1941, GM, 189; Schmidlin, memo, Aug. 1941, ADB, V, 496 n 4; Transcript, Fulda Bishops Conference, 18–20 Aug. 1942, ADB, V, 851.

6. "Tante Johanna": Vogelsberg to Leugers, 27–28 Sept. 1987, and Galandi to Leugers, 13 Oct. 1987, GM, 183.

7. Run over Hitler: Abel to Leugers, 14 Jan. 1988, GM, 300.

8. Franz Halder: Josef Müller managed the initial Jesuit approach to Halder through Berlin Fr. Georg von Sachsen, who met with Halder on 23 Feb. 1941. Halder, diary, 23 Feb. 1941, *Kriegstagebuch*, vol. 2, 291; Müller, transcripts (27 May 1970, IfZ, ZS 659/4, 180; 22 Sept. 1966; c. 1966–1967), HDP, III, 1/7. Father König met Halder on 6 and 7 April ("Datenüberblick," 6–7 April 1941, GM, 376). For Rösch and Halder, see Rösch, memo, c. 20 June 1941, ADB, II, V, 400; Volk, *Akten*, V, 397n; "Anhang," GM, 476 n 459; Bleistein, "Im Kreisauer Kreis," AD, 280. For later Jesuit contacts with Colonel Claus Stauffenberg along the same lines, cf. Delp, "Verteidigung," c. 9 Jan. 1945, GS, IV, 350, 355. "Against a dictator": Halder to Volk, 7 June 1966, AD, 280.

9. Escape detection: Bleistein, "Alfred Delp und Augustin Rösch," AD, 418; Kempner, *Priester*, 66; Delp to Luise Oestreicher, 22 Dec. 1944, GS, IV, 129; Lewy, "Pius XII, the Jews, and the German Catholic Church," *Commentary* 37, no. 2 (Feb.

1964): 23–35; Menke, "Thy Will Be Done: German Catholics and National Identity in the Twentieth Century," *Catholic Historical Review* 91, no. 2 (2005): 300–320.

10. Freethinker . . . headaches: Rösch, "Eine Klarstellung," 6 July 1945, KGN, Doc. 23, 230ff.; Delp, "Bereitschaft," 1935, GS, I, 83; Delp, "Der Kranke Held," GS, II, 205; Delp, "Die Moderne Welt und Die Katholische Aktion," 1935, GS, I, 70; Delp, "Entschlossenheit," 1935, GS, I, 100; Delp, "Kirchlicher und Völkischer Mensch," 1935, GS, I, 102; Kreuser, "Remembering Father Alfred Delp"; Marion Dönhoff, *In memoriam 20 Juli 1944*; Phayer, "Questions about Catholic Resistance," *Church History* 70, no. 2 (2001): 341.

11. "Take action": Hans Hutter to Bleistein, 16 Sept. 1987, AD, 289.

12. Channel to the pope: Rösch to Brust, Feb. 1943, KGN, Doc. 17, 203ff. "I . . . discussed it": Rösch, "Kirchenkampf," 1945, KGN, 222 *("Ich erbat Bedenkzeit, habe mich mit ernsten Leuten besprochen und später zugesagt.")*. "Strongest man in Germany": Roon, *German Resistance to Hitler*, 140; Moltke, 9 April 1943, LF, 294.

13. "Concentration of all forces": Pius XII to Preysing, 30 Sept. 1941, BPDB, no. 76.

14. "Proud to be a Jew!": "A Papal Audience in War-Time," *Palestine Post*, 28 April 1944. Wisla: William Doino to author, 19 Oct. 2015, citing testimony by Herman Herskovic.

15. Yellow star: Klemperer, diary, 7 Oct. 1941, tr. Chalmers, *Witness 1933–1941*, 439. The chaplain [*sic*] was Bernhard Lichtenberg. Klemperer's "vouched for" report perhaps conflated Lichtenberg's public praying for the Jews, which landed him in a concentration camp. "Badly judged": Roncalli, diary entry for 10 Oct. 1941 audience with Pius XII, in Alberto Melloni, *Fra Istanbul, Atene e la guerra. La missione di A.G. Roncalli (1935–1944)* (Rome: Marietti, 1993), 240 ("Si diffuse a dirmi della sua larghezza di tratto coi Germani che vengono a visitarlo. Mi chiese se il suo silenzio circa il contegno del nazismo non è giudicato male").

16. "Blood on his hands": Gumpel, interview, 1 June 2014.

17. *Federalist Papers*: Kennan, *Memoirs*, 121.

18. "I cannot": Roon, *German Resistance*, 82.

19. Wrote in October 1941: Hassell, diary, 4, Oct. 1941, 142–144. Stuttgart and Cologne: Siemer, Erinnerungen, vol. 2, 415, ACDP, I, 096. Catholic Center Party: Gumpel, interview, 17 May 2014; Mommsen, "Nikolaus Gross," *Archiv für Sozialgeschichte* 44 (2004): 704–706; Bücker, "Kölner Kreis"; Bücker, "Mitglieder des Kölner Kreises: Bernhard Letterhaus."

20. Over Christmas: NARA, RG 226, Entry 106, Box 0013, Folders 103–105; Lochner to White House (Lauchlin Currie), 19 June 1942, FDRL, OF 198a; Lochner to Prince Louis Ferdinand and Princess Kira, 2 June 1941, Lochner Papers; John, *Twice*, 69–70, 71–72, 73–74, 127; Lochner, *Stets das Unerwartete*, 355–357; Prince Louis Ferdinand, *Rebel Prince*, 306–324; Lochner, *Always the Unexpected*, 295; Klemperer, *German Resistance*, 132–133, 193, 218, 233–234, 295; Hoffmann, *History*, 109, 214–215; Bartz, *Tragödie*, 229; Rothfels, *German Opposition*, 134–137; Zeller, *Flame*, 252; Fest, *Hitler's Death*, 210.

21. Leaders to tea: MI9, audio surveillance transcript, 26 Jan. 1943, UKNA, SRX 150 (ADG, Doc. 84). "Should be shot": Etzdorf, affidavit, 1947, Weizsäcker trial, IMT, Case XI, Defense Doc. no. 140.

22. Respondek: Dippel, *Two Against Hitler*, 104–106, citing Valeska Hoffmann, interview, 22 March 1986, and Agnes Dreimann, interview, 26 July 1986; Maria Schachtner, letter, 30 Nov. 1986; cf. State Department to Woods, 2 Dec. 1941, no. 2892, RG 59, NARA, RG 59, Woods, Sam E., Decimal File 123; Woods to Cordell Hull, 28 June 1945, NARA, RG 59, 740.00119 Control (Germany)/6–2845. Pearl Harbor: Müller, "Protokoll des Colloquiums am 31. August 1955," IfZ, ZS 659/1, 44; Müller, "Unkorr. NS üb. Gespräch," 1963, IfZ, ZS 659/3, 32; Müller, transcript, 27 May 1970, IfZ, ZS 659/4, 183.

23. Could not win: Tittmann, *Inside the Vatican of Pius XII*, 130. "Most embarrassing": Lochner, *Always the Unexpected*, 295; cf. Donovan to FDR, 24 Jan. 1945, NARA, RG 226, Entry 210, Box 364, and Joseph Rodrigo memo to Hugh Wilson, 27 Aug. 1944, NARA, RG 226, Entry 210, Box 344.

24. Sacked him: Halder, statement, CSDIC, 7 Aug.1945, TRP, DJ 38, Folder 6; Hassell, diary, 21 and 23 Dec. 1941, 150, 152; Halder, *Kriegstagebuch*, vol. 3, 354–356; Hassell, diary, 22 Dec. 1941, 152; Kessel, "Verborgene Saat," 12 April 1945, VS, 216–217, 221; Schwerin, *Köpfe*, 309; surveillance transcript, GRGG 210, 11–12 Oct. 1944, UKNA, WO 208/4364, ADG, Doc. 111. "Image of man": Moltke to Curtis, [15?] April 1942, Balfour and Frisby, *Moltke*, 185 (not in BF or LF).

25. "Guardian angel": Freya von Moltke, *Memories of Kreisau*, 28. "Reborn because of him": Idem to Bleistein, 12 Aug. 1986, AR, 123.

26. "Economic order?": Beate Ruhm von Oppen simplifies the phrase in her English translation as "talks at the Vatican," erasing the agency of the pope precisely where the original German text emphasizes it. Moltke, 9 May 1942, LF, 217, BF, 271. "The stranger": In a footnote to her English translation, Oppen speculates the stranger was "[possibly] Alfred Delp . . . but probably Lothar König . . . often the liaison between Munich and the Kreisauers in Berlin" (LF, 217 n 2). Neither König nor Delp was a stranger to Moltke, however, and throughout his letters he mentions them not by cryptonyms but by name. Neither Jesuit, so far as is known, traveled to Rome during the war to consult Pius or his deputies. By describing the emissary as a liaison between Munich and Berlin, where the original text identifies him as a liaison with the pope, Oppen yet again erases the personal involvement of Pius the Twelfth just where the historical record affirms it. Rösch's Jesuit biographer, Fr. Roman Bleistein, could not determine the identity of the mysterious envoy, but posited that the question about economic issues came from the pope via one of his German Jesuit advisers in Rome—either Fr. Leiber or Fr. Anton Gundlach, professor of social ethics at the Gregoriana, who advised Pius on social questions. Bleistein, AR, 29n. "So was I": Moltke, 9 May 1942, LF, 218. Edited by Rösch: Rösch/König/Delp, "Ziele

und Vorstellungen des Kreises," Erste Kreisauer Tagung, no. 1, DKK, 61–83. Long admired: When the war began, he took to his bed and read the encyclical. Moltke, 3 Sept. 1939, LF, 32, and n. 1.

27. "Communities": Mommsen, *Alternatives*, 31, 140, 54. Vanished with Charlemagne: The champions of *Reichsgedanken*, a nostalgia for the Catholicism of the Holy Roman Empire, started from the notion that the West had begun to go wrong with the Reformation and the loss of the universal Christian church. As argued by Viennese social philosopher Othmar Spann, this was widely accepted in the Catholic resistance. But Protestant authors, taking their cue from the writings of Edgar Julius Jung, also adopted this viewpoint. Mommsen, *Alternatives*, 137; cf. Prittie, "The Opposition of the Church of Rome," in Jacobsen, ed., *July 20, 1944*; Roon, *German Resistance*, 29–99; Rothfels, *German Opposition*, 102; Zeller, *Geist der Freiheit*, 227.

28. Cause civil war: Cf. Aquinas, *In II Sent.*, d. XLIV, Q. ii, a. 2; Suarez, *Def. fidei*, VI, iv, 7; Harty, "Tyrannicide," CE, vol. 15 (1912). Legitimized the plot: Roon, *Neuordnung*, 241; Bleistein, AR, 288; Bleistein, "Delps Vermächntis," AD, 427; cf. Phayer on Delp and tyrannicide in "Questions about Catholic Resistance," *Church History* 70, no. 2 (2001): 341. In the large-group sessions "Moltke condemned all assassinations," presumably so that if the Gestapo interrogated any cell members they could only honestly repeat his disclaimer; Rösch recorded that he had confidential information that Moltke "had thought quite differently." Rösch, "Kirchenkampf," 22 Oct. 1945, AR, 210. "Made public": "Irgendwie war die Rede, dass wieder ein Anschlag auf Hitler gemacht geworden sei, von dem aber nichts in die Öffentlichkeit komme." Rösch, "Kirchenkampf," 22 Oct. 1945, AR, 210.

29. Crosshairs: Roon, *German Resistance*, 152.

CHAPTER 14: CONVERSATIONS IN THE CRYPT

1. Peter's Tomb: Less is known about the content of these talks than about their fact and form, as related in Müller, transcripts (3 Aug. 1963, Tape I, HDP, III, 1/7; 31 Aug. 1955, IfZ, ZS 659/1, 32); Bonhoeffer to Leibholz Family, from Rome, 9 July 1942, DBW, 16, 1/189; Bonhoeffer, LPP, 164, and DBW, 8, 238; Bonhoeffer, letter, 7 July 1942, DBW, 16, 339; Christine Dohnanyi, IfZ, ZS 603, 66–67; Müller, "Fahrt in die Oberpfalz," LK, 241; cf. Hesemann, "Pius XII, Stauffenberg und Der Ochsensepp," *Kath.Net*, 19 July 2009.

2. "Madonna": Müller, "Fahrt in die Oberpfalz," LK, 241. For echoes of the content of these crypt talks in wider resistance circles, see, e.g., Gisevius, "Information given [to Dulles] under date of December 19, 1946," AWDP, Subseries 15c; and Thomas, statement, 6 Nov. 1945, DNTC, vol. V, sec. 10.08. Revenge: "In our conversations about the clergy, he [Bonhoeffer] posited that Catholic priests, as celibates, would have a stronger position in the fight against Hitler, while I thought that the wives of Protestant ministers, when their husbands were arrested, not only helped out

pastorally, but otherwise represented the [minister's] office so well, that they earned respect for it." Müller, "Fahrt in die Oberpfalz," 240.

3. "Human beings": Cologne pastoral letter outline, 28 June 1943, ADB, VI, 195. "Especially the Jews": Dritte Kreisauer Tagung, no. 2, "Zur Befriedung Europas," DKK, 249–259. Route to Switzerland: Bleistein, "Schriftsteller und Seelsorger," AD, 174 ("kümmerte sich um verfolgte Juden und pflegte nicht zuletzt zahlreiche herzliche Freundschaften"). During the prewar persecution of the Jews, Delp and a certain "Annemarie" had founded a group in Munich to help them. Gertrud Luckner, a famous Catholic rescuer of Jews, recalled that she traveled often to Munich to interact with Delp's group. Phayer, "Questions about Catholic Resistance," *Church History* 70, no. 2 (2001): 334, citing Luckner and Marie Schiffer interview transcript, 98.

4. From Warsaw to Brooklyn: "During the Polish campaign . . . I remember that Admiral Canaris told me about his efforts to comply with the request of the US Consul General to safely bring out a high Jewish rabbi from German-occupied Warsaw. The task of fulfilling the American request had characteristically fallen to Admiral Canaris, who took up this task." Bürkner to Wohltat, 15 Jan. 1948, HStAD, NW 10021/49193. Sifton and Stern misidentify the rabbi as "Menachem Mendel Schneersohn" (*No Ordinary Men*, 95n). For the bare facts, see Schneersohn to Cordell Hull, 25 March 1940, WNRC, RG 59, CDF, 811.111. "Ratline": The term "ratline" came into use when fugitive Gentiles later exploited the Church routes and properties that had initially sheltered Jews. A perhaps overcomplicated literature on the ratlines scants the Catholic tradition of sanctuary. On 23 December 1943, when the Gestapo found fifteen Jewish refugees in the Pontifical Russian College, they asked Father Emil Herman why the Jesuits had concealed the Jews, and received the response: "For the same reason which we shall probably be hiding you before long." Herman to Maglione, 22 Dec. 1943, ADSS, IX, no. 482; cf. Wilhelm de Vries to Lapomarda, 3 Nov. 1985, in Lapomarda, *Jesuits*, 220–221. On the use of Catholic monasteries in Jewish rescue, see Gilbert, "Italy and the Vatican," in *The Righteous*, 246–380. For a scholarly treatment of the ratlines, representing the viewpoint of Jewish critics, see Steinacher, "The Vatican Network," *Nazis on the Run*, 101–158; similarly, Phayer, "The Origin of the Vatican Ratlines," *Pius XII*, 173–207. For a Catholic but not uncritical perspective, see Ventresca, "Vatican Ratlines," *Soldier of Christ*, 253–270. The US and British governments asked the Church to facilitate the transit of German scientists and intelligence officers who might prove useful in the Cold War against the Soviets (quintessentially, Gehlen, "From Hitler's Bunker to the Pentagon," *The Service*, 1–20; cf. Naftali, "Reinhard Gehlen and the United States," in Breitman, ed., *U.S. Intelligence and the Nazis*, 375–418). The often overlooked British connection is relevant because the Vatican ratline out of Italy began as a British intelligence operation that helped downed Allied pilots and escaped POWs. See Chadwick, *Britain and the Vatican*, 294ff., and more colorfully but less reliably, Gallagher, *The Scarlet and the Black*; and Derry, *The Rome Escape Line*, passim. From Slovakia to Italy: On Müller and Operation U-7, see Meyer, *Unternehmen Sieben*, 21ff., 18f., 354–358, 363ff., 367–370.

5. Noose: Höhne, *Canaris*, 502. Dealings with Jews: Bartz, *Tragödie*, 129, 133. Bearing down on them: Final Report by Staatsanwalt Dr. Finck, Lüneburg, Verfahren Roeder, Ministry of Justice Archives, Land Niedersachsen, 688, 707, 710; cf. Müller's response to Schmidhuber's allegations, IfZ, ZS 659/3, 2–11.

6. Assassination plots: Müller, transcript, 3 Aug. 1963, Tape I, HDP, III, 1/7. Helped Pius leak: Leiber, "Unterredung," 26–27 Aug. 1960, IfZ, ZS 660, 5–6; Müller, transcripts, 5 and 8 Aug. 1963, Tape III, HDP, III, 1/7. "Gallows with ease": Schmidhuber, "Mitteilungen," c. 1954, Bartz, *Tragödie*, 130–131.

7. "Exterminated": Sapieha to Pius XII, 28 Feb. 1942, ADSS, III, no. 357. Crematoria smoke: Falconi, *Silence*, 148. "Shoot all bishops": Sapieha to Pius XII, 28 Feb. 1942, ADSS, III, no. 357. Secret copy: ADSS, III, p. 15-16. "A child": Stehle, *Eastern Politics*, 214.

8. Reports: "A small group of Catholic activists, deep within the threshold of the episcopacy, had made use of Müller's contacts to the pope under the impression that, if they informed him of the atrocities taking place in the east they could convey several suggestions as to how he could perhaps rouse the conscience of the German faithful." Gisevius, *Wo ist Nebe?*, 233. For "certain death" "gas and lethal injection," "macabre suppositions," "impossible": Hesemann, *Der Papst*, 153-54; cf. Gröber to Pius XII, 14 June 1942, ADB, V, 788; Tittmann to Stettinius, 16 June 1942, Decimal File 1940–1944, Box 5689, File 866A.001/103, RG 59, NARA; Tittmann, *Inside the Vatican of Pius XII*, 115. Dutch Jews: Orsenigo to Montini, 28 July 1942, ADSS, VIII, no. 438; cf. Leugers, "Datenüberblick," GM, 391–392.

9. Early August 1942: Rychlak proposes that since the deportation of Dutch Jews occurred in midsummer, the letter-burning incident "probably took place in the autumn of 1942" (*Hitler*, 302). Yet if the July deportations caused the incident, Pius might have burned his notes in August or even at the end of July, when his Berlin agent raised the issue whether a public protest would hurt or help the endangered (Orsenigo to Montini, 28 July 1942, ADSS, VIII, no. 438). Liberal Catholics later accused the Church of unduly Catholicizing the deaths of Dutch Jewish converts to Catholicism, especially the later sainted Edith Stein. Carroll, "The Saint and the Holocaust," *New Yorker*, 7 June 1999; Wills, *Papal Sin*, 47–60. Jewish critics like Goldhagen, conversely, accused the Church of unduly Judaizing Catholic converts rescued through papal intercession. "What Would Jesus Have Done?" *New Republic*, 21 June 2002. In Goldhagen's view, Jews who converted to Catholicism were not Jews, and therefore papal efforts to save them should not count as papal efforts to help Jews. Holocaust scholars, however, count Jewish converts to Catholicism as Jews for purposes of totaling the 6 million Jewish victims. The same victim, then, would be a Jew if killed by Hitler, but a Gentile if saved by the pope. This position seems open to criticism as a form of rigged discourse. Watched them burn: Lehnert, sworn testimony, 29 Oct. 1968, Tribunal of the Vicariate of Rome (Pacelli), I, 77, 85. Maria Conrada Grabmair, who worked in the pope's kitchen, testified that Pius brought two pieces of paper to the stove and watched them burn completely; this was unusual, because at other times he just handed paper to her and then left. Father Leiber told

her that Pius had decided to burn the document after he was informed about the disastrous consequences of the protest by Dutch bishops. Sworn testimony, 9 May 1969, ibid., I, 173–174; cf. Lehnert, *Servant*, 116–117; Rychlak, *Hitler*, 301–302.

10. "Ethnicity": Pius XII, "Vatican Radiomessage de Noël de Pie XII," 24 Dec. 1942, ADSS, VII, no. 71; cf. Phayer, "Pius XII's Christmas Message: Genocide Decried," *Pius XII*, 42–64: "Historians, myself included, who have been more critical than indulgent in their studies of Pius XII have been rather too dismissive of the 1942 address. . . . I have modified my views to a considerable extent regarding Pius XII's genocide statement of 1942. . . . it was an important step in the pontificate of Pius XII, one that won approval throughout the western world except in Germany." Ibid., 42. Euphemism for Jewry: "Questo voto l'umanità lo deve alle centinaia di migliaia di persone, le quali, senza veruna colpa propria, talora solo per ragione di nazionalità o di stirpe, sono destinate alla morte o ad un progressivo deperimento." Sometimes translated as "race," stirpe is in fact, narrower—connoting stock, ancestry, descent, pedigree, family, birth, extraction, ilk, or family name. From the Latin stirps = lower trunk and roots, stock; plant, shoot; family, lineage, progeny; origin. "Mentioned the Nazis": Office of Taylor to State Department, 28 Dec. 1943, NARA, RG 59, Box 5689, location 250/34/11/1. Cf. Phayer, *Pius XII*, 57; Tittmann to Hull, 30 Dec. 1942, NARA, RG 59, Box 29, Entry 1071; Tittmann to Hull, 7 Jan. 1943, NARA, RG 59, Entry 1071, Box 29, location 250/48/29/05.

11. "War criminals": Chadwick, *Britain and the Vatican*, 219, citing "RSHA report on the broadcast"; Ribbentrop to Bergen, 24 Jan. 1943; Bergen to Ribbentrop, 26 Jan. 1943; Rhodes, *Vatican*, 272–274. Phayer (*Pius XII*, 63) asserts that the pope told Bergen he had really aimed the speech against Moscow, but I do not see how the source Phayer cites supports this reading. To the contrary, Bergen recorded that Pius "avoided bringing in political questions" and responded to baiting remarks about bolshevism only with "appropriate gestures." Bergen to Weizsäcker, 27 Dec. 1942, StS, V, AA Bonn, Friedländer, *Pius XII*, 175–176. "Set himself on fire": "For Berlin, Pius XII Was a Subversive: Radio Operator's Experience of Spreading Papal Christmas Message," Zenit.org, 14 May 2002.

12. "Powerful forces": Rösch, Delp, König, 2 Aug. 1943, DKK, 195ff.

13. Moral dilemma: Final Report by Staatsanwalt Dr. Finck, Lüneburg, Verfahren Roeder, Ministry of Justice Archives, Land Niedersachsen, 688, 707, 710; cf. Müller's response to Schmidhuber's allegations, ZS 659/3, 2–11. Refused: Müller, "Die Depositenkasse," LK, 168. Merano: Verfahren Roeder, MB 6/1, 144. Handcuffs: Sonderegger, "Brief," 17 Oct. 1952, IfZ, ZS 303/1, 32; Ficht, "Eidesstattliche Versicherung," 8 May 1950, IfZ, ED 92, 248; Verfahren Roeder, MB 6/2, 186; Schmidhuber, "Aussage," IfZ, ZS 616, 7; Schmidhuber, deposition, 20 July 1950, LStA, IX, 222; Wappenhensch, deposition, 16 Sept. 1950, LStA, XIV, 23; Huppenkothen, "Verhältnis Wehrmacht Sicherheitspolizei," HDP, 2/10; Müller, transcript, 1958, HDP, III, 1/7; Wild, "Eidesstattliche Versicherung," 15 Nov. 1955, IfZ, ED 92, 245–246.

14. "History of the world": Moltke, 7 Nov. 1942, LF, 259.

CHAPTER 15: SHOOTOUT IN THE CATHEDRAL

1. Quiet: Pannwitz, "Das Attentat auf Heydrich," March 1959, VfZ 33, 681. "Something sunken," "Holy mystery": Muckermann, "In der Tschoslowakei," 26 June 1942, *Kampf*, 469, 468.

2. Foundations hidden: Cf: Deutsch, "Questions," *Central European History*, Vol. 14, No. 4, Dec. 1981, 325.

3. "Ten commandments": "Mitteilung Frau Heydrich," c. 1953, Bartz, *Tragödie*, 83-84; Pannwitz, "Das Attentat auf Heydrich," March 1959, VfZ 33, 681; Müller, "Fahrt in die Oberpfalz," LK, 243; CIA, "The Assassination of Reinhard Heydrich," SI 2-14-1, 1960; MacDonald, *Killing*, 164; Schellenberg, *The Labyrinth*, 405. "The leakages": Brissaud, *Canaris*, 266.

4. Travel schedule: MacDonald, *Killing*, 166–167; Wiener, *Assassination*, 84–86. By some accounts, the castle's clockwinder ripped a page from Heydrich's desk calendar, screwed it into a ball, and threw it into a wastebasket, whence a cleaning lady in the pay of the resistance retrieved it. Yet Heydrich's enemies had better documented and more plausible means of knowing his movements. "We had a very good clandestine connection to an office in the SD," Vatican Jesuit Ivo Zeiger admitted. "It was through a woman whose name is never mentioned, whom I shall call Anita." See "Vernehmung von Pater Zeiger," 9 July 1948, IfZ, ZS A- 49, 25ff. Father Rösch later identified the agent as "Georgine Wagner, now Mrs. Kissler," and said she reported "via an intermediary (Miss Dr. Hofmann)." Rösch, "Kirchenkampf 1937-1945," 22 Oct. 1945, AR, 225. Wagner "had been forced" to join the SS, according to Father König; she was "absolutely reliable," and worked against Heydrich "despite great personal danger." König, "Aufzeichnung," 15 May 1945, ADOPSJ; Leugers, "Die Ordensaussschussmitglieder und ihr Engagement," GM, 328.

5. Preparations for attack: CIA, "The Assassination of Reinhard Heydrich," SI 2-14-1, 1960; Burian, "Assassination," Czech Republic Ministry of Defense, 2002.

6. Attack on Heydrich: Pannwitz, "Das Attentat auf Heydrich March 1959, VfZ 33, 679–680.

7. Caskets: Vanek, "The Chemistry Teacher's Account," in Miroslav Ivanov, *Target Heydrich* (New York: Macmillan, 1974), 223–224.

8. "His mother's head": Pannwitz, "Attentat," 688, citing Amort, *Heydrichiada*, 241.

9. "We summoned the priests": Pannwitz, "Attentat," 695.

10. "Slowly fell silent": Ibid.

11. "Heavy loss": Ibid.

12. Trap door: Ibid., 696.

13. "Immediately be shot": Ibid.

14. Last man: CIA, "The Assassination of Reinhard Heydrich," SI 2–14–1, 1960; Pannwitz, "Attentat," 697.

15. Conversions: Pius XI, *Motu Proprio*, 26 July 1926, Neveu Papers, Archivio dei Padri Assunzionisti, Rome; EPV, 101. Dukla pass: Hartl, interrogation, 9 Jan. 1947, CI-FIR/123. Jesuits disguised as Orthodox: Hartl, "The Orthodox Church," 9 Jan.

1947, CI-FIR/123, Annex VIII. Matěj Pavlík: "Veliky cin male cirkve," 42. Czech Legionnaires: Pannwitz, "Attentat," 700.

16. Albrecht: Jan Krajcar to Lapomarda, 7 Feb. 1984, in Lapomarda, *Jesuits and the Third Reich*, 92; Kempner, *Priester*, 14–15; Gumpel, interview, 1 June 2014, citing information from Father Josef Koláček, SJ. "Settle accounts": Hitler, remarks at dinner, 4 July 1942, TT (Cameron-Stevens), no. 248, 554.

17. "In the sanctuary of the altar": Hitler, remarks at dinner, 4 July 1942, TT (Cameron-Stevens), no. 248, 554.

18. "So-called priests": Hoffmann, *Hitler's Personal Security*, 240 n 33, citing Gerhard Engel, 16 Nov. 1942, and Linge, statement. This suspicion of a Catholic conspiracy accords mathematically with what Hitler, by one account, said eighteen months later, on 4 Aug. 1944: "You won't misunderstand me when I assure you that *for the past eighteen months* I was firmly convinced I would one day be shot" [emphasis added]. He asked his Gauleiters (provincial leaders) to try to imagine how terrible it was to realize that certain violent death could come at any moment. "How much inner energy I had to summon to do all that was necessary for the maintenance and protection of our people! To contemplate, to cogitate, and work out these problems. And I had to do this by myself, without the support of others and with a feeling of depression hanging over me." Toland, *Hitler*, 926, citing Florian, interview.

19. "Come under investigation": Müller, "Depositenkasse," LK, 162–164, citing Huppenkothen trial transcript.

20. Move carefully: Christine von Dohnanyi, IfZ, ZS 603; Ficht, "Eidesstattliche Versicherung," 8 May 1950, IfZ, ED 92, 248; Hettler, "Der Fall Depositenkasse oder die 'Schwarze Kapelle,'" MBM/155, 4.11.1; Huppenkothen, "Verhältnis Wehrmacht Sicherheitspolizei," HDP, 2/10; Müller, transcript, 1958, HDP, III, 1/7; Schmidhuber, deposition, 20 July 1950, LStA, IX, 222; Wappenhensch, deposition, 16 Sept. 1950, LStA, XIV, 23; Sonderegger, "Brief," 17 Oct. 1952, IfZ, ZS 303/1, 32; Ficht, "Eidesstattliche Versicherung," 8 May 1950, IfZ, ED 92, 248; Verfahren Roeder, MB 6/2, 186; Schmidhuber, "Aussage," IfZ, ZS 616, 7; Wild, "Eidesstattliche Versicherung," 15 Nov. 1955, IfZ, ED 92, 245–246. Sentences to its leaders: Roeder, IfZ, ED 92, 356; Schellenberg, *Memoiren*, 326–327.

21. Flew to Rome: DBW, 16, "Chronology," 691. Talks at the Vatican: Huppenkothen, "The 20 July Plot," Interrogation Report, 17 May 1946, DJ 38, Folder 31. Post-Hitler government: Bonhoeffer to Bethge, 29 Nov. 1942, DBW, 16, 1/211. After Hitler's removal: Moltke, 26 Nov. 1942, LF, 265. "Destroyed": Christine Dohnanyi, IfZ, ZS 603, 66–67. Zossen: Müller, 2 Sept. 1954, IfZ, ZS 659 /1, 60; Christine von Dohnanyi, "Aufzeichnung," 3 of 3, c. 1946, IfZ, ZS 603.

22. Schmidhuber case: Verfahren Roeder, MB 6/1, 145. Abwehr sources: Müller, transcript, 3 Aug. 1963, Tape I, HDP, III, 1/7. "That naive?": Müller, "Die Depositenkasse," LK, 165.

23. Müller in Munich: Müller, transcript, 1958, HDP, III, 1/7. Cheek: Müller, "Depositenkasse," LK, 165.

24. Interrogation: Müller, transcript, 1958, HDP, III, 1/7. Seemed shot: Müller, "Depositenkasse," LK, 168.

25. Control the probe: Müller, "Depositenkasse," LK, 166.

26. Downstairs to eat: Ibid.

27. "That criminal": Müller, IfZ, ZS 659/3, 230. Four-course meal: Müller, "Unkorr. NS üb. Gespräch," 1963, IfZ, ZS 659/3, 30.

28. Destroy them: Müller, "Depositenkasse," LK, 168.

CHAPTER 16: TWO BOTTLES OF COGNAC

1. "Their senses": Kreuser, "Remembering Father Alfred Delp."

2. Changed: Müller, testimony to the E.P, 31 Aug. 1953, IfZ, ZS/A 28/13; CHTW, 359; Schlabrendorff, *Revolt*, 68–69; Gersdorff, "Beitrag zur Geschichte des 20. Juli 1944," typescript, 1946.

3. Germany's borders: Hassell, diary, 26 Sept. and 13 Nov. 1942, 174–175, 179–180; Maria Müller, "Aussage," Verfahren Roeder, MB 6/5, 708; Rösch to Brust, Feb. 1943, KGN, Doc. 17, 203ff.

4. Their chance: Schlabrendorff, "Events," 54; Hassell, diary, 4 Sept. 1942, 173; Ritter, *German Resistance*, 233; Schlabrendorff, *Revolt*, 72. Smolensk: Scheurig, *Tresckow*, 136–137; Stieff in Peter, *Spiegelbild*, 87–88, and IMT, XXXIII, 307–308; Ili Stieff to Ricarda Huch, 17 July 1947, IfZ, ZS A 26/3; Stieff, *Briefe*, 170; Hassell, *Vom andern Deutschland*, 350; Gersdorff in Graml, "Militaropposition,"473–474; Hoffmann, *Stauffenberg*, 185. Better elude: Boeselager, *Valkyrie*, 113; Gersdorff, *Soldat im Untergang*, 124; Roon, "Hermann Kaiser und der deutsche Widerstand," VfZ, 1976, 278ff., 334ff., 259. Schlabrendorff: Kaiser, diary 6 April 1943, NARA, RG 338, MS B-285; Schlabrendorff, *Revolt*, 65–66. "Hit man": Bancroft, *Autobiography of a Spy*, 259.

5. As soon as Hitler died: Schlabrendorff, "Events,"55; Indictment against Klaus Bonhoeffer et al., 20 Dec. 1944, DBW, 16, 1/236.

6. Munich Jesuits: "Datenüberlick 1940–1945," TB König, GM, 398.

7. Missionary zeal: Kessel, "Verborgene Saat," 182. Hitler and Mussolini: Under papal leadership, Goerdeler urged, the churches should proclaim that "the world can have a truly just, happy, and permanent peace if it would get rid of these despots." Goerdeler to Pius XII, 23 March 1939, Ritter, *German Resistance*, 123.

8. Security risk: Delp to Tattenbach, 18 Dec.1944, GS, IV, 123–126. "Eradicated": Presying, statement, c. 1950, CH, 14. Faulhaber: Müller, "Unkorr. NS üb. Gespräch," 1963, IfZ, ZS 659/3, 14. Innitzer: Müller, "Aussage," 11 June 1952, IfZ, ZS 659/2, 26. Shared goals: Wuermling, "Der Mann aus dem Widerstand—Josef Müller," 28. Goerdeler's camp: Nebgen, *Kaiser*, 136–138; Kaltenbrunner to Bormann, 18 Sept. 1944, KB, 393–394.

9. Generals trusted: Roon, *German Resistance*, 154. Accept him: Müller, "Aussage," 11 June 1952, IfZ, ZS 659/2, 27. Slip away: Gerstenmaier, "Kreisauer Kreis," VfZ 15 (1967), 228–236.

10. Coup plans: Delp to Tattenbach, 18 Dec.1944, GS, IV, 123–126. Outweighed him: Henk, "Events Leading up to 20 July Putsch," 7th Army Interrogation Center, 22 April 1945, DNTC, vol. XCIX; Müller, "Aussage," 11 June 1952, IfZ, ZS 659/2, 27.

11. Atlantic Charter: Peter, ed., *Spiegelbild*, 2:701–702. "Especially [for] the Jews": Dritte Kreisauer Tagung, no. 2, "Zur Befriedung Europas," DKK, 249–259.

12. Civilian forces: Hoffmann, *Beyond Valkyrie*, 66–67. Did not attend: The 8 Jan. 1943 meeting is among the better documented events of the German resistance to Hitler. The basic sources are Hassell, diary, 22 Jan. 1943, 184–185; Moltke, 8 and 9 Jan. 1943, LF, 270f.; Gisevius, testimony, IMT, II, 240–242; Gisevius, *Bitter End*, 255–256; Gerstenmaier, *Streit und Friede hat seine Zeit*, 169; Gerstenmaier, "Kreisauer Kreis," VfZ 15 (1967): 245; Kaltenbrunner to Bormann, 18 Sept. 1944, KB, 393–394. Valuable secondary treatments include Roon, *Neuordnung*, 270–271, 277; Hoffmann, *Beyond Valkyrie*, 66–67; Hoffmann, *History*, 359; Marion Gräfin Yorck von Wartenburg, interview, 5 Sept 1963, in Kramarz, *Stauffenberg*, 158; Osas, *Walküre*, 16; Mommsen, "Gesellschaftsbild," in *Der deutsche Widerstand*, 73–167; Nebgen, *Kaiser*, 136–138.

13. Complicate consensus: Hassell, diary, 22 Jan. 1943, 184–185. Resign: Hermann Kaiser, diary, BA EAP 105/30.

14. Dictatorship and democracy: Mommsen, "Gesellschaftsbild," in *Der deutsche Widerstand*, 73–167. "Issues": Hoffmann, *History*, 359. During the Russian Revolution: Gerstenmaier, "Der Kreisauer Kreis: Zu dem Buch Gerrit van Roons' Neuordnung im Widerstand," 245; cf. Gerstenmaier, *Streit und Friede hat seine Zeit*, 169. "Long time": Moltke, 9 Jan. 1943, LF.

15. Delp had drawn: Mommsen, "Gesellschaftsbild." Military plotters: Hoffmann, *History*, 360. Strength of their forces: Moltke, 9 Jan. 1943, LF. Occur soon: Hoffmann, *History*, 359.

16. Twenty yards: Kaltenbrunner to Bormann, 3 Aug. 1944, KB, 128; War Office (UK), *Field Engineering and Mine Warfare Pamphlet No. 7: Booby Traps* (1952), 26–28; Hoffmann, *History*, 273, citing information from Gersdorff, 25 May 1964.

17. Hitler's plane: Hoffmann, *History*, 274.

18. "Initial spark": Schlabrendorff, "Events," 1945, DNTC/93, 61.

19. Berlin-Lichterfelde: Liedig, "Aussage," IfZ, ZS 2125, 28; Witzleben, IfZ, ZS 196, 42. Privately with Müller: Müller, "Tresckow Attentat," LK, 159.

20. "Rushed along": Müller, "Protokoll des Colloquiums am 31. August 1955," IfZ, ZS 659/1, 46. Tresckow's plan: Müller, "Aussagen," 4 June 1952, IfZ, ZS 659/2, 27–28. "Finally happen": Müller, "Tresckow Attentat," LK, 159.

21. Secret foreign agent: Müller, "Unkorr. NS üb. Gespräch," 1963, IfZ, ZS 659/3, 25.

22. Sojourn: Triangulated from Bonhoeffer to Bethge, 29 Nov. 1942, DBW, 16, 1/211; DBW, 16, Chronology," 690; Dulles, Telegram 898, 9 Feb.194, NARA, RG 226, Entry 134, Box 307; McCormick, diary, 11 Feb. 1943, ed. Hennessey, 39–40; Goebbels, diary, 3 March 1943, GT, II, 271. These data do not exclude Müller's possibly making two trips, one from about 9–17 Feb., and another from about 20 Feb. to 3 March. If so, Müller during the second trip likely brought Rome a pamphlet

from the White Rose resistance group in Munich; on 18 February, when the White Rose members were arrested, he may have been with Canaris and the Abwehr's Erwin Lahousen at Munich's Hotel Regina (Lahousen, testimony, 1 Dec. 945, IMT/II).

23. Situation report: Rösch to Brust, Feb. 1943, KGN, Doc. 17, 203ff.

24. "Atomic research": Wuermeling, "Der Mann aus dem Widerstand – Josef Müller," 28; Pius XII, "Discorso," Pontificia Accademia Delle Scienze, 21 Feb. 1943; Hartl, "The Vatican Intelligence Service," 9 Jan. 1947, CI-FIR/123, Annex I; Hinsley, *British Intelligence in the Second World War*, Vol. 3, Part 2, 584; Joint Anglo-US Report to the Chancellor of the Exchequer and Major General L.R. Groves, "TA Project: Enemy Intelligence," November 28, 1944, quoted in Hinsley, op. cit., 934; cf. Powers, *Heisenberg's War*, 283, and 542, n. 5. It is possible that Müller received the intelligence not from an American but from a German in the Pontifical Academy, such as Max Planck, who was in Rome for Pius's speech. The Vatican-linked physicist "employed by the U.S." who would seem most likely to have collaborated with German intelligence was Robert Millikan of Caltech. He was accused of anti-Semitism for arguing with Einstein and refusing tenure to Robert Oppenheimer. Millikan was an honorary member of three German science associations, an advocate of pro-Nordic eugenics, and, for some reason, received the only original copy of the Nuremberg Laws from US General George S. Patton in 1945. For these and other controversial aspects of Millikan see: "California Institute of Technology," *Dictionary of American History*, 2003; "Jewish Refugee Scientist Makes Discovery Which May Bring New Era in Technology," *Jewish Telegraph Agency*, 17 Jan. 1944; "Robert A. Millikan," n.d., Pontifical Academy of Sciences; David Goodstein, "In the Case of Robert Andrews," *American Scientist*, Jan-Feb 2001, 54-60; idem, "It's Been Cosmic From the Start," *Los Angeles* Times, 2 Jan. 1991; Ernest C. Watson, unpublished lecture, remarks at the dedication, Millikan Laboratory, Pomona College, Caltech Archives, Watson papers, box 3.12; Harold Agnew, oral history, 20 Nov. 1992 (Los Alamos); Judith R. Goodstein, *Millikan's School* (Norton, 1991), 97; Margaret Rossiter, *Women Scientists in America: Struggles and Strategies to 1940* (Johns Hopkins, 1982), 192; Matt Hormann, "When a Master of Suspense Met a Caltech Scientist, the Results Were 'Explosive,'" *Hometown Pasadena*, 1 Sept. 2011; Sharon Waxman, "Judgment at Pasadena: The Nuremberg Laws Were in California Since 1945. Who Knew?" *Washington Post*, 16 March 2000, C-1.

25. Approached the pope: Müller, "Unkorr. NS üb. Gespräch," 1963, IfZ, ZS 659/3, 25. Postwar plans: Müller, 11 June 1952, IfZ, ZS 659/1, 41. Preparations: Leiber, interview, OSS 2677th Regiment, 18 Aug. 1944, NARA, RG 226, Entry 136, Box 14. For corroboration of Leiber's account (especially on the role of Manstein), see Audiosurveillance, 21 July 1944, CSDIC (UK), SR Report, SRGG 962 [TNA, WO 208/41681371], Neitzel, ed., *Abgehört*, Doc. 146. "Old friendship": Müller, "Tresckow Attentat," LK, 161.

26. Moral sanction: Müller, transcript, 22 Sept. 1966, HDP, III, I/7; Müller, "Aussagen," 4 June 1952, IfZ, ZS 659/2, 27-28. Agrément: Müller, 4 June 1952, IfZ, ZS 659/2, 7; Müller, 11 June 1952, IfZ, ZS 659/2, 24. Separate peace: Stehle, "For

Fear of Stalin's Victory," EPV, 239. "No nation": Leiber, comments, 17 May 1966, 48. Unwelcome: Graham, "Voleva Hitler," 232–233. Chances were good: Müller, 31 Aug. 1955, IfZ, ZS 659/1, 46; Müller, "Aussage," 11 June 1952, IfZ, ZS 659/2, 23, 39. Separate surrender: Hoffmann, *History*, 283–284, citing Gersdorff, "Bericht über meine Beteiligung am aktiven Widerstand gegen Nationalsozialismus," 1963. For possible Nazi-sponsored probes toward a separate peace, which may have been merely ruses to sow discord among the Allies, see Goebbels, diary, 3 March 1943, GT, II, 271; Kallay to Pius XII, 24 Feb. 1943, ADSS, VII, no. 126; Tardini, note, 26 Feb. 1943, ADSS, VII, no. 113, p. 228, n. 6; "Mémorial inédit de la famille Russo," 12 March 1945, ADSS, VII, no. 113, p. 228, n. 6.

27. "London": Müller, "Unkorr. NS üb. Gespräch," 1963, IfZ, ZS 659/3, 25; Leiber, "Unterredung," 26–27 Aug. 1960, IfZ, ZS 660, 11; Sendtner, "Die deutsche Militäropposition im ersten Kriegsjahr," *Die Vollmacht des Gewissens*, 1956, 470-2; Chadwick, *Britain and the Vatican*, 252–253, 274. Philby: Trevor-Roper, "The Philby Affair," in *The Secret World*, 106–107.

28. Müller's messages: McCormick, diary, 11 Feb. 1943, ed. Hennessey, 39–40. "Our agent": Holtsman to X-2, Germany, "Dr. Josef Mueller," 31 Aug. 1945, X 2874, in Mueller, [redacted], CIA DO Records. Hinted broadly: See especially Gisevius, "Information given [to Dulles] under date of December 19, 1946," AWDP, Subseries 15c.

29. "Diplomats concerned": Pfuhlstein, interrogation report, 10 April 1945, DNTC, XCIC, Sec. 3, and CSDIC (UK), GRGG 286, Report on information obtained from Senior Officers (PW) on 19–21 Feb. 1945 [TNA, WO 208/4177], Neitzel, ed., *Abgehört*, Doc. 165. Naming German bishops: Müller, transcript, July 1963, HDP, III, I/7. Over-promise: Müller, transcript, 22 Sept. 1966, HDP, III, I/7. Readiness to mediate: Müller, 4 June 1952, IfZ, ZS 659/2, 7; Müller, 11 June 1952, IfZ, ZS 659/2, 24. "Darkest hour": Müller, "Privataudienz beim Papst," LK, 294.

30. "Manly intercession": Leugers, GM, 188, citing Braun's diary, and Pius to Galen, 24 Feb. 1943, BPDB. "No tyrant": Marianne Hapig, in *Alfred Delp*. "Watch out": Matthias Defregger to Roman Bleistein, 28 Feb. 1980, AD, 288.

31. "Demeanor of the pope": Müller, "Unkorr. NS üb. Gespräch," 1963, IfZ, ZS 659/3, 25. Preysing: Interview with Josef Müller (26 March 1962), at Lewy, 316.

32. "Do something": Müller, "Fehlgeschlagen: Das Tresckow Attentat," LK, 161.

33. Underwear: Scholl, *Die weisse Rose*, 44, 126–128; Scholl, *Briefe und Aufzeichnungen*, 235, 239; cf. Scholl, *Students Against Tyranny*, 17–20, 22–23, 73–74, 76–83, 86–87, 89–90, 93, 129–130.

34. Sister alone: Mayr, "White Rose," EGR, 250–251; Mommsen, *Alternatives*, 187, 295 n 5; Ritter, *German Resistance*, 163, 235–236; Rothfels, *German Opposition*, 13–14; Bethge, *Bonhoeffer*, 778; Hauser, *Deutschland zuliebe*, 293, 341.

35. Beheaded her children: Koch, *Volksgerichtshof*, 227ff.; cf. Hoffmann, *History*, 292; Hassell, diary, 28 March 1943, 192–193.

36. Through a friend: Smolka to Bleistein, 12 April 1979, AD, 284; cf. AD, 278–279; Brink, *Revolutio humana*, 79; Coady, *Bound Hands*, 55–56. Fatal handbill: Moltke, 18 March 1943, LF, 279n; Moltke, BF, 463 n 5, 465 n 1; Balfour and Frisby, *Moltke*, 212. "Via Radio London": Müller, transcript, 24 March 1966, HDP, III, 1/7; cf. Klemperer, *German Resistance*, 311 n 185, citing "Notizen über eine Aussprache mit Dr. Josef Müller, 1 April 1953, BA/K, Ritter 131.

37. Shook the coup plotters: Wheeler-Bennett, *Nemesis*, 540.

38. Through the woods: Boeselager, *Valkyrie*, 116–17. Flight home: Müller, "Tresckow Attentat," LK, 159–160. Canaris and Oster flew: Lahousen, "Zur Vorgeschichte des Anschlages vom 20. Juli 1944," 1953, IfZ ZS 652; Dohnanyi, "Aufzeichnungen," IFZ, ZS 603, 9–10. Only key: Schlabrendorff, "Events," 1945, DNTC/93, 62.

39. "Bottles of cognac": Schlabrendorff, "Events," 1945, DNTC/93, 61.

40. "The spark": Gaevernitz, *They Almost Killed Hitler*, 51.

41. Sistine Chapel: "Pope Marks Anniversary," *New York Times*, 13 March 1939. "Like small horns": Tittmann, *Inside the Vatican of Pius XII*, 145. Osborne through Kaas and Taylor through Müller: Müller, "Protokoll des Colloquiums," 31 Aug. 1955, IfZ, ZS 659/1, 46; Müller, transcript, 22 Sept. 1966, HDP, III/1/7. By 1943, Müller had made contact with Taylor, and told him "in detail about the German military opposition . . . above all, about my Roman negotiations." Müller, "Italien nach der Befreiung," LK, 284, 287. An early postwar OSS assessment of Müller states flatly: "he was our agent and informant during the war with Germany." Holtsman to X-2, Germany, "Dr. Josef Mueller," 31 Aug. 1945, X 2874, in Mueller, [redacted], CIA DO Records.

42. Hitler flew to Smolensk: Gersdorff, "Beitrag zur Geschichte des 20. Juli 1944," 1 Jan. 1946, IfZ; Hoffmann, *Hitler's Personal Security*, 151f. On the stairs: Schlabrendorff, "Events," 1945, DNTC/93, 63.

43. Gladly: Schlabrendorff, "Events," 1945, DNTC/93, 63.

44. Falling snow: Müller, "Tresckow Attentat," LK, 161; Schlabrendorff, "Events," 1945, DNTC/93, 64.

CHAPTER 17: THE SIEGFRIED BLUEPRINTS

1. Word never came: Müller, "Tresckow Attentat," LK, 162.

2. Safely in Rastenburg: Schlabrendorff, "Events," 1945, DNTC/93, 65.

3. "Indescribable agitation": Schlabrendorff, *Secret War*, 230. "Ignition had been set": Schlabrendorff, "Events," 1945, DNTC/93, 65. "Took the fuse out": Ibid., 66.

4. Acid had eaten: Did not ignite: Gersdorff, "Beitrag zur Geschichte des 20. Juli 1944," 1 Jan. 1946, IfZ; Hoffmann, *Hitler's Personal Security*, 151. Unheated, caked with ice: Hoffmann, *History*, 283, citing Hans Baur, 10 Jan. 1969; Schlabrendorff, "Events," 1945, DNTC/93, 66.

5. Second chance: Schlabrendorff, "Events," 1945, DNTC/93, 66.

6. Gersdorff's wife: Schlabrendorff, *Revolt*, 86; Hoffmann, "The Attempt to Assassinate Hitler on March 21, 1943," *Annales Canadiennes d'Histoire* 2 (1967): 67–83.

7. "Death sentence": Schlabrendorff, *Revolt*, 86. "Any breakfast": Schlabrendorff, "Events," 1945, DNTC/93, 67.

8. Down the toilet: On Gersdorff's attempt, see Himmler, Terminkalender, NARA, T-84, Roll R25; Daily Digest of World Broadcasts (From Germany and German-occupied territory), pt. 1, no. 1343, 22 March 1943 (BBC Monitoring Service: London, 1943); U.K. War Office, *Field Engineering and Mine Warfare Pamphlet no. 7: Booby Traps* (1952), 26–28; Hoffmann, *History*, 287, citing information from Gersdorff (16 Nov. 1964) and Strachwitz (20 Jan. 1966); Schlabrendorff, "Events," 1945, DNTC/93, 67; Hoffmann, *History*, 286; Boeselager, *Valkyrie*, 120.

9. "Another height": Moltke, 4 March 1943, BF, 458.

10. Against gas attack: Hoffmann, *Hitler's Personal Security*, 257; Sonderegger, "Mitteilungen," c. 1954, Bartz, *Trägodie*, 168–169. Commandeer: Rösch, "P. Alfred Delp † 2.22.1945 Berlin Plötzensee," 22 Jan. 1956, AR, 305; Rösch, "Lebenslauf," 4 Jan. 1947, AR, 274; Rösch to Ledóchowski, 5 Nov. 1941, KGN, Doc. 8, 106ff. Drinking water: The tap water running through pipes to everyone else was regularly analyzed if it was also used in Hitler's household. Linge, "Kronzeuge Linge," *Revue*, Munich, 1955/56, 4 Folge, 46. Fend off the party: Müller, "Breidbachberichte und Führerbunker," LK, 178.

11. Stayed in Siegfried: Bormann, "Daten," 9 Nov. 1942. Todt corps: Bleistein, "Besuch bei Stauffenberg," AD, 286.

12. Blueprints to Müller: Bleistein to Hettler, 17 July and 17 Oct. 1988, MBM/155, 4.11.2; Bleistein, AR, 31–32. Possibilities: On the vents as possible ingress routes for assassins, see, e.g., Heydrich, "Betrifft: Sicherungsmassnahmen zum Schutze führender Persönlichkeiten des Staates und der Partei 9 March 1940 and Reichssicherheitshauptamt—Amt IV, Richtlinien für die Handhabung des Sicherungsdienstes," Feb. 1940, NARA, T-I 75 Roll 383. An air raid: Roeder, IfZ, ED 92, 264; "Bericht Depositenkasse," NL Panholzer 237, 7; Verfahren Roeder, MB 6/3, 461. 4 April 1943: Müller, "Breidbachberichte und Führerbunker," LK, 179. Through 5 April: Hoffmann, "Hitler's Itinerary," xxx.

13. Plan to rescue Jews: Dohnanyi, statement, 12 May 1943, BA Berlin-Lichterfelde, Nachlass Dohnanyi, 13 II/33,16. Bericht Depositenkasse," NL Panholzer 237, 2; Ficht, "Eidesstattliche Versicherung," 8 May 1950, IfZ, ED 92, 249; Huppenkothen, "Aussage," IfZ, ZS 249/1, 22–23; Kraell to Witzleben, 3 Nov. 1952, IfZ, ZS 657, 1; Verfahren Roeder, MB 6/3, 399–400. Schmidhuber, IfZ, ZS 616, 7; Kraell to Witzleben, 3 Nov. 1952, IfZ, ZS 657, 1; Verfahren Roeder, MB 6/3, 399–400; Hettler, "Das Verfahren beginnt," MBM/155, 4.11.2. Exfiltration of Jews: Roeder, deposition, II, 329.

14. "Z Grau": Roeder, "Deeds of the Accused," 21 Sept. 1943, DBW, 16, 1/229.2. "Those papers"!: Gisevius, *Bitter End*, 472. "Intelligence material": Bethge, *Bonhoeffer*, 686–692. Father Leiber: "Indictment against Dohnanyi and Oster," 9–10.

15. Sheets: Gisevius, *Bitter End*, 472. "Challenged": "Indictment against Dohnanyi and Oster," 9.

16. Days numbered: Müller, "Die ersten Verhaftungen," LK, 168.

17. Time had come: Ficht, Verfahren Roeder, MB 6/1, 146.

18. He wondered: Müller, "Die ersten Verhaftungen," LK, 169. Roeder, Göring, Keitel: Müller, "Statement," OSS/MI6, Capri, 23 May 1945, NARA, RG 226, Entry 125, Box 29. Forged papers and cash: Hoffmann, *Stauffenberg*, 185. "Western powers": Sonderegger, "Bericht," Verfahren Sonderegger, MC-5, 207

19. "*They* are here!": Müller, "Die ersten Verhaftungen," LK, 168.

20. Two places at once: Müller, "Breidbachberichte und Führerbunker," LK, 177.

21. Green necktie: "A list of the items of clothing which his secretary Anni Haaser brought to him in the Munich Wehrmacht prison before she herself was arrested," 4 Aug. 1943, HDP, III, I/7.

22. Family members: Müller, "Die ersten Verhaftungen," LK, 169.

23. Feed the bird: Müller, "Die Ersten Verhaftungen," LK, 173; cf. Ficht, Verfahren Roeder, MB 6/5, 662.

24. Sonderegger: Pfuhlstein, interrogation report, 10 April 1945, DNTC, XCIC, Sec. 31; Müller, "Statement," OSS/MI6, Capri, 23 May 1945, NARA, RG 226, Entry 125, Box 29. Police tape: Müller, "Drohungen und Geschrei," LK, 190.

25. Vanished from their view: Müller, "Lebenslauf," 7 No. 1945, DNTC, vol. XVII, Sub. 53, Pt. 2, Sec. 53.041.

Chapter 18: The White Knight

1. Circled up: Gisevius, *Wo ist Nebe?*, 231.

2. Seemed serious: Ibid., 230–233, 221.

3. "Man in Germany": Moltke, 9 April 1943, LF, 294.

4. "Vacuum": Gisevius, *Bitter End*, 483.

5. Face in his arms: Hoffmann, *Stauffenberg*, 179–180, citing Balser, statements, 23 Jan., 4 March 1991; Schönfeldt, statement, 22 March 1991; Schotts, statement, 13 March, 20, 26 April 1991; Nina Stauffenberg to Hoffmann, 9 Aug. 1991; Schott, statement, 20 April 1991; Burk, statement, 28 Feb. 1991.

6. Left eye: Nina Stauffenberg to Hoffmann, 30 July 1968, SFH, 180; Deutsche Dienststelle, 30 Oct. 1991, BA-MA, 15 Nov. 1991; cf. Zeller, *Flame*, 182, 184, 195; Huppenkothen, "The 20 July Plot," Interrogation Report, 17 May 1946, DJ 38, Folder 31; Schlabrendorff, "Events," 1945, DNTC/93, 71.

7. "The ideal," "good, honest": surveillance, 18–19 Sept. 1944, CSDIC (UK), GRGG 196 [UKNA, WO 208/4363], ADG, Doc. 158. "Cared for his troops": undated

surveillance [after 20 July 1944], CSDIC (UK), GRGG 161 [UKNA, WO 208/4363], ADG, Doc. 145. "Indiscreet," "part of his honesty," "opened his heart": surveillance, 18-19 Sept. 1944, ADG, Doc. 158.

8. "Magnetically attractive": Halder, letter, 26 Jan. 1962, Kramarz, *Stauffenberg*, 81. "Alcibiades": Erwin Topf in *Die Zeit*, 18 July 1946. "Eyes brightened," "bewitched": Trevor-Roper, "Germans," March 1947, *Wartime Journals*, 293. Glass in his right: Reile, statement, 17 March 1991, SFH, 165. *Odyssey:* Berthold Stauffenberg to Fahrner, 2 Sept. 1943, Nachlass Fahrner, StGA, SFH, 190. Criticizing Hitler: Broich, statements, 14 and 20 June 1962, SFH, 164.

9. Aviatrix: Trevor-Roper, "Germans," March 1947, *Wartime Journals*, 294, n 27. Shoah: Herre, statement, 7 Dec. 1986, and Berger, statement, 7 May 1984, SFH, 151–152. Krystalnacht: Walter Reerink, report, June 1963, Kramarz, *Stauffenberg*, 71. "Gleaming eyes" Trevor-Roper, "Germans," March 1947, *Wartime Journals*, 291. Smashing a bust: Hoffmann, *Stauffenberg*, 106. Spoke openly: Zeller, *Flame*, 186.

10. "By the devil": Guttenberg, *Holding the Stirrup*, 194.

11. His faith: The primary evidence on Stauffenberg's Catholic motivation is substantial. See, e.g., Schlabrendorff, "Events," 1945, DNTC/93, 71, 73; Kaltenbrunner to Bormann (22 Oct. 1944, KB, 465–466; 4 Oct. 1944, KB, 435; 7 Aug. 1944, KB, 167; 8 Oct. 1944, KB, 434–439; 4 Oct. 1944, KB, 434–439; Kaltenbrunner to Bormann, 16 Oct. 1944, KB, 448–450); Staedke, statement, 13 Jan. 1963, SFH, 118; Elsbet Zeller, statement, 23 Sept. 1984, SFH, 2, 17; Alfons Bopp, statement, 6 Aug. 1983, SFH, 27; Kramarz, *Stauffenberg* (27–28, citing Dietz Freiherr von Thungen, memo, 1946; Halder, statement, 26 Jan. 1962; Nina Stauffenberg, letter, 17 March 1962; Ulrich de Maizière, statement, 20 Jan. 1963); Pfizer, "Die Brüder Stauffenberg," *Freundesgabe fur Robert Boehringer,* 491; Wassen, "Hie Stauffenberg—Hie Remer," *Die österreichische Furche* 7 (Feb. 1953). "Devout Catholic," "Church ties": Kaltenbrunner to Bormann, 4 Oct. 1944, KB, 434 ("*kirchlichen Beziehungen in der Verschwörer-clique eine* große Rolle *gespielt haben*"). "Catholic reactionary": Kaltenbrunner to Bormann, 7 Aug. 1944, KB, 167. Cathedral canons: Zeller, *Flame*, 173. Playing Mass: Hoffmann, *Stauffenberg*, 15. Luther: Caroline Schenk, "Aufzeichnungen," Sept. 1916, SFH, 8. Holy Roman Empire: Berger, statements, 7 May and 12 July 1984, SFH, 152.

12. Rescue Europe: Stauffenberg to Partsch, 22 April 1940, SFH, 78 (in April 1940, Stauffenberg was reading Frederick II's state papers). Lectured cadets: Zeller, *Flame*, 175. *Civitas Dei:* Hoffmann, *Stauffenberg*, 65.

13. "Murdered": Bussche, statement, 6–7 Dec. 1992, in Baigent and Leigh, *Secret Germany*, 158. "Believing Catholic": Kaltenbrunner to Bormann, 4 Oct. 1944, KB, 435. Political ideals, Aquinas: Berger, statements, 7 May and 12 July 1984, SFH, 152. Preysing: Kramarz, *Stauffenberg*, 148. Delp: See the discussion of his visit to Stauffenberg on 6 June 1944, *supra*.

14. Weekly lectures: Guttenberg, *Holding the Stirrup*, 1972, 190 (Delp was the "famous Jesuit" postulated by deduction; Rupert Mayer was already in Ettal; Friedrich Muckermann was already in exile; Hermann Muckermann lived in Berlin; Delp was

then in Munich). Lay operatives: Angermaier to Berninger, 9 May 1943, in Leugers, *Angermaier,* 111-12.

15. Hiding places: Roeder, "Eidesstattliche Erklärung," 23 May 1947, HStAH, Nds. 721 Lüneburg, Acc. 69/76, II, 213.

16. Official notice: Müller, "Lebenslauf," 7 Nov. 1945, DNTC, vol. XVII, Sub. 53, Pt. 2, Sec. 53.041.

17. Hard man to break: Müller, "Die Ersten Verhaftungen," LK, 173.

18. "Divorce": Müller, "Breidbachberichte und Führerbunker," LK, 180.

19. Guillotine: Müller, "Die ersten Verhaftungen," LK, 170. Fears: "Bericht Depositenkasse," NL Panholzer 237, 7–8; Verfahren Roeder, MB 6/3, 406. "I was afraid": "Die ersten Verhaftungen," LK, 169.

20. "Heil Hitler": Müller, "Die ersten Verhaftungen," LK, 170. Spiral staircases: Hapig, diary, 15 Aug. 1944, *Tagebuch,* 35. Death Row: Maria Müller, statement, 12 Nov. 1948, IfZ, ZS 659, 88.

21. Room: Heinrich Kreutzberg, *Franz Renisch, Ein Märtyrer unserer Zeit* (Limburg, 1952); Müller, "Pfarrer Kreutzer," LK, 205. Window: Müller, "Pfarrer Kreutzberg," LK, 206.

22. Maas: Müller, "Pfarrer Kreutzberg," LK, 206. Hase: Müller, "Die ersten Verhaftungen," LK, 170. Real boss: Müller, "Hart auf hart," LK, 175.

23. Roeder: Müller, "Die ersten Verhaftungen," LK, 169, 173; "Pfarrer Kreutzberg," LK, 206; "Drohungen und Geschrei," LK, 187. "Jesuits in Rome": Müller, "Drohungen und Geschrei," LK, 189.

24. Plans: Müller, "Breidbachberichte und Führerbunker," LK, 177. "Get these?": Müller, "Breidbachberichte und Führerbunker," LK, 179. "My oath": Müller, "Unsichtbare Helfer," LK, 184. Bought time: Roeder, IfZ, ED 92, 264; "Bericht Depositenkasse," NL Panholzer 237, 7; Verfahren Roeder, MB 6/3, 461.

25. "Want to know": Müller, "Aussage," 23 May 1945, 1.

26. Kreutzberg: Müller, "Pfarrer Kreutzberg," LK, 204, 207.

27. Counsel in the case: Kreutzberg, statement, Verfahren Roeder, MB 6/6, 732.

28. König: "Datenüberblick," GM, 402 (König in Munich on 30 April, back to Munich, 2 May; on 4 May, "König: Vortrag in Führerhauptquartier München von Hitler wg. Pullach"; on 6 May, "König sick, fever").

29. "Difficult death": Tacchi Venturi to Maglione, 14 April 1943, ADSS, IX, no. 152. "Killed wholesale": Constantini, diary, 20 April 1943, SVC, 162. "Unlucky innocents": Preysing to Pius XII, 6 Nov. 1943, quoted in BPDB, no. 105.

30. "Reprisals": Pius XII to Preysing, 30 April 1943, BPDB, no. 105. Secret and temperate: "The wording of the [18 Dec. 1942] memorandum, which the German episcopate has sent to the highest offices of the Reich, lies before us. Now you yourself know what slim prospects of success a document, sent in secrecy to the regime, has; however, by all means the memorandum will be a valuable justification of the episcopacy before posterity." Ibid. Prof. Emeritus Phayer, by his own account working from an excerpt of the document rather than the full text, writes: "Unfortunately, the

bishops were advised by Pope Pius XII that what they had already said in 1942 was enough to win them the world's respect. . . . The pope's advice [*sic*] was critical because a faction of the bishops, led by Konrad Preysing, were prepared to set nationalism and patriotism aside and force a showdown with Hitler over the Holocaust. The moment of truth at the height of the Holocaust slipped away. In this way the leaders of the German Catholic Church let the opportunity pass by to seize the moral high ground and openly resist genocide." "Questions about Catholic Resistance," *Church History*, 70: 2 (2001), 332, citing Friedländer, *Pius XII* , 135–145. I do not see how Phayer's statement accords with the evidence cited. (1) Pius did not address the words in question to the German bishops, but only to Bishop Preysing. (2) The words in question did not "advise" Preysing that the bishops had done "enough." Rather, as the context makes clear, Pius consoled Preysing for the failure of the bishops' December 1942 petition to influence the Nazis, by noting that at least the Church had tried—and had, in essence, put down a marker. Pius did not say or imply that the bishops had thereby exhausted their obligations. (3) The petition in question, and the discussion of it by Pius, centered not on Jews or the Holocaust genocide, but the Nazis' persecution of the Church. Therefore, if the pope let the bishops off the hook in this letter, it was not for silence on persecution of the Jews, but for *silence on the persecutions of Catholics*. Pius XII to Preysing, 30 April 1943, BPDB, No. 105: "Der Wortlaut der Denkschrift, den [!] der deutsche Episkopat an die höchsten Stellen des Reichs gelangen liess, liegt Uns vor. Nun wisst ihr ja selbst, wie geringe Aussicht auf Erflog ein Schriftstück hat, das das als vertrauliche Eingabe an die Regierung gerichtet ist; doch wird die Denkschrift auf Fälle den Wert einer Rechtfertigung des Episkopats vor der Nachwelt haben." "Rigid centralization": Cornwell, *Hitler's Pope*, 124, quoting Brüning manuscript, memoirs, 351352, Harvard University Archive FP 93.4, in Patch, *Heinrich Brüning*, 295296.

31. "Never allowed": Preysing, sermon, 15 Nov. 1942, quoted in BPDB, No. 105. "Consoled us": Pius XII to Preysing, 30 April 1943, BPDB, No. 105.

32. "Jewish leadership," "Rabbi of Zagreb," "Our prayers," "way out": Ibid.

33. "Murder unbearable," "Secret intercession," "diplomatic difficulties," "action arms": Ibid.

34. "Decisive intervention": Hoffmann, *Stauffenberg*, 184. Menacing: Zeller, *Flame*, 195.

35. "Bold man": Homer, *Odyssey*, 7:58–59, 235.

36. By 19 July: Moltke, LF, 321. Ghost government: Bleistein, "Dritte Kreisauer Tagung," DKK, 239–240; Delp, "Neuordnung," Dritte Kreisauer Tagung, no. 7, DKK, 278-95; Mommsen, *Alternatives to Hitler*, 218–219; Roon, *German Resistance*, 343–347; Schwerin, *Köpfe*, 313.

37. Coffin: Schmäing, "Aussage," Verfahren Roeder, MB 6/6, 786.

38. "In suspense": Moltke, 20 June 1943, LF, 315. "Protective hand": Müller, transcript, 8 Aug. 1963, Tape VI, HDP, III, I/7. "For the worse": Moltke, 20 June 1943, LF, 315. Keller: Müller, "Drohungen und Geschrei," LK, 189; Keller, "Zeugenschrifttum,"

4 July 1967, IfZ, ZS 2424. "Overlapping connections": "Minutes of Proceedings of an Interrogation of Wilhelm Canaris," 15 June 1943, DBW, 16, 1/227; BA Berlin-Lichterfelde, Nachlaß Dohnanyi 1311/33,17–18; hectograph.

39. Milkau: Müller, "Hart auf hart," LK, 175; Hettler, "Gespräch mit Josef Feulner," 26 Oct. 1989; Hettler, "Die Verhaftung," MBM/155, 4.11.2. Bluff: Müller, "Unsichtbare Helfer," LK, 181.

40. Angry: Müller, "Drohungen und Geschrei," LK, 187.

41. Complaint: Müller, "Unsichtbare Helfer," LK, 182.

42. Himmler: Huppenkothen, "Verhältnis Wehrmacht Sicherheitspolizei," HDP, Box 2, Folder 10. Nonpolitical: Keitel: Huppenkothen, "Verhältnis Wehrmacht Sicherheitspolizei," HDP, Box 2, Folder 10. Treason charges: Kraell, "Bericht Depositenkasse," NL Panholzer 237, 13–14; Roeder, "Aussage," IfZ, ED 92, 266.

43. "First coup": Christine von Dohnanyi, IfZ, ZS 603, 77. "Possible to remove a dictator": "Information obtained from Gentile [Gisevius]," 10 Sept. 1943, AWDP, 15a. Signal: Schwerin, *Köpfe*, 297. "Similar move": Italy: Christine von Dohnanyi, IfZ, ZS 603, 77.

CHAPTER 19: PRISONER OF THE VATICAN

1. "Volcano": Constantini, diary, 27 July 1943, SVC, 186. "Ruins have been ruined": Idem, 19 July 1943, SVC, 172–174.

2. Kessel as plotter's liaison to Pius: Magruder to JCS, 16 March 1945, NARA, RG 226, Entry 180, Box 376. "Down with the Duce!" Weizsäcker, *Memoirs*, 289. Mussolini's' fall: Kessel, "Verborgene," 12 April 1945, VS, 241.

3. "Like this": Müller, transcript, 31 Aug. 1955, IfZ, ZS 659/1, 35. "Vigorously opposed": Müller, "Die Depositenkasse," LK, 167. Propagation of the Faith: Müller, transcript, 31 Aug. 1955, IfZ, ZS 659/1, 34. "Deal with Badoglio": Müller, transcript, 27 May 1970, IfZ, ZS 659/4, 183. Pope and king's backing: Müller, "Colloquium," 31 Aug. 1955, IfZ, ZS 659/1, 35. "Connecting": Müller, "Aussage," 11 June 1952, IfZ, ZS 659/2, 25.

4. Stalled: Müller, "Colloquium," 31 Aug. 1955, IfZ, ZS 659/1, 35. Princess of Piedmont: Montini, notes, 24 Nov. 1942, ADSS, VII, no. 32. Hotel Regina: Müller, "Unkorr. NS üb. Gespräch," 1963, IfZ, ZS 659/3, 30. "Eye to eye": Müller, "Die Depositenkasse," LK, 167. Nephew: Badoglio to Maglione, 21 Dec. 1942, ADSS, VII, no. 67." Same as England," "definitive reading": Müller, "Protokoll des Colloquiums am 31. August 1955," IfZ, ZS 659/1, 44–45.

5. Parallel secret action: Gumpel, interview, 1 June 2014. "You will recall": Taylor to Roosevelt, 10 Nov. 1944, Taylor Papers, FDRL.

6. "Do everything": Pius XII to Mussolini, 12 May 1943, ADSS, VII, no. 186. "Won't go for that": Maglione, notes, 12 May 1943, ADSS, VII, no. 187; Gumpel, interview, 1 June 2014.

7. "How can I help?": Gumpel, interview, 1 June 2014.

8. "Accusations": Gumpel, interview, 1 June 2014. "*Segretissimamente* [secret]": Tardini, notes, 31 May 1943, ADSS, VII, no. 223

9. Political intelligence: Tardini, notes, 11 June 1943, ADSS, VII, no. 242; Montini, notes, 11 June 1943, ADSS, VII, no. 243. No quarter: Borgongini Duca to Maglione, 17 June 1943, ADSS, VII, no. 252.

10. Informed of . . . proceedings: Constantini, diary, 22 July 1943, SVC, 180. "Edge of the abyss": Idem, 18 July 1943, SVC, 171.

11. "Not at all unhappy": Tittmann, *Inside the Vatican*, 172.

12. Fled at dawn: ADSS, VII, p. 55. Via Aurelia: Blet, *Pius XII*, 212. Ruler-straight: Hatch and Walshe, *Crown*, 163. "Their lapels": Derry, *Rome Escape Line*, 61.

13: "Protection": Constantini, diary, 11 Sept. 1943, SVC, 195. "Phone with Roosevelt": Weizsäcker, "Rundbrief," 10 Sept. 1943, WP, 349. Marble floors: Graham, "Voleva Hitler," *Civiltà Cattolica* (1972), 1:319ff. To Munich: Ibid., 321.

14. "Come to light": Transcript, 26 July 1943, 12.25 a.m. to 12.45 a.m., ed. Gilbert, *Hitler Directs*, 54.

15. "All of us," "after midnight": Goebbels, diary, 27 July 1943, ed. Lochner, 416. "World opinion": Ibid., 409.

16. Prepare the operation: Karl Wolff, testimony, IMT, Case 11, Book 1e; Book 5, Doc. 68; Enno von Rintelen, testimony, IMT, Case 11, Book 1e, Doc. 195, also in Rintelen, *Mussolini als Bundesgenosse. Erinnerungen des deutschen Militärattachés in Rom 1936–1945* (Tübingen, 1951), 235; record of Erwin Lahousen interrogation, 15 March 1946, United States Counsel for the Prosecution of Axis Criminality, Interrogations and Interrogation Summaries, NARA, RG 238, Box 11, "Kesselring-Lammers."

17. Make a report: Wolff, "Niederschrift," *Positio Summ* II, 28 March 1972; Wolff, "Excerpts from Testimony," 26 Oct. 1945, IMT, XXVIII; Record of Karl Wolff interrogation, 27 Oct. 1945, NARA, RG-238, Box 24, "Wolf-Zolling"; cf. Müller, "Vor dem Reichskriegsgericht," LK, 197.

18. "What will happen in Germany?" Constantini, diary, 27 July 1943, SVC, 186. Psychological moment: Ritter, *Goerdeler*, 246. "Imminent here": Goebbels, diary, 27 July 1943, ed. Lochner, 411. Valkyrie: Mommsen, *Alternatives*, 243; Rothfels, *German Opposition*, 75; KB, 157; Kramarz, *Stauffenberg*, 135; Hoffmann, *History*, 301–311. Stauffenberg and the Orders Committee (Delp): Balfour and Frisby, *Moltke*, 235; Hoffmann, *History*, 201, 360; Hoffmann, *Stauffenberg*, 187, 190, 295; Kaltenbrunner to Bormann, KB, 145; Osas, ed., *Walküre* (case v. Goerdeler); KB, 357; Zeller, *Flame*, 195, 219, 227, 232, 232–233, 248, 272, 273. "Moral duty": John, *Twice*, 120. Goldmann as cutout to Kessel: Goldmann, *Shadow*, 84–87, 91, 133, 139, 140–146. "Positioned clergy," etc.: Kaltenbrunner to Bormann, 29 Nov. 1944, "Verbindungen zum Ausland," KB, 503. Paul Franken: Schwarz, *Adenauer*, 272. Vatican contacts: By his own account, Franken met with Monsignors Kaas, Krieg, and Schönhöffer; Jesuits Robert Leiber and Ivo Zeiger; Hubert Noots, Abbot-General of the Premonstratensians, and Pancratius Pfeiffer, Superior General of the Salvatorian Fathers, and Father Schulien,

a well-known ethnologist, and a member of the Divine Word Fathers. Graham and Alvarez, *Nothing Sacred*, 34.

19. Grey Sisters: AA, Politisches Archiv, Inland Ilg. 83, Italien, Berichtverzeichnisse des Pol. Att. in Rom, Ka2302: Paul Franken. Call on Franken: Alvarez, *Spies*, 185.

20. "Abandonment of the conspiracy": "An interview with Father Georg [*sic*] Leiber in the Vatican," 18 Aug. 1944, NARA, RG 226, Entry 136, Box 14.

21. They would do it: On the plot c. mid-October 1943, see Goerdeler, "Idee," Nov. 1944, Bundesarchiv, Coblenz, Nachlass Goerdeler, 25; Ritter, *Goerdeler*, 337; Hoffmann, *Stauffenberg*, 188; Rudolf Fahrner, statement, 9 May 1977, SFH, 226; Zeller, *Oberst*, 362; Ritter, *Goerdeler*, 337; Bleistein, "Nach der dritten Kreisauer Tagung," DKK, 301; Alvarez, *Spies*, 186, citing Franken interview, 26 April 1969, Graham Papers; Hesslein, "Material Axel von dem Bussche, Teil I [1968–1993], Kopien Korrespondenz [Franken]," IfZ, ED 447/62; Engert, "Er wollte Hitler töten. Ein Porträt des Axel v. dem Bussche," Sendemanuskript, 20 July 1984 [Franken], IfZ, ED 447/62; Hoffmann, *Stauffenberg*, 225, citing I. Stieff, "Helmuth Stieff," 75; Goerdeler, "Idee," Nov. 1944, Bundesarchiv, Coblenz, Nachlass Goerdeler, 25; Zeller, Oberst, 525 n 1; Schlabrendorff, "Events," 1945, DNTC/93, 84; Leiber, interview, OSS 2677th Regiment, 18 Aug. 1944, NARA, RG 226, Entry 136, Box 14.

22. "Own hand": Gumpel, interview, 17 May 2014; Graham and Alvarez, *Nothing Sacred*, 33, citing information from Mother Pascalina.

23. Nothing happened?: "Mordplan Hitlers gegen den Papst," *Salzburger Nachrichten*, 20 Jan. 1946.

24. International opinion: Lahousen, testimony, 1 Feb. 1946, Nachlass Loringhoven, PWF; Wolff, "Niederschrift," *Positio Summ*, II, 28 March 1972; Nicholas Freiherr Freytag von Loringhoven to Egr. Sig. Dino Boffo, 16 March 2010, PWF.

25. Moment's notice: Toscano, *Nuova Antologia*, March 1961, 299ff., and *Pagine di Storia diplomatica contemporanea* (Milan, 1963), 249–281.

26. Arrested Helmuth von Moltke: Balfour and Frisby, *Moltke*, 300. To act: Deichmann, "Mitteilung," c. 1953; Bartz, *Tragödie*, 189.

27. Hermsdorf: Schwerdtfeger, *Preysing*, 128; Kramarz, *Stauffenberg*, German ed., 160; Knauft, *Christen*, 35f.; Adolph, *Kardinal*, 181; Kaltenbrunner to Bormann, 4 Oct. 1944, *Spiegelbild*, 437f.

28. Alluded: Alexander Stauffenberg, "Erinnerung at Stefan George," address, 4 Dec 1958, Kramarz, *Stauffenberg*, 148. Decision to kill: Wassen, "Hie Stauffenberg— Hie Remer," *Die Österreichische Furche*, 7 Feb. 1953. "Confidential means": Leiber to Preysing, 22 April 1944, ADSS, X, no. 163.

29. "Blessing as a priest": Alexander Stauffenberg, "Erinnerung an Stefan George," address, 4 Dec. 1958; Kramarz, *Stauffenberg*, 148.

30. Military and the SS: Müller, "Aussage," 23 May 1945, 2.

31. Prosecution: Müller, "Vor dem Reichskriegsgericht," LK, 191.

32. Must die: "Bericht Depositenkasse," NL Panholzer 237, 7.

33. Solid proof: Hettler, "Vor dem Reichskriegsgericht," MBM/155, 4.12.5.

34. Proceedings: Müller, transcript, 8 Aug. 1963, Tape VI, HDP, III, 1/7.

35. Own defense: Sonderegger, "Aussage," IfZ, ZS 303/2, 19; Sachs to Witzleben, 19 Nov. 1952, IfZ, ZS 1983, 3.

36. Set him free: Müller, "Statement," OSS/MI6, Capri, 23 May 1945, NARA, RG 226, Entry 125, Box 29.

37. New charges: Müller, "Lebenslauf," 7 Nov. 1945, DNTC, vol. XVII, Sub. 53, Pt. 2, Sec. 53.041.

38. Eye patch: Kraell to Witzleben, 3 Nov. 1952, IfZ, ZS 657, 2–3.

39. Started to leave: Pius XII on Vatican Radio, 2 June 1944; text in Giovanetti, *Roma*, 287–288.

40. "Strafed": Tittmann, *Inside*, 208–209.

41. Jeeps and trucks: Clark, *Calculated Risk*, 365.

42. "Decency, and success": Sevareid, *Not So Wild*, 412. Capitoline Hill: Clark, *Calculated Risk*, 365–366.

43. Pius happy: Giovannetti, *Roma*, 298n.

44. "Color below": Scrivener, *Inside Rome*, 202.

45. "Viva il Papa!": Text of Pius XII's speech in SVC, 297.

46. Your hearts: Giovanetti, *Roma*, 297.

47. Savior of Rome: Kurzman, *Race*, 409–410. Human family: Sevareid, *Not So Wild*, 415.

48. Bless them: Barrett, *Shepherd of Mankind*, 200.

49. Deportations: Chadwick, *Britain and the Vatican*, 288-89; Gilbert, *The Righteous*, 314; Zuccotti, *Under His Very Windows*, 181–186, 200.

CHAPTER 20: IT MUST HAPPEN

1. Sailed for Normandy: On these events, Kershaw, *Nemesis*, accepts Irving, *Hitler's War*, 634–638; cf. Fest, *Hitler*, 704–705, Atkinson, *Guns*, 83–84.

2. Until daybreak: MVD to Stalin, 29 Dec. 1949, CPSU/462a, 2148–2149.

3. Lost France: Below, *Hitler's Side*, 202–203.

4. Catholic youth group: Gerhard Boss to Bleistein, 31 July 1984 and 1 Oct. 1987, AD, 283. Advance work: "Anklage des Volksgerichtshofs gegen Alfred Delp," 16 Dec. 1944, AD, 365.

5. Kleberstrasse rectory: Kaltenbrunner to Bormann, 31 Aug. 1944, KB 331–332; cf. Coady, *Bound Hands*, 65.

6. Certain address: Gerhard Boss to Bleistein, 31 July 1984 and 1 Oct. 1987, AD, 283; cf. Coady, *Bound Hands*, 65.

7. Opened it: "Delp and Stauffenberg's wife, unknown until then, entered the residence. Count Stauffenberg seemed to have been expecting him and retreated with him into a room. Countess Stauffenberg didn't take part in the conversation. Delp lingered with Stauffenberg until about an hour before his train's departure time

of 11:30 PM." Kunigunde Kemmer to Dr. H. Oeller, 25 Feb. 1985, AD, 284. Back to Munich: Bleistein, "Besuch bei Stauffenberg," AD, 286 n 18.

8. Führer's bunkers: Delp, "Gespräch mit Stauffenberg," c. 9 Jan. 1945, GS, IV, 349–356.

9. "Established by nature": Moltke, LF, 400n.

10. "As possible": Smolka to Bleistein, 12 April 1979, AD, 284.

11. "Goes well": Kunigunde Kemmer to Dr. H. Oeller, 25 Feb. 1985, AD, 284.

12. "Let's do it": Hans Hutter to Bleistein, 16 Sept. 1987, AD, 288–289.

13. Happen soon: Bonhoeffer to Bethge, 30 June 1944, LPP, 340–341.

14. Downfall: Müller, "Der 20. Juli 1944," LK, 197–198; Hettler, "Episoden aus der Lehrterstrasse," MBM/155, 4.12.6.

15. Imminent death: For example, Wassen, "Hie Stuffenberg—Hie Remer," *Die österreichische Furche*, 7 Feb. 1953. Reportedly, Stauffenberg asked his wife to ensure that no matter what happened, he should not die without receiving the last rites. Nina Stauffenberg, letter, 17 March 1962; Kramarz, *Stauffenberg*, 27–28. While it cannot be established with certainty that Stauffenberg received last rites during this visit, Church doctrine or practice would not have precluded it. Saint Leo, writing in 442 to Theodore, Bishop of Frejus, says: "Neither is satisfaction to be forbidden nor reconciliation denied to those who in time of need and imminent danger implore the aid of penance and then of reconciliation." Hanna, "Sacrament of Penance," in CE, vol. 11, citing Leo, *Epistles*, cviii. Waiting car: Accounts vary of Stauffenberg's 19 July church visit, raising the question of whether he made similar visits before his previous two assassination attempts. Some retrojection or conflation seems likely; accounts of earlier church visits would naturally cluster onto the eve of the historic event of 20 July, "sacred and awesome in its memory" (Braun, "Widerstand aus Glauben," c. 1951, ACDP, 1–429). One version even has Stauffenberg praying in a *Protestant* church in Dahlem: "It is known that when Stauffenberg was in Dahlem that evening, he went into [Martin] Niemöller's Church, St Anne's, and prayed" (Sykes, *Troubled Loyalty*, 432). This black swan may be significant if, in fact, Bishop Preysing or some other Catholic churchmen had sheltered in St. Anne's after their own churches were destroyed; Moltke had tried to get Preysing space in the Protestant Dom (cathedral) after St. Hedwig's Catholic cathedral was destroyed on 1–2 March 1943 (Moltke, 20 April 1943, LF, 299). For variant accounts, see, esp., SFH, 263: Karl Schweizer, Stauffenberg's driver, statement, 18 June 1965, places the church in Steglitz; Schweizer, interview by Joachim Fest, "Operation Valküre," Bavaria Atelier GmbH, Munich, 1971, places the church in Wannsee; Zeller, *Flame*, 300, 376, citing information from Schweizer's sister, places the church in Dahlem. See also Kramarz, *Stauffenberg*, 200; FitzGibbon, *20 July*, 150–152. Galante, *Valkyire*, 5, asserts (without source) that Stauffenberg met with Chaplain Hermann Wehrle, but likely conflates an episode in December 1943, when Wehrle learned of Stauffenberg's plots through an intermediary.

16. Plastic explosive: Hoffmann, *Stauffenberg*, 263.

CHAPTER 21: HOLY GERMANY

1. Greatest import: Huppenkothen, "Der 20. Juli 1944," HDP, 2/10.

2. Shaky hands: On events at Führer headquarters on 20 July see, esp., Hoffmann, "Zu dem Attentat im Führerhauptquartier 'Wolfschanze' am 20. Juli 1944," VfZ 12 (1964): 266–284. Hitler's hand tremors and his daily routine are well established from the earliest postwar accounts of his surviving entourage and staff. Joachimsthaler, *Last Days of Hitler*, 65, attributes the shaky hands to Parkinson's disease. Concrete bunker: On the timing of the conference: Below to Hoffmann, 15 May 1964; Interrogation Report 032/Case no. 0279, typescript, 23 Jan. 1946; and "Hitlers Adjutant über den 20. Juli im FHQu," *Echo der Woche*, 15 July 1949; Heinz Buchholz, "Das Attentat auf Adolf Hitler am 20. Juli 1944," typescript, Berchtesgaden, 14 July 1945, University of Pennsylvania Library 46 M-25; Buchholz quoted in Knauth, "The Hitler Bomb Plot," *Life*, 28 May 1945, 17–18, 20, 23; and Knauth, *Germany in Defeat*, 175–182.

3. Wood barracks: Peter, *Spiegelbild*, 85; Wehner, "Spiel'," 31. Berthold Stauffenberg told the Gestapo that there was a shirt in the briefcase with the bomb (*Spiegelbild*, 2).

4. One charge: Hoffmann, *History*, 398.

5. Hurry!: Heusinger to Hoffmann, 6 Aug. 1964, in Hoffmann, *History*, 400.

6. Heard an explosion: Peter, *Spiegelbild*, 85–86; "Tätigkeitsbericht des Chefs des Heerespersonalamts," NARA, NA microcopy T-78, Roll 39; Scheidt, "Wahrheit gegen Karikatur," *Neue Politik*, 27 May 1948, 1–2; Hoffmann, *History*, 400–401.

7. Summer cape: Huppenkothen, "The 20 July Plot," Interrogation Report, 17 May 1946, DJ 38, Folder 31; CSDIC, GG Report, RGG 1295(c), 10 June 1945, TRP, DJ 38, Folder 26; BAOR Interrogation Report 032/CAS no. 0279/von Below, 23 Jan. 1946, TRP, DJ-38; Neitzel, ed., Abgehört, Doc. 153, CSDIC (UK), GRGG 183, Report on information obtained from Senior Officers (PW) on 29 Aug. 1944 [TNA, WO 208/4363].

8. Gate rose: "Eyewitness Account July 20th," n.d. [1945–1946], CSDIC, SIR-1583, TRP, DJ 28, Folder 26; Hoffmann, *Hitler's Personal Security*, 248–249.

9. West, for Berlin: Galante, *Valkyire*, 4–5; Hoffmann, *History*, 397; Hoffmann, *Stauffenberg*, 264–267; Fest, *Plotting*, 308; Toland, *Hitler*, 903–904; Papen, *Memoirs*, 496; Schlabrendorff, *Secret War*, 287–288.

10. Famous moustache: Toland, *Hitler*, 799; Loringhoven, *In the Bunker with Hitler*, 49.

11. Maintain order: Zeller, *Flame*, 306.

12. "Arresting you": Gisevius, *Bitter End*, 546–547; Schlabrendorff, *Secret War*, 287–288; SFS, 270; Hoffmann, *History*, 422–423.

13. "Hitler is dead": Hoffmann, *History*, 422–423, 501–503, 507–508; Hoffmann, *Stauffenberg*, 267–270; RSHA Report, 7 Aug. 1944 (US Dept. of the Army, MS, 105/22); Teleprint Message II, 20 July 1944, in Hoffmann, *History*, Appendix 2, 755–756.

14. Maneuvers: Heinz Linge: "Record of Hitler's activities 11 August 1943–30 December 1943," NARA, RG 242 Miscellaneous Box 13 EAP 105/19; Hoffmann, *History*, 300; yet Eugen Gerstenmaier in "Der Kreisauer Kreis: Zu dem Buch Gerritt van Roons "Neuordnung im Widerstand," VfZ 15 (1967): 231 repeats Lukaschek's story as "reliable, I think."

15. Back in the Vatican: Müller, "Aussage," April 1958, HDCP; Müller, "Tresckow-Attentat," LK, 160; Müller, "Der 20. Juli 1944," LK, 198.

16. Soon speak: Tattenbach, "Das entscheidende Gespräch," *Stimmen der Zeit* 155 (1954–1955): 321–329; Delp, GS, IV, 343 n 58; Siemer, AB, 132.

17. Remained normal: Toland, *Hitler*, 799.

18. "Exterminate them!": Bross, *Gespräche mit Hermann Göring*, 221.

19. Drum on the windows: Toland, *Hitler*, 801–802; Hoffmann, *Hitler's Personal Security*, 252.

20. "Decent Germany": Hoffmann, *Stauffenberg*, 193; Hassell, *Vom andern Deutschland*, 394, 399, 418, 608 n 9; Hoffmann, *Widerstand*, 367–368.

21. "Lurch": Buchholz, "Das Attentat Adolf Hitler," University of Pennsylvania Library (manuscript 46M-25).

22. "This afternoon": Hoepner, 7 Aug. 1944, in IMT, XXXIII, 41.

23. "Holy Germany": Hoffmann, *History*, 422ff., 501–503, 507–508; Hoffmann, *Stauffenberg*, 267–270; Speer, *Inside*, 494; RSHA Report, 7 Aug. 1944 (US Dept. of the Army, MS, 105/22).

CHAPTER 22: THE TROVE

1. "Army is accustomed": Hitler, radio speech, 20 July 1944, Domarus, *Reden*, 4:2924–2925; cf. "Hitler's Six-Minute Broadcast," *Guardian* (London), 21 July 1944.

2. Delp to hide: Bleistein, "Die Verhaftung," AD, 294–295.

3. Briefed him: Tattenbach to Volk, 2 Nov. 1964, and Tattenbach to Bleistein, 25 April 1979, AD, 295. "Damn it all": Papecke to Bleistein, 10 Jan. 1979, AD, 293.

4. Farmer's house: Tattenbach, interview by Bleistein, 25 April 1979; and Tattenbach, interview by Volk, 2 Nov. 1964 (AD).

5. Pay for his words: Müller, "Der 20. Juli 1944," LK, 198.

6. Last consequence: Ibid., 199.

7. Danger loomed: Smolka to Bleistein, 12 April 1979, AD, 296.

8. Deliver the message: Kessler, statement, 25 April 1979, AD, 296.

9. "To death": Coady, *Bound Hands*, 70.

10. "Entire will": "Prayer of St. Ignatius of Loyola," in *Handbook for Catholics*, 2. Entered the church: Kessler, statement, 25 April 1979, AD, 296.

11. Approached him: Geisler, "Gespräch," 3 Feb. 1981, AD, 297.

12. "Goodbye": Oestreicher, in Hapig, *Alfred Delp: Kämpfer*, AD, 30.

13. German affairs: Rocca, interview, Jan. 1992.

14. "Territory of the Reich": Frend, "Ein Beweis der tiefen Uneinigkeit," *Frankfurter Allgemeine Zeitung*, 12 July 1997, B3.

15. Monsignor knew: OSS, "Informed German Sources in Rome," 22 July 1944, NARA, RG 226, Entry 16, Box 1015.

16. Catholic resistance: Rocca, interview, Jan. 1992.

17. "Opposition in Germany": OSS, "The Protestant and the Catholic Churches in Germany," 22 July 1944, NARA, RG 59, R&A 1655.22. "Apparatus": Brandt, "Oppositional Movements in Germany," 25 Sept. 1943, NA, RG 226, Entry 100 (AIGR, 103ff). "Underground activities": OSS Morale Branch (London), "The Hamilton Plan and the Organization of the German Underground," 31 Aug. 1943, NARA, RG 226, Box 175, Folder 2316, AIGRH, Doc. 17.

18. "Cautiously": Brandt, "Oppositional Movements in Germany," 25 Sept. 1943, NA, RG 226, Entry 100 (AIGRH, 103ff.). Agreed to see him: Rocca, interview, Jan. 1992.

19. "Informed": Scheffer, Annex E, Poole to Dulles, 10 Oct. 1944, NARA, RG 226, 16/1131.

20. Their designs?: Rocca, interview, Jan. 1992.

21. Conspirators: Leiber, interview, OSS 2677th Regiment, 18 Aug. 1944, NARA, RG 226, Entry 136, Box 14.

22. On Siemer's escape, see: Siemer, DB, 132, 134, 135; "Rundbrief Siemers," 18 Aug. 1945, DPB. For details on Braun's escape, see: Reimann to Leugers, 30 Aug. 1989, GM, 305; Braun, "Lebendig"; Vogelsberg, clandestine message, Feb. 1945, ACDP, I, 429; Bauer, statement, c. Nov. 1979, NLB; Vogelsberg to Leugers, 27/28 Sept. 1987, GM, 185, 305.

23. "Elimination of Hitler": Müller, "Neue Verhöre–alte Fragen," LK, 222.

24. Red sector of Berlin: Müller, "Im Kellergefängnis der Gestapo," ibid., 212.

25. Mortal sin: Ibid., 213.

26. Get out of bed: Although the usually reliable Joachimsthaler (*Last Days*, 65) says that Hitler "collapsed" on 18 September, Bormann's primary evidence dates the episode to 27–28 September: "Unfortunately—but keep this to yourself—the Fuehrer hasn't been at all well these last two days. Because of all the worries . . . he has . . . lost six pounds within two days." Bormann to his wife, 30 Sept. 1944, in *Bormann Letters*, 127. The next day, Bormann referred to "the three days since the Führer fell ill. . . . The situation report had to be canceled today for the third day running!" Bormann to his wife, 1 Oct. 1944, in *Bormann Letters*, 128–129. "Anything anymore": Junge, *Final Hour*, 144.

27. Depressed: Günsche, statement, n.d., in Morrell, *Diaries*, 188.

28. Files on 26 September: Bormann to his wife, 26 Sept. 1944, in *Letters*, 123–124: "Imagine: the murderous plot against the Fuehrer and the National Socialist leadership had been planned as far back as 1939 by Gördeler, Canaris, Oster, Beck and others! In a safe, whose key had been missing so far, incontrovertible proof has been found which should have been destroyed, but was kept through an oversight of one of

the people concerned. The whole plans for our attack in the west were betrayed, they were handed over to the enemy, as evidence shows. It is almost impossible to believe that such vile, bottomless treachery could exist! The fact that we have been getting through this war as we did, in spite of that large-scale betrayal, is nothing short of a miracle." Outcome of the affair: Morrell, entry for 28–29 Sept. 1944, *Diaries*, 190–191 n 2.

29. Examine Hitler: Joachimsthaler, *Last Days of Hitler*, 65–67.

30. "Broken out": Giesing, diary, and statement, 1971, in Toland, *Hitler*, 826.

31. Since August: That Hitler's doctors gave him cocaine is well established in their own accounts. Morrell, *Diaries*, 177; Giesing, "Protokol von Hitlers Hals-, Nasen- und Ohrenarzt Dr. Erwin Giesing vom 12.6.1945 über den 22.7.1944," NARA, RG 242, HL-7241-3; Giesing, in "Hitler as Seen by His Doctors," Annexes II, IV, Headquarters USETMISC Consolidated Interrogation Report no. 4, 29 Nov. 1945. "Hanged": The Gestapo had intercepted and copied the letters. Hitler's valet Linge or adjutant Günsche apparently overheard Hitler's remark. MVD to Stalin, 29 Dec. 1949, CPSU/462a, 160 (giving, however, no date for the quote). Stieff was hanged on 8 August 1944.

32. "Cocaine stuff": Giesing, diary, and statement, 1971, Toland, *Hitler*, 827, cf. Schenk, *Patient Hitler: Eine medizinische Biographie*, 131. "Connections with the pope": Kaltenbrunner to Bormann, 29 Nov. 1944, KB, 509.

CHAPTER 23: HELL

1. Came for Josef Müller: Müller, "Lebenslauf," 7 Nov. 1945. Daughter and wife: Hettler, "In der Prinz-Albrecht-Strasse," MBM/155, 4.13; Müller, "Aussage," Verfahren Huppenkothen, MB/5/T, 157; Müller, "Pfarrer Kreutzberg," LK, 212.

2. Ruin: Kessel, "Verborgene," 12 April 1945, VS, 245. Gestapo headquarters: Müller, "Aussage 10 Oct. 1947, IfZ, ED 92, 59.

3. Pushed him in: Müller, "Im Kellergefängnis der Gestapo," LK, 213.

4. Windowless room: Pfuhlstein, Interrogation Report, 10 April 1945, DNTC, vol. XCIC, Sec. 31; CSDIC (UK), GRGG 286, Report on information obtained from Senior Officers (PW) on 19–21 Feb. 45, Neitzel, ed., *Abgehört*, Doc. 165 (UKNA, WO 208/4177).

5. In the gloom: Müller, "Letztes Gespräch mit Canaris," LK, 226.

6. Toilets: Müller, "Aussage," IfZ, ED 92, 86. Reached Berlin: Müller, "Statement," OSS/MI6, Capri, 23 May 1945, NARA, RG 226, Entry 125, Box 29.

7. Whimpers and moans: Müller, "Neue Verhöre–alte Fragen," LK, 220.

8. "Place is Hell": Müller, "Meine Rettung," LK, 281.

9. Sonderegger: Müller, "Neue Verhöre–alte Fragen," LK, 221.

10. More denials: Sonderegger, "Brief," 14 Jan. 1951, IfZ, ZS 303/1, 13.

11. Wehrmacht: Müller, "Aussage," Verfahren Huppenkothen, MB 3/5/T, 156.

12. Dead man: Hettler, "Der Leiber-Brief," MBM/155, 4.13.1.1.

13. Paper on the table: Müller, "Neue Verhöre–alte Fragen," LK, 222.

14. "Elimination of Hitler": Sonderegger, "Brief," 14 Jan. 1951, IfZ, ZS 303/1, 13; Sonderegger, "Aussage," IfZ, ZS 303/2, 17–16.

15. Whole note down: Müller, "Neue Verhöre–alte Fragen," LK, 223.

16. Death penalty: Moltke, LF, 22. "Round this thing": Moltke, 28 Dec. 1944, LF, 394–395.

17. Dietz: Hapig/Pünder, note, 17 Dec. 1944, Ehrle, 203. Wife gleaned: Moltke, LF, 386.

18. Happen again: Moltke to Freya, 11 Jan. 1945, LF, 397.

19. Catholics and priests: Delp to M., 3 Jan. 1945, GS, IV, 86. Spirit of surrender: Delp, "Mediationen V: Epiphanie 1945," GS, IV, 125–124.

20. "Civilizations": Delp to M., 29 Dec. 1944, GS, IV, 71–72. "Build up": Delp to M., "Neujahrsnacht 1944/45," GS, IV, 78–83.

21. "Died with it": Delp to M., "Neujahrsnacht 1944/45," GS, IV, 78–83.

22. "Proper room for it": Delp to Marianne Hapig and Marianne Pünder, 11 Jan. 1945, GS, IV, 73.

23. Show trials: Balfour and Frisby, *Moltke*, 316. Moltke and Delp: Bleistein, "Prozess," AD, 376. Microphones: Coady, *Bound Hands*, 161.

24. "Someone like you": Kempner, *Priester*, 66; cf. "Prozess," AD, 376. "Other sentence": Delp to Tattenbach, 10 Jan. 1945, GS, IV, 97–98.

25. "What I mean": Kempner, *Priester*, 66; cf. "Prozess," AD, 377.

26. "Father Rösch": "Mitteilung des Oberreichsanwalts beim Volksgerichtshof," 15 Feb. 1945 (O J 21/44 g Rs); Kempner, *Priester*, 70. "Hands of the matter": Bleistein, "Prozess," AD, 380–381. "Pleasing to God": Moltke, 10 Jan. 1945, LF, 400.

27. "Whole man!": Moltke, 11 Jan. 1945, LF, 412.

28. Strode in: Rösch, "Kampf," 17–22 Oct. 1945, KGN, 270ff; Rösch, affidavit, 8 Oct. 1945; Leugers, *Mauer*, 309. "All his strength": Rösch, "Dem Tode entronnen," 1945–1946, KGN, Doc. 29, 301f.

29. To Dachau: Bleistein, "In Händen der Gestapo," AR, 132. "20 July 1944": Bleistein, "König," *Stimmen der Zeit* 204 (1986): 313f. "Hanged you": Rösch, "Konfrontation mit der Gestapo," 10–17 Feb. 1946, AR, 260.

30. Subdued and still: "Lieber ein Schafskopf als gar kein Kopf." Gerstenmaier, "Gespräche," 14 May 1982, AR, 392.

31. "Changed": Delp, "Nach der Verurteilung," c. 11 Jan. 1945, GS, IV, no. 70.

32. To hope: Coady, *Bound Hands*, xiii, 173.

33. 14 January: Delp to Luise Oestreicher, 11 Jan. 1945, GS, IV, no. 72. "Silent": Delp to Hapig and Pünder, 26 Jan. 1945, GS, IV, 146.

CHAPTER 24: THE GALLOWS

1. Six weeks: Hapig, diary, 18 Oct. 1944, *Tagebuch*, 50. Bedbugs: Bleistein, "Im Gestapogefängnis Berlin-Moabit," AR, 135.

2. Delp and Braun: Delp to Braun, 14 and 18 Jan. 1945, GS, IV, 180–184. "Tactical lies": Rösch to Braun, Feb. 1945, ACDP, I, 429 (GM, 308). "For 20 July": Rösch, "Kassiber," 12 Feb. 1945, ACDP, I, 429 (GM, 310). "Inauspicious ending": Rösch, "Kirchenkampf," 22 Oct. 1945, AR, 229. First Communion: Leugers, *Mauer*, 309, citing Simmel, "Rösch," 101.

3. Exercise hour: Rösch, "Escape," 321; Rösch, "Lebenslauf," 4 Jan. 1947. "Community grew": Bleistein, "Im Gestapogefängnis Berlin-Moabit," AR, 135.

4. "Pleased at this": Rösch, "Kirchenkampf 1937–1945," 22 Oct. 1945, AR, 230. Delp alive: Rösch, "Zum Gedächtnis von P. Alfred Delp SJ," 26 Jan. 1946, AR, 255. Their stories: Coady, *Bound Hands*, 209.

5. "Postponed": Rösch, "Zum Gedächtnis von P. Alfred Delp SJ," 26 Jan. 1946, AR, 257.

6. Death for noon: Bleistein, "Verhaftung," AD, 302.

7. "Bird of prey": Gerstenmaier, *Streit*, 204f.; cf. Schlabrendorff, *Offiziere*, 138; Bleistein, "Verhaftung," AD, 305–306. 20 July 1944: Kempner, *Priester*, 64; cf. Hartl on Neuhaus, "The Orthodox Church," 9 Jan. 1947, CI-FIR/123, Annex VIII.

8. "I wanted to know": Neuhaus to Bleistein, 11 July 1989, AD, 307. Line of inquiry: Rösch, "Gedächtnis," 26 Jan. 1946, AR, 255.

9. Nail heads: Delp said of the scars on his back: "That was done by Neuhaus." Gerstenmaier in Delp, *Kämpfer*, 41; Gerstenmaier to Bleistein, 22 Jan. 1988, AR, 304. Neuhaus later served two years in prison for abusing prisoners. High as it would go: Hoffmann, *History*, 522–523.

10. Death hut: Thus it is "no wonder that not so much as a hint of a statement from Delp is to be found in the Kaltenbrunner Reports from the RSHA." Bleistein, "Verhaftung," AD, 305. Color film: Hoffmann, *History*, 528, citing Erich Stoll, statement, 1 July 1971; and Heinz Sasse, statement, 20 Nov. 1964; Maser, *Hitler*, 255, 472; Stegmann, "Betreft: Filmmaterial zum Attentat auf Hitler am 20. July 1944," typescript, Deutsche Wochenschau GmbH, 3 June 1970; Kiesel, "SS-Bericht uber den 20 Juli: Aus den Papieren des SS-Obersturmbannführers Dr Georg Kiesel," *Nordwestdeutsche Hefte* 2 (1947), no. 1/2, 34. Piano wire: Fraser, "Révélations sur l'exécution des conjures antinazis," *XX Siècle*, 3 Jan. 1946.

11. Twenty-five minutes: Helmsdorffer, "Scharfrichter seit 200 Jahren," *Pivatal* 7 (1949): 22–24; "Der Henker des 20. Juli," *Hannoversche Neuste Nachrichten*, 24 Aug. 1946; Rossa, *Todesstrafen*, 31–40; Poelchau, *Die letzten Stunden*, 53–54, 86–87, 100, 107–108. "Thank you": Coady, *Bound Hands*, 199–200.

12. Hard to bear: Leugers, *Mauer*, 309, citing Hapig/Pünder notes of 13 Feb. and 5 March 5 1945, in Ehrle, *Licht über dem Abgrund*, 221, 223.

13. "Very great": Rösch, letter [to unknown person], after 15 Feb. 1945, ACDP/St. Augustin, Estate of Odilo Braun, 1–429–008/3.

14. "File card": Edmund Rampsberger SJ, "Einige Angaben zur Flucht von P. August Rösch," 26 Feb. 1982, AR, 199. "Executed": Rösch to Leiber, 8 July 1945, KGN, Doc. 24, 234ff.

15. February cold: Schlabrendorff, "In Prison," IKDB, 218; Müller, "Letztes Gespräch mit Canaris," LK, 230.

16. Gallows, as Christians: Ibid., 231.

17. Empty space: Huppenkothen, "The 20 July Plot," Interrogation Report, 17 May 1946, DJ 38, Folder 31. On the Mausterstrasse: O'Donnell, *Bunker*, 181n. No record: Müller, "Wieder in Deutschland," LK, 303.

18. Dirtied by it: Müller, "Statement," OSS/MI6, Capri, 23 May 1945, NARA, RG 226, Entry 125, Box 29.

19. Sprinkled with lime: Müller, "Letztes Gespräch mit Oster," LK, 233.

20. Stalin's son: He was Jakob Dzhugashvili. Tracked them down: After their recapture, Dzhugashvili had made a movement toward the electrically charged barbed wire, and the guards shot him dead (14 April 1943). 25,000 civilians alive: Müller, "Buchenwald," LK, 238.

21. "Loved ones": Müller, "Flossenbürg," LK, 246.

22. "Diaries": Huppenkothen, transcript, 5 Feb. 1951, HDP, 2/10.

23. Buhle: Hoffmann, *Stauffenberg*, 476. Rattenhuber: Höhne, *Canaris*, 591. Kaltenbrunner: Huppenkothen deposition, record of witnesses' testimony, 4–14 Feb., Day 1, 193; photocopy in IfZ.

24. Southward: The contingent in Müller's van included Kokorin, Captain Gehre, Hugh Falconer, the former ambassador to Spain, Dr. Erich Heberlein and his wife, Lieutenant Commander Franz Liedig, the former foreign minister, Hermann Pünder, Generals Falkenhausen and von Rabenau, Dietrich Bonhoeffer, as well as the notorious SS doctor, Sigmund Rascher.

25. "My fiancée": Müller, "Fahrt in die Oberpfalz," LK, 243.

26. As celibates: Müller, Ibid., 242

27. At noon: According to Brissaud, *Canaris*, 330, Rattenhuber gave Kaltenbrunner the "diaries" on 6 April.

28. "At once": Buchheit, *Der deutsche Geheimdienst*, 445; Fest, *Plotting*, 310; Höhne, *Canaris*, 591.

29. Drove on: Müller, "Fahrt in die Oberpfalz," LK, 243. Telex from Berlin: Sullivan and Frode, "Facsimile of the Message Forms for Nr. 14 and 24." Diverted to Flossenbürg: Höhne, *Canaris*, 592.

30. Russian way: Dünninger, "Prisoners," 11; Müller, "Fahrt in die Oberpfalz," LK, 244.

31. Like a moat: Irmingard, *Jugend-Erinnerunge*, 313ff.

32. General view: Müller, "Flossenbürg," LK, 247. Broke the silence: Brissaud, *Canaris*, 328.

33. Heads underwater: Thompson, "Flossenbürg," 14 Jan. 1989; Müller, "Augenzeuge," LK, 256.

34. Any counsel: Müller, "Eidesstattliche Erklärung," 16 Jan. 1946, S.3, WNRC, RG 332, ETO-MIS-YSect., Box 66

35. Did it for Germany: Buchheit, *Geheimdienst*, 478.

36. Would do it again: Höhne, *Canaris*, 594.

37. Understand that?: Augsburg Judgment, 31.

38. "No": *Die Welt*, 14 Feb. 1951.

39. "Gallows-bird!": Toland, *Last 100 Days*, 404.

40. "I die for peace!": Müller, "Ein Augenzeuge berichtet," LK, 256.

41. Bread of life: Müller, "Flossenbürg," LK, 246.

42. Barking of dogs: Müller, "Flossenbürg," LK, 251; cf. Bonhoeffer, "Night Voices in Tegel," c. 8 July 1944, LPP, 349–356. Guards took Bonhoeffer: Müller, "Augenzeuge," LK, 256.

43. Kicked the steps aside: Müller, "Lebenslauf," 7 Nov. 1945, DNTC, vol. XVII, Sub. 53, Pt. 2, Sec. 53.041; Fischer, "Aussage," Augsburg, c. Oct. 1955, Bartz, *Downfall*, 198.

CHAPTER 25: A DEAD MAN

1. Feet or skull: Kirschbaum, in Hollis, *The Papacy*; Guarducci, *Retrouvé*, 118–122.

2. At the ankles: Curran, "Bones of Saint Peter?" *Classics Ireland*, vol. 3 (1996).

3. Threads of gold: "St Peter's Bones," *The Express*, 21 April 2000. Vatican later announced: Guarducci, *Reliquie-messa*, 65–74; "Pope Says Bones Found Under Altar Are Peter's," *New York Times*, 27 June 1968, 1; Guarducci, *Retrouvé*, 147–148; Guarducci, *Le Reliquie di Pietro*, 96–103.

4. "Turning point!": Inge Haberzettel, debriefing, c. Nov. 1945, Trevor-Roper, *Last Days*, 100; cf. Fest, *Hitler: Eine Biographie*, 734; cf. Rösch, "Kirchenkampf 1937–1945," 22 Oct. 1945, AR, 231.

5. "Done away with": Müller, "Meine Rettung," LK, 280.

6. Plaut a copy: Plaut, "Report on Trip to Italy," 5 May 1945, NARA, RG 226, Entry 174, Box 123, Folder 933.

7. "Cornerstone": "Verborgene," 12 April 1945, VS, 252.

8. Extend the tenure: Pius XII to Truman, 13 April 1945, ADSS, XI.

9. "Change the heart": Pius XII, "Interpreter of Universal Anguish," 15 April 1945.

10. "Gain time!": Schroeder, shorthand notes, May 1945; Irving, *Hitler's War*, 794.

11. "Arose among us": Rösch, "Kirchenkampf 1937–1945," 22 Oct. 1945, AR, 232. Reichsmarks: Leugers, *Mauer*, 312; Rösch, "Dem Tode Entronnen," KGN, 328.

12. "Take him away": Guttenberg, *Holding the Stirrup*, 255. Their heads: One of the prisoners, Herbert Kosney, turned his head as the shot came, and the bullet went through his neck and cheek. He collapsed and feigned death. After the Gestapo left, Kosney crawled away and later led victims' families back to the scene, where the SS had buried the others in a bomb crater. Rösch, "Dem Tode," 1945/46, KGN, 313.

13. "Small bones": Thompson, "Flossenbürg Concentration Camp," 14 Jan. 1989.

14. "Dead man": Müller, "Meine Rettung," LK, 280.

15. Transferees: Müller, "Dachau," LK, 259. Letters from the dead: Müller, "Schlusswort," LK, 360–361. Hanged him: Müller, "Dachau," LK, 260.

16. Belonged to Joey Ox: Ibid., 260.

CHAPTER 26: THE EMERALD LAKE

1. Steel door: Anni Oster to Richardi, 25 June 2004, SSHAF, 338 n 8. Story to tell: Loringhoven, transcript, 13 March 1948, MMC, FF 51, Folder 41.

2. Wild turn: Matteson, "Last Days of Ernst Kaltenbrunner," CIA, 1960, NARA, 263, 2–11–6; Lischka, interrogation, 10 April 1946, and Kopkow, report, 9 April 1946, TRP, DJ 38, Folder 25; Deutsch, "Questions," *Central European History* 14, no. 4 (Dec. 1981): 325. "Greatest center of espionage": report of Interrogation No. 5747 (von Rintelen), 6 Sept. 1945, DNTC, vol. VIII, Sec. 14.07.

3. Not be revealed: Judgment v. Huppenkothen, 2 Dec. 1952, HJ, I, 1 StR 658/51; Kunkel, transcript, 8 Oct. 1951, 2nd Regional Court, File 1 Js Gen. 106/50, Dachau Memorial Archive; Kaltenbrunner to Bormann, 20 Aug. 1944, Anlage 1, KB, 275–278; cf. Hitler, "Night and Fog Decree," 7 Dec. 1941 NCA, vol. 7, Doc. No. L-90. ("In case German or foreign authorities inquire about such prisoners, they are to be told that they were arrested, but that the proceedings do not allow any further information.")

4. Wave of the hand: Müller, "Meine Rettung," LK, 280.

5. Germany's internal enemies: Müller, "Statement," OSS/MI6, Capri, 23 May 1945, NARA, RG 226, Entry 125, Box 29."

6. Keller: Russo, "Mémoire," 12 March 1945, 7–18, 10–14, 16, HDP, III, 1/9.

7. "In safety": Anni Oster to Richardi, 25 June 2004, SSHAF, 338 n 8.

8. Detonations: Müller, "Flossenbürg," LK, 249. Camp gate: Loringhoven, "Kaltenbrunner und 'Der Ochsensepp' Josef Müller," May 2010; Müller, "Statement," OSS/MI6, Capri, 23 May 1945, NARA, RG 226, Entry 125, Box 29.

9. "Just numbers!": Müller, "Statement," OSS/MI6, Capri, 23 May 1945, NARA, RG 226, Entry 125, Box 29. "Walking around!": Müller, "Flossenbürg," LK, 249.

10. Gallows yard: Gumpel, interview, 1 June 2014; Müller, "Statement," 23 May 1945, NARA, RG 226, Entry 125, Box 29. Below the noose: Müller, "Unkorr. NS üb. Gespräch," 1963, IfZ, ZS 659/3, 25. No idea how: Müller, "Flossenbürg," LK, 250.

11. His pallet: Müller, "Statement," 23 May 1945, NARA, RG 226, Entry 125, Box 29.

12. Could not sleep: Müller, "Aussage," Verfahren Huppenkothen, MB 3/5/T, 182–183; Thomas, "Gedanken und Ereignisse," IfZ, ZS 310/1, 21; Bonin, "Aussage," 21 Nov. 1951, IfZ, ZS 520, 3. Kept barking: Müller, "Flossenbürg," LK, 250–251. Silence fell: Loringhoven, "Kaltenbrunner und 'Der Ochsensepp' Josef Müller," May 2010; Müller, "Flossenbürg," LK, 252.

13. Müller's leg shackles: Müller, "Statement," OSS/MI6, Capri, 23 May 1945, NARA, RG 226, Entry 125, Box 29. Do with him: Müller, "Flossenbürg," LK, 251–252. Circulate his blood: Müller, "Aussage," Verfahren Huppenkothen, MB 3/5/T, 183–184.

14. "Behind the ridge": Müller, Verfahren Huppenkothen, MB 3/5/T, 184. Remained of his friends: Müller, testimony to E.P., 31 Aug. 1953, IfZ.

15. Approaching front: Fest, *Plotting Hitler's Death*, 310. Stand in the Alps: Müller, "Augenzeuge," LK, 254.

16. Across the moors: Müller, "Statement," 23 May 1945, NARA, RG 226, Entry 125, Box 29; Richardi, "Consolidation of the Special Prisoners," SSHAF; Müller, "Augenzeuge," LK, 257.

17. Stacked with corpses: Müller, "Buchenwald," LK, 238.

18. "Free at once!": Müller, "Dachau," LK, 263.

19. Last gamble: Weidling, *Voennoistoricheskii Zhurnal*, Oct.-Nov. 1961.

20. Steiner stalled: Trevor-Roper, *Wartime Journals*, 247, dating the scene to 22 April; cf. Trevor-Roper, *Last Days*, 127, dated to 23 April, and with Trevor-Roper's description of Hitler put in Berger's voice.

21. "Shoot them all!": Berger, debriefing, c. Nov. 1945, in Trevor-Roper, *Wartime Journals*, 247.

22. Had survived: Müller, "Dachau," LK, 265.

23. "This man": Müller, "Dahinten ist Schuschnigg," LK, 269.

24. Wrong he had done: Rösch, "Kirchenkampf 1937–1945," 22 Oct. 1945, AR, 234. Shouting the news: Rösch, "Zum Gedächtnis von P. Alfred Delp SJ," 26 Jan. 1946, AR, 257; Rösch, "Dem Tode entronnen," 1945/1946, KGN, Doc. 29, 332f.

25. "Came down on us": Rösch, "Kirchenkampf 1937–1945," 22 Oct. 1945, AR, 235. Safe house: Bleistein, "Dem Tode Ertronnen," KGN, 332.

26. "Killed by bombs": James, "Great Escape."

27. "Accepted this": Müller, "Dachau," LK, 265. Squad at Buchenwald: Bader "was only called by his first name." Müller, "Dahinten ist Schuschnigg," LK, 268.

28. "Enemy alive": Müller, "Protokoll des Colloquiums am 31. August 1955," IfZ, ZS 659/1, 45. Carried a pistol: Müller, "Dahinten ist Schuschnigg," LK, 271.

29. "Got drunk": James, "Great Escape."

30. Attack the SS guards: Müller, "Dahinten ist Schuschnigg," LK, 271.

31. "Special room": James, "Great Escape."

32. Dawn the next day: Müller, "Dahinten ist Schuschnigg," LK, 271. Reach the area: Müller, "Befreiung und Abschied," LK, 274. His rectory: On Saturday, 29 April, the Catholic priests had effectively freed themselves by looking for private quarters at the Niederdorf parish rectory, without paying much regard to the orders of Obersturmführer Stiller. The Bishop of Clermont-Ferrant, Gabriel Piquet, his friend Dean Johannes Neuhäusler, and the two chaplains Dr. Anton Hamm and Karl Kunkel, as well as several relatives of the Stauffenberg and Goerdeler families, found a welcome reception with the parish priest. Müller, "Befreiung," LK, 273.

33. Turned and fled: Müller, "Dahinten ist Schuschnigg," LK, 271. "Partisans to attack": James, "Great Escape."

34. Small groups: Trevor-Roper, *Last Days*, 193.

35. Double doors: Payne, *Life and Death*, 567.

36. Squeezed the trigger: MVD to Stalin, 29 Dec. 1949, CPSU/462a, 268–269, 271, 288; Joachimsthaler, *Ende*, 339, 346–347, 349.

37. Smell of gunpowder: Payne, *Life and Death*, 568; O'Donnell, *The Bunker*, 230. Vase of flowers: CSDIC, interrogations of Kempka, Gerda Christian, Traudl Junge, and Ilse Krüger, TRP.

38. Twitching in the fire: Fest, *Inside Hitler's Bunker*, 188.

39. "Very moving": James, "The Great Escape." The BBC transcript erroneously identifies the rescue force as the US Army, but the American troops did not arrive until 4 May. Luck with the Allies: Müller, "Befreiung," LK, 273. "Strung up": James, "Great Escape."

40. Werewolf units: Heiss-Hellenstainer, "[Original Report],"13 Aug. 1945, Heiss family (Dr. Caroline M. Heiss), 2f.; Niemöller, diary entry, 30 April 1945, Lutheran Archives Hesse/Nassau, vol. 35/376; Auer, "Fall Niederdorf," 23 June 1956, IfZ, ZS 1131; Bonin, "Aussage," 21 Nov. 1951, IfZ, ZS 520, 5. "Cold in the hotel": Müller, "Befreiung und Abschied," LK, 274.

41. "That whore": This designation dated to the Crimean War, when England backed the Turks and defeated the Russians. Twenty-five miles south: Müller, "Befreiung," LK, 275. Vanished into the night: Müller, "Befreiung," LK, 276.

42. Russian zone: Reitlinger, *SS*, 439.

43. Schultheiss brewery: Junge, *Final Hour*, 193.

44. "Surrender": Ibid., 193–194.

45. Emerald lake: Müller, "Italien," LK, 282. Turned in their weapons: Thomas, "Thoughts and Events," 20 July 1945, DNTC, vol. II, 6.13.

46. Naples: Neuhäusler, "Nochmals in grösster Gefahr," AH, 200.

47. Barracks at Verona: Müller, "Meine Rettung," LK, 277. Shaped like a key: Müller, "Italien," LK, 282.

Epilogue

1. "Better universe": "Pope Pius XII's Radio Broadcast on War's End," *New York Times*, 9 May 1945.

2. Liaison to the pope: Gisevius, *Wo Ist Nebe?*, 221, 230–233; cf. Müller, "Unternehmen Avignon," LK, 197.

3. Give an opinion: Gaevernitz, *They Almost Killed Hitler*, 2.

4. Signed his pass: Ibid., 3.

5. "Murder squad": Gaevernitz, "Between Caserta and Capri," 5.

6. Ischia and Sorrento: Müller, "Italien," LK, 281.

7. American secret agent: Gaevernitz, "Between Caserta and Capri," 6.

8. Whole story: Müller, "Italien nach der Befreiung," LK, 285.

9. Other Germans: Gaevernitz, *They Almost Killed Hitler*, 6.

10. Christian Democratic Union: Müller thought that "this man [Dale Clark] should not be forgotten." Müller, "Italien," LK, 283.

11. "Uninteresting": Hartl, interrogation, 9 Jan. 1947, CI-FIR/123.

12. "I witnessed"; "sexually impotent": Ibid., Annex IX, "Hartl's Trip to Russia."

13. "Abnormality": Hartl, interrogation, 9 Jan. 1947, CI-FIR/123.

14. Whole foods: Hartl, *Lebe gesund, lange und glücklich!*

15. Nuns' quarters: Leugers, *Mauer*, 312. "Back to Germany": Rösch, "Dem Tode entronnen," KGN, Doc. 29, 334–335.

16. American Zone: Bleistein, "Heimweg nach München," 22 Oct. 1945, AR, 140–141.

17. Disappeared: Rösch, "Dem Tode entronnen," 1945/1946, KGN, Doc. 29, 375f.

18. By the stars: Bleistein, "Heimweg nach München," AR, 142.

19. Met with Pius the Twelfth: Neuhäusler to Pius XII, [11] May 1945, ADSS, X, App. 8, n. 6, ref. "fogli d'Udienze."

20. Terrible danger: Müller, "Privataudienz beim Papst," LK, 291.

21. "My audience": Ibid., 292.

22. Every day: Müller, "Privataudienz beim Papst," LK, 293; Müller, "Befragungen [Widerstand II]," 26 March 1963, IfZ, ZS 659/4, 217–218.

23. Hitler's Reich: Müller, "Privataudienz beim Papst," LK, 294; "Besprechung mit Josef Müller," Feb. 1952, IfZ, ZS, A-49, 22.

24. Fatherland: Müller, "Privataudienz beim Papst," LK, 295; Gumpel, interview, 1 June 2014; Leiber, "Gespräch mit Elsen," 10 and 23 April [no year], NL Elsen.

25. "Diabolical forces": Müller, "Privataudienz beim Papst," LK, 294–295; Müller, transcript, 22 Sept. 1966, HDP, III, 1/7.

26. All meant?: Müller, "Privataudienz beim Papst," LK, 294–295; Müller, transcript, 3 Aug. 1963, Tape I, HDP, III, 1/7.

27. "Great joy": Müller, "Privataudienz beim Papst," LK, 295; Müller to CSU, 5 April 1978, HDP, IV, 20/5.

28. "By the sword": Pius XII, Address to Sacred College, 2 June 1945, ADSS, III, no. 600. "Widespread criticism": Tittmann to Taylor, 4 June 1945, Taylor Papers, FDRL.

29. "Robot": SCI Detachment, Munich to Commanding Officer, OSS/X-2 Germany, "Semi-Monthly Operations Report SCI Munich," 30 September 1945, G-TSX-3747, in DO Records, [redacted] Box 3, Folder 21, CIA ARC; Ruffner, "Eagle and Swastika," CIA, Draft Working Paper, II 37, citing "SC Munich Present and Discontinued Contacts"; NARA, "Research Aid: Cryptonyms and Terms in Declassified CIA Files, Nazi War Crimes and Japanese Imperial Government Records Disclosure Acts," June 2007, pp. 40, 50 (PDF). "Leadership in Bavaria": Franklin Ford [Perry Miller], "Political Implications of the 20th of July," 15 Oct. 1945, US Army Military Archives, Lexington, VA. Francis P. Miller Papers, Box 8, Folder 10. Oppressed: Müller, "Buchenwald," LK, 239.

30. Human rights: See, in particular, Kaiser, *Christian Democracy and the Origins of European Union*, 119, 193, 214, 242, and, more generally, 22–42, on European

unification as an outgrowth of political Catholicism, Catholic transnationalism, left-Catholic cooperation, and supranational party networks tracing to wartime contacts between exiled or underground leaders. "The Euro": The creator of the euro, Theo Waigel (later German finance minister and the author of *Pact for Stability and Growth*, adopted by the European Council in Dublin in 1996), was "inspired all his life" by Müller and frequently quoted from a 1946 speech in which Müller said, "If the European peoples wish to have security today, then I would see the best security in having a single currency. If there is only one currency in Europe, no country can mobilize against another. That is the best guarantee for the security of the European people." Collignon and Schwarzer, *Private Sector Involvement in the Euro*, 179.

31. "Advice throughout the war": Tittmann to Taylor, 4 June 1945, Taylor Papers, FDRL.

32. "Ostrichlike policy": Tittmann, *Inside the Vatican*, 116, citing his memo to the State Department, 16 June 1942. "Part of the mediator": Ibid., 117. "Ruthless furor": Ibid. 123. "Political repercussions": F.C.G. [Francis C. Gowen] to Taylor, 7 Nov. 1944, NARA, RG 59, Entry 1069, Box 4, location 250/48/29/05.

33. "One time or another talk?": SSU (London), covering memorandum to Müller CIC Interrogation, 24 Oct.1945, in Ruffner, CIA Draft Working Paper, April. 2003, III, 32. A captured transcript from the Führer's stenographic service quoted him saying to General Keitel on 25 July 1943: "One has to be very careful. Our people have to be arrested and locked up along with others, so that the others don't notice what they are. They are even tried and convicted along with the others. Actually, though, they are our agents. The others must never realize who has sold them out." Hitler, conference transcript, 25 July 1943, ed. Gilbert, 46. Two days earlier, Keitel had orally ordered treason charges dropped against Müller, Dohnanyi, Schmidhuber and Bonhoeffer; one day later, he put the order to Judge-Advocate Roeder in writing (Kraell, "Bericht Depositenkasse," NL Panholzer 237, 13–14; Roeder, "Aussage," IfZ, ED 92, 266). Nothing in the stenographic transcript, however, indicates that Hitler was speaking of Müller. Further, even if Hitler or Keitel had seen Müller as a loyal informant, this might have merely shown how clever Canaris had been in camouflaging Müller's treason as an investigation of treason. "Well corroborated": AB-17 [identity unknown] to Holtsman, "Summary of Preliminary Vetting of Dr. Josef Mueller," 31 December 1945, LX-003-1231, in Ruffner, CIA Draft Working Paper, April 2003, III, 33. No. 10 Schaflachstrasse: 30 Oct. 1955 debrief, "Johan [*sic*] Rattenhuber (Brigadenführer, Chef RSD)," IfZ, ZS 0637.

34. "Last moment": Loringhoven, "Kaltenbrunner und 'Der Ochsensepp' Josef Müller." On Müller's luck, cf. Nazi court politics in April 1945 as an agglomeration of "random influences" and the machinations of "flatulent clowns" at Trevor-Roper, *Last Days of Hitler*, 33. Lose it: Cf. Luke 17:33, Matthew 16:25, Mark 8:35.

SOURCES

This list excludes editions of classic authors (e.g., Aquinas) referenced by standard chapter/section numbers. Where a source appears just once in the Notes, bibliographical information is provided there and reference to the source omitted here.

Abshagen, Karl Heinz. *Canaris: Patriot und Weltbürger.* Stuttgart: Union Deutsche Verlagsantalt, 1950.

Actes et Documents du Saint Siège relatifs à la période Seconde Guerre mondiale. Ed. Pierre Blet et al. 11 vols. Vatican City: Liberia Editrice Vaticana, 1965–1981. In English: Vol. 1 (only), *The Holy See and the War in Europe March 1939–August 1940.* Ed. Gerard Noel. Dublin: Clonmore and Reynolds, 1968.

Albrecht, Conrad. "Kriegstagbuch, 22 August 1939," in Winfried Baumgart, "Zur Ansprache Hitlers vor den Führern der Wehrmacht am 22. August 1939," VfZ 16:2, 120–149.

Albrecht, Dieter, ed. *Der Notenwechsel zwischen dem heiligen Stuhl und der deutschen Reichsregierung.* 2 vols. Mainz: KfZ, 1965.

Albrecht, Johannes. "Erinnerungen (nach Diktat aufgez. v. P. Thomas Niggl . . .)." Ettal [Benedictine Monastery], private printing, 1962.

Alvarez, David. "Faded Lustre: Vatican Cryptography, 1815–1920." *Cryptologia* 20 (April 1996): 97–131.

———. *The Pope's Soldiers.* Lawrence: University Press of Kansas, 2003.

———. "The Professionalization of the Papal Diplomatic Service, 1909–1967." *Catholic Historical Review* 72 (April 1989): 233–248.

———. *Secret Messages: Codebreaking and American Diplomacy, 1930–1945.* Lawrence: University Press of Kansas, 2000.

————. *Spies in the Vatican*. Lawrence: University Press of Kansas, 2003.

Alvarez, David, and Robert Graham. *Nothing Sacred: Nazi Espionage Against the Vatican, 1939–1945*. London: Frank Cass, 1997.

Amè, Cesare. *Guerra segreta in Italia, 1940–1943*. Rome: Gherado Casini, 1954.

Amort, Cestmir. *Heydrichiada*. Prague: Nase Vojsko-SPB, 1965.

Anon. "Roman Tombs Beneath the Crypt of St. Peter's." *Classical Journal* 42, no. 3 (1946): 155–156.

Appolonj-Ghetti, B. M., et al., eds. *Esplorazioni sotto la Confessione di san Pietro in Vaticano*. 2 vols. Vatican City: Tipografia Poliglotta Vaticana, 1951.

Atkinson, Rick. *Guns at Last Light: The War in Western Europe 1944–1945*. New York: Henry Holt, 2013.

Aveling, J. H. C. *The Jesuits*. New York: Stein and Day, 1982.

Baigent, Michael, and Richard Leigh. *Secret Germany: Claus von Stauffenberg and the True Story of Operation Valkyrie*. New York: Skyhorse, 2008.

Baker, W. J. *A History of the Marconi Company, 1874–1965*. London: Routledge, 2013.

Balfour, Michael, and Julian Frisby. *Helmuth von Moltke: A Leader against Hitler*. London: Macmillan, 1972.

Bancroft, Mary. *Autobiography of a Spy*. New York: Morrow, 1983.

Barrett, William. *Shepherd of Mankind: A Biography of Pope Paul VI*. New York: Doubleday, 1964.

Bartoloni, Bruno. *Le orecchie del Vaticano*. Florence: Mauro Pagliai Editore, 2012. Excerpted as "All the Mystery Surrounding St. Peter's Tomb." *L'Osservatore Romano*, 29 Aug. 2012, 6. Weekly edition in English.

Bartz, Karl. *Die Tragödie der deutschen Abwehr*. Salzburg: Pilgrim, 1955. In English: *The Downfall of the German Secret Service*. Tr. Edward Fitzgerald. London: William Kimber, 1956.

Bauer, Klaus. "Die Tätigkeit von Pater Johannes Albrecht für das Kloster Ettal und seine Verbindung zum Müllerkreis während der nationalsozialistischen Herrschaft (Facharbeit für das Abitur)." Ettal [Benedictine Monastery], private printing, 1979.

Baumgart, Winfried. "Zur Ansprache Hitlers vor den Führern der Wehrmacht am 22. August 1939 (Erwiderung)." VfZ 19 (1971): 301ff.

Bedeschi, Lorenzo. "Un episodio di spionaggio antimodernista." *Nuova revista storica* 56 (May-Aug. 1972): 389–423.

Begsen, Achim. *Der stille Befehl. Medizinairat Kersten, Himmler und das Dritte Reich*. Munich: Nymphenburger, 1960.

Below, Nicholas von. *At Hitler's Side: The Memoirs of Hitler's Adjutant 1937–1945*. South Yorkshire: Pen and Sword, 2012.

Belvederi, G. "La tomba di san Pietro e i recenti lavori nelle Grotte Vaticane." *Bollettino degli Amici Catacombe* 13 (1943): 1–16.

Benz, Wolfgang, and Walter H. Pehle, eds. *Lexikon des deutschen Widerstandes*. Frankfurt am Main: S. Fischer, 1994. In English: *Encylopedia of German Resistance to the Nazi Movement*. Tr. Lance W. Garmer. New York: Continuum, 1997.

Berger, John. "High Treason." Unpublished manuscript, 21 March 2000. Author's collection.

Bernabei, Domenico. *Orchestra Nera*. Turin: ERI, 1991.

Bertolami, Ugo. "Dossier: La Vera Tomba Di San Pietro." Unpublished paper, 2008, author's collection.

Besier, Gerhard. *Die Kirchen und das Dritte Reich*. Berlin: Propyläen, 2001. In English: *The Holy See and Hitler's Germany*. Tr. W. R. Ward. New York: Palgrave, 2007.

Best, S. Payne. *The Venlo Incident*. London: Hutchinson, 1950.

Bethge, Eberhard. *Dietrich Bonhoeffer: A Biography*. Rev. ed. Minneapolis: Fortress, 2000.

Bierbaum, Max. "Pius XII. Ein Lebensbild." Pamphlet. Cologne: Bachem, 1939.

Biesinger, Joseph A. "The Reich Concordat of 1933." In *Controversial Concordats*, ed. Frank J. Coppa. Washington, DC: Catholic University of America Press, 1999.

Biffi, Monica. *Monsignore Cesare Orsenigo: Nuncio Apostolico in Germania*. Milan: NED, 1997.

Bleistein, Roman. *Alfred Delp: Geschichte eines Zeugen*. Frankfurt am Main: Knecht, 1989.

———. *Augustinus Rösch: Leben im Widerstand: Biographie und Dokumente*. Frankfurt am Main: Knecht, 1998.

———. *Dossier: Kreisau Kreis. Dokumente aus dem Widerstand gegen den Nationalsozialismus Aus dem Nachlass von Lothar König, SJ*. Frankfurt am Main: Knecht, 1987.

———. "Jesuiten im Kreisauer Kreis." *Stimmen der Zeit* 200 (1982): 595–607.

———. "Josef Roth und Albert Hartl: Priesterkarrieren im Dritten Reich." *Beiträge zur altbayerischen Kirchengeschichte* 42 (1996): 71–109.

———. "Kirche und Politik im Dritten Reich." *Stimmen der Zeit* 205 (1987): 147–158.

———. "Lothar König." *Stimmen der Zeit* 204 (1986): 313–126.

———. "Nationalsozialischte Kirchenpolitik und Katholische Orden." *Stimmen der Zeit* 203 (1985).

———. "Rösch Kreis." In Benz and Pehle, eds. *Lexikon des deutschen Widerstandes*. Frankfurt am Main: S. Fischer, 1994.

Blet, Pierre. *Pius XII and the Second World War*. New York: Paulist Press, 1999.

Boberach, Heinz. *Berichte des SD und der Gestapo über Kirchen und Kirchenvolk in Deutschland, 1934–1944*. Mainz: Kommission für Zeitgeschichte, 1971.

Boeselager, Phillipp Freiherr von. *Valkyrie: The Story of the Plot to Kill Hitler, by Its Last Member*. Tr. Steven Rendall. New York: Vintage, 2010.

Bolton, John Robert. *Roman Century: A Portrait of Rome as the Capital of Italy, 1870–1970*. New York: Viking, 1971.

Bonhoeffer, Dietrich. *Ethics*. Ed. Eberhard Bethge. Tr. Neville Horton Smith. New York: Touchstone, 1995.

———. *Works*. 16 vols. Minneapolis: Fortress, 1993–2006.

Boothe, Claire. *Europe in the Spring*. New York: Knopf, 1940.

Bormann, Martin. *The Bormann Letters: The Private Correspondence Between Martin Bormann and His Wife from January 1943 to April 1945*. Ed. H. R. Trevor-Roper. London: Weidenfeld and Nicholson, 1954.

Brakelmann, Günter. *Peter Yorck von Wartenburg 1904–1944. Eine Biographie*. Munich: C.H. Beck, 2012.

Braun, Odilo. "Lebendig in der Erinnerung." In Alfred Delp, *Kämpfer, Beter, Zeuge*, 111–114. Freiburg: Herder, 1962.

———. "Wie sie ihren Kreuzweg gingen: Ansprache zur Gedenkfeier der Opfer des 20. Juli 1944 in Berlin-Plötzensee am 20 Juli 1954." In *Bekenntnis und Verpflichtung: Reden und Aufsätze zur zehnjährigen Wiederkehr des 20. Juli 1944*. Stuttgart: Stuttgart Vorwerk, 1955.

Breitman, Richard. *Architect of Genocide: Himmler and the Final Solution*. New York: Knopf, 1991.

———. *Official Secrets: What the Nazis Planned, What the British and Americans Knew*. New York: Hill and Wang, 1998.

Breitman, Richard, ed. *U.S. Intelligence and the Nazis*. Washington, DC: National Archives Trust Fund Board, n.d. [2005].

Breitman, Richard, and Norman J. W. Goda. "OSS Knowledge of the Holocaust." US National Archives Trust Fund Board, Nazi War Crimes, and Japanese Imperial Government Records Interagency Working Group, Washington, DC, 2005.

Brissaud, André. *Canaris*. Tr. and ed. Ian Colvin. New York: Grosset and Dunlap, 1970.

Broszat, Martin. *Der Staat Hitlers*. Wiesbaden: Marix, 2007.

———. *Nationalsozialistische Polenpolitik, 1939–1945*. Stuttgart: Deutsche Verlagsanstalt, 1961.

———"Zur Perversion der Strafjustiz im Dritten Reich." *Vierteljahrshefte für Zeitgesichte* 4 (1958).

Broszat, Martin, with E. Frohlich and F. Wiesemann, eds. *Bayern in der NS-Zeit: Soziale Lage und politisches Verhalten der Bevölkerung im Spiegel vertraulicher Berichte*. Munich: Institute für Zeitgeschichte, 1977.

Browder, George. *Foundations of the Nazi Police State: The Formation of Sipo and SD*. Lexington: University Press of Kentucky, 1990.

Buchheit, Gert. *Der deutsche Geheimdienst*. Belthheim-Schnellbach: Lindenbaum, 2010.

Buchstab, Gert, et al. *Christliche Demokraten gegen Hitler: Aus Verfolgung und Widerstand zur Union*. Freiburg: Herder, 2004.

Bunson, Mathew. *The Pope Encyclopedia*. New York: Crown, 1995.

Burian, Michal, et al. "Assassination: Operation Anthropoid, 1941–1942." PDF file. Prague: Czech Republic Ministry of Defense, 2002.

Burleigh, Michael. *The Third Reich: A New History*. New York: Hill and Wang, 2001.

Burns, James MacGregor. *Roosevelt: The Soldier of Freedom, 1940–1945*. Francis Parkman Prize ed. History Book Club, 2006.

Burns, Tom. *The Use of Memory*. London: Sheed and Ward, 1993.

Burton, Katherine. *Witness of the Light: The Life of Pope Pius XII*. New York: Longmans, Green, 1958.

Butow, Robert. "The FDR Tapes." *American Heritage*, Feb./March 1982, 13–14.

———"How FDR Got His Tape Recorder." *American Heritage*, Oct./Nov. 1982, 109–112.

Cabasés, Félix Juan, ed. "Cronistoria Documentata e Contestualizzata della Radio Vaticana." Radio Vaticana, Vatican City, 2011, www.radiovaticana.va/it1/cronistoria.asp?pag. Accessed 22 May 2014.

Cadogan, Alexander. *The Diaries of Sir Alexander Cadogan, 1938–1945*. Ed. David Dilks. New York: G. P. Putnam's Sons, 1971.

Castagna, Luca. *A Bridge Across the Ocean: The United States and the Holy See Between the Two World Wars*. Washington, DC: Catholic University of America Press, 2014.

Cavalli, Dimitri. "Jewish Praise for Pius XII." *Inside the Vatican*, Oct. 2000, 72–77.

Chadwick, Owen. *Britain and the Vatican During the Second World War*. New York: Cambridge University Press, 1986.

———. *A History of the Popes, 1830–1914*. New York: Oxford University Press, 1998.

Chalou, George, ed. *The Secrets War: The Office of Strategic Services in World War II*. Washington, DC: National Archives and Records Administration, 1992.

Charles-Roux, François. *Huit ans au Vatican, 1932–1940*. Paris: Flammarion, 1947.

Cheetham, Nicolas. *A History of the Popes*. New York: Scribners, 1982.

Chenaux, Philippe. *Pio XII, Diplomatico e Pastore*. Milan: Cinisello Balsamo, 2004.

Cianfarra, Camille. *The Vatican and the War*. New York: Dutton, 1944.

Ciano, Galeazzo. *The Ciano Diaries*. Ed. Hugh Gibson. New York: Doubleday, 1946.

Clark, Mark W. *Calculated Risk*. New York: Enigma Books, 2007.

Coady, Mary Frances. *With Bound Hands: A Jesuit in Nazi Germany. The Life and Selected Prison Letters of Alfred Delp*. Chicago: Loyola Press, 2003.

Collignon, Stefan, and Daniela Schwarzer, eds. *Private Sector Involvement in the Euro: The Power of Ideas*. London: Routledge, 2003.

Colvin, Ian. *Chief of Intelligence*. London: Victor Gollancz, 1951.

———. *Master Spy*. New York: McGraw-Hill, 1951.

———. *Vansittart in Office*. London: Victor Gollancz, 1965.

Connelly, John. *From Enemy to Brother: The Revolution in Catholic Teaching on the Jews, 1933–1965*. Cambridge, MA: Harvard University Press, 2012.

Constantini, Celso. *Ai margini della Guerra (1838–1947): Diario inedito del Cardinale Celso Constantini*. Venice: Marcianum Press, 2010. In English: *The Secrets of a Vatican Cardinal: Celso Constantini's Wartime Diaries, 1938–1947*. Ed. Bruno

Fabio Pighin. Tr. Laurence B. Mussio. Montreal: McGill-Queen's University Press, 2014.

Conway, John. "The Meeting Between Pope Pius XII and Ribbentrop." *CCHA Study Sessions* 35 (1968): 103–116.

———. "Myron C. Taylor's Mission to the Vatican, 1940–1950." *Church History* 44, no. 1 (1975): 85–99.

———. *The Nazi Persecution of the Churches, 1933–1945*. New York: Basic Books, 1968.

———. "Pope Pius XII and the German Church: An Unpublished Gestapo Report." *Canadian Journal of History* 2 (March 1967): 72–83.

Cooper, H. H. "English Mission: Clandestine Methods of the Jesuits in Elizabethan England as illustrated in an Operative's Own Classic Account." *Studies in Intelligence* 5, no. 2 (Spring 1961): A43–A50.

Coppa, Frank. *Cardinal Giacomo Antonelli and Papal Politics in European Affairs*. Albany: State University of New York Press, 1990.

———. *The Italian Wars of Independence*. New York: Longman, 1992.

———. *The Modern Papacy Since 1789*. New York: Addison Wesley Longman, 1998.

Coppa, Frank, ed. *Controversial Concordats: The Vatican's Relations with Napoleon, Mussolini, and Hitler*. Washington, DC: Catholic University of America Press, 1999.

Cormenin, Louis Marie de. *A Complete History of the Popes of Rome*. 2 Vol. Philadelphia: J. B. Smith, 1850.

Cornwell, John. *Hitler's Pope: The Secret History of Pius XII*. New York: Viking, 1999.

———. *The Pontiff in Winter: Triumph and Conflict in the Reign of John Paul II*. New York: Doubleday, 2005.

Cousins, Norman. *The Improbable Triumvirate: John F. Kennedy, Pope John, Nikita Khrushchev*. New York: W. W. Norton, 1972.

Curran, John. "The Bones of Saint Peter?" *Classics Ireland* 3 (1996): 18–46.

Dederichs, Mario. *Heydrich: The Face of Evil*. London: Greenhill, 2006.

Delp, Alfred. "Bereitschaft." *Chrysologus* 75 (1935): 353–357.

———. "Die Moderne Welt und Die Katholische Aktion." *Chrysologus* 75 (1935): 170–178.

———. *Gesammelte Schriften*. Ed. Roman Bleistein. 5 vols. Frankfurt am Main: Knecht: 1982–1984, 1988.

———. *Kämpfer, Beter, Zeuge*. Freiburg: Herder, 1962.

Derry, Sam. *The Rome Escape Line*. New York: Norton, 1960.

Deschner, Gunther. *Heydrich: The Pursuit of Total Power*. London: Orbis, 1981.

Deutsch, Harold C. *The Conspiracy Against Hitler in the Twilight War*. Minneapolis: University of Minnesota Press, 1968.

———. "The German Resistance: Answered and Unanswered Questions." *Central European History* 14, no. 4 (1981): 322–331.

———. Letter to Josef Müller. 2 Dec. 1965, HDP, II, 1/7.

———. "Pius XII and the German Opposition in World War II." Paper read to the Congress of the American Historical Association, Dec. 1965, HDP, VII, 4/8.

Dippel, John V. H. *Two Against Hitler: Stealing the Nazis' Best-Kept Secrets.* New York: Praeger, 1992.

Documents on British Foreign Policy, 1919–1939. D Series, Vol. 5. London: Her Majesty's Stationery Office, 1956.

Dohnanyi, Christine von. "Aufzeichnung (über das Schicksal der Dokumentensammlung meines Mannes)." IfZ, ZS 603.

———. Statement, 26 June 1958, HDP.

Domarus, Max, ed. *Hitler: Reden und Proklamationen, 1932 bis 1945.* Wiesbaden: Löwit, 1973. In English: *Hitler—Speeches and Proclamations, 1932–1945.* Tr. Mary Fran Golbert. Wauconda, IL: Bolchazy-Carducci, 1990.

Dornberg, John. *Munich 1923: The Story of Hitler's First Grab for Power.* New York: Harper and Row, 1982.

Doyle, Charles Hugo. *The Life of Pope Pius XII.* Sydney: Invincible Press, 1947.

Dreher, K. *Der Weg zum Kanzler: Adenauers Griff nach der Macht.* Düsseldorf: Econ, 1972.

Duce, Alessandro. *Pio XII e la Polonia (1939–1945).* Rome: Edizioni Studium, 1997.

Duffy, James P., and Vincent Ricci. *Target Hitler.* Boulder: Praeger, 1992.

Dulles, Allen. *Germany's Underground.* New York: Macmillan, 1947.

Eddy, Mary Frances Coady. *With Bound Hands: A Jesuit in Nazi Germany. The Life and Selected Prison Letters of Alfred Delp.* Chicago: Loyola University Press, 2003.

Edsel, Robert. *Saving Italy: The Race to Rescue a Nation's Treasures from the Nazis.* New York: W. W. Norton, 2013.

Ehrle, Gertrud, and Regina Broel. *Licht über dem Abgrund.* Freiburg im Breisgau: Herder, 1951.

Eidenschink, Georg. "Interrogation [statement taken] by Capt. O. N. Nordon (Present: Dr. Josef Müller)." 6 Nov. 1945. DNTC, vol. XVII, Sec. 53.015.

Ennio, Caretto. "Olocausto, le denunce ignorate dagli Alleati." *Corriere della Sera,* 4 Sept. 2001, 16.

Epstein, Klaus. *Mathias Erzberger and the Dilemma of German Democracy.* Princeton, NJ: Princeton University Press, 1959.

Evans, Richard J. *The Coming of the Third Reich.* New York: Penguin, 2004.

———. *The Third Reich at War.* New York: Penguin, 2009.

———. *The Third Reich in Power.* New York: Penguin, 2005.

Falconi, Carlo. *Silence of Pius XII.* Tr. Bernard Wall. Boston: Little, Brown, 1970.

Fattorini, Emma. *Germania e Santa Sede: Le nunziature de Pacelli tra la Grande guerra e la Repubblica di Weimar.* Bologna: Societa editrice il Mulino, 1992.

Faulhaber, Michael von. *Judentum, Christentum, Germanentum: Adventspredigten gehalten in St. Michael zu München.* Munich: Druck und Verlag der Graphischen Kunstanstalt A. Huber, 1934.

Feldkamp, Michael F. "Paul Franken." In Gert Buchstab et al. *Christliche Demokraten gegen Hitler: Aus Verfolgung und Widerstand zur Union*, 172–178. Freiburg: Herder, 2004.

———. *Pius XII und Deutschland*. Göttingen: Vandenhoeck and Ruprecht, 2000.

Ferdinand, Louis. *The Rebel Prince: Memoirs of Prince Louis Ferdinand of Prussia*. Chicago: Henry Regnery Co., 1952.

Ferrua, Antonio. "Il sepolcro di san Pietro è di certo nella Basilica Vaticani." *Il Messaggero*, 16 Jan. 1952.

———. "La crittografia mistica ed i graffiti Vaticana." *Rivista di Archeologia Cristiana* 35 (1959): 231–247.

———. "La storia del sepolcro di san Pietro." *La Civiltà Cattolica* 103 (1952): 15–29.

———. "Nelle Grotte di san Pietro." *La Civiltà Cattolica* 92 (1941): 358–365, 424–433.

———. "Nuove scoperte sotto san Pietro." *La Civiltà Cattolica* 92 (1942): 72–83, 228–241.

———. "Sulle orme di san Pietro." *La Civiltà Cattolica* 94 (1943): 81–102.

Fest, Joachim C. *Hitler: Eine Biographie*. 2 vols. Frankfurt am Main: Ullstein, 1978. In English: *Hitler*. Tr. Richard and Clara Winston. New York: Harcourt Brace, 1974.

———. *Plotting Hitler's Death: The Story of the German Resistance*. New York: Owl, 1996.

FitzGibbon, Constantine. *20 July*. New York: Norton, 1956.

Flynn, George Q. "Franklin Roosevelt and the Vatican: The Myron Taylor Appointment." *Catholic Historical Review* 58, no. 2 (July 1972): 171–194.

Forschback, Edmund. *Edgar J. Jung: Ein konservativer Revolutionär 30. Juni 1934*. Pfullingen: G. Neske, 1984.

Frale, Barbara. "Petrusgrab: Ort einer Verschwörung gegen Hitler?" Vatikanische Dokumente (rv 21.03.2012 gs), Radio Vatikan (de), 2 Feb. 2012.

Frank, Hans. *Im Angesicht des Galgens: Deutung Hitlers und seiner Zeit auf Grund eigener Erlebnisse und Erkenntnisse*. Munich: Neuhaus, 1953.

Franken, Paul. "20 Jahre später." In *Akademische Monatsblätter des KV* 68 (Jan. 1956).

Freemantle, Anne, ed. *A Treasury of Early Christianity*. New York: Viking, 1953.

Frend, William. "Ein Beweis der tiefen Uneinigkeit." *Frankfurter Allgemeine Zeitung*, 12 July 1997, B3.

———. "The Vatican Germans and the Anti-Hitler Plot." *History Today* 54 (2004): 62ff.

Friedländer, Saul. *Pius XII and the Third Reich*. New York: Knopf, 1966.

———. *The Years of Extermination: Nazi Germany and the Jews 1939–1945*. New York: HarperCollins, 2007.

Frohlich, Elke, ed. *Die Tagebücher von Joseph Goebbels, Teil I Aufzeichnungen 1923–1941*. Munich: K. G. Saur, 1998.

Gaevernitz, Gero von. "From Caserta to Capri." In Schlabrendorff, *They Almost Killed Hitler*, 1–7. New York: Macmillan, 1947.

Galante, Pierre. *Operation Valkyrie: The German Generals' Plot Against Hitler.* New York: Harper and Row, 1981.

Gallagher, Charles. "Cassock and Dagger: Monsignor Joseph P. Hurley and American Anti-Fascism in Mussolini's Italy, 1938–1940." Paper presented at the meeting of the American Catholic Historical Association, Indianapolis, 28 March 1998.

———. "Personal, Private Views: Newly Discovered Report from 1938 Reveals Cardinal Pacelli's Anti-Nazi Stance." *America* 189, no. 5 (2003).

———. *Vatican Secret Diplomacy: Joseph Hurley and Pope Pius XII.* New Haven, CT: Yale University Press, 2008.

Gallagher, J.P. *The Scarlet and the Black: The True Story of Monsignor Hugh O'Flaherty.* San Francisco: Ignatius Press, 2009.

Gasbarri, Carlo. *Quando il Vaticano confinava con il Terzo Reich.* Padua: Edizioni Messaggero, 1984.

Gerard, John. *The Autobiography of a Hunted Priest.* Tr. Philip Caraman. San Francisco: Ignatius Press, 1988.

Gersdorff, Rudolf-Christoph von. *Soldat im Untergang.* Berlin/Frankfurt a-M: Ullstein, 1977.

Gerstenmaier, Eugen. *Streit und Friede hat seine Zeit.* Berlin: Propylaen: 1981.

———. "Zur Geschichte des Umsturzversuchs vom 20. Juli 1944." *Neue Züricher Zeitung*, 23–24 June 1945.

Ghetti, B. M., et al. *Esplorazioni Sotta La Confessione Di San Pietro in Vaticano Eseguite Negli Anni, 1940–1949.* 2 vols. Vatican City: Tipografia Poliglotta Vaticana, 1951.

Gilbert, Felix, ed. *Hitler Directs His War: The Secret Records of His Daily Military Conferences.* Oxford: Oxford University Press, 1950.

Gilbert, Martin. *Auschwitz and the Allies.* London: Michael Joseph/Rainbird, 1981.

Giovanetti, Alberto. *Roma: Città aperta.* Milan: Àncora, 1962.

Gisevius, Hans Bernd. "Political Background of the German Resistance Movement and of the Events Which Led to the Conspiracy Against Hitler and the Up-Rising Attempt of July 20th, 1944." Undated [1945–1946]. AWDP, Box 29 Folder 2 (PDF, 29–37).

———. *To the Bitter End: An Insider's Account of the Plot to Kill Hitler.* New York: Da Capo, 1998.

———. *Wo ist Nebe?* Zurich: Droemersche Verlangstalt, 1966.

Giskes, Hermann J. *Spione überspielen Spione.* Hamburg: Thoth, 1951.

Godman, Peter. *Der Vatikan und Hitler.* Munich: Knaur TB, 2005. In English: *Hitler and the Vatican.* New York: Basic Books, 2004.

Goebbels, Josef. *Final Entries 1945: The Diaries of Josef Goebbels.* Tr. Richard Barry. New York: G. P. Putnam's sons, 1978.

———. *The Goebbels Diaries 1939–1941.* Tr. Fred Taylor. New York: G. P Putnam's Sons, 1983.

———. *The Goebbels Diaries 1942–43.* Ed. Louis P. Lochner. Garden City, NY: Doubleday, 1948.

———. *Journal 1939–1942*. Paris: Tallandier (Archives contemporaines), 2009.

Goldmann, Gereon Karl. *The Shadow of His Wings*. San Francisco: Ignatius Press, 2000.

Gordon, Harold J. *Hitler and the Beer Hall Putsch*. Princeton, NJ: Princeton University Press, 1972.

Graham, Robert A. "II vaticanista falsario: L'incredibile successo di Virgilio Scattolini." *Civiltà Cattolica* 3 (Sept. 1973): 467–478.

———. "La strana condotta di E. von Weizsäcker ambasciatore del Reich in Vaticano." *Civiltà Cattolica* 2 (1970): 455–471.

———. "The 'Right to Kill' in the Third Reich: Prelude to Genocide." *Catholic Historical Review* 62, no. 1 (Jan. 1976): 56–76.

———. "Spie naziste attorno al Vaticano durante la seconda guerra mondiale." *Civiltà Cattolica* 1 (Jan. 1970): 21–31.

———. *The Vatican and Communism During World War II: What Really Happened?* San Francisco: Ignatius, 1996.

———. *Vatican Diplomacy: A Study of Church and State on the International Plane*. Princeton, NJ: Princeton University Press, 1959.

———. "Voleva Hitler allontanare da Roma Pio XII?" *Civiltà Cattolica* 1 (Feb. 1972): 319–327.

———. "Voleva Hitler Che Fosse Pio XII A Negoziare La Pace?" *La Civiltà Cattolicà* 4 (1976): 219–233.

Griesinger, Theodor. *The Jesuits: A Complete History of Their Open and Secret Proceedings from the Foundation of the Order to the Present Time*, 2nd ed. London: W. H. Allen, 1885.

Grisar, Hartmann. *Analecta Romana*. Vol. 1. Rome: Desclée Lefebvre, 1899.

———. *Le Tombe Apostoliche di Rome*. Rome: Tipografia Vaticana, 1892.

Gritschneder, Otto. "Die Akten des Sondergerichts über Pater Rupert Mayer S.J." *Beiträge zur altbayerischen Kirchengeschichte* 28 (1974).

Groscurth, Helmuth. *Tagebücher Eines Abwehroffiziers, 1938–1940. Mit weiteren Dokumenten zur Militäropposition gegen Hitler*. Ed. Harold C. Deutsch et al. Stuttgart: Deutsche Verlags-Anstalt, 1970.

Guarducci, Margherita. *Cristo e san Pietro in un documento presconstantiniano della Necropoli Vaticana*. Rome: Bretschneider, 1953.

———. *Dal gioco letterale alla crittografia mistica*. Berlin: Walter de Gruyter, 1978.

———. *I Graffiti sotto La Confessione di san Pietro in Vaticana*. 3 vols. Vatican City: Libreria Editrice Vaticana, 1957.

———. "Il fenomeno orientale del simbolismo alfabetico e i svoi svilluppi nel mondo cristiano d'occidente." *Accademia Nazionale dei Lincei* 62 (1964): 467–497.

———. "Infondate reserve sulle Reliquie di Pietro." *Archeologia Classica* 2 (1968): 352–373.

———. *Le Reliquie di Pietro*. Vatican City: Libreria Editrice Vaticana, 1965.

———. *Le Reliquie di Pietro: Una messa a punto*. Rome: Coletti Editore, 1967.

————. *Peter: The Rock on Which the Church Is Built. A Visit to the Excavations Beneath the Vatican Basilica.* Vatican City: Rev. Fabricca di S. Pietro, 1977.

————. *St. Pierre Retrouvé.* Paris: Editions St. Paul, 1974.

————. *The Tomb of St. Peter.* New York: Hawthorn, 1960.

Guiducci, Pier Luigi. *Il Terzo Reich Contro Pio XII: Papa Pacelli nei documenti nazisti.* Milan: Edizioni San Paolo, 2013.

Gumpel, Peter. Interviews by author, 17 May and 1 June 2014.

Guttenberg, Elisabeth von und zu. *Holding the Stirrup.* New York: Little, Brown, 1952.

Guttenberg, Karl Ludwig Freiherr von und zu. "Zusammenfassung meiner Angaben vor Standartenführer Huppenkothen," 7 Nov. 1944. Reprinted in Donahoe, *Hitler's Conservative Opponents in Bavaria,* Appendix F, 258–267.

Gvosdev, Nikolas K. "Espionage and the Ecclesia." *Journal of Church and State,* 22 Sept. 2000, 803ff.

Haasis, Hellmut G. *Tod in Prag: Das Attentat auf Reinhard Heydrich.* Reinbek: Rowohlt, 2002.

Halder, Franz. *The Halder War Diary, 1939–1943.* Eds. Charles Burdick and Hans-Adolf Jacobsen. Novato, CA: Presidio, 1988.

————. *Kriegstagebuch: Tägliche Aufz. des Chefs des Generalstabes des Heeres, 1939–1942.* 3 Vols. Stuttgart: Kohlhammer, 1962–1964.

Hales, E. E. Y. *The Catholic Church in the Modern World: A Survey from the French Revolution to the Present.* Garden City, NY: Hanover House, 1958.

Hapig, Marianne. *Tagebuch und Erinnerung.* Ed. Elisabeth Prégardier. Plöger: Edition Mooshausen, 2007.

Harrison, E. D. R. "The Nazi Dissolution of the Monasteries: A Case-Study." *English Historical Review* 99 (1994).

Hartl, Albert [as Dieter Schwarz, with Reinhard Heydrich]. *Attack Against the National Socialist World-View.* Lincoln, NE: Preuss, 2001. Translation of *Angriff auf die nationalsozialistische Weltanschauung* (1936).

Hartl, Albert [as Alfred Harder]. "Papst Pius XII. Der Mensch—der Politker." Berlin: Theodor Fritsch, 1939. Pamphlet prepared under SS auspices; references no events after mid-March 1939.

Hartl, Albert [as Anton Holzner]. *Priestermacht.* Berlin: Nordlandverlag, 1939. In English: *Priest Power.* Lincoln, NE: Preuss, 2001.

Hartl, Albert, ed. *Lebe gesund, lange und glücklich!* Schlachters bei Lindau: Wohlmuth, 1956.

Hassell, Ulrich von. *Die Hassell-Tagebücher, 1938–1944: Aufzeichnungen vom Andern Deutschland.* Berlin: Siedler, 1988.

————. *The Ulrich von Hassell Diaries: The Story of the Forces Against Hitler Inside Germany.* Tr. Geoffrey Brooks. South Yorkshire, UK: Frontline Books/Pen and Sword, 2011.

Hastings, Derek. *Catholicism and the Roots of Nazism: Religious Identity and National Socialism.* New York: Oxford University Press, 2010.

Hatch, Alden, and Seamus Walshe. *Crown of Glory: The Life of Pope Pius XII*. New York: Hawthorn Books, 1956.

Hebblethwaite, Peter. *In the Vatican*. Bethesda, MD: Adler and Adler, 1968.

———. *Paul VI: The First Modern Pope*. New York: Paulist Press, 1993.

Hehl, Ulrich von. *Priester unter Hitlers Terror: Eine biographische und statistische Erhebung*. Mainz: Matthias Grünewald, 1985.

Heiden, Conrad. A *History of National Socialism*. Reprint ed. London: Routledge, 2013.

Held, Heinrich. "Diktiert Ministerpräsident Dr. Heinrich Held unmittlebar nach dem 9 März 1933 über die Vorgänge bei der Machtübernahme der Nationalsozialisten in Bayern." Müller, "Niederschrift," LK, 373–378.

Held, Joseph. *Heinrich Held: Ein Leben für Bayern*. Regensburg: Held, 1958.

Helmreich, Ernst. *The German Churches Under Hitler*. Detroit: Wayne State University Press, 1979.

Hennessey, James. "An American Jesuit in Wartime Rome: The Diary of Vincent A. McCormick, S.J., 1942–1945." *Mid-America* 56, no. 1 (Jan. 1974).

Hesemann, Michael. *Der Papst, der Hitler trotzte: Die Wahrheit über Pius XII*. Augsburg: Sankt Ulrich, 2008.

———. "Pius XII, Stauffenberg und Der Ochsensepp," *Kath.Net*, 19 July 2009.

Hettler, Friedrich Hermann. "Josef Müller (Ochsensepp): Mann des Widerstandes und erster CSU-Vorsitzender." *Miscellanea Bavarica Monacensia*, vol. 55, Kommissionsverlag UNI-Druck München, Neue Schriftenreihe des Stadtarchivs. Munich, 1991.

Heydecker, Joe J., and Johannes Leeb. *The Nuremberg Trial: A History of Nazi Germany as Revealed Through the Testimony at Nuremberg*. Tr. R. A. Downie. London: Heinemann, 1962.

Hilberg, Raul. *The Destruction of the European Jews*. New York: Octagon, 1978.

Hilgenreiner, K. "Tyrannenmord." In *Lexicon für Theologie und Kirche*, 10:346–348. Freiburg im Breisgau: Herder, 1938.

Hill, Leonidas. "The Vatican Embassy of Ernst von Weizsäcker, 1943–1945." *Journal of Modern History* 39 (June 1967): 138–159.

Hilton, Stanley E. "The Welles Mission to Europe, February-March 1940: Illusion or Realism?" *Journal of American History* 58, no. 1 (June 1971): 93–120.

Himmler, Heinrich. *Rassenpolitik*. Pamphlet. Berlin, n.d. [c. 1943]. Tr. Randall Bytwerk. German Propaganda Archive.

Hinsley, F. H. *British Intelligence in the Second World War*. Abridged ed. New York: Cambridge University Press, 1993.

Hitler, Adolf. *Hitlers Tischgespräche*. Ed. Henry Picker. Wiesbaden: VMA-Verlag, 1983.

Hoek, Kies van. *Pope Pius XII: Priest and Statesman*. New York: Philosophical Library, 1945.

Hoffmann, Peter. *The History of the German Resistance 1939–1945*, 3rd ed. Cambridge, MA: MIT Press, 1996.

———. *Hitler's Personal Security*. New York: Da Capo, 2000.

———. *Stauffenberg: A Family History*. New York: Cambridge University Press, 1995.

Hoffmann, Peter, ed. *Beyond Valkyrie: German Resistance to Hitler: Documents*. Montréal: McGill-Queen's University Press, 2011.

Hofmann, Paul. *O Vatican! A Slightly Wicked View of the Holy See*. New York: Congdon and Weed, 1982.

Hofmeister, Corbinian. Transcript. 6 Aug. 1963, HDP, III, 1/7.

Höhne, Heinz. *Canaris: Hitler's Master Spy*. New York: Doubleday, 1979.

———. *The Order of the Death's Head: The Story of Hitler's S.S.* Tr. Richard Barry. New York: Coward-McGann, 1970.

Höllen, Martin. *Heinrich Wienken, der "unpolitische" Kirchenpolitiker. Eine Biographie aus drei Epochen des deutschen Katholizismus*. Mainz: Veröffentlichungen der Kommission für Zeitgeschichte, 1981.

Hollis, Christopher. *The Jesuits: A History*. New York: Macmillan, 1968.

Holmes, Derek J. *The Papacy in the Modern World: 1914–1978*. New York: Crossroad, 1981.

———. *The Triumph of the Holy See*. London: Burns and Oates, 1978.

Höttl, Wilhelm [*sic*, under pseud. Walter Hagen]. *Die geheime Front*. Vienna: Nibelungen, 1950. In English: Wilhelm Hoettel [*sic*], *The Secret Front: The Inside Story of Nazi Political Espionage*. London: Phoenix, 2000.

Hudec, L. E. "Recent Excavations Under St. Peter's Basilica in Rome." *Journal of Bible and Religion* 20, no. 1 (1952): 13–18.

Hughes, John Jay. "Hitler, the War, and the Pope." *First Things*, Oct. 2000.

Huppenkothen, Walter. "Der 20. Juli 1944." Undated statement. HDP, 2/10.

———. "The 20 July Plot Answers of Walter Huppenkothen." USFET/CIC Interrogation Report, Hersbruck, 17 May 1946. Answers in German (19 pp.) to a 3-page English questionnaire. Carbon copies. Lord Dacre Papers, DJ 38, Folder 21.

———. "Verhältnis Wehrmacht Sicherheitspolizei. . . ." Statement, n.d., HDP, 2/10.

Ihnhass, Michael J. [L. M. Telepun]. "The Bloody Footprints." Privately printed, 1954.

Irmingard von Bayern. *Jugend-Erinnerungen: 1923–1950*. Erzabtei St. Ottilien: EOS, 2010.

Irving, David. *Hitler's War*. New York: Viking, 1977.

Jacobsen, Hans-Adolf. "10. Januar 40–Die Affäre Mechlin." *Wehrwissenschaftliche Rundschau* 4 (1954): 497–515.

———. *Fall Gelb*. Wiesbaden: Steiner, 1957.

Jacobsen, Hans-Adolf, ed. *July 20, 1944: Germans Against Hitler*. Bonn: Federal Government of Germany, 1969.

Joachimsthaler, Anton. *Hitlers Ende*. Munich: Herbig, 2004.

Joachimsthaler, Anton, and Helmut Bögler. *The Last Days of Hitler*. London: Brockhampton, 1999.

John, Otto. *Twice Through the Lines: The Autobiography of Otto John*. New York: Harper and Row, 1972.

Josi, Enrico. "Gli scavi nelle Sacre Grotte Vaticana," 2–13. In *Il Vaticano nel 1944*. Rome: Tipographia Vaticane, 1945.

———. "Ritrovamenti Archeologici." *L'Osservatore Romano*, 13 March 1941, 6.

Junge, Traudl. *Until the Final Hour: Hitler's Last Secretary*. Tr. Anthea Bell. New York: Arcade, 2004.

Kaas, Ludwig. "The Search for the Bones of St. Peter." *Life*, 27 March 1950, 79–85.

Kahn, David. *The Codebreakers: The Story of Secret Writing*. New York: Macmillan, 1967.

———. *Hitler's Spies: German Military Intelligence in World War II*. New York: Macmillan, 1978.

Kaiser, Wolfram. *Christian Democracy and the Origins of European Union*. New York: Cambridge University Press, 2007.

Kaltefleiter, Werner, and Hanspeter Ochswald. *Spione im Vatikan: Die Päptse im Visier der Geheimdienste*. Munich: Pattloch, 2006.

Kaltenbrunner, Ernst. "The Defense Case. VII. Final Argument" with "Final Plea," 20 Nov. 1945, NCA, II, Pt. 1, 275ff. Kurt Kauffmann was defense counsel.

Keitel, Wilhelm. *The Memoirs of Field-Marshal Keitel*. Ed. Walter Görlitz. New York: Stein and Day, 1966.

Keller, Hermann. "Zeugenschrifttum," 4 July 1967, IfZ, ZS 2424.

Kempner, Benedicta Maria. *Priester vor Hitlers Tribunalen*. Leipzig: Rütten u. Loening, 1966.

Kennan, George. *Memoirs, 1925–1950*. New York: Pantheon, 1983.

Kershaw, Ian. *Hitler 1889–1936: Hubris*. New York: W. W. Norton, 1998.

———. *Hitler 1936–1945: Nemesis*. New York: W. W. Norton, 2000.

———. *The 'Hitler Myth': Image and Reality in the Third Reich*. New York: Oxford University Press, 2001.

———. *Hitler, the Germans and the Final Solution*. New Haven, CT: Yale University Press, 2008.

———. *Popular Opinion and Political Dissent in the Third Reich: Bavaria, 1933–1945*. Oxford: Clarendon, 1983.

———. *The Nazi Dictatorship: Problems and Perspectives of Interpretation*, 3rd ed. London: Arnold, 2000.

Kertzer, David I. *The Pope and Mussolini: The Secret History of Pius XI and the Rise of Fascism in Europe*. New York: Random House, 2014.

Kessel, Albrecht von. "Umschwung in D." Handwritten manusucript, n.d., c. 6 Nov. 1942, Nachlass Kessel. Reprinted in Schwerin, *Köpfe*, 447–452.

———. *Verborgene Saat: Aufzeichnungen aus dem Widerstand, 1933 bis 1945*. Ed. Peter Steinbach. Berlin: Ullstein, 1992.

Kimball, Warren F., ed. *Churchill and Roosevelt: The Complete Correspondence*. Vol. 3, Alliance Declining, February 1944–April 1945. Princeton, NJ: Princeton University Press, 1984.

Kirschbaum, Engelbert. "Gli scavi sotto la Basilica di San Pietro." *Gregorianum* 29: 3–4 (1948): 544–557.

———. *The Tombs of St. Peter and St. Paul*. New York: St. Martin's, 1959.

———. "Zu den Neuesten Entdeckengen unter der Peterskirche in Rom." *Archivum Historiae Pontificiae* 3 (1965): 309–316.

Klemperer, Klemens von. *German Resistance Against Hitler: The Search for Allies Abroad, 1938–1945*. New York: Oxford University Press, 1992.

Knauth, Percy. *Germany in Defeat*. New York: Knopf, 1945.

Koch, Laurentius. "Die Benediktinerabtei Ettal." In Schwaiger, ed. *Das Erzbistum München und Freising in der Zeit der nationalsozialistischen*, 2:381–413.

Kochendörfer, Sonja. "Freising unter dem Hakenkreuz Schicksale der katholischen Kirche." In Schwaiger, ed., *Das Erzbistum München und Freising in der Zeit der nationalsozialistischen*, no. 1: 676–683.

Kolakovic, Tomislav. *God's Underground*. New York: Appleton-Century Crofts, 1949. [Originally bylined: "Father George as told to Greta Palmer."]

Kordt, Erich. *Nicht aus den Akten*. Stuttgart: Union Deutsche Verlagsgesellschaft, 1950.

Kramarz, Joachim. *Stauffenberg: Architect of the Famous July 20th Conspiracy to Assassinate Hitler*. Tr. R. H. Barry. New York: Macmillan, 1967.

Kurtz, Lester. *The Politics of Heresy: The Modernist Crisis in Roman Catholicism*. Berkeley: University of California Press, 1986.

Kurzman, Dan. *Special Mission: Hitler's Secret Plot to Seize the Vatican and Kidnap Pius XII*. New York: Da Capo, 2007.

Kwitny, Jonathan. *Man of the Century: The Life and Times of Pope John Paul II*. Henry Holt, 1997.

Ladd, Brian. *The Ghosts of Berlin: Confronting German History in the Urban Landscape*. Chicago: University of Chicago Press, 2008.

Lahousen, Erwin. "Testimony of Erwin Lahousen taken at Nürnberg, Germany, 1 Feb. 1946 1330–1430 by Lt Col Smith W. Brookhart, Jr., IGD. Also present: Leo Katz, Interpreter; John Wm. Gunsser, Reporter." Facsimile, 16 March 2010, Nachlass Loringhoven, PWF.

Lapide, Pinchas. *Three Popes and the Jews*. New York: Hawthorn, 1967.

Lapomarda, Vincent A. *The Jesuits and the Third Reich*. Lewiston, NY: Edwin Mellen, 1989.

Laqueur, Walter. *The Terrible Secret*. Boston: Little, Brown, 1980.

Large, David Clay. *Where Ghosts Walked: Munich's Road to the Third Reich*. New York: Norton, 1977.

Lavelle, Elise. *The Man Who Was Chosen: Story of Pope Pius XII*. New York: McGraw-Hill, 1957.

Lease, Gary. "Denunciation as a Tool of Ecclesiastical Control: The Case of Roman Catholic Modernism." *Journal of Modern History* 68, no. 4 (1996): 819–830.

Lees-Milne, James. *Saint Peter's: The Story of Saint Peter's Basilica in Rome.* Boston: Little, Brown, 1967.

Lehnert, Sister M. Pascalina. *His Humble Servant.* Tr. Susan Johnson. South Bend, IN: St. Augustine's Press, 2014. In German: *Ich durfte ihm dienen: Erinnerungen an Papst Pius XII*, 10th ed. Würzburg: Naumann, 1996.

Leiber, Robert. "Bandaufnahme eines Vortrages von HH Pater Leiber am . . . mit angeschliessender Diskussion." Undated transcript from tape-recorded lecture and discussion, Berlin Pastoral Conference [c. Autumn] 1963. Title: Juliusz Stroynowski Collection (CN 92019), Hoover Institution, Palo Alto, CA.

———. "Mit Brennender Sorge." *Stimmen der Zeit* 169 (1961–1962): 417–426.

———. "Pius XII." *Stimmen der Zeit*, Nov. 1958. Reprinted in *Der Streit um Hochhuth's Stellvertreter* (Basel: Basilius Presse, 1963); and in Bentley, ed. *The Storm Over the Deputy*, tr. Salvator Attars, 173–194.

———. "Pius XII and the Third Reich." Written comments. Tr. Charles Fullman. Excerpted in *Look*, 17 May 1966, 36–49.

———. "Unterredung," 26–27 Aug. 1960. IfZ, ZS, 660, 2–7.

———. "Zum Gutachten Seiner Eminenz Card. Faulhaber," 5 [or 6] March 1939, ADSS, II, Annex IV, "Note du Secrétariat privé de Pie XII."

———. "Zweite Konferenz des Heiligen Vaters mit den deutschen Kardinälen 9 März 1939. Zu behandelnde Punkte," 7 [or 8] March 1939, ADSS, II, Annex VII, "Note du Secrétariat privé de Pie XII."

Lernoux, Penny. *People of God.* New York: Viking, 1989.

Lesourd, Paul. *Entre Rome et Moscou: Le jésuite clandestin, Mgr Michel d'Herbigny.* Paris: Editions Lethielleux, 1976.

Leugers, Antonia. *Gegen eine Mauer bischöflichen Schweigens: Der Ausschuss für Ordensangelegenheiten und seine Widerstandskonzeption, 1941 bis 1945.* Frankfurt am Main: Knecht, 1996.

Lewy, Guenter. "Pius XII, the Jews, and the German Catholic Church," *Commentary* 37:2 (Feb. 1964): 23–35.

———. "Secret Papal Brief on Tyrannicide." *Church History* 26:4 (1957), 319–324.

Lichten, Joseph. *A Question of Judgment.* Washington, DC: National Catholic Welfare Conference, 1963.

Lochner, Louis. *Always the Unexpected: A Book of Reminiscences.* New York: Macmillan, 1956.

Loringhoven, Bernd Freytag von. *In the Bunker with Hitler: The Last Witness Speaks.* London: Weidenfeld and Nicolson, 2006.

———. "Kaltenbrunner und 'Der Ochsensepp' Josef Müller." *Austria-Forum*, May 2010.

Ludecke, Kurt G.W. *I Knew Hitler.* London: Jarrolds, 1938.

Ludlow, Peter. "Papst Pius XII, die britische Regierung und die deutsche Opposition im Winter 1939/40." VfZ no. 3 (1974).

Lugli, G. "Recent Archaeological Discoveries in Rome and Italy." *Journal of Roman Studies* 36, no. 1–2 (1946): 1–17.

Lukacs, John. *At the End of an Age.* New Haven, CT: Yale University Press, 2002.

———. "The Diplomacy of the Holy See During World War II." *Catholic Historical Review* 60 (July 1974).

———. *Historical Consciousness: Or, the Remembered Past.* New York: Harper and Row, 1968.

———. *The Hitler of History.* New York: Knopf, 1997.

———. "In Defense of Pius." *National Review* 51, no. 22, 22 Nov. 1999.

———. *The Last European War, 1939–1941.* New York: Doubleday, 1976.

———. "Questions About Pius XII." *Continuum*, Summer 1964, 183–192. Reprinted in Mark G. Malvasi and Jeffrey O. Nelson, eds., *Remembered Past: John Lukacs on History, Historians, and Historical Knowledge.* Wilmington, DE: ISI Books, 2005.

Machiavelli, Niccolò. *Discourses on the First Decade of Titus Livius.* Tr. Ninian Hill Thomson. Pennsylvania State University Electronic Classics, 2007.

Marchasson, Yves. *La Diplomatie Romaine et la République Française.* Paris: Beauchesne, 1974.

Matteson, Robert E. "The Last Days of Ernst Kaltenbrunner." *Studies in Intelligence* (CIA), Spring 1960; CIA Historical Review Program Release, 22 Sept. 1993, NARA, RG 263, 2–11–6.

McCargar, James [as Christopher Felix]. *A Short Course in the Secret War*, 3rd ed. Lanham, MD: Madison, 1992.

McKay, C.G. *From Information to Intrigue: Studies in Secret Service Based on the Swedish Experience, 1939–1945.* London: Frank Cass, 1993.

Meehan, Patricia. *The Unnecessary War: Whitehall and the German Resistance to Hitler.* London: Sinclar-Stevenson, 1992.

Menges, Franz. "Müller, Josef." *Neue Deutsche Biographie* 18 (1997): 430–432.

Meyer, Winifred. *Unternehmen Sieben: Eine Rettungsaktion für vom Holocaust Bedrohte aus dem Amt Ausland/Abwehr im Oberkommando der Wehrmacht.* Frankfurt am Main: Hain, 1993.

Moltke, Freya von. *Memories of Kreisau and the German Resistance.* Tr. Julie M. Winter. Lincoln: University of Nebraska Press, 2005.

Moltke, Helmuth James von. *Briefe an Freya, 1939–1945.* Munich: C. H. Beck'sche Verlagsbuchhandlung, 1988. In English: *Letters to Freya.* New York: Knopf, 1990.

———. "Ueber [*sic*] die Grundlagen der Staatslehre" [On the Foundations of Political Science], Oct. 1940. In Moltke, Papers, Bundesarchiv, Koblenz N 1750 Bd. 1, tr. Hoffmann, BV, 44–53.

Mommsen, Hans. *Alternatives to Hitler: German Resistance in the Third Reich*. Tr. Angus McGeoch. Princeton, NJ: Princeton University Press, 2003.

Moorhouse, Roger. *Berlin at War*. New York: Basic Books, 2012.

Morrell, Theo. *The Secret Diaries of Hitler's Doctor*. Ed. David Irving. New York: Macmillan, 1983.

Morsey, Rudolf. "Gelehrter, Kulturpolitiker und Wissenschaftsorgnisator in vier Epochen deutscher Geschichte: Georg Schreiber (1882–1963)." In Bastin Hein et al., eds. *Gesichter der Demokratie: Porträts zur deutschen Zeitgeschichte: Eine Veröffentlichung des Instituts für Zeitgeschichte München-Berlin*, 7–20. Munich: Oldenbourg, 2012.

Muckermann, Friedrich. *Der Deutsche Weg: Aus dem Widerstandsbewegungen der deutschen Katholiken von 1930–1945*. Zurich: NZN, 1945.

———. *Im Kampf zwischen zwei Epochen*. Ed. Nikolaus Junk. Mainz: Matthias Grünewald, 1973.

Muckermann, Hermann. "April 2, 1946-Friedrich Muckermann SJ." *Mitteilungen aus den deutschen Provinzen der Gesellschaft Jesu XVII* 113–116 (1953–1956): 325–328.

Mueller, Michael. *Canaris: The Life and Death of Hitler's Spymaster*. Tr. Geoffrey Brooks. Annapolis, MD: Naval Institute Press.

Mueller, Richard, and Allan J. Lichtman. *FDR and the Jews*. Cambridge, MA: Belknap Press of Harvard University Press, 2013.

Müller, Josef. "Besprechung in Rom beim Vatikan 612.11.39." Reprinted in Groscurth, *Tagebücher*, 506–509.

———. "Betrifft: Halder." Unsigned, undated statement of early postwar origin, probably prepared for US Office of Strategic Services, HDP.

———. *Bis zur letzten Konsequenz*. Munich: Süddeutscher, 1975.

———. "Fragen und Erläuterungen von Dr. Müller," July 1947. LStA (Roeder), Vol. 5, Land Niedersachsen, Lüneburg, 1951.

———. [Josef Müller Private Papiere, 1947–1956.] IfZ, ED 63.

———. "Lebenslauf," 7 Nov. 1945. 5 pp, German (typewritten carbon), DNTC, vol. XVII, Subdivision 53, "Others Investigated or Interrogated," 53.041.

———. [Papers and documents.] IfZ, ZS 659.

———. "Protokoll der Siztung vom 1.2.1952." IfZ, ZS 603.

———. "Statement by Josef Müller," 21 Oct. 1948. LStA (Roeder), Vol. 5, Land Niedersachsen, Lüneburg, 1951.

———. "Statement of Mueller Josep[f], Lawyer (Munich) Gedonstrasse A. Munich." Capri, 23 May 1945, NARA, RG 226, Entry 125, Box 29.

———. Transcripts of debriefings by Harold C. Deutsch (1958; April 1958; 5 and 31 May 1958; June 1958; 31 June 1958; 3 Aug. 1958; 12 Aug. 1958; 4 Aug. 1960; July 1963; Aug. 1963; 5 Aug. 1963; 6 Aug. 1963; 8 Aug. 1963; 1966–1967?; 23 and 24 March 1966; Sept. 1966; 22 Sept. 1966; c. 1966). HDP, III, 1/7.

———. "Vernehmung des Zeugen Dr. Josef Müller, 49 Jahre Alt, Rechtsanwalt in München." Unpublished manuscript, 29 April 1947, HDP.

Müller, Klaus-Jürgen. *Der deutsche Widerstand 1933–1945*. Paderborn: Schöningh, 1990.

Murphy, Paul I. *La Popessa*. New York: Warner, 1983.

Naftali, Timothy. "ARTIFICE: James Angleton and X2 Operations in Italy." In *The Secrets War: The Office of Strategic Services in World War II*, 218–245. Ed. George C. Chalou. Washington, DC: National Archives and Records Administration, 1992.

National Security Agency [US Signal Security Agency]. "Vatican Code Systems," n.d. [25 Sept. 1944]. NARA, RG 437, HCC, Box 1284 (document NR 3823 ZEMA100 37012A 19430000 Cryptographic Codes and Ciphers: Vatican Code Systems).

Nebgen, Elfriede. *Jakob Kaiser*. Stuttgart: Kohlhammer, 1967.

Neitzel, Sönke. *Abgehört: Deutsche Generäle in britischer Kriegsgefangenschaft, 1942–1945*. Berlin: Ullstein Buchverlage, 2005. In English: Tapping Hitler's Generals: Transcripts of Secret Conversations, 1942–45. Tr. Geoffrey Brooks. St. Paul: MBI, 2007.

Neuhäusler, Johannes. *Amboss und Hammer: Erlebnisse im Kirchenkampf des Dritten Reiches*. Munich: Manz, 1967.

———. *What Was It Like in the Concentration Camp at Dachau?* 31st ed. Dachau: Trustees for the Monument of Atonement in the Concentration Camp at Dachau, 2002.

Nicolosi, Giuseppe. "I lavori di ampliamento risanamento e sistemazione delle Sacre Grotte Vaticane." *L'Osservatore Romano*, 13 March 1941, 6.

O'Callaghan, Roger T. "Recent Excavations Underneath the Vatican Crypts." *Biblical Archaeologist* 12, no. 1 (Feb. 1949): 1–23.

———. "Vatican Excavations and the Tomb of Peter." *Biblical Archaeologist* 16, no. 4 (Dec. 1953): 69–87.

O'Donnell, James. *The Bunker*. New York: Da Capo, 2001.

Oesterreicher, John M. *Wider die Tyrannei des Rassenwahns: Rundfunkansprachen aus dem ersten Jahr von Hitlers Krieg*. Vienna: Geyer, 1986.

Osas, Veit. *Walküre*. Hamburg: Adolf Ernst Schulze, 1953.

Pacelli, Eugenio. *Gesammelte Reden*. Ed. Ludwig Kaas. Berlin: Buchverlag Germania, 1930.

Pacepa, Ion Mihai, and Ronald J. Rychlak. *Disinformation*. Washington, DC: WND, 2013.

Padellaro, Nazareno. *Portrait of Pius XII*. Tr. Michael Derrick. New York: Dutton, 1957.

Pagano, Sergio. "Documenti sul modernismo romano dal Fondo Benigni." *Ricerche per la storia religiosa di Roma* 8 (1990): 223–300.

Papen, Franz von. *Memoirs*. Tr. Brian Connell. New York: Dutton, 1953.

Parparov, Fyodor, and Saleyev, Igor [MVD/NKVD]. "Dyelo" [Dossier] [to Stalin], 29 Dec. 1949, CPSU, Doc. 462a. In English: *The Hitler Book: The Secret Dossier*

Prepared for Stalin from the Interrogations of Hitler's Personal Aides. Eds. Henrik Eberle and Matthias Uhl. Trans Giles Macdonough. New York: Public Affairs, 2005.

Patin, Wilhelm. "Beiträge zur Geschichte der Deutsch-Vatikanischen Beziehungen in den letzten Jahrzehnten. Quellen und Darstellungen zur politischen Kirche, Sonderband A." Copy 0470 SD, 1942, author's collection. Internal SS study for Heinrich Himmler.

———. "Document Room Intelligence Analysis: Dr. Wilhelm August Patin." Office of US Chief of Counsel for the Prosecution of Axis Criminality [Col. Brundage], Nuremberg, 24 Sept. 1945.

———. "Preliminary Interrogation Report: Patin, Wilhelm," US 7th Army Interrogation Center, 14 July 1945. Author's collection.

———. "Testimony of Dr. Wilhelm August Patin, taken at Nuremberg, Germany, 24 Sept 1945, 1050–1230, by Howard A. Brundage, Colonel." Office of US Chief of Counsel for the Prosecution of Axis Criminality [Nuremberg].

———. "Testimony of Wilhelm Patin, taken at Nurnberg, Germany, 3 November 1945, 1030–1130, by Lt. John B. Martin." Author's collection.

Pawley, Edward. *BBC Engineering, 1922–1972.* London: British Broadcasting Corporation, 1972.

Payne, Robert. *The Life and Death of Adolf Hitler.* New York: Barnes and Noble, 1995.

———. *The Rise and Fall of Stalin.* New York: Macmillan, 1968.

Perrin, Henri. *Priest-Workman in Germany.* Tr. Rosemary Sheed. New York: Sheed and Ward, 1948.

Persico, Joseph. *Roosevelt's Secret War: FDR and World War II Espionage.* New York: Random House, 2001.

Peter, Karl Heinrich, ed. *Spiegelbild einer Verschwörung.* Stuttgart: Seewald, 1961.

Peters, Walter H. *The Life of Benedict XV.* Milwaukee: Bruce Publishing, 1959.

Petrarch [Francesco Petrarca]. *Petrarch's Remedies for Fortune Fair and Foul.* Ed. Conrad H. Rawski. 5 vols. Bloomington: University of Indiana, 1991.

Petrova, Ada, and Watson, Peter. *The Death of Hitler: The Full Story with New Evidence from Secret Russian Archives.* New York: Norton, 1995.

Phayer, Michael. *The Catholic Church and the Holocaust, 1930–1965.* Bloomington: Indiana University Press, 2000.

———. *Pius XII, the Holocaust, and the Cold War.* Bloomington: Indiana University Press, 2008.

———. "Questions about Catholic Resistance." *Church History* 70, no. 2 (June 2001): 328–344.

Pius XII. *Summi Pontificatus.* Vatican City: Libreria Editrice Vaticana, 1939.

Pollard, John. *The Papacy in the Age of Totalitarianism.* New York: Oxford University Press, 2014.

———. *The Unknown Pope: Benedict XV (1914–1922) and the Pursuit of Peace.* London: Geoffrey Chapman, 1999.

———. *The Vatican and Italian Fascism, 1929–32.* New York: Cambridge University Press, 1985.

Poulat, Emile. *Intégrisme et Catholicisme intégral.* Tournai: Casterman, 1969.

Prados, John. *The White House Tapes: Eavesdropping on the President.* New York: New Press, 2003.

Prandi, Adriano. *La zona archeologica della Confessio Vaticana del II secolo.* Vatican City: Tipografia Poliglotta Vaticana, 1957.

Pridham, Geoffrey. *Hitler's Rise to Power: The Nazi Movement in Bavaria, 1923–1933.* New York: Harper and Row, 1973.

Prittie, Terence. *Germans Against Hitler.* Boston: Little, Brown, 1964.

Quigley, Martin. *Peace Without Hiroshima: Secret Action at the Vatican in the Spring of 1945.* Lanham, MD: Madison, 1991.

Radio Vaticana. "Summario," 1 April 2014, www.aireradio.org/articoli/img/vaticano _2.pdf. Accessed 27 May 2014.

Rauscher, Anton, ed. *Wider den Rassismus: Entwurf einer nicht erschienenen Enzyklika (1938). Texte aus dem Nachlass von Gustav Gundlach SJ.* Paderborn: Ferdinand Schöningh, 2001.

Rauschning, Hermann. *The Revolution of Nihilism and Warning to the West.* New York: Alliance Book Corporation, 1939.

Reck-Malleczewen, Friedrich Percyval. *Diary of a Man in Despair.* Tr. Paul Rubens. London: Duck Editions, 2000. In German: *Tagebuch eines Verzweifelten.* Stuttgart: Buerger, 1947.

Reese, Thomas J. *Inside the Vatican.* Cambridge, MA: Harvard University Press, 1996.

Reilly, Michael F. *Reilly of the White House.* New York: Simon and Schuster, 1947.

Reitlinger, Gerald. *The SS: Alibi of a Nation, 1922–1945.* New York: Viking, 1957.

Respighi, C. "Esplorazioni recenti nella Confessione Beati Petri." *Rivista di Archeologia Cristiana* 19 (1942): 19–26.

Rhodes, Anthony. *The Power of Rome in the Twentieth Century.* New York: Franklin Watts, 1983.

———. *The Vatican in the Age of the Dictators.* New York: Holt, Rinehart and Winston, 1973.

Ribbentrop, Joachim von. "Testimony of Joachim von Ribbentrop taken at Nürnberg, Germany, on 5 October 1945, by Mr. Justice Robert H. Jackson, OUSCC." Office of United States Chief Counsel for Prosecution of Axis Criminality. *Nazi Conspiracy and Aggression. Supplement B* [Red Book], 1232–1239. Washington, DC: US Government Printing Office, 1948.

Ritter, Gerhard. *Carl Goerdeler und die deutsche Widerstandsbewegung.* Stuttgart: Deutsche Verlags-Anstalt, 1956.

———. *The German Resistance: Carl Goerdeler's Struggle Against Tyranny.* Tr. R. T. Clark. London: Allen and Unwin, 1958.

Roon, Ger van. *German Resistance to Hitler: Count von Moltke and the Kreisau Circle.* Tr. Peter Ludlow. London: Van Nostrand Reinhold, 1971.

———. *Neuordnung im Widerstand: Der Kreisauer Kreis innerhalb der deutschen Wider-standsbewegung*. Munich: Oldenbourg, 1967.

Rösch, Augustinus. "Dem Tode entronnen," 1946, KN, 398–301.

———. "Gottes Gnade in Feuer und Flamme," 1947, KN, 412–453.

———. *Kampf gegen den Nationalsozialismus*. Ed. Roman Bleistein. Frankfurt am Main: Knecht, 1985.

———. "Kampf gegen den NS," 22 Oct. 1945, KN, 268–270.

———. "Lebenslauf," 14 Dec. 1916, BHStAM, War Archives Department, OP2455.

———. "Zum Abschiedsbrief Moltkes," 1945–1946, KN, 286, 288f.

Rothe, Alfred. "Pater Georg von Sachsen." *Mitteilungen aus den deutschen Provinzen der Gesellschaft Jesu* 17, no. 113 (1953–1956).

Rothfels, Hans. *The German Opposition to Hitler: An Assessment*. Tr. Lawrence Wilson. London: Oswald Wolff, 1961.

Ruffner, Kevin Conley. "Eagle and Swastika: CIA and Nazi War Criminals and Collaborators." Draft Working Paper, US Central Intelligence Agency History Staff, Washington, DC, April 2003. Declassified in 2007.

Rürup, Reinhard, ed. *Topographie des Terrors*, 4th ed. Berlin: Verlag Willmuth Arenhövel, 1987.

Russo, Domenico. Untitled manuscript ["Mémoire"], 12 March 1945. (20 pp.), HDP, III, 1/9.

Rychlak, Ronald J. *Hitler, the War and the Pope*. Huntington, IN: Genesis Press, 2000.

Safire, William. "Essay: Happy to Watergate You." *New York Times*, 14 June 1982.

Sale, Giovanni. "L'Attentato a Hitler, La Sante Sede e i Gesuiti." *La Civiltà Cattolica* 1 (2003): 466–479.

Sanchez, José. *Pius XII and the Holocaust: Understanding the Controversy*. Washington, DC: Catholic University of America Press, 2002.

Schellenberg, Walter. *The Labyrinth*. Harper and Brothers, 1956.

———. *Memorien*. Cologne: Verlag für Politik und Wirtschaft, 1956.

Scheurig, Bodo. *Henning von Tresckow ein Preuße gegen Hitler*. Berlin: Propyläen, 2004.

Schlabrendorff, Fabian von. "Events Leading Up to the Putsch of 20 July (1944)." Typescript for US Office of Strategic Services, (copy), n.d. [c. July 1945]. DNTC, vol. XCIII.

———. *Offiziere gegen Hitler*. Berlin: Siedler, 1984.

———. *Revolt Against Hitler: The Personal Account of Fabian von Schlabrendorff*. London: Eyre and Spottiswoode, 1948.

———. *The Secret War Against Hitler*. Tr. Hilda Simon. Boulder: Westview, 1994.

———. *They Almost Killed Hitler*. New York: Macmillan, 1947.

Schmuhl, Hans-Walter. *The Kaiser Wilhelm Institute for Anthropology, Human Heredity, and Eugenics, 1927–1945*. Dordrecht: Springer Science and Business Media, 2008.

Schneider, Burkhart, ed., with Pierre Blet and Angelo Martini. *Die Briefe Pius' XII an die Deutschen Bischöfe, 1939–1944*. Mainz: Matthias Grünewald, 1966.

Scholl, Inge. *Students Against Tyranny: The Resistance of the White Rose, Munich, 1942–1943*. Tr. Arthur R. Schultz. Middletown, CT: Wesleyan University Press, 1970.

———. *The White Rose: Munich, 1942–1943*. Tr. Arthur R. Schultz. Middletown, CT: Wesleyan University Press, 1983.

Schramm, Percy Ernst. "Ahlmann, Wilhelm." In *Neue Deutsche Biographie*. Berlin: Duncker and Humblot, 1953.

Schuschnigg, Kurt. *Im Kampf gegen Hitler: Die Überwindung der Anschlussidee*. Vienna and Munich: Fritz Molden, 1969.

Schwaiger, Georg ed. *Das Erzbistum München und Freising in der Zeit der nationalsozialistischen*. 2 vols. Munich: Schnell and Steiner, 1984.

Schwarz, Hans-Peter. *Konrad Adenauer: A German Politician and Statesman in a Period of War, Revolution, and Reconstruction*. Vol. 1. Providence, RI: Berghahn, 1995.

Schwerin, Deltef von. *"Dann Sind's die Besten Köpfe, Die Man Henkt." Die junge Generation im deutschen Widerstand*. Munich: Piper, 1991.

Scoccianti, Sandro. "Appunti sul servizio informazioni pontificio nelle Marche nel 1859–60." *Atti e memorie della deputazione di storia patria per le Marche* 88 (1983): 293–350.

Scrivener, Jane. *Inside Rome with the Germans*. New York: Macmillan, 1945.

Sevareid, Eric. *Not So Wild a Dream*. New York: Knopf, 1946.

Sheridan, Michael. *Romans: Their Lives and Times*. New York: St. Martin's, 1994.

Shuster, G. N. *In Amerika und Deutschland: Erinnerungen eines amerikanischen College Präsidenten*. Frankfurt am Main: Knecht, 1965.

Siemer, Laurentius. *Erinnerungen: Aufzeichnungen und Briefe*. Frankfurt am Main: Knecht, 1957.

Slezkine, Yuri. *The Jewish Century*. Princeton, NJ: Princeton University Press, 2004.

Smothers, Edgar. "The Bones of St. Peter." *Theological Studies* 27 (March 1966): 79–88.

———. "The Excavations Under St. Peter's." *Theological Studies* 17 (1956): 293–321.

Sorondo, Marcelo Sánchez. "The Pontifical Academy of Sciences: A Historical Profile." *Pontificia Academia Scientiarum*, extra series 16, 2003.

Speer, Albert. *Inside the Third Reich*. Tr. Richard and Clara Winston. New York: Macmillan, 1970.

Spengler, Oswald. *The Decline of the West*. Vol. 2, *Perspectives of World-History*. Tr. Charles Francis Atkinson. New York: Knopf, 1928.

Stehle, Hansjakob. *Eastern Politics of the Vatican, 1917–1979*. Athens: Ohio University Press, 1981.

———. "Ein Eiferer in der Gesellschaft von Mördern: Albert Hartl, der Chef des anti-kirchlichen Spitzeldienstes der SS." *Die Zeit*, 7 Oct. 1983, www.zeit.de/1983/41/ein-eiferer-in-der-gesellschaft-von-moerdern. Accessed 28 Aug. 2104.

Stehlin, Stewart. *Weimar and the Vatican, 1919–1933: German-Vatican Diplomatic Relations in the Interwar Years*. Princeton, NJ: Princeton University Press, 1983.

Steigmann-Gall, David. *The Holy Reich: Nazi Conceptions of Christianity, 1919–1945*. Cambridge, UK: Cambridge University Press, 2002.

Steinacher, Gerald. *Nazis on the Run: How Hitler's Henchmen Fled Justice*. New York: Oxford University Press, 2012.

Steinhoff, Johannes, et al. *Voices from the Third Reich: An Oral History*. Washington, DC: Regnery Gateway, 1989.

Stickler, Wolfgang. "Odilo Braun: Dominikaner im Nationalsozialismus." Unpublished paper, Oct. 1998, Cloister of the Dominican Order, Braunschweig.

Stone, I. F. *The War Years, 1939–1945: A Nonconformist History of Our Times*. Boston: Little, Brown, 1988.

Strauss, Franz Josef. Address, 6 April 1978, Munich. HDP, IV, 20/5.

Sullivan, Geoff, and Frode Weierud. "Breaking German Army Ciphers." *Cryptologia* 29, no. 3 (2005): 193–232.

Sykes, Christopher. *Troubled Loyalty: A Biography of Adam von Trott*. London: Collins, 1968.

Tardini, Domenico. *Memories of Pius XII*. Tr. Rosemary Goldie. Westminster, MD: Newman Press, 1961.

Tattenbach, Franz von. "Das enstscheidende Gespräch." *Stimmen der Zeit* 155 (1954–1955): 321–329.

Thompson, Leslie A. "Flossenbürg Concentration Camp." 14 Jan. 1989. Unpublished paper in the author's collection.

Tilley, John, and Stephen Gaselee. *The Foreign Office*. London: Putnam's, 1933.

Tittmann, Harold H. *Inside the Vatican of Pius XII*. New York: Image, 2004.

———. "Vatican Mission." *Social Order* 10 (March 1960): 113–117.

Toland, John. *Adolf Hitler*. New York: Doubleday, 1976.

Townend, Gavi. "The Circus of Nero and the Vatican Excavations." *American Journal of Archaeology* 62, no. 2 (1958): 216–218.

Toynbee, Jocelyn. "The Shrine of St. Peter and Its Setting." *Journal of Roman Studies* 43 (1953): 1–26.

Toynbee, Jocelyn, and J. W. Perkins. *The Shrine of St. Peter and the Vatican Excavations*. New York: Pantheon, 1957.

Trevor-Roper, Hugh. "Admiral Canaris." In *The Philby Affair: Espionage, Treason, and Secret Services*, 102–120. London: William Kimber, 1968.

———. "The European Witch-craze of the Sixteenth and Seventeenth Centuries." In *The Crisis of the Seventeenth Century: Religion, the Reformation, and Social Change*, 90–192. New York: Harper and Row, 1968.

———. *The Last Days of Hitler*. New York: Macmillan, 1947.

———. *The Philby Affair*. London: William Kimber, 1968.

———. *The Secret World*. Ed. Edward Harrison. London: I. B. Tauris, 2014.

———. *The Wartime Journals*. Ed. Richard Davenport-Hines. London: I. B. Tauris, 2012.

Tully, Grace. *F.D.R.: My Boss*. New York: Charles Scribner's Sons, 1949.

United Kingdon War Office. *Field Engineering and Mine Warfare Pamphlet no. 7: Booby Traps*. London: The Office: 1952.

US Army. Headquarters Counter Intelligence Corps. "Dr. Mueller, a Good German, Tells of 'Resistance in Reich.'" Allied Force Headquarters, Naples, 9 June 1945. NARA, RG 226, Entry 125, Box 29.

US Forces in Austria, Air Division Headquarters. "The Last Days in Hitler's Air Raid Shelter." Interrogation summary, 8 Oct. 1945. 16 pp. DNTC, vol. IV, 8.14.

US National Security Agency. *Eavesdropping on Hell: Historical Guide to Western Communications Intelligence and the Holocaust, 1939–1945*, 2nd ed. Ed. Robert J. Hanyok. United States Cryptologic History, Series IV, Vol. 9. Washington, DC: Center for Cryptologic History, 2005.

US Seventh Army. "Hitler's Last Session in the Reichs Chancellery, 24 Feb 45." Interrogation report, Karl Wahl and Max Amann, 24 May 1945, DNTC, vol. IV, 8.14.

Ventresca, Robert A. *Soldier of Christ: The Life of Pope Pius XII*. Cambridge, MA: Belknap Press of Harvard University Press, 2009.

Veyne, Paul. *Writing History: Essay on Epistemology*. Tr. Mina-Moore Rinvolucri. Middletown, CT: Wesleyan University Press, 1984.

Vocke, Harald. *Albrecht von Kessel. Als Diplomat für Versöhnung mit Osteuropa*. Freiburg: Herder, 2001.

Volk, Ludwig, ed. *Akten Kardinal Michael von Faulhabers (1917–1945)*. 3 Vols. Mainz: VfZ, 1975, 1984.

Vollmer, Antje. *Doppelleben. Heinrich und Gottliebe von Lehndorf im Widerstand gegen Hitler und von Ribbentrop*. Berlin: Die Andere Bibliotek, 2012.

Waigel, Theo. *Pact for Stability and Growth*. Brussels: Europe Documents No. 1962 (24 Nov. 1995), 1–3.

Wall, Bernard. *The Vatican Story*. New York: Harper and Brothers, 1956.

Wall, Donald D. "The Reports of the Sicherheitsdienst on the Church and Religious Affairs in Germany, 1939–1944." *Church History* 40, no. 4 (Dec. 1971): 437–456.

Wallace, Robert, H. Keith Melton, and Henry R. Schlesinger. *Spycraft: The Secret History of the CIA's Spytechs from Communism to Al-Qaeda*. New York: Dutton, 2008.

Walpole, Hugh. "The Watch on St. Peter's Square." Excerpted from idem, *Roman Fountain* (London: Rupert Hart-Davis, 1940), reprinted in Sweeney, ed., *Vatican Impressions*, 205–221.

Walsh, John Evangelist. *The Bones of St. Peter: The First Full Account of the Search for the Apostle's Body*. New York: Doubleday, 1982.

Ward, Geoffrey C., ed. *Closest Companion: The Unknown Story of the Intimate Friendship Between Franklin Roosevelt and Margaret Stuckley*. New York: Simon and Schuster, 1989.

Weber, Max. "Politik Als Beruf." In *Gesammelte Politische Schriften*, 2nd ed., 533–548. Tübingen: J. C. B. Mohr (Paul Siebeck), 1958. In English: "Politics as a Vocation," 212–225. *Max Weber, Selections in Translation*. Ed. W. G. Runciman. Tr. E. Matthews. New York: Cambridge University Press, 1978.

Wehner, Bernd. "Das Spiel ist aus." *Der Spiegel*, no. 12, March 1950, 31.

Weigel, George. *Witness to Hope: The Biography of Pope John Paul II*. New York: Harper Perennial, 2005.

Weinberg, Gerhard. *The World at Arms: A Global History of World War II*. New York: Cambridge University Press, 1994.

Weisbrod, Bernd. "Terrorism and Performance: The Assassinations of Walther Rathenau and Hanns-Martin Schleyer." *Control of Violence* 2011, 365–394.

Weissauer, Ludwig. *Die Zukunft der Gewerkschaften*. Stuttgart: Neske, 1970.

Weitz, John. *Hitler's Diplomat*. London: Ticknor and Fields, 1992.

Weizsäcker, Ernst von. *Die Weizsäcker-Papiere, 1933–1950*. Ed. Leonidas E. Hill. Frankfurt am Main: Propyläen, 1974.

———. *Memoirs*. Chicago: Regnery, 1951.

Welles, Sumner. "Report by the Under Secretary of State (Welles) on His Special Mission to Europe," 29 March 1940, FRUS, 1940, I, 21–113.

———. *Time for Decision*. New York: Harper Brothers, 1944.

Wenger, Antoine. *Catholiques en Russie d'après les archives du KGB, 1920–1960*. Paris: Desclee de Brouwer, 1998.

———. *Rome et Moscou, 1900–1950*. Paris: Desclée de Brouwer, 1987.

Wheeler-Bennett, John W. *The Nemesis of Power: The German Army in Politics, 1918–1945*. London: Macmillan, 1953.

Wiener, Jan G. *Assassination of Heydrich*. New York: Grossman, 1969.

Wilson, Hugh. *Diplomat Between the Wars*. New York: Longmans, 1941.

Wistrich, Robert S. *Hitler and the Holocaust*. New York: Modern Library, 2001.

———. "Reassessing Pope Pius XII's Attitudes toward the Holocaust." Interview by Manfred Gerstenfeld. Jerusalem Center for Public Affairs, 19 Oct. 2009.

Wolf, Hubert. *Papst and Teufel: Die Archive des Vatikan und Das Dritte Reich*, 2nd ed. Munich: C.H. Beck, 2009. In English: *Pope and Devil: The Vatican's Archives and the Third Reich*. Tr. Kenneth Kroneburg. Cambridge, MA: Belknap Press of Harvard University Press, 2010.

Wolf, Kilian. "Erinnerungen [und] Erlebnisse des Ettaler Konvents während der Nazizeit." Ettal [Benedictine Monastery], private printing, 1979.

Wolff, Karl. "Excerpts from Testimony of Karl Wolf [*sic*], taken at Nuremberg, Germany, 26 October 1945, 1430–1650, by Col. Curtis L. Williams, IGD," IMT, Vol. XXVIII.

———. "Niederschrift über meine Besprechungen mit Adolf Hitler September 1943 über die Anweisungen zur Besetzung das Vatikans under die Verschleppung des Papstes Pius XII." *Positio Summ*, Pars. II, 836 ff, 28 March 1972, PWF.

World Jewish Committee et al. *The Black Book: The Nazi Crime Against the Jewish People*. New York: Jewish Black Book Committee/American Book-Stratford Press, 1946.

Wuermeling, Henric L. *Die weisse Liste*. Frankfurt am Main: Ullsteinhaus, 1981.

Wulf, Peter. "Vom Konservativen zum Widerständler. Wilhelm Ahlmann (1895–1944). Eine biografische Skizze." *Zeitschrift für Geschichtswissenschaft* 59, no. 1 (2011): 5–26.

Wyman, David. *The Abandonment of the Jews: America and the Holocaust, 1941–1945.* New York: Pantheon, 1984.

Wytwycky, Bohdan. *The Other Holocaust.* Washington, DC: Novak Report, 1982.

Zeiger, Ivo. "Betr.: Vernehmung von Pater Zeiger durch Dr. Kempner und Dr. Becker, Nürnberg, 9. Juli 1948." Aktennotiz Nr. 12 Prinz Konstantin [ed. Pflieger], IfZ, ZS A-49, 25ff.

Ziegler, Walter. "Nationalsozialismus und kirchliches Leben in Bayern, 1933–1945." In Schwaiger, ed., *Das Erzbistum München und Freising in der Zeit der nationalsozialistischen*, 2:49–76.

Zeller, Eberhard. *The Flame of Freedom: The German Struggle Against Hitler.* Tr. R. P. Heller and D. R. Masters. Boulder: Westview, 1994.

———. *Oberst Claus Graf Stauffenberg: Ein Lebensbild.* Paderborn: Schöningh, 2008.

Zipfel, Friedrich. *Kirchenkampf in Deutschland 1933–1945.* Berlin: Walter De Gruyter, 1965.

Zuccotti, Susan. *Under His Very Windows: The Vatican and the Holocaust in Italy.* New Haven, CT: Yale University Press, 2000.

INDEX

Laurie Lambrecht

Mark Riebling is a pathbreaking writer on secret intelligence. The author of *Wedge: The Secret War Between the FBI and CIA*, he lives in New York City.